MODERNISM AND THE MIDDLE PASSAGE

MODERNIST LATITUDES

MODERNIST LATITUDES

Jessica Berman and Paul Saint-Amour, Editors

Modernist Latitudes aims to capture the energy and ferment of modernist studies by continuing to open up the range of forms, locations, temporalities, and theoretical approaches encompassed by the field. The series celebrates the growing latitude ("scope for freedom of action or thought") that this broadening affords scholars of modernism, whether they are investigating little-known works or revisiting canonical ones. Modernist Latitudes will pay particular attention to the texts and contexts of those latitudes (Africa, Latin America, Australia, Asia, Southern Europe, and even the rural United States) that have long been misrecognized as ancillary to the canonical modernisms of the global North.

Shir Alon, *Static Forms: Writing the Present in the Modern Middle East*

Mat Fournier, *Dysphoric Modernism: Undoing Gender in French Literature*

Nergis Ertürk, *Writing in Red: Literature and Revolution Across Turkey and the Soviet Union*

Cate I. Reilly, *Psychic Empire: Literary Modernism and the Clinical State*

Adam McKible, *Creating Jim Crow America: George Horace Lorimer, the Saturday Evening Post, and the War Against Black Modernity*

Hannah Freed-Thall, *Modernism at the Beach: Queer Ecologies and the Coastal Commons*

Daniel Ryan Morse, *Radio Empire: The BBC's Eastern Service and the Emergence of the Global Anglophone Novel*

Jill Richards, *The Fury Archives: Female Citizenship, Human Rights, and the International Avant-Gardes*

Claire Seiler, *Midcentury Suspension: Literature and Feeling in the Wake of World War II*

Elizabeth Outka, *Viral Modernism: The Influenza Pandemic and Interwar Literature*

Ben Conisbee Baer, *Indigenous Vanguards: Education, National Liberation, and the Limits of Modernism*

Aarthi Vadde, *Chimeras of Form: Modernist Internationalism Beyond Europe, 1914–2014*

Eric Bulson, *Little Magazine, World Form*

Eric Hayot and Rebecca L. Walkowitz, eds., *A New Vocabulary for Global Modernism*

For a complete list of books in this series, see the CUP website.

MODERNISM AND THE MIDDLE PASSAGE

LAURA WINKIEL

Columbia University Press
New York

Columbia University Press
Publishers Since 1893
New York   Chichester, West Sussex

Copyright © 2025 Columbia University Press
All rights reserved

Library of Congress Cataloging-in-Publication Data
Names: Winkiel, Laura A. author
Title: Modernism and the Middle Passage / Laura Winkiel.
Description: New York : Columbia University Press, 2025. | Includes index.
Identifiers: LCCN 2025011706 (print) | LCCN 2025011707 (ebook) |
ISBN 9780231217248 hardback | ISBN 9780231217255 trade paperback |
ISBN 9780231561631 ebook
Subjects: LCSH: Literature, Modern—20th century—History and criticism |
Literature—Black authors—History and criticism | American literature—African
American authors—History and criticism | Slavery in literature |
Other (Philosophy) in literature | Modernism (Literature) |
LCGFT: Literary criticism
Classification: LCC PN771 .W585 2025 (print) | LCC PN771 (ebook) |
DDC 809.9112—dc23/eng/20250514

Cover design: Elliott S. Cairns
Cover image: Emma Langdon Roche, "Wreck of the 'Clotilde,'" from *Historic Sketches of the South* (Knickerbocker Press, 1914). Schomburg Center for Research in Black Culture, Jean Blackwell Hutson Research and Reference Division, The New York Public Library. New York Public Library Digital Collections.

GPSR Authorized Representative: Easy Access System Europe, Mustamäe tee 50, 10621 Tallinn, Estonia, gpsr.requests@easproject.com

TO MY FEMINIST MENTORS AND FRIENDS.
IN MEMORIAM, SUSAN STANFORD FRIEDMAN.

CONTENTS

Acknowledgments ix

OVERTURE 1

1. READING WITH THE SEA 23

2. ALLUVIUM: LANGSTON HUGHES,
ZORA NEALE HURSTON, AND CLAUDE McKAY 60

(INTERLUDE) 102

3. WAVES: VIRGINIA WOOLF AND KABE WILSON 115

4. ARCHIPELAGO: JEAN RHYS, MARLON JAMES,
AND JAMAICA KINCAID 150

5. DELTA: WILLIAM FAULKNER AND AMOS TUTUOLA 192

CODA 228

Notes 237
Index 291

ACKNOWLEDGMENTS

This book is about long, deep, occluded histories that are brought to the surface for all to see. Given this, it is eminently fitting that I can, at long last, acknowledge the quiet, submarine work of many people and institutions that have sustained me in bringing this project to completion. To begin, I wish to thank the Modernist Latitudes series editors, Jessica Berman and Paul Saint-Amour, for supporting this project even before I knew what it was going to be. They coaxed it along patiently, shook it up occasionally, and celebrated its success. They are the editors one hopes to be lucky enough to find. Deep gratitude goes also to Philip Leventhal at Columbia University Press for his guidance, support, and good humor. The anonymous manuscript readers provided excellent directives for sharpening the argument. I greatly appreciate them for giving their time and expertise to make this a better book. I recognize, too, the production staff at Columbia, especially Lis Pearson, for bringing the manuscript to press.

Besides enjoying the benefits of working in a place with such stunning natural beauty that it still takes my breath away, the University of Colorado at Boulder's English Department has been a collegial and stimulating place in which to write this book. I thank my chairs, Sue Zemka, Jeff Cox, and William Kuskin, for their support of this project that included a sabbatical leave and another course release that helped me to finish drafting. The environmental studies working group, spearheaded by

Karen Jacobs and maintained by Jason Gladstone, sparked my interest in the oceans, shorelines, and the animacy of the more-than-human. I thank Maria Windell whose Ethnic Studies reading group created a space for cross-disciplinary conversations on Sylvia Wynter, Katherine McKittrick, and many others. The Center for the Humanities and Arts provided a faculty fellowship that came at the perfect time. I thank the Director, Jennifer Ho, for her encouragement, assistance, and institutional savvy. Donna Axel at the Research Innovation and Opportunity office was an invaluable collaborator in helping me to make the project compelling to readers outside my discipline. Many colleagues read this work at various stages and got me over hurdles in my writing. Janice Ho and Ramesh Mallipeddi were incredibly generous with their time and, as always, super smart in their interventions. Emily Harrington, Jill Heydt-Stevenson, Cheryl Higashida, Maria Windell, and Nicole Wright pushed me to finish chapters and make them better. Thora Brylowe was a wonderful summer writing partner and got me dancing. Jane Garrity took me on hikes. Tiffany Beechy came into the project at a key moment: I greatly appreciate her support. Much gratitude goes to Reiland Rabaka for spearheading the long overdue CAAAS (Center for African and African American Studies) on the heels of the Black Lives Matter movement. Thanks to the graduate students who cheered me on to the finish. Finally, I thank the University of Colorado for awarding this book the Kayden Book Prize prior to its publication.

Farther afield, I was able to share work in progress at the University of Chicago's 20th and 21st Century Cultures Workshop, Pennsylvania State University's English Department, and the Glascock Center for Humanities Research at Texas A&M. I thank Brandon Truett, Rivky Mondal, Sonali Thakkar, and Janet Lyon for their invitations and for hosting my visits. I've also benefited from panels and seminars held at the Modernist Studies Association, the American Comparative Literature Association, and the Association for Postcolonial Thought and from readers of the manuscript at other institutions. Special thanks go to Jed Esty, Harris Feinsod, Yogita Goyal, Peter Kalliney, Jessie Matz, Nels Pearson, Nicole Rizzuto, Sonita Sarkar, and Cherene Sherrard-Johnson for their excellent comments on the manuscript. Amanda Golden was an important interlocutor and editor at an early stage of the writing. BK Clapham worked tirelessly over the summer to format the manuscript and to start seeking permissions. A shout out goes to Gary Holcomb and Bill Maxwell for bringing Claude McKay's *Romance in Marseille* into the light of day and for encouraging new scholarship on the novel. The Schomburg Center for Research in Black Culture and the McFarlin Library at the University of Tulsa were welcoming and generative places for delving deeper into the work of Sylvia Wynter and Jean Rhys, respectively. Kara Walker and Ellen Gallagher were extremely generous in making reproductions of their work available to the readers of this book for little to no permissions fees. On a more personal level, Ali Hasan has been the bedrock in my life while bringing this book into being. I thank him for his steadfast support, general goofiness, excellent kebabs, and willingness to help out during the final crunch. Endless amazement goes to my daughter, Atiya: it's been a delight to watch you grow up. You truly are a gift. I thank my father, Joe, for his support. Finally, I thank the kids at the majority African American, far west side Chicago Public School where I attended elementary school early on. There, I learned by age six that I had white privilege and that it wasn't fair, that the adults in Chicago didn't think much of the children in my school, judging from our broken glass and gravel playground, and that my schoolmates had some pretty boss street games to share. Soon after, my family became part of white flight from the city, but I never stopped asking, what about the Black community?

I'm grateful to *English Language Notes* and its publisher, Duke University Press, for permission to reprint in chapter 2 a revised, excerpted version of "Shoreline Thinking: Alluvial Entanglements in *Romance in Marseille*," *English Language Notes* 59, no. 1 (April 2021): 146–65. Taylor & Francis gave its permission to reprint in chapter 3 a revised, excerpted version of "A Queer Ecology of the Sea: Reading Virginia Woolf's *The Waves*," *Feminist Modernist Studies* 2, no. 2 (July 2019): 1–23. Much appreciation goes to Cassandra Laity for this journal's existence and for her support of my article. Portions of Langston Hughes's "A Negro Mother" and "To the Little Fort in San Lazaro" are used by permission of Harold Ober Associates and International Literary Properties LLC. Présence Africaine gave their permission for the republication of an excerpt from Aimé Césaire's *Cahier d'un retour au pays natal*. The New Mrs Partington (1910), London Museum ref 50.82/864; is used by permission of the artist's estate.

Finally, I dedicate this book to the wonderful, generous feminist mentors whose brilliance, friendship, and support have sustained me these many years. I hope that I have paid forward to the next generation even some of the comradery, brilliant guidance, and inspiration I've received. These women include: Gloria-Jean Masciarotte, Barbara Green (Djuna Barnes stayed in!), Ewa Ziarek, Rita Barnard (a partner in glorious mountain adventures), and the late Susan Stanford Friedman. Susan's trailblazing scholarship, collaborative networking, and high level of worldly engagement set the bar high for scholars of global modernisms. This book is dedicated to her memory.

MODERNISM AND THE MIDDLE PASSAGE

OVERTURE

In October 2019, at the Tate Modern's Turbine Hall exhibition space, Kara Walker's massive sculpture *Fons Americanus* opened to the public. Standing forty-two feet high, the sculpture mirrors the scale and grandiosity of the Victoria Memorial that it confronts and rewrites. The earlier monument to empire was unveiled in 1911, completed in 1924, and stands just outside of Buckingham Palace in London. In this revision of the early twentieth-century tribute to empire and the monarchy, *Fons Americanus*, subtitled "The Daughter of the Waters," foregrounds the aquatic, comprised of bodily fluids, oceanic terror, and connective space. It depicts the long history of the Black Atlantic, as Walker states in an explanatory video: "This is a piece about oceans and seas traversed fatally. . . . *Fons Americanus* is an allegory of the Black Atlantic and really all global waters which disastrously connect Africa to America, Europe, and economic prosperity."[1] Inverting the celebratory and elevating impulse of public monuments, *Fons Americanus* instead manifests that a primary fount or source of the Americas and empire is an ongoing catastrophe of violence against African and African-descended peoples and others that took place on the ocean's surface, within its depths, and skimming its circum-Atlantic shores during the era of European colonization and slavery, from roughly the mid-fifteenth century to its afterlife in the present. The sculpture's mobility—figures snorkeling, rowing, begging for their lives, spilling their blood and breast milk, and more—suggests a relationality with the imperial monumental past that opens into the present. Walker's fountain presents Black Atlantic history in dialogue with empire such that it puts in motion and in question space, time, and what constitutes the human.

This history from the water meets the spectator even prior to viewing the main sculpture. In Figure 0.1, a small child gazes at the exhibit in horror. A tear runs down their face, linking bodily fluids with surrounding water. The vestibular placement of this smaller sculpture, prior to and yet inextricably linked to the central fountain mirrors the child's own undecidability. While the child's head sits where the pearl of an oyster should be, the shell is not enclosed; its bottom where the pearl should rest is instead an indeterminate passageway. Are the cave-like circular walls a birth canal and the waters amniotic fluid and life-giving? Or do the walls resemble a grave to suggest that the child is drowning and soon to be engulfed by the dangerous marine depths? This death-in-life greeting

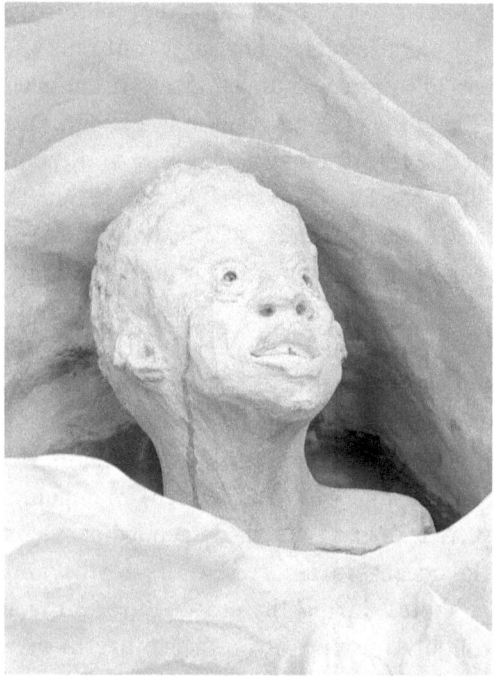

FIGURE 0.1 Kara Walker, *Fons Americanus*. Detail, shell grotto. 2019

announces Blackness itself as a liminal condition of waiting for death *and* reaching for life, the consequence of slavery as social death.[2] Further, the ambiguity queries whether the child is a witness to the terrors of the slave trade or soon to be just another aspect of its absent archive. The question of transmission allegorizes the role of the reader/spectator to ask how the fountain might aid them in the creative praxis of world-imagining from the waters, an activity that the sculpture pedagogically models.

Walker's sculpture teaches its viewers to rethink the human from the perspective of Black Atlantic history. It emphasizes the violent proximity of Afro-diasporic peoples with the sea, marine animals, and inorganic materiality. This linkage, both metonymic and metaphoric, demands a speculative kind of reading and imagining. It moves beyond realism, or what is concretely knowable, to the uncertain, the unreliable, and the opaque. In the figure mentioned above, the small child substitutes for a pearl (in satirical reference to anti-Black imagery of the late nineteenth century) and asks the reader/viewer to think of the two together. Nurtured by the oyster, the pearl signals both an irritant (an inorganic grain of sand) and the shellfish's organic response to the foreign particle. In a parallel metamorphosis, the child can be thought of as both human and nonhuman since they occupy the place of the pearl. Given that the oyster lives underwater, the child may even be imagined to breathe underwater in reference to the Atlantis myth of Black fetuses who, thrown overboard slave ships while in utero, survived on liquid oxygen and founded an underwater utopia.[3] This reinvention of the category of the human through assemblage with fish, bird, ghost, plant, and even compost, I'm arguing, allows for a world-imagining that strikes at the nature-culture and materiality-form division so central to modernity and coloniality alike.[4]

Reading from the sea, as artists such as Kara Walker have done, confronts and disperses the unified, hierarchical memory of empire and colonization, as exemplified by the Victoria Memorial.[5] It challenges aesthetic form, spatial and temporal grids, and allows for an understanding of the co-constitution of the human and nonhuman. For example, the poster that accompanies *Fons Americanus*, an amalgamation of nineteenth-century slave auction notices with circus fair and Wild West show advertisements, proclaims the fountain to be "A Gift and Talisman Towards a reconciliation of Our Respective Mother-Lands ... Afrique and Albion." It places that reconciliation in the turbulent seas: "Behold the

Swirling Drama of the Merciless Seas, Routes, and Rivers upon which our dark fortunes were traded and on whose frothing shores lay prostrate Captain, Slave, and Starfish alike."[6] That the beneficiary of empire, the Captain, lies inert next to an enslaved person and a starfish makes plain Walker's investment in foregrounding Anthropocene-era crises: rising seas, ocean acidification, species extinction, melting ice caps, and rising temperatures that threaten the entire human species and most forms of planetary life. This emphasis on the sea links empire to climate change and environmental destruction. Although all are threatened, *Fons Americanus* places the mobility, experience, and resistance of Afro-diasporic persons as a primary means by which to reimagine the human in an open-ended relation with the planet. Crucially, that inventive process occurs within slavery and its afterlife, a condition in which, as Saidiya Hartman writes, "black lives are still imperiled and devalued by a racial calculus and a political arithmetic that were entrenched centuries ago." Slavery's afterlife, she continues, manifests as "skewed life chances, limited access to health and education, premature death, incarceration, and impoverishment."[7] Christina Sharpe calls this extended duration of slavery being "in the wake," a place and consciousness of precarity and mourning for the dead. As a place, the wake repeats the material semiotics of the slave ship, "from the forced movements of the enslaved to the forced movements of the migrant and refugee, to the regulation of Black people in North American streets and neighborhoods, to those ongoing crossings of and drownings in the Mediterranean Sea, to the brutal colonial reimaginings of the slave ship and the ark; to the reappearances of the slave ship in everyday life in the form of the prison, the camp, and the school."[8] Walker's installation reveals Black life in the wake: despite the seeming equivalence of Captain, African captive, and starfish in death, it also confronts the living hierarchies of the human in empire. Walker displaces these hierarchies by elevating a Black woman, her jugular vein cut, her breasts spewing milk, to the apex of the monument as the stolen life force that motors the vast accumulation of wealth and power that is empire.

Extending the sculpture's antagonism toward empire to its spatial technologies, Walker's counter-monument rejects European cartographic practices that abstract space into the gridded divisions of latitude and longitude that separate here from there. Instead, she reveals a Black planetary imaginary that moves flexibly across and amid multiple scales and dimensions that include ocean surface and depths, geophysical "deep" time, and the entangled, heterotemporal dimensions of human histories. The latter blends divisions of past and present by presenting time as an all-encompassing now that includes the long era of the slave trade, the Queen Victoria monument, Emmet Till, and the contemporary; finally, its affective register shifts between the terror of the Middle Passage and the joyous vitality of Black resistance. In another detail of *Fons Americanus*, the figure in the boat references Winslow Homer's painting *The Gulf Stream* (1893) in which a Black man struggles to navigate a boat in a storm without a rudder or sail [see Figure 0.2]. Like Homer, Walker fills the sea with sharks to index how slave ship crews encouraged sharks by feeding them to terrorize captives during the Middle Passage. Further, the sharks metaphorize the racial straits of the Jim Crow South and beyond. Behind the man in the dinghy, another figure *snorkels* through the shark-infested water. The anachronism is striking, but what is more surprising is that the snorkeler is there at all. The incongruity between the imminent danger of the sea and the figure's obvious pleasure in swimming and exploring the sea depths through the prostheses of breathing tube, mask, and, most likely, fins, instances the cultural, historical, and affective work that I intend this book to do: to be with and read from the sea itself. The Atlantic Ocean hosts the lingering history of the slave trade *and* supports Black liveliness, creativity, and relationality as an Afro-diasporic reinvention of the human from which all can learn.

Walker's work demonstrates how to think relationality across time periods, geographies, humans and nonhumans, terror and pleasure, and archival facts and what Hartman calls "critical fabulation," a method of telling the stories of slavery that "are impossible to tell" due to the near total absence of Black perspectives in the slavery archive.[9] Reading modernism through the lens of Afro-diasporic art, theory, and literature reveals that while *Fons Americanus* targets the monumentalization of empire underway in the early twentieth century, many modernists—Black and white—were undermining those same certainties. In the United States, Zora Neale Hurston introduces her ethnography of one of the last living Africans to endure the transatlantic slave trade, *Barracoon*

FIGURE 0.2 Kara Walker, *Fons Americanus*. Detail, main. 2019

Nontoxic acrylic and cement composite, recyclable cork, wood, and metal. Main: 43 × 50 × 73.5 feet (13.2 × 15.2 × 22.4 meters). Grotto: 10.8 × 10.2 × 10.5 feet (3.3 × 3.1 × 3.2 meters). Installation view: Hyundai Commission: Kara Walker—Fons Americanus, Tate Modern, London, UK, 2019. Photo: Tate (Matt Greenwood). Artwork © Kara Walker, courtesy of Sikkema Jenkins & Co. and Sprüth Magers.

(completed in 1931, published in 2018), by calling the slave trade "the most dramatic chapter of the story of human existence," three years before W. E. B. Du Bois makes a similar pronouncement in *Black Reconstruction* (1934).[10] White writers and some Black writers are more circumspect: recall the racial mayhem and oceanic burial of West Indian sailor James Wait in Joseph Conrad's *The Nigger of the 'Narcissus'*; Virginia Woolf's Bernard in *The Waves* who muses, "We have destroyed something by our presence, . . . a world perhaps"; and Jean Rhys's Anna in *Voyage in the Dark* who reminds herself that "This is England, and I'm in a nice, clean English room with all the dirt swept under the bed."[11] More, William Faulkner's screenplay of *The Last Slaver* (1936) features the uncanny doubling of Captain Lovett's fiancée's bracelet with that worn by an

African woman captive on the so-called last slave ship. In a mirroring reminiscent of Conrad's women characters in *Heart of Darkness*, Faulkner connects white femininity (both Northern and Southern) with the spoils of the slave trade. Meanwhile, Langston Hughes, Claude McKay, and Amos Tutuola invoke the slave trade through tropes of containment, dismemberment, ghost ships, and a "body in a bag," as I discuss in the chapters to come.[12] In sum, these authors pull a thread from the fabric of empire to reveal how the specter of the slave trade haunts modernism.

The wager of this book is that reading from the sea, as Walker's sculpture prompts us to do, reveals the atrocious racist and sexist violence inherent in the commodification of humans and that modernist aesthetic innovation by Hughes, Hurston, McKay, Rhys, Tutuola, and Woolf contests this commodity structure. Still, the claim that the legacy of the Middle Passage is important to modernism goes against the grain of critical common sense. Even in Black modernist studies, the prevailing literary historical narrative emphasizes the new militancy in African American arts and politics that broke from late nineteenth-century accommodationism. Black modernism tends to embrace urban life, with its anonymity, innovation, experimentation, and stylized self-fashioning. Slavery, much less the slave trade, was not on these artists' minds, so the story goes, except as what they must escape.[13] In her recent prize-winning book on the afterlives of neo-slave narratives in contemporary Anglophone literature, Yogita Goyal concurs that Black modernists seldom engaged with the slave past. She writes that it wasn't until the 1960s that writers began to do so, "after a gap of almost a century, barring exceptions like Arna Bontemp's 1936 *Black Thunder*."[14] Certainly, this claim can be upheld in terms of a realist retelling of slave revolt history, such as Bontemp's. But I disagree that the slave past is put to rest in modernism. Unlike previous accounts that explore how white modernists held unacceptable racial biases that have since been overcome, or how modernists understood racial difference through orientalist and primitivist frameworks, this book argues that the legacy of the Middle Passage reveals to readers how modernist literature addresses the trauma of empire's racist and sexist violence *and* reimagines the human in a manner not predicated on exclusion.[15]

As I explore in the chapters to come, references to the Middle Passage in modernism also occur through tropes of suffocation, drowning, bondage, and psychological and physical suffering. In conceptualizing this figuration as representing the multigenerational effects of trauma, I draw upon Laura T. Murphy's examination of "the hidden though significant role the transatlantic slave trade has played in the West African Anglophone imagination." The lingering presence of the slave trade, she writes, occurs "beyond the layer of explicit historical setting and into the realm of metaphor, the rumor, the bodily expression of a long-resident wound. The slave trade hides in the proverbial bush of ghosts, a past always alive in the present, though it is sometimes unnoticed or obscured."[16] In contrast to West African literature, Afro-diasporic writing locates this haunting, wounded sensibility elsewhere. Hartman, in her critical memoir, *Lose Your Mother*, moves the site of loss from Tutuola's bush (where slave raids, kidnapping, and forced marches in West Africa occurred) to the sea, writing, "I needed to see the Atlantic, which was where I reckoned with the dead, the men and women and children who were all but invisible in most of the history written about the slave trade.... The ocean never failed to remind me of the losses, and its roar echoed the anguish of the dead."[17] Here, it is the seeming emptiness of the sea's shifting nonplace and the "roar" of affective nonsignification that marks the unmarked dead. Commenting more generally on the slave trade's impact on African American cultural imagination, Maria Diedrich, Henry Louis Gates Jr., and Carl Pedersen remark that the Middle Passage "emerges not as a clear break with the past and present but as a spatial continuum between Africa and the Americas. Submerged beneath the surface of the dominant language, it constantly seeps through and inevitably affects it."[18] Following these critical predecessors, this book is not a history of the slave trade; rather, it explores how modernist polysemy and experimental aesthetics engage with the legacy of the slave trade, lost beneath the waters, but nonetheless "seeping" into collective memory and literary form.

The modernist writers in this study, I argue, engage with the extremist prejudices of the early twentieth century—the explosion of public misogyny and sexual violence aimed at British and US women agitating for citizenship; the mass mutilations and deaths during the First World War; the increased racist and gendered violence of anti-Blackness, anti-Semitism, and other forms of bigotry—by reaching back in time to the lexicon of the slave trade's history and abolition debates. This history also appears, I show, when writers assess the British Empire in its waning years. The legacy of empire and slavery results in the dehumanization of marginalized peoples, including unruly white women and, across an ontological divide that is the legacy of chattel slavery, Black women and men. But more than finding metaphors and historical references to the slave trade in modernist literary texts, this book argues that modernism's allusions to the slave trade make visible the exploitative structural relations between the metropole and the colonies and between the liberal subject and its others, as well as contests the commodification of persons and art. In sum, my analysis is twofold. First, reading from the slave trade history of the sea uncovers the longue durée violence of slavery that turned humans into inhuman objects that lived or died according to the whims of their captors. I read less for historical continuity than for the haunting, hallucinatory effects of terror and for the metamorphosis of humans into commodities. Attention to the ungroundedness at the crux of modernity—the slave ship as a factory/prison/school that transformed captive persons into objects—allows for a critique of the structures that modernity imposes: if they are made, they can be unmade.[19] I foreground how modernists made this critique available through experiments with literary form that refer back, sometimes unconsciously, to slavery's violent legacy at sea. Second, I argue that by denaturalizing geographies, commodities, and the human, modernists make space for, as Frantz Fanon puts it, "introducing invention into life."[20] I emphasize modernist fiction's speculative elements—the creative unleashing of new, utopian possibilities—as a constructive project concerned with building new spaces and establishing new relationalities.[21] While I draw out alternatives to the liberal subject only momentarily glimpsed in the modernist texts I examine, the coda addresses new routes for global race studies in modernism and beyond. Throughout these pages, I explore ways of reimagining the human through the lens of Black Caribbean writers' critical tools, especially Édouard Glissant's poetics of relation and Sylvia Wynter's being human as praxis.[22] These conceptualizations highlight relationality such that the ontological dividing line between humans and animals, plants, water, rocks, air, spirits, aliens, and other humans, gives way and reassembles into something other than European Man while still keeping human agency in the foreground.

The task of rethinking the human is an urgent one. The dominant model of the human I reference above is shorthand for European humanism, a category of philosophical doctrines "that affirm the dignity and worth of humans, based on the ability to determine right and wrong by appeal to universal human qualities—particularly rationality."[23] Very briefly, humanism, especially as it was variously conceptualized during the Enlightenment (1685–1815), holds that rationality rather than adherence to religious doctrine is humankind's chief attribute. In the colonies, this doctrine helped to justify how through scientific reason, Europeans are fit to govern the world. The more recent form of humanism, liberal subjectivity, emphasizes the subject's autonomy—its apartness from others and nature—and self-interest in economics, politics, and society. The problem with European humanism is that it is built upon metaphysical hierarchies, including the elevation of mind (exemplified by European men) over bodies (especially Indigenous and Afro-diasporic peoples), as I explore in chapter 1. Blackness, in this schema, functions to define Man as universal in opposition to his other: the "uncivilized savage."[24] In his universality, Man narrates his exploits as the progressive, positive overcoming of obstacles, including superstition and unreason. These latter qualities characterize "savages" in their entwinement with "uncivilized" nature, a mute, irrational particularity in need of Man's direction. The alternatives to this model, envisioned by Glissant, Wynter, and others, reject this model of anti-Blackness. Instead, as Alexander G. Weheliye argues:

> Afro-diasporic cultures provide singular, mutable, and contingent figurations of the human and thus do not represent mere bids for inclusion in or critiques of the shortcomings of western liberal humanism. . . . Black studies, especially as it is imagined by thinkers such as Spillers and Wynter, is engaged in engendering forms of the human vital to understanding not only black cultures but past, present, and future humanities. As a demonic island, black studies lifts the fog that shrouds the laws of comparison, particularity, and exception to reveal an aquatic outlook "far away from the continent of man."[25]

Because African and Afro-diasporic peoples have been excluded from conceptions of European Man, they are less constrained by its structures. Their cultures, as envisioned by modernist writers, exhibit open-ended, particular, and changeable experiments in how to think human-nonhuman relationality. And these experiments, because they are open-ended, have the potential to impact positively all of humanity, not just Black peoples. As a "demonic island," Black Studies injects what Wynter understands the demonic to be—uncertainty and nonlinearity—into how knowledge and being unfold.[26] The singularity of the island perspective "lifts the fog" to reveal what European Man disavows, namely, an aquatic outlook where the grounds for comparison and exclusionary belonging fall away. I read the phrase "aquatic outlook" as a swirling, mobile conflation of traumatic memories, creative mutations, impurity, and unboundedness that dismantle categories of race, gender, language, species, and more. By contrast, the continent of Man is fixed, territorial, and warlike.

Spurred by the fluidity afforded by an "aquatic outlook," this book moves across the color line to place the racial categories of white and Black in relation to each other as both conjoined and divided. This lens confronts the reification of racially and geographically defined fields of knowledge to move toward knowledge of the open-ended whole, premised on the "dark underside of modernity" that includes Black Atlantic histories.[27] It asks, how can African and Afro-diasporic thought allow for a rethinking of modernism outside of its provincially constituted categories, including European Man himself? In posing this question, this project extends critical efforts in the new modernist studies to articulate Black and postcolonial modernisms with and against white Euro-modernisms begun decades ago by Houston A. Baker, Simon Gikandi, George Hutchinson, Michael North, Jahan Ramazani, and many others.[28] Laura Doyle and I in *Geomodernisms: Race, Modernism, Modernity* argue for the spatial expansion of modernism beyond Europe and North America where in myriad "contact-zone clashes and reversals" global modernity spawned modernisms informed "by the repressed ghosts of an African modernity, an Atlantic modernity, a subaltern modernity."[29] In this formulation, one might hear an echo of Fredric Jameson's influential argument in "Modernism and Imperialism," that "colonialism means that a significant structural segment of the economic system as a whole is now located elsewhere, beyond the metropolis in colonies over the water whose own life experience and life world—very different from that of the imperial power—remain unknown and unimaginable for the subjects of the imperial power, whatever social class they may belong to."[30] The invisible colonies and their ghostly presence, Jameson argues, produce in Euro-modernists their distinctive styles and formal experimentations as a means of registering (but not solving) this historical problem. *Modernism and the Middle Passage* extends Jameson's influential thesis beyond labor to engage with questions of Black fungibility and commodification that, as Tiffany Lethabo King argues, "defines and organizes Black value within relations of conquest."[31] Colonizers imagine and shape Black bodies and their metonymic relation to land in ways that legitimize colonial expansion. In addition, they naturalize these activities to render them unremarkable—indeed, invisible—to the metropole. Conversely, Black and postcolonial modernisms arise in contact zones that host clashes of incommensurable cultures and values. Chinua Achebe's *Things Fall Apart*, Ngũgĩ wa Thiong'o's *A Grain of Wheat*, and Nella Larsen's *Quicksand*, to name just a few examples, imaginatively inhabit both sides of the modernity/coloniality divide and therefore can denaturalize the denigration of Blackness and revalue it as a means of being human otherwise.[32] The critical project of comparing postcolonial, Black, and white modernisms, as Laura Doyle and I say in *Geomodernisms*, "is not to dilute [the historic and local] specificity of [these texts] or the term [modernism] but rather to concretize both ... insofar as they share a global horizon that effects both content and form. The question of whether we should name these various works 'modernist' is less pressing than the need to understand the circuits they share."[33]

Modernism and the Middle Passage emphasizes oceanic, rather than geo, circuits: the shorelines, docks, deltas, and archipelagos of the Atlantic World. Although it doesn't consider other oceans, the open-endedness of relation acknowledges the transoceanic connectedness of the world-system. It also doesn't offer a linear historical narrative: its metaphors are not lines, exchanges, or webs. Rather, it proceeds by nonlinear swirls: the argument moves backward through the long history of modernity/coloniality, forward to contemporary rewritings of modernist texts, and drifts in the modernist historical now: the early to mid-twentieth century. Reading from the sea allows two critical moves: 1) rather than compare two discrete modernist entities through the seeming fixity of Western-derived categories, the extremity of the Middle Passage reveals how these categories, and even the human itself, are malleable and in flux; and 2) attention to the absent presence of the Middle Passage underscores the uneven circulations of Atlantic modernisms and beyond. The latter aim raises questions about the global circulation of modernist texts. By attending to modernity's counter-history of slavery, this book addresses the formation of what Jennifer Wenzel calls, "traffic lines of power and modes of inequality" that determine which texts circulate globally, what counts as universal, what can be narrated, and what is cast off as refuse or inessential backdrop.[34] Wenzel's critical object is "world literature" that, during the first decades of the twenty-first century, eclipsed the older, field-specific work of comparative literature. Global modernisms are, to be sure, a subset of this endeavor. In addressing the shortcomings of world literature as a field of inquiry, Wenzel joins other critics, including Emily Apter, Pheng Cheah, and Aamir Mufti, who caution against an uncritical acceptance of a frictionless circulation of global literature, especially in English. Wenzel's project of reading for the planet from the perspective of those dispossessed by modernity seeks to "imagin[e] across social divides and break[] through what [she] calls *quarantines of the imagination*."[35] Without attending to the unevenness by which literature circulates, she warns, readers "can effect a *gentrification* of the imagination, displacing communities and epistemologies in the name of breaking down barriers."[36] Even more damaging, the displacement caused by gentrification is quickly forgotten in the name of the greater good of world literary expansion. Mufti writes that the process of determining what gets to circulate is naturalized and normalized in a manner that "eras[es] the scene of politics and power that marks its emergence. This retroactive ability of English in its contemporary 'global' form to suspend its own prehistory should be of interest and concern to criticism and to humanistic study more broadly."[37] Part of this amnesia, he suggests, stems from an emphasis on creolization and métissage that assimilates writers from the non-West into the global republic of literature. A presentist emphasis on hybridity and assimilation fails to attend to the long history of empire's violence and to its seemingly intractable structures.

Within the specific field of global modernist studies, this amnesia appears when critics focus strictly on the ways in which modernism circulates globally or when they posit modernity as the only horizon of political possibility. This danger continues under the new rubric of "weak modernisms," a critical trend that focuses on what Paul Saint-Amour calls "the dissidence of the weak," the formerly overlooked activities and stances of women, queers, and the disabled who occupy "the everyday, the domestic, the affective, the middlebrow, the infrastructural, the doctrinal."[38] As pliable as these new modernisms are, Saint-Amour wonders whether they rhetorically mask a power play of the same order as exclusionary "strong" modernisms once did. He asks, "When does the weakening of a field's central term participate, deliberately or not, in a 'lose to win' strategy, a performatively submissive showing of the belly that draws attention away from a territorial dominance-bid?"[39] In the terms I am presenting here, the concern is whether the global horizon of modernism and the expansion of weak modernisms ultimately function to assimilate different points of views and geographies into the umbrella of liberal subjectivity, effectively extending empire's reach. Does the new modernist studies and its affiliate, weak modernisms, function as what Mufti claims is "*a border regime*, a system for the regulation of movement, . . . a regime of *enforced* mobility and therefore of *immobility* as well?"[40] Ultimately, Saint-Amour suggests that weak modernisms, like all critical work, must be self-reflexive about the power/knowledge it produces.

It is one aim of this book to show how white modernist writers Joseph Conrad, Virginia Woolf, Jean Rhys, and William Faulkner partake in the power granted by racial supremacy while also reading them against the grain to show how they write against the fixed category of race, whether consciously or not. White modernists, in my analysis, are chiefly concerned with the waning of their power, rather than with their race, at the end of empire. (Although power and race, of course, are related.) However, I locate places in their texts that begin to break down or displace racial categories, especially when they reassess empire in its terminal crisis.[41] I liken this endeavor to Mara de Gennaro's methodology of reading modernism *after* postcolonialism. Specifically, she demonstrates how "literary form can evoke alternative possibilities for thought and action even in texts that ostensibly deny their viability."[42] In early twentieth-century literary texts, those alternative possibilities appear as uncertainty and unreliability, especially at moments of hallucinatory extremis and catastrophe where the poetics of the text "exceeds the ostensible control of the narrator."[43] I extend this methodology not only to account for, as de Gennaro does, the "refusal of secure knowledge and fearless belief" in modernist and postcolonial texts, but also to avoid Wenzel's "quarantines of the imagination" that preclude thinking the historical relation between white and Black modernists.[44] This book shows how both critical endeavors—a critique of modernism as it has been historically configured as an object of knowledge and a counterfactual reading against the grain of the text—are needed to rethink white modernisms with the Middle Passage.

In considering uneven circulations in the circum-Atlantic world, this book would not be possible without *The Black Atlantic*. Paul Gilroy's book began the process of reading Black artists and writers from the sea. It foregrounds the Atlantic as the shifting, rhizomatic grounds of cultural exchanges between Afro-diasporic peoples across the North Atlantic world. For Gilroy, attention to the Atlantic signaled that Afro-diasporic subjects could not be defined strictly through the bounded, minoritizing scope of national belonging, especially in the United States and United Kingdom. Configured doubly, as both internal and external to national time and space, Black cultural production, in Gilroy's view, serves as an important counterculture of modernity and a crucial resource for bringing to fruition the delayed promise of modernity: freedom and equality for all. Gilroy's chronotope of the ship crossing and recrossing the Atlantic allows him to draw attention to the Middle Passage, the idea of Africa as a redemptive homeland, and the international circulation of Black texts, music, and activist activity from the eighteenth century to the present. By foregrounding the vital contributions by Afro-diasporic subjects to modern thought and culture, Gilroy omits, even as he gestures toward it, as Gikandi points out, "the story of black suffering and the occlusion of Africa in the moral and social geography of the black Atlantic."[45] Sharpe puts the matter in succinct phenomenological terms: "While the air of freedom might linger around the ship, it does not reach into the hold, or attend the bodies in the hold."[46] Here, uneven circulations attend the slave ship itself. Replacing Gilroy's chronotope of the sailing ship as a vehicle for masculine freedom with what Elizabeth DeLoughrey calls the "condensed chronotope of the belly of the slave ship," the Atlantic becomes, for critics after Gilroy, an abject place of wreckage and stasis.[47] But it is also a place that reimagines the world. *Modernism and the Middle Passage* demonstrates how imaginative accounts of the belly of the ship figure the human in lateral, inventive relations with the nonhuman: animals, elements, plants, and more.

While this book attends chiefly to how Afro-diasporic thought transforms modernism, it also contributes to Middle Passage studies by conjoining catastrophe with ecology. It does this not to affirm an apocalyptic vision of climate change, but rather to rethink the catastrophe of the transatlantic slave trade in order to advance a decolonial critique of posthumanism, new materialism, and other Western versions of ecological thought.[48] It asks, how did the African captives reinvent their humanity in the face of atrocious violence and radical displacement? How is it possible to read what Wynter calls the "narratively condemned status" of Blackness as a disruption of thought itself and, in particular, of the current trend to rethink the human through posthumanism, new materialism, and Anthropocene discourse?[49] Addressing the critical need to move "beyond the human," Zakiyyah Iman Jackson pointedly asks, "What and crucially whose conception of the human are we moving beyond?" Even the spatial gesture of "beyond," she continues, "takes for granted Man's authority over the entire contested field pertaining to matters 'human.' Thus praxes of humanity illegible from within the logic of Man are simply rendered void or made to accord with Man's patterned logics by acts of presupposition."[50] The disavowal of racial matters in posthumanist and new materialist criticism is not simply a failure to address inclusivity. Rather, critics' inattention to how race frames the very nature of their perceived reality results in their ignorance at how Blackness, Jackson writes, "conditions and constitutes the very nonhuman disruption and/or displacement they invite."[51] Posthumanism and new materialism, then, carry forward the human qualities aligned with whiteness in a differential and hierarchized opposition to Blackness.[52]

Instead, attention to Blackness as it was violently formed in the Middle Passage disrupts certainties of knowledge. The event of transatlantic slavery, according to novelist and poet Dionne Brand, enacts "a tear in the world." Jared Sexton glosses this phrase as "an offering or gift, really, for thinking differently about space, time, being, existence and so on—a whole series of ontological matters—*through* an inextricable and inescapable nexus of sociopolitical problems giving rise to divergent ethical dilemmas."[53] The question of race, and especially Blackness, Sexton continues, "is a dangerous, disorienting offering because it opens the space for articulating what is unthought—and encountering the unthinkable—in the material-discursive activity involved."[54] As this book explores, thinking the nonplace of the slave ship hold where the captor reduced African captives to a state of death-in-life produces what Sexton calls, "demand in excess of any presently imaginable form of realization."[55] It is this demand to which this book attends in order to allow for new ways of thinking the human in mutually constitutive relations with the nonhuman. Further, the chapters to come offer a counter-history of Blackness from which to think and organize an adequate social response to our present, planetary catastrophe of climate change that exacerbates racism, xenophobia, and misogyny. Sexton eloquently summarizes the challenge of thinking Blackness:

> I might call this blackness as persistence, which suspends the differences between life and death, and between life (and death) and non-life. Living things persist, non-living things persist, dead things persist, undead things persist. The slave is the threshold of legal non-personhood, communing among other things, where the damned coexist with this bitter earth, with nonhuman animals, wild and hunted, domesticated and slaughtered, with aspects of the natural landscape like plants and rivers despoiled, and mountains and mineral deposits blown apart and mined out, all the fauna and flora, all the inorganic matter and the immaterial stuff that is split off from the world of proper human beings and corporations.[56]

In tracing Black coexistence with the nonhuman and the dead, this book corrects the racial blindness of Western ecological thought, including work by Stacy Alaimo, Jane Bennett, and Bruno Latour, that assumes that European Man is the only model for being human and leap over Indigenous and Afro-diasporic possibilities to embrace the posthuman and postmodern, as if all peoples have already achieved full humanity in the European humanist sense.[57]

The implied narrative linearity of the posthuman is suspect. Part of my project to attend to the reimagining of the human depends upon a reconsideration of narrative form. If the bildungsroman represents modernity through narratives of national and individual development, as Jed Esty argues, *Modernism and the Middle Passage* shows what happens to narrative when it strives to represent an unbounded and intra-animated world.[58] It demonstrates the ways in which the experience and legacy of the Middle Passage have impacted narrative form by means of attending to description, settings, atmospheres, minor characters, and other instances of backdrop and detail. So, too, this study transvalues historical significance by holding up the Middle Passage as the crux of modernity. Such a reversal—that opposes the African captives' invisibility in the making of modernity—instantiates my critical thought experiment and methodology: What happens to conceptions of modernism when modernity signifies the racial and sexual violence of slavery and colonization? How might we read modernist texts then? How can the mobility and relationality of modernist writings in the circum-Atlantic Anglophone world (the delimitation of this book, but not at all the limit of modernist circulations) yield an ethics of reading in common, across difference that nevertheless registers the collective and ongoing suffering of untold millions of humans in the making and sustaining of modernity?

In order to achieve these ends, this book expands the Middle Passage archive by featuring Hurston's *Barracoon* and McKay's *Romance in Marseille* (published for the first time in 2020). Hurston's and McKay's texts tell a tale of loss and dehumanization rather than assimilation into the nation, a critical narrative that contributed to their unpublished, uncirculated status. Their newly visible texts, confined no longer to the dusty archive shelf, aid in restructuring and ungrounding modernism such that the whiteness of modernism may no longer be a given. I don't mean by this statement that I'm endeavoring to change the modernist canon—who's in and who's out—but, rather, I seek to break modernism open to the past and future so that it interweaves with the long history of slavery and anti-racist counter-histories. Only by confronting the foundations of geographic and racial divides can anti-racist and decolonial modernist studies be possible.[59]

THE CHAPTERS

The reader, I'm sure, has already noticed a penchant for musical vocabulary and a mixed-media presentation of the argument. Both choices reflect the ungroundedness of the Middle Passage where the Africans' metaphysical certainties fell away and the enslavers violently imposed a metaphysics of race that was belied by the captives' resistance to their degradation. The multimedia contents disrupt a continuous narrative and consolidate my argument through what Walter Benjamin calls the "dialectical image." Reproductions of Kara Walker's sculpture, Ellen Gallagher's painting, Ernestine Mills's suffrage postcard, and Emma Langdon Roche's photograph pepper this book and are formally homologous to the unmaking and remaking of enslaved people: the images show both the promise and violence of modernity/coloniality *and* the possibility of synthesis: a way forward through catastrophe. The musical vocabulary—interlude, overture, coda—and emphasis on sound underscore the performativity of the scripts for being human. This book's argument performs the human differently by denaturalizing the narrative of European Man. In addition, I enact a method of reading from the sea that keeps the transatlantic slave abyss always in view to emphasize the ungrounded, and hence contingent, nature of time, space, race, and the human. My argument in each chapter begins with an element of an ecotonal seascape—waves, alluvium, delta, archipelago—to emphasize the agential features of the sea and landscape and how modernist writers structured their remembrance of the Middle Passage through the nonrepresentational but lively voices of those terraqueous zones.

Taking its cue from Kara Walker's installation, this book follows the Atlantic Ocean's movements: it is as much about Britain and West Africa as it is about North American and Caribbean slavery and its afterlife. (An analysis of Latin American oceanic entanglements is beyond the Anglophone purview of this study.) The introductory chapter 1, "Reading with the Sea," further lays out the stakes of my argument and key analytic terms: geography, animism, and being human as praxis. Its frame begins with the commodification of African captives in the slave trade to build the argument that being human otherwise arises from this event in the "new" world. Rethinking the human demands an attention to geography as lively in order to contest the abstractions of European Man and his cartography. Geography instead produces dynamic form that revalues and resignifies materiality. Finally, animism serves as a crucial term for understanding the interactions between these subjects and their surrounds. I strengthen these claims through readings of Zora Neale Hurston's *Barracoon* (1931), Joseph Conrad's *The Nigger of the 'Narcissus'* (1897), and the slave trade archive.

Following the ocean's remixing and recycling of matter, my argument and presentation of texts, as mentioned earlier, do not proceed in a linear fashion. My approach instead begins from material-formal (empirical and imaginative/conceptual) aspects of the seas and shoreline. I do this to read imminently from the sea rather than from the abstractions of nation and the individual. Chapter 2, "Alluvium," draws on Glissant's notion of how alluvium is indistinct, unexplored, and discounted as waste. It begins with the premise that Black lives are also treated as sea-born refuse and that Hughes's *The Big Sea* (1940), Hurston's *Their Eyes Were Watching God* (1937), and McKay's *Romance in Marseille* (1931–1934) revalue Blackness by means of their characters' material interdependence with one another and with the nonhuman. It argues that these narratives reinvent being human as malleable and permeable to others and to their surroundings and that, in so doing, they transform an exclusion from liberal subjectivity into a riotous experiment of living otherwise together.

An interlude pauses to bridge and register the absent presence of the slave abyss that divides the Black writers in chapter 2 from the historical limitations of white modernist writers who nonetheless draw from the legacy of the Middle Passage. To illustrate the conjunctions and disjunctions between the two sides of history, it discusses Jamaican novelist Marlon James's assessment of Rhys and Woolf as well as Djuna Barnes's performative journalism in "How It Feels to be Forcibly Fed" (1914). The next two chapters focus on only one primary author, Woolf in chapter 3 and Rhys in chapter 4, and then consider Black rewritings of each author, Kabe Wilson on Woolf and Marlon James and Jamaica Kincaid on Rhys. Chapter 3, "Waves," argues that the disciplining of white femininity is intimately entangled with the long history of slavery and conquest and that Woolf figures this imbrication in her novel *The Waves* (1931). She explores this violence by drawing from abolition discourse on slavery, but the connection between patriarchal violence toward white women and racial and sexual violence toward African descended peoples is then put to rest with the drowning suicide of Rhoda. Further, the chapter argues that Woolf's experimental aesthetics produces a queer ecology that, while keeping racial dominance in place, nevertheless challenges the liberal subject. I end the chapter with Black British performance artist Kabe Wilson's "Dreadlocks Hoax" that recycles Woolf's *A Room of One's Own* into a twenty-first century tale of disidentification from Woolf's racial biases.

In chapter 4, "Archipelago," white Caribbean writer Jean Rhys presents this geographical formation as chaos, wildness, and movement. Unlike the uninterrupted rhythm of waves on the English shore in chapter 3, Rhys's archipelagic imagination openly acknowledges the catastrophic racial violence of the Middle Passage as part of the melancholic geography of the Caribbean. From *Voyage in the Dark* (1934) to *Wide Sargasso Sea* (1966), Rhys's archipelagic imagination breaks down signification, fragments narrative, and fleetingly asserts Black Creole understandings of being human otherwise through the animism of the land- and seascapes as well as through obeah practices. In addition, Rhys's novels interrogate the destructive nature of white privilege (to which her protagonists nevertheless succumb) and contest the commodification of white women and art through abjection and self-destruction. The chapter concludes by reading Jamaica Kincaid's *The Autobiography of My Mother* (1996) and Marlon James's *The Book of Night Women* (2009) as Afro-diasporic revisions of Rhys's work. They demonstrate the importance of Rhys's texts across the color line as well as the need for ongoing critique of her work.

Chapter 5, "Delta," pairs the Mississippi Delta with the Niger Delta. There, I argue that Faulkner's and Tutuola's novels express a dialectic between the lure of extractive wealth and ruination, decades before the oil industry had fully taken over the Mississippi and Niger Deltas. I show how their fictions rewrite the geological grammar of extraction that legitimates the forcible removal of Africans, as nonhuman "natural resources," as well as valuable minerals from the earth. I track how the category of Blackness as inhuman slides—i.e., fails to remain fixed and inert—to reveal Black agency that reorders and rehumanizes relations between humans and the earth. I link this agency on the threshold of life and death to Faulkner's writings on the Middle Passage: the short story "Red Leaves" (1930), the screenplay of *The Last Slaver* (1936), *Absalom, Absalom!* (1936), and *Go Down, Moses* (1941). Quite differently from Faulkner, but with surprising formal convergences of sedimentation, Tutuola's mid-century novels, *The Palm-Wine Drinkard* (1952) and *My Life in the Bush of Ghosts* (1954) caution against historical amnesia. They do so by referencing the slave trade and foregrounding West African cosmologies where life and death exist on a continuum and where the forest seethes with spirits, animals, and plants that exist on the same ontological plane as their human visitors. On the eve of Nigeria's independence, Tutuola's novels offer West Africans a strident warning against the dangers of historical amnesia.

The "Coda" pauses to note the limitations that an emphasis on Middle Passage history has on the formation of Afro-diasporic belonging. From there, it offers an alternative genealogy of global racial formations that begins with W. E. B. Du Bois's characterization of World War One as the violence of colonialism and slavery arriving at Europe's doorstep. Postwar crises of statelessness, genocide, mass migrations, and refugees result in "surplus" populations who live in the interstices of global capitalism and persist in decolonial forms of sociality: nomadic, Indigenous, fugitive, and more. These populations cross all the oceans and bring with them urgently needed alternatives to our Anthropocene present.

1

READING WITH THE SEA

> *The ocean had*
> *no memory of the wanderings of Gilgamesh, . . .*
> *It was an epic where every line was erased*
> *yet freshly written in sheets of exploding surf*
>
> —DEREK WALCOTT, *OMEROS*

Reading with the sea demands a rethinking of time and space, nature and culture, and the human itself. Water is a medium that circulates both within bodies and without.[1] It necessitates new critical methods, scales, and objects. Water is agential: it erodes rocks and shorelines, nurtures life, absorbs carbon, produces energy, inundates boats and shores, and decomposes organisms. Its actions compost and recirculate; its unmaking of organic matter allows new life to occur. Water unsettles forms, overflows boundaries, and refuses any fixed categories of thought, including the divisions between land and sea. Marine geographer Philip E. Steinberg asserts that the production of space is part of the sea's unfolding: space is constituted by and constitutive of the sea's tidal movements. The interaction of land and sea consists of silting, eroding, and pressuring that continually reshapes coastlines. In so doing, it challenges "the Euclidian conception of space as a stable surface . . . that separates[s] space from the matter and meanings that occur within. From a Euclidean perspective, the foundational 'space' that remains after substance is stripped away is empty, abstracted, and atemporal, and this provides a poor foundation for theorizing relational geographies of imminence."[2] Abstract space depends upon a clear distinction between inside and outside. It marks territorial boundaries of sovereignty and a bounded sense of society whose national historical development overcomes obstacles and transcends the past. And while mariners map their positions by means of the abstract measurements of latitude and longitude, the sea itself does not signify through linear narrative or fixed space. Hester Blum argues that the oceans provide "a methodological model for nonlinear or nonplanar thought."[3] She draws upon Steinberg's assertion that the oceans are "continually being reconstituted by a variety of elements: the nonhuman and the human, the biological and the geophysical, the historic and the contemporary."[4] There is no autonomous vantage point from without; reading from the sea results in relational geographies of immanence since even the perceiving human subject is co-constituted with matter. As water dissolves and recirculates human and animal bodies, plant life, and human-derived detritus, history from an oceanic perspective accumulates and metamorphoses. It becomes, as Steve Mentz writes, "a comingling and fecund process, a fertilizing combination of the living and the dead" that produces both noise and meaning; blockage and circulation.[5] More, the sea's mixture of life and death serves as a medium for a transhistorical sensibility.[6] The old becomes newly relevant, revived from the disremembered, and the present becomes answerable to a reawakened past and a moment for imagining futures that do not resemble the present.

To begin to conceptualize this three-dimensional, nonlinear, shifting space from the event of the Middle Passage, this introductory chapter provides vital theoretical and historical backgrounds that inform the chapters to come. First, it discusses historians and critics of transatlantic slavery who emphasize the significance of human commodification. This body of work contributes to theories of Blackness that highlight the structural divide between European Man and enslaved persons who are commodified. Then, it considers how experimental modernist literature contests the commodity structure. From there, the chapter outlines the ways in which the modernist experimental literature explored in this book reimagines geography, the human, and the animism of the nonhuman. After this theoretical foray, it turns to the history of modernity/coloniality and the archives of the transatlantic forced passage. Last, it demonstrates how attention to the Middle Passage imagines the human in lateral relations to the sea via readings of Zora Neale Hurston's *Barracoon* and Joseph Conrad's *The Nigger of the 'Narcissus.'*

I begin the discussion of my framework with the powerful revisionist historical account of transatlantic slavery, Stephanie Smallwood's *Saltwater Slavery* (2007). Her history begins by positing the "traumatic echo of commodification" that manifested in Afro-diasporic subjects each time a new cargo of "saltwater" enslaved people arrived from Africa to the United States and Caribbean.[7] Commodification, for Smallwood, marks the singular innovation of transatlantic slavery. The captives, she writes, "were represented [in European records] merely as ciphers in the political arithmetic, [and] thus feature in the documentary record not as subjects of social history but as objects or quantities."[8] Smallwood builds upon Orlando Patterson's understanding of slavery as "social death" (i.e., the loss of kinship ties and social dishonor) by highlighting the extreme self-alienation of commodification. She argues that "the Africans revealed the boundaries of the middle ground between life and death where human commodification was possible."[9] She emphasizes how slave ship owners and captains wielded "the rationalized science of human deprivation" by keeping the captives barely alive through reduced rations and extremely crowded holds in order to guarantee profits.[10] By means of this ongoing deprivation and violence, the captives' wills were stripped away. They became "bodies animated only by others' calculated investment in their physical capacities."[11] Despite these brutal conditions, Smallwood says, "we find a stark contest between slave traders and slaves, between the traders' will to commodify people and the captives' will to remain fully recognizable as human subjects."[12] The captives fought back and found inventive measures by which to maintain their humanity.

Hortense J. Spillers's foundational essay, "Mama's Baby, Papa's Maybe: An American Grammar Book" extends Smallwood's formulation by theorizing the captives' humanity on board the slave ship in terms of how the ongoing violence they sustained foundationally altered their gendered, cultured being. Spillers writes that the captives became a cultural "vestibularity"—at the borders of the human—insofar as their lacerated "flesh," their wounded body, "exposes" or makes available to others the captives' sense of self.[13] They are ungendered, "reduce[d] to a thing, becoming being for the captor."[14] But in this dissolving of boundaries and will—in this "monstrosity"—there is, at the same time, the possibility for a new human, what she calls a "different social subject."[15] Spillers argues for a "wild and unclaimed richness of possibility that is not interrupted, not 'counted'/'accounted,' or differentiated, until its movement gains the land thousands of miles away from its point of departure."[16] Moving beyond Smallwood's normative "humanity," Spillers finds the potential at sea, at the captives' greatest extremity, for recreating the human, beyond gender and sexual norms and the autonomous subject. This transformation occurs just prior to the captives' (re)quantification as commodities upon landing. On the one hand, slave traders made African captives just prior to auction into objects of exchange, or commodities (oiling and feeding them better to assert their capacity for work); on the other, the bondspersons' injured flesh reveals the flip side of commodity: devalued, unformed materiality (bodies on the verge of death) through which one might glimpse the possibility of being human otherwise, an absent presence that upends the grammar of the subject.

It's important to underscore the fleeting and speculative nature of this glimpse. Saidiya Hartman builds upon Spillers's theorization of the captive's flesh by reflecting on the impossibility of its representation. In an interview with Frank Wilderson III, she states, "Every attempt to emplot the slave in a narrative ultimately resulted in his or her obliteration [into national narratives of assimilation]. What I was trying to do [in *Scenes of Subjection*] was to narrate a certain impossibility, to illuminate those practices that speak to the limits of the most available narratives to explain the position of the enslaved."[17] The impossibility of narration arises due to the captive's existence in the liminal space between life and death and between commodification and resistance. Hartman acknowledges Spillers's influence in her argument: she says that because the female captive has no ability to consent to sexual relations given her object status, even the material shaping of her body and subjectivity through gender and sexuality are negated (impossible to think) under these conditions. Hartman puts it thus, "the slave occupies the position of the unthought.... So what does it mean to try to bring that position into view without making it a locus of positive value, or without trying to fill the void?"[18] In other words, how to represent enslaved people when chattel slavery takes away their subject position and leaves in its place traumatic unrepresentability?

What kind of agency is available then? Hartman answers that, for the bondsperson, "existence is the space of death, where negation is the captive's central possibility, whether we think of that as a radical refusal in terms of the social order or these acts that are sometimes called suicide or self-destruction, but which are really an embrace of death."[19]

What might look at first like the reader's sympathetic (or worse, voyeuristic) dwelling on the captives' suffering is instead a necessary critical consideration for theorizing freedom in the interstices of captivity and at the margins of European Man. It is a sketchy, barely imaginable agential space that conjoins the flesh with its proximity to the mutable materiality of the nonhuman. Both critics theorize this liminal agency through the excessive sexual violence that turns female captives into empty vessels for male fantasies and which also renders captives into commodified units of value. I first detail how the commodification of flesh supports colonization, then I turn to how it can become resistant. Hartman states that as a commodity, the captive body is "vulnerable to the projection of other's feelings, ideas, desires, and values."[20] She uses the term "fungibility" to refer to the "interchangeability and replaceability" of commodified Black bodies, that is, how they are rendered identical units of labor power.[21] Hartman also insists, as does Spillers, that the fungibility of Blackness goes far beyond labor power to include its "metaphorical aptitude."[22] A metaphor, as we know, depends upon figurative slippage and thus, as Tiffany Lethabo King writes, "the signified and signifier fail to line up squarely at the sign of the intended commodity with which it is to be exchanged."[23] In addition to being rendered abstract units of exchange, the Black enslaved body also generates fluid symbolic, sexual, and metonymic meanings, becoming "liquid, dust, and more."[24] These tropes frequently supported the colonizing project. King argues that they not only linked captives to "nature" and the exotic (a claim that has long been established), but they also forged a symbolic connection to the Americas that legitimized the exploitation and occupation of colonized land, domination of the "free" seas, and gender and racial violence itself.

An example that King uses will clarify the stakes of this argument. Jennifer L. Morgan shows how in Richard Ligon's *A True and Exact History of the Island of Barbados* (1657), he struggled to make sense of the cognitive dissonance at seeing African women working as agricultural laborers in the Caribbean. Ligon was familiar with West African societies and became disoriented by seeing the radical displacement of Africans set to work in the plantation economy. To account for this cognitive and geographical aphasia—i.e., a conceptual impasse—Ligon turns to metaphor. He recounts a scene in which African men and women transport bunches of plantains, writing "'Tis a lovely sight to see a hundred handsom [sic] Negroes, men and women, with every one a grasse-green bunch of these fruits on their heads . . . the black and green so well becoming one another."[25] Morgan writes, "[Ligon] compares African people to vegetation; they are passively and abstractly beautiful as blocks of color."[26] Here, African men and women are rendered symbolic. They are not merely compared to "nature" or to atavistic ways of life, as common racist tropes would have it. They are *aestheticized* as decorative features intended to accentuate the civilizational prowess of white European masters. In short, Black bodies authorize modernity in the slave trade and plantation economies. Both instances work to shore up European mastery. Like nature itself, Blackness is available to advance the will of European conquest. Black bodies became metonymically and metaphorically associated with the mute materiality of land and sea. This figurative association renders Black bodies, as King puts it, a "manipulable and an open landscape of flux" that includes relations with "plants, objects, and non-human life forms."[27] Paradoxically, the malleability of Blackness also becomes a potential for "escape from the current entrapments of the human."[28] As King argues, the porousness and instability of Blackness threatens to unravel white spaces of conquest and control. It becomes agential. The fungibility of Black flesh connotes unstable borders, processes, and shifting power relations as opposed to the geography of reason enforced by European colonists and settlers that maps land and sea through the abstract, fixed grids of longitude, latitude, and equivalent exchange, as I discuss later in this chapter.

In sum, I have delineated two aspects of fungibility. The first refers to the commodified exchange of bodies and the violent repression that turns subjects into objects. By transforming persons into property, they are excluded from normative ideas of the subject. Second, that exclusion provides the conditions that allow fungibility, as C. Riley Snorton argues, "to become fertile ground for flight. . . . Indeed, in one key sense, . . . fungibility and fugitivity figured two sides of a Janus-faced coin, in which the same logic that figured blackness as immanently interchangeable would also engender its flow."[29] The second form of fungibility is inventive and agential. This book traces how modernist texts critique the first notion and experiment with the second aspect of fungibility. It is here that my framework addresses how the second notion of Black fungibility is also ecological. Rather than conflate Blackness with nature, I trace how the fungibility of Blackness reassembles the human in relation to its surrounds. I show this through the poetics developed by Afro-American and Afro-Caribbean writers. My claim is that modernist experimental aesthetics makes space for thinking the human in a manner that imagines future possibility as radically different from the narratives of Man.

To understand how modernist aesthetics does this requires that I analyze the commodity form. The critique of existing structures built through the transatlantic slave trade begins with the commodity and its fetishization since it is the foundational form of the capitalist world-system and what the African captives and their progeny became under transatlantic slavery. The commodity is fetishized (overvalued), as Marx writes, because it embodies social relations between things, or exchange value, and represses its material remnants (the exhausted, violated bodies of workers and enslaved people and waste material from the production process, including a devastated biosphere). The commodity is abstracted, or severed, from what Marx calls "material [dinglich] relations between persons," or the ways in which communities reproduce themselves via food, shelter, leisure, kinship, etc.[30] I argue that references to the Middle Passage in modernist experimental texts contest the commodity structure. This is so because the trauma of the slave trade makes visible that which is disavowed in commodity fetishism: the constitutive outside of the commodity—broken flesh, abandoned refuse, mutilated bodies, destroyed landscapes, and more.[31] Trauma, as Ewa Płonowska Ziarek argues, is formalized in experimental modernist literature in ways that revalue damaged materialities and contest the hierarchical split between chaotic matter, including bodies, and the commodity form.[32] A primary instance of this contestation, according to Fred Moten and drawn upon by Ziarek, is the commodity who speaks, i.e., the enslaved person, and the ways in which they unsettle the form/matter divide. They do so by resisting their status as a mute, exchangeable object. Instead, they speak their material, lived reality as violated flesh through affective language. Moten's paradigmatic example is Aunt Hester's scream in *Narrative of the Life of Frederick Douglass, an American Slave* (1845). Matter speaks and takes form. Aunt Hester, in signifying her violation, occupies the border between subject and object. Her scream, according to Moten, is "the performance of the object and the performance of humanity" whose "inspirited materiality," an amalgamation of spirit and flesh, disrupts the commodity system by giving value to that which slavery holds to have no intrinsic worth at all.[33]

Besides fetishizing bodies, the commodity structure also impacts how literary form appears to be autonomous or separated from its social and material conditions. Theodor Adorno urges the recognition of history's presence in what looks like art's autonomy. This history, he writes, can be "sought in the recognition of aesthetic form as sedimented content."[34] By this, he means that art originates in a social context, such as religious ceremony or dance, and that the trace of this social origin lives on in aesthetic form. Ziarek's powerful revision of Adorno in the context of gender and race politics in modernism emphasizes the paradox of what Adorno calls art's "heteronomous autonomy," namely, that art stands apart from social divisions of labor and is also a product of it.[35] Ziarek writes, "This contradictory status of modern art situates women's modern literature *between* economic exchange and utopian political praxis, between political domination and the possibility of freedom."[36] This fraught, ambivalent positioning of art, she continues, results in both a "subversion of and complicity with domination."[37] Adding male authors to the mix, as I do, allows me to survey works of art that range widely along the spectrum between domination and freedom. But what joins together all the authors I study is the articulation of enslavement within modernity. Often despite these authors' intentions, the liminality of enslaved persons, as Ziarek argues by drawing on Patterson's *Slavery and Social Death*, contests divisions between the human and nonhuman, the monstrous and normal, life and death, order and chaos, being and nonbeing.[38] Rather than assuming an unchanging dualism between matter and form, modernist texts make visible that which is violently excluded from form—abject bodies, pestilential, contaminated locations, the monstrous, the invisible—in order to challenge the violence of the abstract (exchange value). Matter and form, in this experimental writing, intra-act in dynamic ways, with form serving "as an active intelligible principle of the work."[39] Dynamic form, in revaluing damaged materialities, demonstrates a new way of relating and building collectivities. It reveals co-constitutive, intra-active relations across the human and nonhuman divide such that matter actively shapes and form passively bends. Adorno writes, "Scars of damage and disruption are the modern's seal of authenticity; explosion is one of its invariants."[40] The human as form begins to shape-shift to reveal that which has been excluded from modernity's narrative of development. Loss, violence, and mutilation create the conditions for a new mode of envisioning the world through an Afro-diasporic reinvention of the human.

An awareness of how modernist experimental texts contest the division between materiality and form allows me to make three key interventions in reassessing modernism from the vantage point of the slave trade: geography, animism, and being human as praxis. All of these components arise from trauma that shatters the self-contained subject.

GEOGRAPHY

The texts in this study stand on the edges of the known world. Each chapter is organized by the interaction of land and sea—alluvium, waves, archipelago, and delta—in order to foreground how geography unfolds in material *and* metaphorical terms. By materiality, I refer to how geography actively shapes human and more-than-human possibilities. Space is produced by its inhabitants who are also co-constituted by it. By metaphoricity, I address how language alters human perception of geography in a manner that is ongoing and inventive, as we saw in Morgan's example. Reconfiguring geography as material and metaphorical contests the division of abstract form and inert, passive materiality. I begin each chapter with geography to decenter the human, to listen to and feel the shifting sands and water as they create new interpretive possibilities for what modernism's engagement with the Middle Passage might mean. These shifting, amphibious locations repel aims of anchoring knowledge through fixed coordinates of measurement and meaning. Instead, these texts narrate how geographical zones of waste, contamination, and wetlands might be recovered and revalued as Black, feminist, and queer places of possibility and liberation in relation to the nonhuman. This transvaluation occurs as bodies interact with their surrounds such that, as Katherine McKittrick argues, they forge a "process of self-assertion and humanization."[41] Thus, the geographies of land and sea in this study do not serve as inert, mute backgrounds for the liberal subject. They are not rendered abstract through geometrical measurement (longitude and latitude) and property relations (exchange value). Instead, this book underscores how geography is reenvisioned in modernism as what Édouard Glissant calls "a poetics of landscape."[42]

Glissant shifts the geographic center of modernity from Europe to the Black Atlantic and the Caribbean. In so doing, geography—the sea and shoreline—serves as a place of memory and site of trauma. For him, the sea is opaque; it materially registers how Middle Passage trauma is obscured from history and memory. Nonetheless, the inaccessible trauma produces in subsequent generations a felt sense of absence, loss, and a disconnection from the "new" world. The past haunts the present and prevents the linear unfolding of time. Despite this melancholic haunting, Glissant finds in the unmaking of the self and the collective in trauma the means for what one of his commentators, John E. Drabinski, calls, "*A revolutionary thinking, creating another world.*"[43] The forcibly displaced African-descended peoples, according to Glissant, negotiate their trauma by rerooting themselves in the shifting ecotone of the shoreline, a rooting that is partial, mobile, and subject to ongoing reinvention. The rhythmic settling and unsettling of water and sand serve as a means of articulating a felt sense of an unknown past. This relation becomes for Glissant, as Drabinski writes, "an aesthetics [that] is tantamount to a defense of the elusive utterance, its opacity and murky depth."[44] This aesthetics is speculative; it registers the absent presence of trauma and the liminality of enslavement to reconfigure the dualism between form and matter and between the human and nonhuman. *Modernism and the Middle Passage* draws upon Glissant's groundbreaking work to decenter modernity through Black Atlantic history; to posit trauma as a necessary condition for reinventing the subject and its relation to the world; and to envision geography as entwined with the human as part of "a revolutionary thinking, creating another world."

ANIMISM

Just as geography is envisioned as both metaphor and materiality, so, too, is the nonhuman and both function in modernist literature on the slave trade to contest the form/matter divide. In a recent book, Jay Rajiva critiques the Eurocentrism of trauma studies by suggesting other ways of working through trauma besides the individualist, therapeutic model of the West. He proposes animism, "the belief, common to many parts of the world, in the spiritual [or enlivened] properties of nonhuman matter (including objects, organic substances, and animals)" as an effective remedy for working through trauma.[45] Trauma, he continues, effects a sense of isolation in its victims:

> [It] deadens or dampens the subject's ability to access the world outside of their own pain. . . . The task is to live again, or to derive some measure of healing from trauma within structures of meaning larger than the single person traumatized. The world must be enlivened, but without dismissing or reducing the trauma victim's experience. As a foundation for this enlivening, animism offers, in its very ontology, an ethnically vibrant housing for traumatic experience. It points to phenomena that are not visible through empirical observation, it draws on and emanates from cultures and traditions that have a rich account of being in the world and it posits a fundamental inter-implication between all matter in a given environment.[46]

According to Rajiva, postcolonial trauma is given voice and negotiated through a sense of the nonhuman world's aliveness. In these pages, I discuss animism's function in modernist experimental writing. For my purposes, the term *animism* has clear advantages over primitivism in describing Black modernist writing.[47] Because animism is a quality attributed to the nonhuman in the present, it subverts the linearity of development from tradition to modernity; whereas primitivism, as a supposedly premodern, immediate (instinctual or essential) quality, does not. In addition, animism exists side by side with modern science and technology. As Harry Garuba writes, "animist logic destabilizes the hierarchy of science over magic and the secularist narrative of modernity by reabsorbing historical time into the matrices of myth and magic."[48] Below, and in the chapters to come, I consider how obeah, animated landscapes, and river and sea goddesses, enfold humans within a world not determined strictly by rationality and human will. At the same time, animism criticizes scientific rationalism that has justified racism, sexism, and the destruction of nature. While Conrad, Woolf, and Faulkner are decidedly not influenced by African and Afro-diasporic animist practices, the concept of animism underscores and provincializes their experimental and fleeting notions of the object world's liveliness. Finally, animism precedes new materialist theories by Stacy Alaimo, Karen Barad, Jane Bennett, Mel Y. Chen (who examines animacy in linguistics), and others. I discuss new materialist understandings of more-than-human aliveness in chapter 3; and elsewhere I refer to animism as a multitude of beliefs long practiced by Indigenous and diasporic communities around the globe. I do this in order to entwine environmental thinking with antiracist and decolonial critique.

In addition, the animism of the nonhuman includes literary texts themselves. As Rajiva argues, "All matter is storied matter," but equally "all [written] stories are matter"; they are physical objects that are animated by their content.[49] Books are part of the tissue of the world. They "story" the world and, in so doing, co-constitute it by animating within their readers a vision of what is or could be and thus instituting ethical or destructive actions. In the pages to come, I show how Hughes, Rhys, and Woolf explicitly comment on the status of the literary object as living matter. In Hughes's case, the book as object references Olaudah Equiano's slave narrative in which Equiano describes literacy as a "talking book," a trope of animism in which the book exerts magical powers. This formulation gives more agency to the book as object to shape the world than to the individual reader. Addressing the book as a material object, Hughes, Rhys, and Woolf make visible the text's frame, the social and political effects of that framing, and then dissolve the object back into the unformed materiality from whence it came. In so doing, they comment on the dynamic form/matter interaction of experimental modernist aesthetics.

BEING HUMAN AS PRAXIS

Enlightenment humanism posits Man as a form. Its being comes from its ability to reason and observe: he renders in literate form the objects he observes in order to know and unilaterally act on them. Thus, his narrative of development subordinates nonhumans and less-than-humans (white women and non-Europeans) to his needs and desires. He is autonomous and clearly demarcated from unformed materiality. In later centuries, this understanding of the human informs the liberal subject, defined as a universal ideal, the normative model for peoples around the world. In contrast, modernist questioning of Man as human, as these pages will show, challenges this form/materiality divide and anticipates ecocritical scholarship that offers a lateral, nonhierarchical idea of the human. Chief among these writers is Black studies theorist Sylvia Wynter whose notion of being human in relation, or "as praxis," acknowledges the plasticity and fungibility of being human "as genre" or as a socially and biologically constituted entity that is always being reshaped and reinvented.[50] Rather than posit Man as a biological given, "naturally" superior in race and gender qualities to his subordinates, Wynter borrows from Frantz Fanon the concept of "sociogeny" that refers to how social relations constitute the biological. However, Wynter broadens Fanon's sociogeny to include gender and sexuality. In a conversation with McKittrick, Wynter recalls how she derived "being human as praxis" from Judith Butler's notion of the performative enactment of gender:

> I am suggesting that the enactments of such gender roles are always a function of the enacting of a specific genre of being hybridly [socially and biologically] human. Butler's illuminating redefinition of gender as a praxis rather than a noun, therefore, set off bells ringing everywhere! Why not, then, have the performative enactment of all our roles, of our role allocations as, in our contemporary Western/Westernized case, in terms of, inter alia, gender, race, class/underclass, and, across them all, sexual orientation?[51]

This process is in evidence in the archives of the Middle Passage, as I will show. The horrific racialization on board ship makes visible the contingency and openness of the human itself. And while that openness resulted in the captives' metamorphosis into commodities, we should remember that it's only a partial transformation. This book asks, how might the captives have transformed the residual materiality of the commodity form in order to reshape their humanity under slavery? How might they have formed new relations to the nonhuman, to one another, and to the shifting, unstable geographies and heterotemporalities at sea? The work of Black studies scholars, such as Alexander G. Weheliye and King, have brilliantly opened new avenues of thought in pursuing these questions. These critics, in many different ways, have denaturalized the process of racialization by showing how relation is always mobile: its metaphorical, linguistic, and spatial exchanges, slippages, and resonances exceed racializing categories that aim to fix identities and stabilize geographies. Accordingly, being human as genre (a particular version of a socially organized form) presents sites of resistance and agency that, as Weheliye writes, are "other than that of full, self-present, and coherent subjects."[52] Rather than read for assimilation into modernity as a full citizen modeled on European Man, these critics read against the grain of Western narratives for Black practices of freedom dreams and the "possibilities of other worlds."[53] Reading for being human otherwise shows the limits of liberal subjectivity (its racial and historical blindnesses and power differentials) and opens the horizon of political possibility to a decolonial futurity. The next section outlines the problem of focusing solely on modernity without also treating its socioeconomic basis in colonization. It provides a history of modernity through the lens of the slave trade and exploration at sea, and it demonstrates how modernity/coloniality continues to structure liberal thought. Finally, it argues that without taking into account the uneven system of modernity/coloniality, critics risk reinscribing the same divisions.

MODERNITY/COLONIALITY

To examine the work of white modernist authors in terms of the slave trade is to dwell on a combination of appalling ignorance and bald face appropriations of abolitionist discourse and Black culture. In part, these authors were operating under the conditions of modernity hegemonic in the early to mid-twentieth century. I say this not to excuse their erasure of Black history, but rather to use this problem as a catalyst for opening the archive of modernism to an examination of the centuries-long conditions that fostered this disarticulation. Many scholars, have documented extensively how liberalism, including philosophy, the arts, economics, and government, was co-constituted with colonialism, slavery, capitalism, and empire.[54] I build upon their efforts by examining the maritime world because the European dominance of the oceans was essential to the formation of the modern/colonial system upon which modernity is based. This system involved not only the atrocious theft of land and genocide of Indigenous peoples in the Americas and beyond, but also the forced conscription of millions of people, mostly African from across the Atlantic, to work the mines and plantations under conditions of chattel slavery.

The oceans were charted in a manner that enabled modernity to unfold in tandem with colonization. The modern/colonial world system simultaneously unites and divides the globe into two legal, historical, and economic worlds. A founding instance of this relation occurred on June 7, 1494, when Pope Alexander VI in the Treaty of Tordesillas drew an imaginary line bisecting the Atlantic Ocean from north to south one hundred leagues (approximately 320 miles) west of the Cape Verde Islands. Spain claimed all lands west of this line (occidentalis) while Portugal declared sovereign access to the newly discovered lands east of the line (Indias, or the Orient). In 1506, Pope Julius II moved the line to 370 leagues west of Cape Verde, a shift that allowed Portugal access to all of Brazil. Although these divisions were continuously disputed and did not take into account the later colonial pursuits of other European nations, the epistemological importance of this mapping can hardly be overstated.[55] Carl Schmitt argues that the treaty ushered in the "new nomos of the earth," a cognitive and international legal system that constituted the modern/colonial world system. It mapped the globe into the system of nation-states under the rule of law in Europe and the "free" seas and "heathen" lands governed by the state of exception (the suspension of the rule of law). He writes:

> At this "line" [the western meridian at the Azores], Europe ended and the "New World" began. At any rate, European law, i.e., "European public law," ended here. Consequently, so, too, did the bracketing of war achieved by traditional European international law, meaning that here the struggle for land-appropriations knew no bounds. Beyond the line was an "overseas" zone in which, for want of any legal limits to war, only the law of the stronger applied.[56]

Schmitt argues that the international legal system arose in tandem with commercial interests to sanction the brutal conquest and pillage of the "new" world and other non-European territories.

Crucially enabling this geographical bifurcation of the world was the European scientific method. Mignolo argues that the performative instantiation of dividing the globe into European zones of influence and power allowed for the extension of the new scientific method of observation and a new epistemic foundation for understanding Europe's dominance of the rest of the world. He writes, "this sense of 'newness' will become one of the anchors of all rhetoric of modernity, from the sixteenth century to the twenty-first. The Columbian philosopher Santiago Castro-Gómez described it as 'the hubris of the zero point. It sets the stage for the imperial control and colonization of knowledge and of being.'"[57] Scientific rationality substituted for Divine Will, with the effect that the embodied and local particularity of the observing scientist was bracketed.[58] This transcendental move enabled European observers to discern the universal "natural laws" governing the newly encountered lands. This authority was enforced by means of the rapacious violence of European conquest, the "hubris of the zero point." Scientific knowledge, then, is co-constituted with imperial power in a manner that produces the fantasy of mastery, a delusion because it is based on the violence that enforces it rather than on the indisputable nature of its truth. At the same time, the power/knowledge of Western scientific thought serves to legitimate Europe's rule over the "discovered" lands.[59] Summarizing this mutually constitutive process, Mignolo calls zero point epistemology, "the ultimate grounding of knowledge which paradoxically is ungrounded, or grounded neither in geo-historical location nor in bio-graphical configuration of the bodies. The geopolitical and bio-graphic politics (e.g., body-politics, not bio-politics) of knowledge is hidden in the transparency and universality of the zero point. It is grounding without grounding; it is in the mind and not in the brain and in the heart."[60] The paradoxical grounding of something that is also ungrounded points to the forgetting of the particularities that institute abstract scientific laws.[61] Latitude and longitude, for instance, hide the particularity of their location and value under the guise of an abstract, nonhistorical measurement of space. The fact that the prime meridian bisects the Greenwich Observatory in England, an indicator of England's imperial mastery and the zero point of reference for the rest of the world, does not factor into the utility of the global measurement.

The force and newness of these abstract laws displaced traditional and local knowledges and inaugurated what Mignolo calls "global linear thought" that underlies the rhetoric of modernity.[62] Scientific discovery, allied with imperial commerce, constantly renews modernity by innovating thought, developing technologies, and arriving at scientific breakthroughs. The accumulation of great wealth and scientific knowledge justifies the violent means by which this process occurs. With the ends of wealth and power overriding contested methods, civilizational superiority displayed as good taste and finery legitimated the subordination and enslavement of non-Western peoples.[63] Finally, the bifurcation of the globe between the rule of law in Europe and the state of exception on the seas and in the colonies worked to conceal the connection between violent overseas activities and new liberal freedoms at home. The vast geographical sweep of the oceans, as well as their construction by Europeans as empty, wasted space, aided in divorcing metropolitan and national history from colonial conquest. Steinberg asserts, "The ocean ... was idealized as an empty transportation surface, beyond the space of social relations."[64] The sea, in this formulation, is a space of amnesia. Its scale dwarfs human history and resists human signification. The sea, as Roland Barthes writes, "bears no message."[65] Refusing inscription, the ocean's lack of social meaning instead suggests elemental forces of deep time and space. Gaston Bachelard argues, "To disappear into deep water or to disappear toward a far horizon, to become part of depth or infinity, such is the destiny of man that finds its image in the destiny of water."[66] Rather than dwell on the certainty of death and the smallness of human endeavor on the seas that Bachelard points to, fictional and nonfictional accounts of maritime exploratory voyages, as Michelle Burnham shows, demonstrate a temporality of deferral that justifies the means of present-tense violence for the future ends of colonial conquest and riches: "These narratives ... reveal that commerce didn't so much eliminate violence as conceal it within a narrative temporality of prolonged promise [risk management]."[67] Sea-travel narratives order the chaos at sea by providing a telos that subsumes violence into the celebrated goal of wealth and power.

Meanwhile, the Cartesian divide transforms non-Europeans (including African and African-descended peoples) "into the physical referents" of nature.[68] This division, between rational, scientific Man and the subhuman other, associates the latter with the sensory, externally oriented, nonhuman world. Crucially, this narrative of Man's overcoming of nature through scientific rationality works to disregard African and Afro-diasporic ways of knowing and being because they are irrational in terms of European scientific methods.[69] King summarizes this watertight alibi for the overrepresentation of Man: "These scientific and cultural discourses function as a recursive feedback loop that justifies and legitimizes itself while hiding the ways that humans are both produced by and produce these codes. The notion that humans are external to—or can gaze on—these natural and self-writing codes is a form of autopoiesis."[70] By "autopoiesis," King refers to the circularity, or self-reinforcing logic, of whiteness that both legitimates itself through writing and forecloses other modes of being and knowing, especially those conjoined with "the natural, or sensory bound, elements of the world."[71] Because African and Afro-diasporic peoples have not transcended the natural world to become scientific observers and explorers, European thought denies them the status of historical subjects. Because they appear to Europeans as irrational, they are uncivilizable.

Crucial to this book's consideration of early to mid-twentieth-century literature, the end of slavery did not alter this power dynamic. Lisa Lowe argues, "What some have represented as a linear temporal progression from colonial abjection to liberal freedom actually elides what might be more properly conceived as a spatial dynamic, in which forms of both liberal subject and society in the imperial center are possible only in relation to laboring lives in the colonized geographies of 'zones of exception' with which they coexist, however disavowed."[72] The point here is that white modernist authors operate within a system that actively excludes non-Western territories and racialized people from participation in the history-making society of the European nation-state. This exclusion occurs, in part, due to the form in which the liberal subject and society are represented. In the colonial "zones of exception," reason and narrative founder. This is so because the dehumanizing traumatic violence in the colonies and on the oceans exceeds representation. The breakdown of form, reason, and language in the face of Blackness and the alterity of African and Afro-diasporic geographies presents an intractable problem for white modernism, however much it begins to break away from a mimetic relation between words and things.[73] While an important component of modernism is an attempt to rescale literature in order to move beyond the nation form, its representational purview is still defined by the structure of the modern/colonial system.[74] It narrates history from the vantage point of the liberal subject of modernity, grounded through the particularities of racial and national identities. This problem cannot be resolved by pluralizing or expanding the various kinds of modernisms around the world.[75] Because modernity is configured at its outset as the birth of the new in historical time and, conversely, by the ascendance of scientific and human universality seemingly outside the contingency of history, this structure remains even when adding more or expanded modernisms. In this model, cultural difference (comprised here of subjected peoples in the colonies and internal others in the West) is brought into modernity when that difference narrates itself as realizing universality (the human as transparent and fully recognizable by Europeans) and historicity (narratives of individual and social development). This pluralized model of various cultural, geographical, and racialized modernisms is insufficient for dismantling the Eurocentrism of modernism as it still stands.

A view from the other side of slavery's legacy is missing as a decolonial counterweight. This critique does not suggest that there's a hidden modernism waiting to be discovered. Rather, it argues that Black writers inject into their representational and formal strategies figures, affects, and structures that refuse the tenets of Man and take their force from the transformation of African captives into fungible (commodified) objects and, from there, to a reconception of being human in ongoing, contingent relations to alterity. Rather than examining how these writers assimilate into the universalism and historicity of the liberal subject, I emphasize how a counter-history of slavery, as imagined by Black modernists and available as speculative glimpses into the slave trade archive, reveals another way of being that resists the power and normativity of Man's overrepresentation as human. Blackness, in these texts, is a resistant practice and way of being that unsettles Man's foundational authority.[76] More, a counter-history of Blackness, especially as it is embodied in the "material capacities" of Black maternity, as Zakiyyah Iman Jackson writes, "destabilizes and even ruptures the reigning order of representation that grounds the thought-world relation."[77] As I will discuss, chattel slavery figured Black maternity as sheer matter, a monstrous source of human difference. The inventive, improvisational practice of representing Blackness against the grain of its imposition by modernity/coloniality questions the hegemony of Man. It suggests a mode of being that is neither self-contained and individuated nor imitative of European Man as its normative ideal. Because of its rejection of Man as ideal, Black resistance derived in part from a counter-history of slavery disrupts the very system of modernity/coloniality. In light of this understanding of Blackness, it becomes evident that the pluralizing model of the new modernisms, one that adds new versions of modernism without interrogating how modernism upholds modernity/coloniality, is insufficient for rethinking the historical relation of race and modernism. In saying this, I do not mean to imply that efforts of inclusion and recognition within liberalism should be suspended. However, I am arguing that these efforts alone cannot overcome the hierarchization of peoples and the instrumentalization of nature. Instead, exciting new studies of race and modernism seek to decolonize inherited conceptual and interpretive reading practices. These include Joshua Bennett's *Being Property Once Myself*, Mara de Gennaro's *Modernism After Postcolonialism*, Nadia Nurhussein's *Black Land: Imperial Ethiopianism and Africa America*, and Sonya Posmentier's *Cultivation and Catastrophe: The Lyric Ecology of Modern Black Literature*.[78] I hope that *Modernism and the Middle Passage* will further the inroads they have so brilliantly made.

In the next section, I turn to the Middle Passage archive and the longue durée of racialization. I seek to posit continuities between Middle Passage history and modernist literature that will unfold over the course of the chapters to come. First, I provide a brief reference to the atrocious conditions that dehumanized the captives, and then, I consider ways in which the enslaved people remade their humanity during the maritime passage by forging relations with the wooden boat and the turbulent water as conveyed by eyewitness accounts and fictional imaginings. These historical traces provide a speculative glimpse and counter-history of ways of being human as praxis.

THE MIDDLE PASSAGE

Any attempt to read against the grain of the slavery archive is necessarily speculative. It involves telling an impossible story, conveyed by, as

Hartman writes, "listening for the unsaid, translating misconstrued words, and refashioning disfigured lives—and intent on achieving an impossible goal: redressing the violence that produced numbers, ciphers, and fragments of discourse, which is as close as we come to a biography of the captive and the enslaved."[79] Speculation on what may have occurred on the slave ships is only that—guesswork based on fragmentary textual evidence and historical context. But I do so in order to posit brief flickers of freedom and resistance by the captive Africans that, as I'll show, return in modernist literature. In each instance, resistance is forged through relating to the nonhuman in terms other than European dualism between form and materiality.

The Middle Passage is the indeterminant ground upon which European Man rests and a place from which a transformational being human as praxis emerges. Despite what little is known from the captives themselves, it is evident that the Middle Passage from the west coast of Africa to the Americas intensified the process of metamorphosizing humans into chattel slaves. From scattered evidence, historians including Sowande' M. Mustakeem, Marcus Rediker, and Smallwood surmise their experience as follows. On board the slave ship, the captives were greeted by guns lining the top of the barracoon, or barrier wall, between the slaves' area on deck and the crew's. Their confinement below deck was horrifically cramped, with no space to stand, or even to sit erect, much less to crawl to latrine buckets or to vents that brought insufficient fresh air. Death by suffocation in the hold was a common occurrence. In inclement weather, bondspeople languished in these unbearably dark, cramped spaces, lying spoon-wise or head to foot with others, for upward of sixteen hours a day. The conditions of lying in toxic waste, the frequent asphyxiation from fetid, noxious fumes, and the quick transmission of disease contributed to the characterization of slave ships as "coffin ships" and of sick, disabled, and older slaves as "refuse."[80] Because male captives were chained to one another to prevent insurrection, many became lashed to a dead person. Both on deck and in the hold, the African transportees were terrorized into submission by means of indiscriminate violence that was sexual, physical, and psychological.

In addition to the violence on board ship, the sea itself was a medium of terror. Smallwood speculates on the effects of the transatlantic crossing on African captives whose cultures contained no reference to travel on the open seas with which to relate their predicament. She writes, "The sheer scale of the unknown element disabled many of the cognitive tools supplied by African epistemologies, which attributed dangerous supernatural powers to the watery realm. The slave ship at sea reduced African captives to an existence so physically atomized as to silence all but the most elemental bodily articulation, so socially impoverished as to threaten annihilation of the self, the complete disintegration of personhood."[81] The slave ship, combined with the vast and unknown scale of the sea itself, had the effect of decontextualizing the captives from their known world where the ancestors established a continuity between the past and future. On the "vastus" of the sea, a term that links etymologically the sea to waste and nothingness, the forcibly transported Africans were confronted with a potential loss of self through the oceanic boundlessness of space and time, the terror of tumultuous, life-threatening storms and disorienting waves, as well as from the sharks that followed the slave ships across the ocean.[82] Although the ship's location on the seemingly endless reaches of the Atlantic aided the crewmen in transforming their human cargo into commodities, the captives fought back. The death ships pushed the struggle against the dehumanizing forces of Western slavery into the elemental realms of life and death itself where the bondspersons struggled "to maintain bodily and cognitive integrity."[83] The conditions on the ships demanded that the forced migrants construct new narratives and forge new lines of kinship and connection to the ancestors even within the hostile maritime environment. Smallwood says, "[the] connection Africans needed [on board the slave ship] was a narrative continuity between past and present—an epistemological means of connecting the dots between there and here, then and now, to craft a coherent story out of incoherent experience."[84] Vincent Brown corroborates this view that the captives reinvented themselves on board the slave ship. Describing a women-led protest aboard the *Hudibras* in 1786, Brown relates how the women convinced the captain to let them observe the dignified lowering of the corpse of a beloved woman elder into the ocean precisely in order to remap their worlds as Smallwood describes, by amalgamating African traditions with the disorientation of their present. The captives, Brown says, made "their cultural practices from the stuff of death and dissolution."[85] It was in administering funeral rites on board ship, as Brown argues, and in resistance by drowning, that the transatlantic depths became part of an Afro-diasporic cosmology.

The captive Africans created a diasporic sensibility on board ship that could make sense of exile and homelessness. To achieve this reconfiguration under extreme duress, they adapted West African beliefs that saw death as a continuation of life, not a fundamental division from it. The ancestors play a vital role in the ongoing life of the community and its kinship networks. The dead are not relegated to a prior time but instead participate in a cyclical temporality in which the past is continuous in the present. The captives' sense of time is not one of narrative deferral in favor of future development as it is in global linear thinking, but instead, past, present, and future combine to produce the temporal sense, as Toni Morrison memorably put it, that "all of it is now."[86] The temporality of duration finds particular resonance in water. In many African spiritual traditions, water is a central medium for connecting people to the ancestral spirits and to water deities who inhabit the past and future. Unlike Europeans who saw water as a dangerous void to be crossed as quickly as possible, Africans living near seacoasts, lakes, and rivers incorporated water activities into their everyday lives, although they did not venture significantly into open oceans. They were expert at swimming, boating, fishing, even surfing, much to the surprise of European mariners, traders, and explorers who usually could not swim. Kevin Dawson writes:

> Water dominates much of Atlantic Africa. Stretching from Senegal to Angola, this region is rimmed by thousands of miles of coastline, bisected by rivers and streams, and pockmarked by lakes, while the Niger River's sweeping arch frames its northeastern limits and the Congo plunges through its southern reaches. Here, Africans maintained intimate interactions with water during work and personal time; regarding it as social and cultural spaces, not as intervals between places. . . . Many Africans were fishing-farmers and farming-fishermen who wove terrestrial and aquatic experiences into amphibious lives, interlacing spiritual and secular beliefs, economies, social structures, and political institutions— their very way of life—around relationships with water.[87]

Many captives carried these aquatic skills to the Americas and used them to carve out within slavery a sense of semiautonomous life along coastal, lakefront, and riverine areas. They possessed distinct physical advantages over white people in swamps through which they often fled slavery. The bondspeople passed this knowledge along to African-descended (and sometimes white) children whom they taught to swim. In addition, captives brought this intimate relation to water on board the slave ships.

Along with a familiarity with water and a belief in its supernatural attributes, the wooden slave ship may have been reimagined by the captives as affording a diasporic connection to the ancestors. The wooden barque may have echoed the material significance of African canoes with which many of the captives were familiar. Atlantic Africans, accustomed to building canoes for transport across local waters and coastal seas, frequently saw in these wooden vessels a crossroads to the spirit world. Dawson states, "Canoes conjoined the sacred and the earthly, making them secular workplaces and spiritual objects hewn from revered [cottonwood] trees capable of serving as conduits to the watery spirit world.... Reverence for cottonwoods was commonly based on beliefs that the trees interlaced the living, ancestral spirits, and deities by connecting earth, sky, and water."[88] Knowledge of Africans' relationship to water and wood as well as slave trade abolition testimony potentially changes how their plunge into the Atlantic depths—suicide by drowning—may have been self-understood.

Although the experiences of enslaved peoples are seldom registered in the colonial archive, it is possible to glean indirectly the African captives' survival mechanisms from testimony offered to the British House of Commons by eyewitnesses (sympathetic captains, chaplains, clerks, doctors, merchants, overseers, planters, sailors, and shipboard surgeons who had spent years in the colonies or in Africa from the Gold Coast to Angola) concerning the abolition of the slave trade. While much of their testimony involves the captives' melancholy from homesickness and exile, other accounts suggest that they remade themselves and their social networks through an embrace of death that could facilitate a return to Africa.[89] In these cases, death was actively sought and a source of triumph. Captain Thomas Wilson, an officer of the Royal Navy, recounts the pleasure and triumph of captives who resorted to suicide in order to escape their fates at the hands of the whites. He says of hunger-striking captives, "It hurt his feelings much to be obliged to use the cat [o'nine tails whip] so frequently to force them to take their food. In the very act of chastisement, they have looked up at him with a smile, and in their own language have said, *'presently we shall be no more.'* "[90] The captives in this instance, as Mustakeem states, "recogniz[e] that freedom existed within another cosmic space... the continuation of life beyond the human world" where their spirits, liberated by the physical death of their bodies, would "transcend into a different realm, thus freeing them from captivity."[91]

Referencing more active instances of self-destruction, Wilson recalled how sailors closely watched captives on deck for fear that they would throw themselves overboard. Most slave ship decks were encased in netting to prevent such actions. Even the terrifying presence of sharks that followed slave ships was not a deterrent. Wilson states, "At another time, when at sea, the captain and officers, when at dinner, heard the alarm of a slave's being overboard, and found it true, for they perceived him making every exertion to drown himself. He *put his head under water,* but *lifted his hands up*; and thus went down, *as if exulting that he had got away.*"[92] A ship surgeon, Mr. Claxton, corroborates this occurrence by means of another account of slave suicide:

> Some of the slaves on board... had such an aversion to leaving their native places, that they threw themselves overboard, on an idea that they should get back to their own country. The captain, in order to obviate this idea, thought of an expedient, viz. to cut off the heads of those who died, intimating to them, that if determined to go, they must return without their heads. The slaves were accordingly brought up to witness the operation. One of them seeing, when on deck, the carpenter standing with his hatchet up ready to strike off the head of a dead slave, with a violent exertion got loose, and flying to the place where the nettings had been unloosed, in order to empty the tubs, he darted overboard. The ship brought to, and a man was placed in the main chains to catch him, which he perceiving, dived under water, and rising again at a distance from the ship, made signs, which words cannot describe, expressive of the happiness in escaping.[93]

While the ocean occasioned imminent death, it also was a realm of freedom from captivity. Hence, it provoked in these instances expressions of happiness or elation at odds with the grim reality of certain death. The suiciding captive's sentiment may indicate a belief in the coexistence of the spiritual and material world. Mustakeem states, "[some of the captives] believed water encompassed the primary pathway to reincarnation. For slave ship runaways, the sea encompassed an underwater railroad and passage to freedom they pursued in jumping overboard to their deaths."[94] In such a world, gravity, vertical orientation, and stable ground disappear.[95] The human is reinvented as part of a watery world of spirits that mediate continuity with past and future, as well as the freedom to journey home. Slave masters, in these instances, could not control or contain the captives given that death was not a limit for these particular persons. Although these bids for freedom met with death, these disruptive acts nonetheless, as Jackson argues, are part of the "inchoate and incomplete nature of [the bondspeople's] intervention and an effort to refuse modes of relating that were established under slavery."[96] The potentiality of their acts signifies an interdependent relation to wood and water that conjoins their humanity to that of the earth and sea.

Fred D'Aguilar's novel *Feeding the Ghosts* (1997) imagines the healing relationship between an African captive and the wooden slave ship. It portrays the protagonist, Mintah, pressing her forehead against the deck and thinking, "To be truly like wood, indifferent to everything, grain fixed for all time, unchanging, she would have to be still, reduce her heavings in this stale, airless grave to nothing, be as still as wood, collect warmth, wet and shed skin, grow indifferent."[97] To become wood is to reimagine agency and to channel energy into living amid death.[98] This felt relation to the ship's wood resurfaces later in the novel in Maryland, when Mintah expresses memories of the passage by carving wood into sculpture. In transforming her trauma into art, Mintah gives critical and aesthetic shape to her ordeal: "[People] said the wood I worked resembled water in its curves and twists. The very element I sought to escape rose out of wood shaped by me. Trees became waves. Waves sprouted roots, branches, and leaves. My carvings exchanged the two and made the sea home, at least in my head."[99] Wood and water interpenetrate, marking each other through Mintah's memory of the slave ship hold and expressing the animism of the nonhuman in lateral relation to Mintah during the passage.

For those who stayed on board the ship, the space of confinement in the hold as well as the theater of terror on deck were mechanisms by which

African captives were turned into European signifiers of Blackness as matter. To conclude this section on the Middle Passage, I return attention to the (un)making of gendered African captives on the ship. The slave trade archive is filled with unspeakable scenes of the torture and murder of babies and young children, often right before their mothers' eyes, along with rampant sexual violence against pregnant and other women. These practices instituted chattel slavery, and more specifically, they produced the Black maternal person as monstrous and a primary source of human difference. While kinship structures order the chaos of generation, abduction and transport on the slave ship destroyed the purposefulness of African reproduction. Sailors deliberately dispelled meaning and dignity in the female (and other) captives' lives through the arbitrary, excessive, and inventive use of sexual and other violence. By destroying babies, fetuses, and children, the crew halted African mothers' linear generation and instead proliferated a nonlinear, hybrid, toxic, monstrous progeny of rape, torture, and fungibility. The Latin word mater (mother) is etymologically connected to matter and mare (the sea). The crew reduced maternity, the interconnection of mother and child, into formless matter and plasticity whereby bodies are turned into flesh, or brute existence as I discussed at the outset of this chapter.[100]

The attention to gender and sexuality on board the slave ship serves as an important corrective to the notion of the generic enslaved person who is assumed to be male. It moves against an antagonistic and protonationalistic model of predominantly male shipboard revolts. Instead, to speculate on the counter-history of female captives is to reimagine the fungibility of the human as a porous, unstable site of maneuver within the confined constraints of anti-Blackness. This creative resistance to sexual violence, as King argues, "is as unpredictable and uncontainable [as the inflicted violence itself]. As a Black mode of critique, it elaborates and gives texture to various forms of violence while also revealing unexpected and ever emerging modes of freedom."[101] What appear as lifeless and inert—the wooden ship, the confining hold—become instead a potential "loophole of retreat." Scripts are reinvented for a diasporic world of exile and its subsequent rerooting. I turn next to these scripts as they appear in both white and Black modernist texts in vastly different yet connected ways.

MODERNISM AND THE MIDDLE PASSAGE

I focus on Atlantic slave trade history not because I'm positing a single origin of modernity and a linear history that extends outward from the Atlantic deeps, but because I believe that Black and white modernisms unevenly share a critique of the power dynamics that commodified African persons in the transatlantic slave trade. In what follows, I read Zora Neale Hurston's *Barracoon: The Story of the Last "Black Cargo"* as an instance of a modernist engagement with the Middle Passage so as to find there the agency of the sea and the irruptive force of the commodity who speaks, the enslaved person themself. After this reading, I turn to Conrad's novella *The Nigger of the 'Narcissus'* in order to compare the two texts from opposing sides of the color line. I also consider commonalities between the experiences of two Black men crossing the Atlantic, one as an enslaved captive in 1859, the other a West Indian sailor on a British merchant ship in the later nineteenth century. I begin with Hurston to demonstrate the far-reaching possibilities of reimagining the human from a Black modernist account of the Middle Passage. That Conrad's imagination cannot accept the relational perspective he reveals in his Black sailor is symptomatic of the disjunction between Black and white modernist imaginations, shaped through the modernity/coloniality divide discussed earlier.

In 1931, Hurston introduces her ethnography of one of the last known survivors of the Middle Passage, Oluale Kossula, renamed in slavery Cudjo Lewis, as follows:

> The African slave trade is the most dramatic chapter in the story of human existence. Therefore a great literature has grown up about it. Innumerable books and papers have been written. These are supplemented by the vast lore that has been blown by the breath of inarticulate ones across the seas and lands of the world.... All the talk, printed and spoken, has had to do with ships and rations; with sail and weather; with ruses and piracy and balls between wind and water; with native kings and bargains sharp and sinful on both sides; with tribal wars and slave factories and red massacres and all the machinations necessary to stock a barracoon with African youth on the first leg of their journey from humanity to cattle; with storing and feeding and starvation and

suffocation and pestilence and death; with slave ship stenches and mutinies of crew and cargo; with the jettying of cargoes before the guns of British cruisers; with auction blocks and sales and profits and losses. All these words from the seller, but not one word from the sold. The Kings and Captains whose words moved ships. But not one word from the cargo. The thoughts of the "black ivory," the "coin of Africa," had no market value. Africa's ambassadors to the New World have come and worked and died, and left their spoor, but no recorded thought.[102]

If the "black ivory" and "coin of Africa" could speak, what would they say? Despite the slave trade being "the most dramatic chapter in the story of human existence" and despite the "innumerable books and papers" on the topic, the commodified captives' voices are missing. To fill this gap, Hurston introduces Kossula as the last survivor of and witness to the Middle Passage undergone by millions. He was illegally transported to Alabama in 1859 in a bravado act of defiance on the part of two Southern slave owners during the run-up to the American Civil War. Hurston introduces Kossula as "the only man on earth who has in his heart the memory of his African home [and] the horrors of the slave trade."[103] As such, Hurston presents him as the lone witness who joins the past to the present and future of African Americans. Beyond the facts of the slave trade, listed earlier as an accumulation of sordid, lifeless details, Hurston queries Kossula about his experience of the maritime passage into slavery in order to recover the continuity between Africa and the New World. But the promise that Kossula will adequately represent his experience of the passage from West Africa to Alabama falls short. Here is Kossula recounting his journey on the slave ship crossing the Atlantic: "De boat we on called de Clotilde.[104] Cudjo suffer so in dat ship. Oh Lor!' I so skeered on de sea! It growl lak de thousand beastes in de bush. De wind got so much voice on de water. Oh Lor!' Sometimes de ship way up in de sky. Sometimes it way down in de bottom of de sea. Dey say de sea was calm. Cudjo doan know, seem lak it move all de time."[105] This account is all that Kossula provides concerning his seventy-day voyage at sea.[106] Rather than narrate the events and conditions on board ship, he describes his affective and embodied state in relation to the open seas. Elsewhere, when telling Hurston about the raid and extermination of his village, he becomes "inarticulate" and gets lost in gazing at his "smoke pictures."[107] In foregrounding Kossula's failure to adequately represent his experience, Hurston inverts the trajectory of classic slave narratives. Deborah G. Plant notes that *Barracoon* does not tell an assimilation-in-America story, nor does it triumphantly tell of obstacles overcome and freedom and literacy gained. Instead, she describes it as "a slave narrative in reverse," where belonging, peace, and harmony are realized in Africa prior to Kossula's descent into the horrors and barbarity of slavery.[108] Further, the narrative discloses the materiality of Kossula's racialization, understood "as a physical condition of experience," that takes shape through an ongoing configuration of language, embodiment, and the physical world.[109]

On board the slave ship, tossed up and down continually, unanchored from any fixed marker of position, Kossula recalls the overwhelming seascape in which wind and water exhibit affect, mobility, and a seeming animality that suggests its liveliness and agency. The sea "growl lak de thousand beastes in de bush" and the wind "got so much voice." Their active, terrorizing, sonic forces converge on Kossula to shift his ontological sense of himself. Disorientation at sea, as Kossula relates, is a proprioceptive, embodied experience as well as an epistemological one.[110] In emphasizing the wind and water's vibratory and physical agency that threatens him physically, Kossula describes how he is dehumanized. As he attributes to the sea a vast power and liveliness, he renders himself paralyzed—unlively—with fear. Chen argues that "Language users use animacy hierarchies to manipulate, affirm, and shift the ontologies that matter the world."[111] Here, Kossula relies on ontologies that reflect his African sense of the world as animated and inclusive of humans. Ontologies do not need to be shifted because they already affirm being human in relation. But the relation is overwhelming. The sea functions here to unmake his previous sense of self. The wind and sea diminish Kossula's capacity to preserve his life. Perhaps it was when he hovered at the edge of physical annihilation that he began to objectify his consciousness of self as Cudjo, a disassociation that splits him from his previous sense of personhood as Kossula. Kossula's metamorphosis from African captive to Cudjo, an American enslaved person, occurs by means of proximity to death and a sustained physical condition of life-threatening experience. The slave ship, as Kossula understands it, marks him as equivalent to death.[112] As he later says to Hurston, "[W]e from cross de water know dat he [Death] come in de ship wid us."[113]

As Kossula relates, the ever-present threat of annihilation by immersion in the sea arrests his social and cognitive facilities. His experience recalls Equiano's 1789 slave narrative when, upon arriving on the slave ship, Equiano recounts: "I no longer doubted my fate; and quite overpowered with horror and anguish, I fell motionless on the deck and fainted."[114] However similar in this respect, Hurston's narrative refuses the univocality of Equiano's speaking subject. She conveys the discrepancies in Kossula's narrative from standard English. His grammatical shift to the third person (Cudjo) attests to his commodified objectification (as "black ivory" and the "coin of Africa") while on board the *Clotilda*. "Cudjo" references neither Kossula as he was when he was kidnapped from his Yoruba village in present-day Nigeria nor to another person. His performative enunciation is neither subject nor object, but an indeterminate third space between the two. Further, Hurston stylizes Kossula's speech in such a way that we hear echoes of the wind and sea in the liminal space through which Kossula arrays himself. Hurston emphasizes the long e sound above—"skeered"—and throughout the text—by adding it to nearly every verb Kossula uses ("tellee" "gittee" "makee" "astee") as well as to other parts of speech.[115] The sound echoes the moaning and howling of the wind and water and their transitive power to dehumanize the captives. Kossula's voice and those of the elements intermingle to produce a single vibratory, mobile resonance, both auditory and affectual. The sounding of the sea in Kossula's account is both the terrifying element of open water and his recounting of it: the moaning ee's convey his experience of the crossing and the loss of his African and American kin through slavery and its aftermath. The resonance of his account, as Julie Beth Napolin argues, occasions a spaciotemporal delay.[116] There is no fixed location or emitter of sound. It comes from everywhere and nowhere at once. Sound refracts, travels, and decays. It is not a determinate voice but rather a re-voicing by Kossula, an echo of the absent presence of the slave abyss.[117]

As an ethnologist, Hurston emphasizes Kossula's memories and customs from West Africa. These include the family's compound built after slavery's end for his eldest son: "Aleck, dat de oldest one, you unnerstan me, he married and live wid his wife. We buildee him a house right in de yard, jus lak in de Africky soil" and technologies, such as a garden gate lock made of "an ingenious wooden peg of African invention."[118] Prompted by Hurston, Kossula relates his African community's rituals, system of justice, religious beliefs, folktales, and initiation ceremonies: Hurston even includes Yoruba proverbs transcribed in the original language. Crucial to my argument, Kossula describes his felt relation to his place of origin by means of its materiality. He longs for African *soil*, a geography and relation of material belonging, and he embodies this desire when he poses for a photograph. Hurston recalls, "When he came out [for the picture] I saw that he had put on his best suit but removed his shoes. 'I want to look lak I in Affica 'cause dat where I want to be,' he explained."[119] The intimacy of bare feet in soil translates to Kossula's felt memory of place, belonging, and community. In contrast, Kossula recalls the violence and anti-African discrimination he experienced in Alabama by both African Americans and whites following Emancipation. One by one, his wife and six children die or are murdered. He describes these losses as mutilations of his body: "I say dey cut off de feet, he got hands to 'fend hisself. Dey cut off de hands he wiggle out de way when he see danger come. But when he lose de eye, den he can't see nothin' come upon him. He finish. My boys are my feet. My daughter is my hands. My wife she my eye. She left, Cudjo finish."[120] For Kossula, embodiment is grounded in soil and entangled with kin. The narrative bares his wounds and lets them linger, as Hurston speculates in conclusion that Kossula "does not fear death."[121]

Rather than expose slavery's unhealed wounds as does Hurston, Joseph Conrad's injuriously titled novella, *The Nigger of the 'Narcissus,'* depersonalizes and naturalizes racism. The harmful term seems to come from everywhere and nowhere at once. It is bandied about by the crew, and the title also names the anti-Black atmosphere of the intended English-speaking audience, an environment established prior to the narrative's commencement.[122] More, the novel extends this attitude past the novel's ending, as the novel's lone West Indian sailor, James Wait, dies and is buried at sea. Thus "unburdened," the doldrums off the coast of West Africa vanish and the *Narcissus* is able to complete its voyage around Africa and land in England. Once disembarked, the sailors inform the shipping company of Wait's death. The Marine Office clerk, viewing the employment records, declares, "James Wait—deceased—found no papers of any kind—no relations—no trace."[123] In disappearing Wait, the novel encodes a willful amnesia and exclusion of racialized subjects from the British mainland, apostrophed by the narrator as, "A ship mother of fleets and nations! The great flagship of the race; stronger than the storms! And anchored in the open sea."[124] Wait is neither allowed to circulate unimpeded and arrive in England, nor has the offensive term been refuted in any way. In effect, the anti-Black atmosphere becomes one with the elemental temporality that describes sailing the open ocean:

> The passage had begun: and the ship, a fragment detached from the earth, went on lonely and swift like a small planet. Round her the abysses of sky and sea met in an unattainable frontier. A great circular solitude moved with her, ever changing and ever the same, always monotonous and always imposing. The smiling greatness of the sea dwarfed the extent of time. The days raced after one another, brilliant and quick like the flashes of a lighthouse.[125]

While the novel lauds the British Empire and the ways in which its history and geopolitical dominance unfolded at sea, other passages, such as the one above, undercut this temporality. The planetary timescale, Maxwell Uphaus writes, "casts ideas of transition and progress into doubt."[126] Instead, faced with the immense geophysical scale of the oceans, historical progress "reverts to aporia, an impasse that is depicted in the novel as a state of drift and stasis."[127] Crucially, in order to solve this impasse and enter into the national time of his adopted country, Conrad "attempts to reframe the sea's anti-progressive temporality as an essentially racial condition," a displacement that elicits the atrocities and trauma of slavery and colonization.[128] Moreover, that racial history extends into the novel's diegetic present through the anachronistic presence of the oldest sailor, John Singleton, who speculates on whether Wait is actually ill or just pretending: "'And a black fellow, too,' went on the old seaman. 'I have seen them die like flies.' He stopped, thoughtful, as if trying to recollect gruesome things, details of horrors, hecatombs of [niggers] They looked at him fascinated. He was old enough to remember slavers, bloody mutinies, pirates perhaps: who could tell through what violences and terrors he had lived!"[129] Singleton explicitly connects the uncertainty on board *The Narcissus*—is Wait really dying?—to the slave trade and the anarchy of the seas. He connects Wait's Blackness with abducted Africans who "die like flies," a simile that links racialized bodies with pestilential nature and mass death. But the causal connection between the later nineteenth-century setting of *The Nigger of the 'Narcissus'* and the anarchic seas of the early nineteenth century remains unspoken. When Singleton pauses, the narrator fills in his silence with conjecture: "*as if* trying to recollect." Similarly, the crew, gathered around the ancient mariner, also speculates, "*who could tell* through what violences and horrors he had lived!" This history is repressed even as it is inferred and denied the specificity of actual events and individuals. Singleton makes an impression—the defining feature of Conrad's modernist aesthetic—that serves as a symbolic link between imperial conquest and slavery and the diegetic moment in which the novel's actions occur. Singleton claims to read Wait clearly: he insists that he is near death and not shamming sick. But Wait's "passive, terminal lingering," configures him as poised undecideably between life and death.[130] Even his first spoken utterance—"Wait!"—both conveys his identity and brings the crew's activities to a halt.

In associating Wait with death's imminent arrival, the novel reduces Wait to flesh: sheer matter from which labor is to be extracted. Other descriptions of Wait in these terms abound. Singleton pronounces that "the sea will have her own," a statement that consigns Wait to the ocean floor.[131] His coughing "tossed him like a hurricane"; he was "mute as a fish," and a "black phantom."[132] In the end, Wait is unknowable because "he is nothing," in Conrad's own words.[133] Elsewhere, the crew yell: "Yer nobody!" and "You're a thing—a bloody thing. Yah—you corpse."[134] He's ungendered, referred to as "it." He's nonhuman, agentless and opaque: his name is both a smudge and polysemic. He won't signify properly. He is portrayed as inert matter, an elementalism that is reducible to the geophysical substrate of the watery abyss with which he is identified. Given the unperturbed racism of the novella, it is startling to find a moment that reveals how the flesh might conjoin with the elements in a nonhierarchical form of being human as praxis. The narrator first describes the Atlantic's faint nocturnal whisperings: "For long hours she [the ship] remained lost in a vast universe of night and silence, where gentle sighs wandering here and there like forlorn souls, made the still sails flutter as in sudden fear, and the ripple of a beshrouded ocean whisper its compassion afar—in a voice mournful, immense, and faint. . . ."[135] The ellipses push the boundaries of language by registering nonhuman agencies and affects. The passage prefigures Conrad's description of the uncanny Congo in *Heart of Darkness*. Unlike the Congo's seething life, however, the description figures the ocean as a graveyard where unquiet ghosts wander. Next, the narrative turns to Wait's perception of the nighttime sea and the lightning flashes of a squall. In doing so, the novella breaks its convention of conveying only Wait's exterior. Instead, it deploys free indirect narration. Jimmy, the crew's diminutive name for Wait:

> turning on his pillow, could see vanishing beyond the straight line of topgallant rail, the quick, repeated visions of a fabulous world made up of leaping fire and sleeping water. The lightening gleamed in his big sad eyes that seemed in a red flicker to burn themselves out in his black face, and then he would lay blinded and invisible in the midst of an intense darkness. He could hear on the quiet deck soft footfalls, the breathing of some man lounging on the doorstep; the low creak of swaying masts; or the calm voice of the watch-officer reverberating aloft, hard and loud, amongst the unstirring sails. . . . Life seemed an indestructible thing. It went on in darkness, in sunshine, in sleep; tireless, it hovered affectionately round the imposture of his ready death. It was bright, like the twisted flare of lightning, and more full of surprises than the dark night. It made him feel safe, and the calm of its overpowering darkness was as precious as its restless and dangerous light.[136]

Opposed to the mournful, deathly sea in the earlier passage, here, from Wait's interior point of view, the sea is a place of life-giving. It is calm, peaceful, and safe. When the lightning ceases to flash, Wait merges with the opacity of darkness and silence. He perceives the continuity of life, a co-constituted intrarelation of humans, ship, fire, and water. Wait experiences his embeddedness in life, a force that supersedes his individual life and impending death. Michael North calls this passage "the oddest violation of point of view" in the novel as the reader witnesses Wait perceive the "voice of the ship, if not of life itself."[137] North argues that "sensing the voice at the most basic level, the level of rhythm, of pure, asignifying sound, is [more important than the ability to see that is emphasized in the preface]."[138] This sound, moreover, says North, is a language of action, the unconscious language of solidarity between the crew that is heard as a "phatic communion that exists far below the level of discourse, that comes from national and racial commonality."[139] It is also a language shared between the crew, the ship, and the sea. But North doesn't pursue the nexus with the environment and the ship. Instead, he likens

Conrad to Wait's positioning as both an insider and outsider to the crew defined by race and nation. By the end of the voyage, Wait has been eliminated and the narrator, a stand-in for Conrad, shifts to a first person voice and takes his place among the crew as both part and outside of its phatic community. The narrator concludes, "Haven't we, together and upon the immortal sea, wrung out a meaning from our sinful lives? Good-bye brothers! You were a good crowd. As good a crowd as ever fisted with wild cries the beating canvas of a heavy foresail; or tossing aloft, invisible in the night, gave back yell for yell to a westerly gale."[140] Here the images are of a battle against nature. With Wait's departure, a hierarchy is restored. Conrad, the European immigrant, proves his right to belong to the English nation by excluding the racial other.

But what if the reader holds forth in Wait's solidarity with water, wood, and life itself? The narrative pauses; the reader is enveloped by the creak of the swaying masts, the rhythmic footfalls, heavy, sleeping breaths, and a matter-of-fact voice. Can they hear Kossula's moaning ee sounds? Unlike Hurston's narrative of racist exclusion, here, they are folded into the dynamic materiality of racial immanence where hierarchies are dismantled. Background, infrastructure, and atmosphere join with Wait and the crew to reinvent the harsh life at sea as a more-than-human assemblage. Even so, this collective is shot through with the atrocities of slavery and empire, figured as Wait's slow dying. But for this moment, he becomes fugitive and blends with the silent dark, comforted and held, even while in movement and transformation. The atmosphere is briefly anti-racist.

Conrad, however, cannot allow the solidarity with water, wood, and the crew that Wait evinces to persist. A few pages later, the reader is again privy to Wait's inner thoughts. Here, though, the seaman's frame of mind is diametrically at odds with the calm peacefulness he describes just before. In the latter passage, Wait is filled with petty resentment and grievance—"That lunatic Belfast will bring me some water if I ask. Fool"—that then turns into a hallucinatory free association in which Wait imagines he is deprived of both air and water and confined to jail, ostensibly due to his illness.[141] He deliriously envisions:

> A ship whose mastheads protruded through the sky and could not be seen, was discharging grain, and the wind whirled the dry husks in spirals along the quay of a dock with no water in it. He whirled along with

the husks—very tired and light. All his inside was gone. He felt lighter than the husks—and more dry.... There was no more air—and he had not finished drawing his long breath. But he was in gaol! They were locking him up. A door slammed.[142]

In contrast to the felt and heard solidarity of the sea, the ship, and the crew, in this passage, Wait is desiccated and his thoughts entangled with his illness. His creative relationality dries up and he resumes the novella's racist caricature of Wait as a hollow, masked enigma. Finally, he likens his restricted breath to penal confinement. In order for the narrator to take his place in England, Wait must be sacrificed. His slow suffocation, dehydration, and incarceration evokes the historical slave trade and renders his death and burial at sea as inexorable as Singleton predicts.

This chapter has moved from the seas, to the hold, and into the archive. It has introduced how reading with the sea can shift geography, animate the nonhuman, and reimagine the human itself. I've argued that the slave trade archive can be read against the grain to offer speculative instances of freedom in the face of death. Finally, this chapter offered readings of texts by Hurston and Conrad to show how they briefly converge when articulating the trauma of slavery at sea. The next chapter, "Alluvium," focuses on how Black modernists Langston Hughes, Hurston, and Claude McKay engage with the opaque, unformed, and unwanted detritus of oceanic and shoreline flux to resignify Blackness as being human in and through lateral relation with the seashore and with one another. While *Barracoon* and *The Nigger of the 'Narcissus'* take place on the sea and describe the undoing of their respective Black characters, the authors in chapter 2 (including Hurston in *Their Eyes Were Watching God*) inflect their meditations on the Middle Passage with possibilities for ways of living otherwise.

2

ALLUVIUM

Langston Hughes, Zora Neale Hurston, and Claude McKay

In a postcolonial rewriting of Caribbean poetics and history, poet, novelist, and theorist Édouard Glissant posits the Middle Passage as the "abyssal" beginnings of Caribbean thought. He writes:

> Experience of the abyss lies inside and outside the abyss. The torment of those who never escaped it: straight from the belly of the slave ship into the violent belly of the ocean depths they went. But their ordeal did not die; it quickened into this continuous/discontinuous thing: the panic of the new land, the haunting of the former land, finally the alliance with the imposed land, suffered and redeemed. The unconscious memory of the abyss served as the alluvium for these metamorphose.[1]

The abyss is both literal and sedimented into the history, memory, and the location of the Caribbean archipelago. It is the watery grave of an estimated 1.8 million men, women, and children thrown or suicided overboard the slave ships *and* the residual trace, or absent presence, of the abyss that is metamorphosed into, as Sylvia Wynter puts it, "new natives in a new world."[2] This newness was born of terror and loss: the enslaved survivors and their descendants were both dehumanized by the plantation economies in which they found themselves and rehumanized by "rerooting" in the Caribbean archipelago. This rerooting is open, discontinuous, and shot through with the sediments of the abyss. Glissant calls these sediments of the Middle Passage that wash up on shore, "a whole alluvium."[3] They are both literal, the "balls and chains gone green," and symbolize the memories of slavery that haunt the descendants of survivors. This alluvium, "indistinct and unexplored," is usually discounted as waste.[4] It appears to be formless; its opacity rebuffs possession or exchange. And therein, Glissant says, lies its promise. According to him, the "unconscious memory" of the Middle Passage provides "a whole alluvium" for the poetic relations and affectual practices of Black life.[5] Glissant's unconscious memory is a forgotten "chasm" that is "furrowed with fugitive memories."[6] There is neither origin nor ground here, but only loss and uncertain sensory and affective remembrance. The chasm paradoxically figures an absence that "in the end became knowledge."[7] Glissant figures memory as akin to the sea: indeterminate, groundless, and yet material and present. The absence of origins, rather than producing nonbeing, instead proliferates possibilities: Africa becomes "the birthplace of multiplicity" and the Caribbean, a "cradle of multiple diasporas."[8] Freed from fixed meanings, origins, and territories, alluvium conjoins multiple sources, overlapping memories and practices, and the damaged, discarded materiality of bodies and nature.

To begin again, to re-create the world from the shards of a broken, dispossessed people, Glissant says, depends upon the cultural process of creolization by means of relation. Glissant's notion of relation, according to An Yountae, is the poetic sacralization of the local shoreline and landscape that memorializes the unknown and the unimaginable: the ordeal of crossing the Atlantic on a slave ship and the loss of the living and dead who were unceremoniously thrown into the sea or left behind in Africa. Until recently, memorials to the Middle Passage in the "new" world consisted strictly of the found landscape. Glissant says in *Caribbean Discourse*, "Our landscape is its own monument: its meaning can only be traced on the underside. It is all history."[9] Valérie Loichot connects this early statement with Glissant's *Philosophie de la Relation* (2009) where "the recurring image of a 'renfoncement de terre,' or 'hollowing out of earth,' acts simultaneously as the site of the beginning and end of life; as the mother's birth and death; and as the refuge for what Glissant calls le poeme."[10] Le poeme collapses background and foreground as well as linear temporality. It expresses what Glissant calls *entour*, a term, Loichot explains, that "establishes a continuum between the natural environment and its historical surroundings."[11] *Entour* indicates for Glissant, "the whole environment comprising the poem, human and nonhuman animals, vegetation, rocks, lavas, and 'nature' and 'culture.' The latter terms lose meaning since they exist on a continuum, not in a system of opposition."[12] *Entour* claims place as sacred. Yountae argues that its sacredness, expressed through love and care, enables a rerooting and a re-creation of self in relation to place.[13] It's important to note that the re-creation of self through place is mobile and open-ended. Unlike the static universals of the colonizer, Glissant's poetics of relation occupy the shifting ground of seaside alluvium that open to the unbounded ocean. Yountae argues that "by reconceptualizing the world otherwise [than the colonizer], [Glissant's] poetics gives life to relations that were deemed unrecognizable, unreadable, absent [by the colonizer]. These social relations reconstitute the self in return."[14] The traces of past atrocity and ongoing dispossession open the self to alterity in a manner that the colonizer, who insists on what is empirically knowable, cannot discern. And that alterity is always mobile, a force that creolizes the subject. We can understand Glissant's poetics of relation through Ewa Płonowska Ziarek's glossing of Theodor Adorno's materialist aesthetics that concern "the coimplication of matter and form in the creation of meaning." She argues, "By preserving rather than obliterating the otherness of materiality, aesthetic form foregrounds the conflicting but inseparable interrelation of the intelligible and material, the conceptual and the sensual in the creation of meaning."[15] This materialist aesthetic actively contests the colonizer's abstractions, including narrative form whereby the autonomous subject sublates racialized, feminized bodies and nature into passive background. Instead, the particularity and contingency of matter continually draw the subject into dialogue with opacity, novelty, and the absent presence of trauma.

As discussed in chapter 1, the colonizer's knowledge is abstract and totalizing. He commodifies labor power and renders each enslaved persons equivalent and hence exchangeable for a specified monetary value. So, too, he reduces geography and history into gridded cartographies and linear projections of future profitability. These abstractions externalize damage to laboring bodies and the ecosystem as unclaimed waste. Additionally, the owner's anticipation of future capital accumulation subsumes the ever-present, daily violence that enforces the bondspeople's enslavement and destroys the ecosystem as the means of reaching production goals. By setting his sights on future wealth, the colonizer renders invisible the particularity of his bondspeople's labor and lives as well as nature itself. He abstracts himself from the means by which he accumulates wealth and even from the surroundings in which he lives. And he fails to recognize the mutually constitutive relations between himself and the bondspeople, favoring instead metaphysical categories of geography, race, and gender that naturalize his dominance and deny relation.

This chapter argues that alluvium's shifting, semiaquatic ground undercuts the colonizer's abstract categories and revalues the damaged materiality of Black bodies and the wasted landscape. Using Glissant's poetics of relation, I find in Black modernist aesthetics references to the absent presence of the slave trade abyss that resist narrative form and the colonizer's abstractions. Additionally, Black aesthetics animate and hence foreground alluvial settings: sea- and landscape, infrastructure, and the nonhuman, usually treated as inert by the colonizer. I argue that Black aesthetics instead synthesize materiality and form by means of "noncoercion" toward the otherness of materiality. (We'll see this aesthetic method again in Virginia Woolf's composting technique.) Materiality and form, Adorno writes, "communicate with one another, thus the synthesis is itself a product of otherness."[16] Alluvium speaks, remembers, memorializes, and this activity opens the artist to an ongoing creolizing synthesis that changes subject and object alike. Because readers are trained to attend to narrative and character development, they often overlook the alluvial settings in Black texts, but Glissant's poetics of relation alerts us to how the unformed materiality of this liminal location signifies the overlooked presence of the Middle Passage and the possibility of being human in lateral, communicative relation with the nonhuman. Reading Black modernist texts in light of Glissant's generative work allows me to locate instances, rather than sustained narratives, where Langston Hughes, Zora Neale Hurston, and Claude McKay attempt to bring the "unthought" into speculative representation to challenge the colonizer's knowledge. These moments reinvent the world from an anti-racist, ecological perspective.

Second, this chapter links unstable alluvium (comprised of water, rocks, debris, rusting ships, logs, and "muck") to the porous, indeterminate status of Black fungibility. As discussed in chapter 1, the metaphorical and material fungibility of Black bodies arises from the sexual violence in the hold but this chapter shows that it doesn't remain there. Attention to embodiment braids Glissant's alluvium together with fungibility to address a crucial shortcoming in Glissant's visionary work. His notion of the slave ship as a "womb abyss" deploys a familiar feminine gendering of the ship to highlight a maternal rather than paternal force in the formation of Black Atlantic histories.[17] But he neglects the ungendering of captive bodies that renders them commodified property and erases the sexual violence that occurred on board ship and afterward. This critique of Glissant's gender blindness is important to understanding how Hughes, Hurston, and McKay address Black reinventions of race, gender, and the human that began in the Middle Passage and continue to challenge anti-Black racism. To make this critique, I turn to C. Riley Snorton's important reading of Glissant in terms of Black transgendering. Snorton elaborates on how the event of forced deportation from Africa allows for the reinvention of the human across the subsequent centuries, including the early to mid-twentieth century. To do so, Snorton builds upon Glissant's notion of "transversality" defined as the Caribbean's "multiple converging paths."[18] Snorton remarks, "transversality articulates submerged forms of relationalities that need not be visible to have effects."[19] These relations are opaque; they offer the unthinkable rather than the historically knowable: the passing into another condition, from human to thing to animal, from gendered to ungendered. When the unthinkable makes itself felt, it puts into question a single history of Man. Snorton says, "history becomes less a program for examining change over time and more an examination of disruptions in linear time."[20]

This chapter also confronts the race blindness of new materialist theories that seek to dislodge the long-standing division between symbolic form (the political, the literary, and the constructed), on the one hand, and materiality (nature, geography, and the body, often seen as inert, given, and essential), on the other. Katherine McKittrick who draws upon Sylvia Wynter's notion of "demonic grounds," for instance, recalibrates the seeming fixity of space and built environments, such as the slave ship, that "contains and regulates" the captives as chattel slaves while "it hides black humanity."[21] She argues that the notion of fixed space, such as naturalized boundaries of the slave ship, the plantation, the ghetto, the prison, and the nation, "while materially and ideologically enclosing black subjects... also contribute to the formation of an oppositional geography."[22] This geography reconfigures space as entwined with and coproduced by being human otherwise, "infused with sensations and distinct ways of knowing" that are imaginative and continually being shaped anew.[23] This turn to human geography in Black Studies adds an important racial dimension to new materialist studies in which geographies, bodies, and things are malleable, porous, and subject to imaginative and real reconfigurations.[24] Namely, it emphasizes how Black people have long practiced and understood animative and intra-active relations with the nonhuman and that they address issues of power and racism that new materialist theories generally avoid.

In this chapter, I draw upon all of these critical efforts to think the material and metaphorical together. I demonstrate how texts by Hughes, Hurston, and McKay work to configure a geography of tumult, upheaval, and loss. Hughes, Hurston, and McKay convey Black sex workers, migrant workers, and sailors in their alluvial locations and how they are both foreclosed from European notions of the human and offer a glimpse of the human as praxis, an open-ended, sacred, and practical relation between the human and nonhuman. In this endeavor, I am influenced by Robert Reid-Pharr's *Archives of the Flesh* where he diagnoses white modernism and the racial divide:

> It is true that our enslaved ancestors formed new modes of relation and belief from out of the detritus of their lost traditions. What remains largely unspoken, however, is the simple fact that modern forms of European culture were also established by the history of contact, conquest, colonization and travel to which we attach many names, most notoriously, "the Middle Passage." Or, to push my readers beyond the boundaries of polite irritation, the celebrated objects of Goya, Velazquez, Murillo, Cervantes, Picasso, and Lorca are themselves examples of slave culture, cleverly wrought articulations of complex procedures by which the repression and exploitation of humanity are at once ritualized and ignored.[25]

Reid-Pharr's phrase, "at once ritualized and ignored," expresses the workings of Black fungibility on the part of the colonizer. The master engages in fantastical and metaphorical projections onto Black bodies that act as a screen. Their aestheticization as primitive both defines whiteness as civilized and authorizes Western transgressions of the primitive in order to energize and re-enchant modernity. What is disavowed, or ignored, through these symbolic or ritual meanings is the resistance generated by the same Black bodies. This chapter asks, what happens when the master's appropriative mechanism of slave culture is represented critically, through an interrogation of the Middle Passage that stalls progress narratives and contests European models of the human that continue to repress and exploit the humanity of peoples living in alluvial, unstable, and environmentally harmful locations?

The pages to follow demonstrate how Hughes, Hurston, and McKay interrogate the formation of Blackness during the Middle Passage and beyond, a transhistorical linkage that rubs against the grain of the emphasis on newness and nowness in modernism that is part of global linear thinking. Some of the difficulty in locating Middle Passage rewritings in the modernist era is that they occur not as plot or realist reference, but as transversality that makes itself manifest as absence, chiasmus, silence, indirection, and lingering, impersonal affect, as we saw in the chapter 1 with Zora Neale Hurston and Joseph Conrad. Not only does the archive foreclose captives' experience, as they were deemed to be of no value to those who kept records, but the slave trade at sea was a singular zone of violence and terror. The groundbreaking work by Black feminist critics such as Saidiya Hartman, Tiffany Lethabo King, McKittrick, Christina Sharpe, Snorton, Hortense Spillers, Alexander G. Weheliye, Wynter, and others follow Glissant's lead and direct us to look beyond the liberal subject and its nation-centered progress narratives to alternative geographies in which the legacy of the slave trade and slavery is sedimented into bodies, land, and sea. These material and shifting sites continually remix and reshape the past, present, and future via geophysical forces that extend beyond the nation. Alluvial zones are infused with what Avery Gordon calls, "living effects, seething and lingering, of what seems over and done with."[26] Reading for affect, opacity, and resistant, wayward desire reveals Black geographies at odds with the universalizing abstractions of modernity/coloniality. The Middle Passage isn't often directly represented in Black modernist literature, but its living effects, as I'll show, are clearly registered.

LANGSTON HUGHES AND
THE REVERSE MIDDLE PASSAGE

Langston Hughes's first autobiography, *The Big Sea* (1940), famously opens with his twenty-one-year-old self throwing books into the water. The young Hughes had just embarked on his maiden voyage as a seaman on a merchant ship, the fictionalized S.S. *Malone*, and was on route to Africa from New York. As the books "went down into the moving water," he says, "it was like throwing a million bricks out of my heart."[27] Critics often accept Hughes's older persona's diagnosis of this scene as simply a youthful, melodramatic gesture. But if we read the literary history of racial difference into the episode, more is at stake. In a reversal of the slave narrative trope of the Talking Book, in which Olaudah Equiano, Frederick Douglass, and others equate freedom with the literate ability to hear books speak to them, Hughes finds mobility and affectivity in *removing* its voice—concretized as bricks—from his heart.[28] He explains his actions by saying, "You see, books had been happening to me."[29] Their agency exceeds his own through the circularity of whiteness that both legitimates itself through writing and forecloses other modes of being and knowing. The dumping of books at the outset of Hughes's autobiography declares his need to cast away the authority of literary tradition, including that of the Talking Book in African American slave narratives. In these narratives, formerly enslaved authors both recognize the power of literacy and respond at first by putting the book to their ear and hoping that the book will "talk" to them. This trope both acknowledges African and Afro-diasporic oral traditions, and it mocks their so-called lack of civilization. In contrast, Hughes rejects the weight of the written word, and rather than reading this gesture solely as an instance of romantic rebellion, I believe it has greater critical purchase. Hughes recognizes that the Talking Book has written him out of humanity and silenced his very being. He associates books with his experience of poverty, racism, and social uncertainty:

> For it wasn't only the books that I wanted to throw away, but everything unpleasant and miserable out of my past: the memory of my father, the poverty and uncertainty of my mother's life, the stupidities of the color-prejudice, blacks in a white world, the fear of not finding a job, the bewilderment of no one to talk to about things that trouble you, the feeling of

always being controlled by others—by parents, by employers, by some outer necessity not your own.[30]

In this passage, Hughes comments on "the double bind of freedom" that constitutes most African American lives in the post-Reconstruction United States. Hartman describes this double bind as "being freed from slavery and free of resources, emancipated and subordinated, self-possessed and indebted, equal and inferior, liberated and encumbered, sovereign and dominated, citizen and subject."[31] Hughes likewise relates how Blacks have been brought under the umbrella of liberal individualism with few of the benefits and all of the burdens. The racial order of the republic, as Hartman says, had been preserved postslavery. Blacks were simultaneously included as citizens and liberal subjects of the nation and excluded from it by being figured as "abject, threatening, servile, dangerous, dependent, irrational, and infectious."[32] This contradiction stands at the center of the dilemma of the Talking Book. How do African American writers strategically use the Western literary tradition to argue for Black *inclusion* rather than *exclusion* in civilization, reason, and equality? Houston A. Baker figures the impasse between the white man's Talking Book and the particularity of Blackness as a chiasmus, what he calls "mastery of form, deformation of mastery."[33] Henry Louis Gates Jr. terms the dilemma a crossroads whereby the enslaved person or descendent writes to demonstrate their membership in the already existing white community.[34] In either case, the Black writer faces a double bind of writing the Black subject while using the master's literary tradition that configures Black people as subhuman. How to solve this problem? The youthful Hughes, at the outset of his maiden voyage to Africa, appears to reject the dilemma entirely. I suggest that he looks elsewhere for his subject matter: in the watery depths of the sea, the crew's cabins, an anchorage, and in a West African harbor to render in literary form the constitutive outside of Man. He seeks out the political unconscious of marine infrastructure, waste, and sexual violence. By connecting the abstraction of written form with the unseen history of Black disposability in the slave trade and beyond, he reverses and inextricably links aesthetic form to abject materiality. Books become garbage; Black modernist writers (in a society in which Blackness is synonymous with "refuse") reinvent literary form and the human itself. I linger with Hughes in his contemplations of moving water, shifting alluvium, and Black fungibility. In these overlooked spaces, other possibilities besides assimilation arise.

To make this claim, it is necessary to posit that Hughes articulates submerged forms of relationality to the ancestors and to African and Afro-diasporic peoples across the circum-Atlantic world. Hughes's desire to recover a pan-African history and identity is notable from his first published poem, "The Negro Speaks of Rivers" (1921). The poem expresses primitivism, or an essential, unchanging timeless "I," that unites the eternity of the speaker's soul with the Euphrates at the dawn of human history, the Congo, Nile, and Mississippi Rivers. Hughes's watery transversality becomes more historical and disruptive as he matures. In "Sea Charm," published in *The Weary Blues* (1926), the speaker is "the sea's own children" who "do not understand / They know . . . that the sea holds / A wide, deep death."[35] Here, the "sea's own children" speak from the perspective of the drowned and share a deep-seated affective knowledge of abyssal slave history. Also published in *The Weary Blues*, "Caribbean Sunset" turns paradise into a violent reverberation of the slave trade's violence: "God having a hemorrhage, / Blood coughed across the sky, / Staining the dark sea red."[36] For Hughes, as Gilroy suggests, reference to ships (and oceans) immediately recall the Middle Passage. The reddened ocean bespeaks the many below. In "The Negro Mother" (1932), the first-person speaker carries in her blood the genealogy of her matrilineal ancestors: "I am the child they stole from the sand / Three hundred years ago in Africa's land. / I am the dark girl who crossed the wide sea / Carrying in my body the seed of the free."[37] Shane Graham reads this poem as Hughes's assertion of continuity among Blacks throughout history using the "I" pronoun.[38] He argues that Afro-diasporic writers "imagined, disseminated, adapted, and repurposed a skein of ancestral pan-African memory."[39] But the image of a skein of yarn suggests a continuity between past and present whereas I am positing a transversal, discontinuous relation that is much more powerful in its reimagining of the slave trade past. It combines the rupture of the Middle Passage with creolizing "new" world knowledge. For example, freedom, in "The Negro Mother," is embodied and carried aboard the ship. It exists as the Janus-face of the mother's fungiblity. And that hidden freedom exists in the poem's present in its ability to contest the domination of Man. Such a freedom dream is ambiguous in this poem given that the mother expresses a determined drive for her children to succeed (assimilate) in the United States. However, that narrative arc is missing in "To the Little Fort of San Lazaro on the Ocean Front, Havana" published in *New Masses* in 1931. The poem begins with "Watch tower once for pirates... / DRAKE / DE PLAN, / EL GRILLO."[40] The fort had effectively protected against the "pirate" explorers and slave traders, but the current pirate, "THE NATIONAL CITY BANK," one of the largest investors in the Cuban sugar industry in the 1930s, cannot be overcome by the outdated fort. Instead, the poem constellates the past and present to foment a political awakening in its audience. Hughes's poetry, as Graham argues, seeks "to reanimate and 'organize the past.'"[41] Graham claims that Hughes's goal in so doing was "to guarantee black people a place in modern culture," but I hold that poem juxtaposes the slave trade past with National City Bank such that the speaker hopes that the remembrance of slave trade atrocities will fan the flames of international struggle against capitalist accumulation.[42] The speaker calls for a leap out of temporal continuum into an apocalyptic life and death struggle. Hughes continues, "Bear in mind / That death is a drum / Beating forever / Till the last worms come / To answer its call, / Till the last stars fall, / Until the last atom / Is no atom at all."[43] The world tears; apocalypse ruptures the quality of being and the cosmos.

I have considered Hughes's poetic transversality in order to posit how reading the slave trade history into Hughes's seemingly presentist autobiography is affirmed by his poetic imagination. I return now to *The Big Sea* and Hughes's account of his maiden sea voyage as it insistently points to the ocean. He speculates on the absent history of the debris lying on the bottom of the ocean. Not only are his books submerged, but "All the filth and garbage that has accumulated in the harbor was dumped into the ocean, and the limpid blue-green of the sea received the garbage and swill, and didn't seem dirtied at all. This is one of the many wonders of the sea—that the garbage and bilge water of ten thousand ships is dumped into it every day, and the sea is never dirty."[44] Hughes's faux-naif tone both acknowledges the common Western assessment of the sea as a space of emptiness, purity, and erasure and indirectly comments on what might be lingering in its depths. Anticipating Glissant's notion of the importance of sediments that wash up on shore for articulating Black memory and geography, Hughes ponders the absent presence of what is dumped uneceremoniously into the oceans. As he underscores the disconnect between dirty, unwanted refuse and clean, limpid water, Hughes makes plain the hidden connection between the sea and what was thrown into it. Referring to a later scene in Hughes's autobiography but applicable here as well, Reid-Pharr remarks, "Though Hughes never bothers to say so, it is obvious that what haunts this scene is the specter of the Middle Passage."[45] While Reid-Pharr focuses on the circulation of flesh in *The Big Sea* and elsewhere, I seek to more widely interrogate the ghostly presence of the Middle Passage in Hughes's first autobiography.

In the scene just prior to Hughes's first voyage to Africa, Hughes finds himself hired as a mess boy on a fleet of ships "going nowhere."[46] Over one hundred freighters commissioned for World War One had been declared unseaworthy soon after the war, due to shoddy construction overseen by shady contractors. Towed up the Hudson River to Jones Point, the "dead ships" sat anchored and connected to one another by means of planks without railings.[47] Overseen by a "skeleton crew," Hughes reads a lot, talks to sailors, and revises his poem, "The Weary Blues," writing and rewriting its ending without satisfaction, "something that seldom happens to any of my poems."[48] This scene of stasis, with its "long winter nights," and "the old ships rocking and creaking in the wind, and the ice scraping and crunching against their sides, and the steam hissing in the radiators," not only allows Hughes to read voraciously, but it also focuses attention on marine infrastructure.[49] Rather than sailing unimpeded, Hughes's first nautical encounter underscores the ship as a built environment and disconnects it from its purpose of transportation. The ship's flaking, rusting hull, the movement on the water, the weather, and its emptiness draw attention to what typically goes unnoticed, the decaying alluvial materiality that undergirds travel and transport.[50] Hughes connects the ship's lack of purpose and decay to his own writing that cannot be brought to satisfactory closure. Speaking of his typical process of writing poems, Hughes says, "There are seldom many changes in my poems, once they're down. Generally, the first two or three lines come from me from something I'm thinking about, or doing, and the rest of the poem (if there is to be a poem) flows from the first few lines, usually right away."[51] Hughes's composition of "The Weary Blues," as Nadia Nurhussein has argued, rather than flowing unimpeded, is a mechanical and repetitive process.[52] The narrative arc is missing as is the teleology of the ship's voyage. What this scene conveys, instead, is an atmosphere of the haunted maritime past. Time dilates and space hangs suspended without resolution.

Not only that, but this haunted past is explicitly racialized. While the fleet's history is firmly grounded in World War One, the racial difference that Hughes makes plain throughout—"I was the only Negro in the whole fleet"—insists on a longer history.[53] Besides Hughes's speculation on what lies buried in the water, he underscores his confinement within "the mother ship" from which he seldom ventures away for an entire season.[54] More, Hughes is anxious to disprove to his fellow crewmen the stereotype that Black people are superstitious and frightened. This desire prompts him to spend a night on a dead ship supposedly haunted by a mutineer. No other sailor would dare to do the same. Hughes inhabits the uninhabitable, a nowhere zone that spatializes the otherness of his Blackness. He occupies a scene of rebellion from the nation's war efforts, rendering him akin—indeed he sleeps in the same cabin—to the murdered, treasonous sailor. The sailor's ghost floats between the past and present, animation and death, national belonging and traitorous betrayal. Blackness occupies a similar state, although the connection between the two remains unremarked in Hughes's account. Once on board for a few hours, Hughes confronts the possibility of a ghost, yelling at the watchman, "Beat it, Pug, and lemme alone! You're no ghost!"[55] His bravado successfully negates the crew's expectation of him. Soon after, Hughes falls soundly asleep. He exorcises the history of shipboard violence, both the specific instance of a recent mutiny, and, through his representativeness as a Black man, the longer history of the slave ship. Rather than being haunted by this past, Hughes faces the violence held in the "dead" vessel directly. The ship, in this scene, is an actant, raising both fears and horrific memories. It interrupts the presumed role of ships as facilitators of smooth, efficient transport and instead foregrounds the violence of the past as it lingers in a creaky, echoing stillness. An absent presence resounds. But is this exorcism a final overcoming of the past?

To answer this question, let us return to the last line of "The Weary Blues," the line that Hughes says he struggled to write during the long, cold winter on the mother ship. It reads, "He slept like a rock or a man that's dead."[56] Hughes closes the poem with the undecidability of whether the blues player can best be likened to a rock or to someone dead. In either case, he resembles the nearly dead, fungible state of human cargo, lingering in a state of suspended animation.[57] As Nurhussein points out, Hughes's biographer, Arnold Rampersad, attributes this condition to Hughes himself while serving on the dead ship and likens it to a fetus in the womb.[58] This description also aligns with Glissant's term for the slave ship, the "womb abyss." I suggest that Hughes's state of suspended animation, especially while sleeping in the bunk of a murdered mutineer, revisits the grim origins of Blackness. The blues player's metamorphosis from a haunted, melancholic musician to someone close to death may have occurred while Hughes was on board the dead ship fleet. Might the atmosphere of the creaking, rusting, empty vessels have prompted this vision of a zombified Black man? The connection is opaque and submarine because the alluvial memory of the Middle Passage, as Glissant states, sits offshore from the mappable geography and history of the nation. To further explore this sense of Blackness as alterity, let us next consider Hughes's initial voyage to Africa.

Critics often consider Hughes's pre–World War Two writings as romanticizing Africa, but in *The Big Sea*, his paeans to Africa are immediately undercut by critical observations of West Africa's poverty and colonization.[59] Crucially, Hughes includes West Africans in his interrogation of Blackness, noting that the coastal Africans he meets affirm Blackness, calling a particularly dark sailor, George, "black," despite his protestations to the contrary.[60] Moreover, Hughes writes that West Africans "did not laugh at Marcus Garvey, as so many people laughed in New York. They hoped what they had heard about him was true—that he really would unify the black world, and free and exalt Africa."[61] These positive comments on the term "Black" suggest that Hughes is speculating about how Africans might be as a possible source of pan-African identity and resistance given that they treat Hughes as fully assimilated into the West. They call him white and exclude him from religious rituals. Blackness, in Hughes's treatment, is a contested, differential, and shifting category, one that is open to new meanings that do not always arise directly from forced transport during the slave era. Extending his earlier reflections on the sea as a receptacle for waste, he now associates the sea as dumping grounds for Africans. He describes a scene in which young African boys are swimming alongside the ship. A "dozen black Kru boys" dive beneath massive mahogany logs being exported in order to place chains around them so that they can be hauled on board the ship.[62] Hughes states matter-of-factly that if they were caught between the logs or between the logs and the ship, they would be crushed to death. "Or if the sharks came, death would come, too."[63] The boys' vulnerable bodies float next to the logs in an image that places African life and the natural world on the same existential plane. By quantifying the boys—"a dozen"—locating them in the water, and identifying their disposability, Hughes presents the bifurcation of the world between Westerners who export valuable African resources for trade and manufacture, and the marginally human, or expendable persons, who often risk their lives for those endeavors. In this scene, Blackness is associated with death-defying work, specifically in the oceanic chaos in which Black bodies are vulnerable to the sudden movements of the mahogany logs, the ship, and sharks.

As Hughes gazes down at the swimmers, he mingles Black alterity and beauty with the unfathomable scale of lives drowned at sea. His matter-of-fact tone conceals and reveals these depths: "It was beautiful and dangerous work, those Black boys swimming there in the tossing waves."[64] Black liveliness intermingles with the violence that threatens and the history that decimates. The massive wooden objects (the logs) and the (now) metal ship figure the holds wherein Africans were held captive; the chains and sharks also metonymically reanimate the legacy of the forced transport of Africans to the Americas. I ask the reader to speculate on a transversal history in this scene. Hughes's lexicon is explicitly presentist but might we connect sharks, disposable people (who are not enslaved but exploited), the boat, and chains to the longer history of the West African coast? To argue for the racial longue durée in *The Big Sea*, I compare this scene to Guyanese writer Eric Walrond's short story "Wharf Rats" that is part of the 1926 short story collection, *Tropic Death*, which Hughes reviewed favorably. "Wharf Rats" narrates a shark attack and subsequent death of a boy (Philip) in the Panama Canal where Philip and his brother Ernest dive for coins tossed by rich passengers from ocean liner decks. The narrator recounts, "It was a suction sea, and down in it Philip plunged. And it was lazy, too, and willful—the water. Ebony-black, it tugged and mocked. Old brass staves—junk dumped there by the retiring French—thick, yawping mud, barrel hoops, tons of obsolete brass, a wealth of slimy steel faced him."[65] Harris Feinsod argues that this detritus "prefigure[s] the Middle Passage chains rolling at the bottom of Édouard Glissant's Atlantic, but Walrond's story is shaped less by the history of slavery than by the specific disaster of the 'Panama Panic.'"[66] Unlike Walrond's Panama Canal, Hughes's parallel scene occurs in deep African coastal waters where the past is an echoing void rather than filled with the detritus of a recently failed infrastructure project. Unlike Walrond's story, Hughes sees potentiality in the boys rather than desperate pathos. Amid the chaotic dangers of impending death—the tossing waves, the massive logs—Hughes glimpses beauty in Black liveliness amid horrible circumstances. The boys' bodies float, dive, and risk being crushed or eaten so that, from Hughes's elevated, spectatorial perspective (occupying the position of the rich passengers in Walrond's story), they are associated with matter. Like the logs, they are also unmoored and floating in the sea. Yet, at the same time, their youthful liveliness indexes Black promise; their beauty yields a space of resistance within their disposable existence. Hughes reads for Black life and particularly for the erotic power of these Black youth to resist the configuration of Blackness as disposable.

In figuring the Kru boys metonymically with the mahogany logs, Hughes draws attention to the boys' expendability in a manner that shifts attention to labor. These swimmers are not merely waged laborers. By putting their lives at risk in the sea, they become equivalent with the exchangeability of the logs, although less valued. To the employer, their lives are disposable; they are the refuse that cannot be sold. They are akin to natural resources expropriated from a colonized land and thus rendered less than human. Each boy is equivalent to the next—there are twelve—and easily replaced. They are dispensable through the coercive and oppressive mechanisms of global networks of imperial trade.[67] These logs, Hughes casually remarks, "would perhaps someday be somebody's grand piano or chest of drawers made of wood and life, energy and death out of Africa."[68] The labor and lives of African workers congeal to the wooden object, rendering its fetishistic power. Natural and human resources are coterminous with energy and death; in his treatment, the human joins with the organic and nonorganic (wires, nails, varnish, etc.) in a material unity of the piano or chest of drawers that underscores art's (music in this instance) dependence upon labor, expendable bodies, and materials. While Hughes envisions energy and death attached to the production of the commodities, he also sees it taking place in the present scene of colonial expropriation: one of mixing, diving, hauling, and floating.

Such activity—flashes of limbs and heads in movement—eroticizes the youths, although Hughes's detached narration disavows such physical attraction. Rather, he displaces his reaction onto another scene. He likens the spectacle of the swimming boys to "the same feeling I had had in Mexico, watching Sanchez Mejias turning his red cape so gracefully before a bull's horns."[69] In both, beauty and death are aestheticized, a move that mediates the scene through an artistic appreciation that removes Hughes from admitting a direct personal response. He assumes a mask of impersonality which prevents, as Omri Moses suggests, the assigning of identity.[70] Many critics have noted in frustration that Hughes dissembles, displaces, or masks his sexual attractions that the confessional mode of the autobiography requires.[71] But if we understand Hughes's narrative as a revaluing of damaged materiality (boys risking death, the deforestation of Africa) rather than asserting an autonomous identity, we can understand this scene as a heterogenous mixing of the nonidentical—the disposable boys, the logs, boat, and chains—to reveal scars of the past and the active, shaping force of damaged materialities. Without the boys and the forest, how can art be possible? This rhetorical move inverts the colonizer's line of reasoning whereby European culture originates modernity and "civilizes" the rest of the world. Such a presentation not only, in Ziarek's words, "preserv[es] ... the otherness of materiality" (emphasizing its liveliness, agency, and beauty), but it also creates an "aesthetic form [that] foregrounds the conflicting yet inseparable interrelation between the intelligible and the material."[72] The actively shaping materiality of the boys' labor and the wood contests the colonizer's abstractions. It inserts otherness and the objectivity of art into Hughes's autobiographical narrative.

The eroticism that Hughes underscores is first introduced to readers directly after he tosses his books into the sea. If the books exclude Hughes from the category of the human, the scene that occurs just afterward, below decks in the mess boys' cabin, demonstrates exactly what those books foreclose. Hughes enters his shared room to find one of them, George, "lying stark naked in a lower bunk, talking and laughing and gaily waving his various appendages around."[73] This possibly homosexual scene is interrupted by the narrator's observation that "George was talking about women, of course."[74] Specifically, he complains about his landlady in Harlem who had pawned his clothes. He speculates that when he returns, he might "pay her the month's back rent he owed her.... Or else—and here he waved one of his appendages around—she could have what he had in his hand."[75] Brian Loftus reads this scene as an instance in which "the erotic potential is immediately rendered impotent and represented in terms of its economic implication."[76] The possible homoerotic content, according to Loftus, is evacuated by impotent braggadocio of a heterosexual "payment." But if we remember that these racialized "mess boys" are traveling to Africa, below decks, in a "hot cabin," this scene echoes the ways in which sexuality became a form of resistance to the economic exchange of captive Africans during the slave trade. Omise'eke Natasha Tinsley argues for queer desire as resistance to the dehumanization on board the slave ships. She writes, "the emergence of intense shipmate relationships in the water-rocked, no-person's-land of slave holds created a Black Atlantic same-sex eroticism: *a feeling of, feeling for* the kidnapped that asserted the sentience of the bodies that slavers attempt to transform into brute matter."[77] Although the slave trade voyage renders African captives into socially dead slaves, the erotic bonds between captives affirmed their "sentient selves" in their gender and sexual fluidity. Queer, in this sense, Tinsley states, "mark[s] disruption to the violence of the normative order ... by forging interpersonal connections that counteract imperial desires for African's living deaths."[78] These captive bodies enter into exchange, becoming fungible, within slave economies and this same fluidity allows for Glissant's "transversality," an opaque connection that produces relation.[79] The mutable nature of "trans," as Snorton phrases it, "provides critical insight into the transubstantiation of things...'black' and 'trans' ... are brought into the same frame by the various ways they have been constituted as fungible, thingified, and interchangeable, particularly within the logics of transatlantic exchange."[80]

In Hughes's reverse crossing of the Middle Passage, its history—as a forced transportation that violently imposed a transmutation of the self into brute matter—reverberates in its ever-present, but opaque, nowness. Keeping this crossing at the forefront of awareness, we discern that George's body forges an erotic, but unspoken and indirect, connection with the other men even as his words assert a normative heterosexual exchange. His queerness, in the sense of an unanchored crossing between hetero- and homo-object attachments, resists capture by the racist structures that encircle these men on the ship and in colonial Africa. The fluidity of sexual orientation in this scene is heightened by the description of another mess "boy" in the cabin, Ramon, who, we learn, "didn't care much for women."[81] Instead, he "preferred silk stockings—so halfway down the African coast, he bought a pair of silk stockings and slept with them under his pillow."[82] Hughes describes how Ramon relates to the silk stockings in terms of commodity fetishism and leaves unsaid an opaque insinuation that this item may also express a transgender identification. Here, Ramon's gender becomes a "territory of cultural and political maneuver," in which his racialized body shape-shifts via a transgender fluidity that is both material and symbolic.[83] The transversal fluidity of gender identifications, as Snorton argues, is "a concept that encompasses 'categorical crossings, leakages, and slips of all sorts.'"[84] The racial, gender, and sexual crossings of these "mess boys" resist the racist and heteropatriarchal social order that surrounds their cabin. The queer and racialized community among whom Hughes sails revel in transversality, one which eludes knowability by the colonial apparatus based on the exchangeability of Black bodies. Such a resistant practice, manifest in the slave ship hold, suggests far more creative potentiality than the overrepresentation of Man as human can account for. The cabin "mess boys" perform within the confines of their cabin a Black liveliness that resists the abstract categories of the racist world in which they must otherwise live.

Contrast this laughing, transgendered, homoerotic space of color with the horrific scene of gang rape on board ship that occurs once arrived in West Africa. Hughes recounts, "One night, very late, two little African girls rowed through the surf in a boat to our vessel, hoping to make some money."[85] The bo'sun, in charge of the crew, takes one girl to his cabin while the other is thrown down on the floor of the sailors' quarters where the rest take turns with her. Hughes describes the scene, "Each time man would rise, the little African girl on the floor would say: 'Mon-nee! Mon-nee!' Finally, I couldn't bear to hear her crying: 'Mon-nee!' any more so I went to bed. But the festival went on all night."[86] The spelling of her cry for money, in French, puns with "my birth," signifying a primal scene of Blackness and fungibility. Her words name herself as currency or pure exchangeability of value. Her body is a screen for male fantasies and insatiable desire. Despite this, Reid-Pharr argues:

> The multiracial crew, the naked African girl were lost together atop the aloofness and depth of the Atlantic, their revelry a type of theater, a ritualized evocation of a never quite palpable certainty.... What they attempt to defeat is the sense of possibility she represents, that spectacular and elusive virgin animality that might leave both men and cultures adrift forever. They press her down, moor and anchor her, just as their predecessors carved their bows into images of half-naked women.[87]

The opacity of the African girl's existence reverberates in the scene as a "spectacular and elusive virgin animality" that the men attempt to possess and destroy. That Hughes leaves the scene without intervening permits the torture of anti-Black violence to remain ongoing. But it also demonstrates Hughes's refusal to participate in a homosocial male order founded on sexual and racial violence. The unspeakability of the violence along with the unrepresentability of the girl's alterity resound as a gap in narrative, a suspension of action and denouement. It suspends mimeticism and instead reverberates as a horrific, outraged scream across the centuries.

ZORA NEALE HURSTON'S LIFE ON THE MUCK

Their Eyes Were Watching God explicitly links Janie's quest for freedom to her maternal genealogy of interracial rape. It is not until Janie meets Tea Cake, her third husband, that she understands that freedom lies in a turn away from respectability and racial uplift. For Janie, Black patriarchy mirrors too closely the plantation structure of white male violence and power. Instead, she finds creativity and joy when she and Tea Cake join a community of migrant farm workers in the Everglades:

> To Janie's strange eyes, everything in the Everglades was big and new. Big Lake Okeechobee, big beans, big cane, big weeds, big everything.

Weeds that did well to grow waist high up the state were eight and often ten feet tall down there. Ground so rich that everything went wild. Volunteer cane just taking the place. Dirt roads so rich and black that a half mile of it would have fertilized a Kansas wheat field. Wild cane on either side of the road hiding the rest of the world. People wild too.[88]

The Florida Everglades, for Hurston's Janie, is an alluvial site par excellence. "The ground so rich that everything went wild" relates plant life, soil, water, and people in an abundance of growth and mobility. The people who live there, a mixture of migrant African Americans and Bahamians along with Seminoles, revel in the exuberance of vegetal proliferation whose wildness spreads to them as well. The cane, rather than being stringently cultivated, is decidedly postplantation. It grows unbidden, bursts boundaries, and hides the people on "the muck" from the rest of the world, carving out a Black geography that is decidedly different from the Jim Crow South. But this secluded enclave is hardly separate from the wider world, after all, the soil "would have fertilized a Kansas wheatfield." The Everglades is both particular to an Afro-diasporic and Indigenous geography *and* part of settler colonial industrial agriculture in the Americas. This uncertain zone of flux gives the lie to the myth of landscape as stable and uncontested geography. Rather than naturalize the distinction between land and water, alluvium troubles those boundaries. But more than merely delineating an ecological zone of transition, or ecotone, alluvium has vital resonances for being human otherwise. As Hurston's description of the Everglades above suggests, the rich ground of "the muck" sets people wild as well.

As a material accumulation, alluvium has always been an enemy of ports. Port authorities must constantly dredge alluvium in order to maintain the smooth flow of incoming and outgoing ships. Not only does dredging assert control over the flow of goods and people, it also poses ecological harm to plant and animal life. It destroys marshes and other wetlands that provide natural flood protection and damages coral and other underwater ecologies. Given that alluvium slows the steady flow of global trade, it also impacts narratives of colonizers and settlers. Time dilates and momentum slows. More, visibility clouds, frustrating the ongoing efforts at surveillance and control of Black fugitivity and resistance. It blocks the state's intentions to assert totalizing borders. As

Isabel Hofmeyr argues, ports serve as a "hydroborder" that aim "to pave the ocean and assert sovereignty over the conjunction of land and sea."[89] Such a desire—to pave the ocean and achieve total control over the coastal ecotone—is manifest by means of constant surveillance of borders, goods, and peoples that circulate across zones. Maritime boundary-making, Hofmeyr continues, has long had a "seminal function in terms of creating racialized identities, paranoid styles of governmentality, and epidemiological forms of statecraft."[90] The connotations of waste, pollution, and contamination that ports carry extends to those who inhabit the squalid and often transient living quarters nearby. Alternatively termed by Hurston and, we'll see next McKay, the bottom, the muck, and the ditch, these zones of "low" life featured drinking dens, gambling sites, and bordellos where prostitution of all types and contraband items circulate along with "alien" and other unwanted peoples.

Hurston's "muck" is not an ocean port; instead, it lies inland along the southern edge of Florida's Lake Okeechobee, the eighth largest freshwater body in the United States. But this fact, as Brian Russell Roberts argues, works to disturb the distinction between inside and outside the continental United States. When the hurricane hits Okeechobee and the lake breaches its "seawalls," Roberts writes, the "continent becomes sea-scape."[91] Fish swim in yards and hills become islands.[92] Even prior to the storm, the denizens of the muck carve out an Afro-diasporic geography—comprised of African Americans, Bahamians, and inflected by Seminoles—that sits in liminal relation to the white settler's geography of reason. Akin to Hughes's night in the haunted dead ship marked by treason, Black migrant workers occupy a liminal zone that renders them disposable by being external to secure land. This geography is perpetually making and unmaking itself, like the migrant culture itself: "All night now the jooks clanged and clamored. Pianos living three lifetimes in one. Blues made and used right on the spot. Dancing, fighting, singing, crying, laughing, winning and losing love every hour. Work all day for money, fight all night for love. The rich black earth clinging to bodies and biting the skin like ants."[93] The precarious nature of migrant farm labor demands, for survival purposes, sole attention to the present as the future is always uncertain. This now time is further condensed as pianos, like the life force of the migrants, work triple overtime. Songs are created on the spot, but the genre of the blues remains, insisting that the past is not overcome. The pianos are animated alongside the performers and the crowd, blurring together subjects and instruments in performance. The scene is mobile, alive, and seething in the continuous present of making and unmaking. The jooks emerge from the muck, as the soil "clings to bodies" and "bites the skin like ants." The dirt focuses attention on the body's permeable surface where external elements turn inward, biting the skin "like ants," alive and agentic. This formulation renders the inhabitants of this community a living threshold between the nonhuman and human.

More, their "wildness" rejects the mimicry by liberal subjects of an ordered nature in favor of a Black sociality that is open-ended and fecund with possibilities of living otherwise together. Hortense Spillers calls this liminality "vestibular" and links it specifically to the flesh of Black women as they are ungendered on board the slave ship and on the plantation: "A female body strung from a tree limb, or bleeding from the breast on any given day of field work because of the 'overseer,' standing at the length of a whip, has popped her flesh open, adds a lexical and living dimension to the narratives of women in culture and society. This materialized scene of unprotected female flesh—of female flesh 'ungendered'—offers a praxis and a theory, a text for living and for dying."[94] In order to fully grasp the implications of the alluvial as Hurston describes it, it's important to understand the fungibility of Black female bodies in the context of Black insurgent geographies. Spillers writes that flesh carries men and women (the mother's progeny) "to the frontiers of survival" and in the process turns the cultural text of the nation inside out.[95] The founding event of race is inscribed on Black women's bodies. Those who own and dominate Black women are defined as white. They become national subjects who make history while Black women become cousins to beasts, not quite human, and lacking gender. Black women are variously seen as things, animals, or objects. By means of their exclusion from the human, exiled "to the frontiers of survival," Black flesh constitutes national narratives by defining the center. Paradoxically, this exclusion can become a strength. Because Black women are positioned as subhuman, they are not burdened by the dualism of scientific thought where "nature" can only be known through empirical observation and universal laws. They are instead proximate—although not identical—to nonhuman worlds. Because of this positioning, they invent a poetics of relation with the nonhuman that is opaque to the colonizer because it does not follow dualistic structures of thought. Spillers's notion of "female flesh 'ungendered' " enacts a marginal cultural geography where the human is in open-ended relation with the nonhuman. It serves as a text for living anew.

On the muck, Janie rejects the imposed gentility that her previous husband Jody had demanded of her in order to participate fully in the Black sociality she finds there. She adopts the blue denim overalls and heavy shoes of the farmworkers and voluntarily joins them in their work. In the rough and tumble of the muck, Janie becomes jealous, chases after a rival Nunkie, and threatens violence; Tea Cake and Janie physically strike one another; and Tea Cake worries that a "boogerman" will take Janie away.[96] Love, violence, and folk beliefs characterize the "wildness," or exorbitant behavior and sensibility, of the migrant community. Tall tales, "skin games" (rigged games, swindles, and fraud), and card games like "woof" and "boogerboo" are raucous, performative, and improvised on the spot. As Janie's grandmother tells her, "us colored folks is branches without roots and that makes things come round in queer ways."[97] Excluded from the rootedness of national narratives and identities, the Black workers revel in disruptive cultural exchanges and inventiveness, including, at times, with the Bahamians and, to a lesser extent but still manifest, the Seminoles. More, their sexual desires are wayward, multiple, and unconfined to monogamy. The migrants' boisterous manipulation of appearance and language claims a proximity to animals and spirits, thereby engaging in a joyous fungibility at odds with the dehumanizing fungibility that Janie's grandmother endured in slavery when she was used "for a work-ox and a brood-sow."[98] More, her grandmother considers Black women's role in postslavery society to be continuous with the past in many respects. They are "de mule uh de world so fur as Ah can see."[99] The migrants' resistant fungibility continues to blur the lines between animal, plant, the sea, and the human.[100]

Hurston highlights these nonhuman connections made via alluvial geographies by means of the hurricane that strikes the camp. The sublime scale of the storm allows her to represent what Glissant calls the "other of Thought," an encounter with an unfathomable totality that alters the subject by opening them to an "aesthetics of turbulence."[101] This aesthetics undoes hierarchies of the human and recalls the foundational unsettling of Black humanity during the Middle Passage. During the hurricane, plants talk, a monstrous sea walks the land, wild animals fearlessly shelter with humans, humans become animals, and life and death become almost indistinguishable. Sonya Posmentier argues that the hurricane "marks a shift in narrative structure, evoking both the physical horrors of the middle passage and the indignities of Jim Crow racism."[102] She draws on Hurston's description of living through a hurricane while doing fieldwork in Nassau, Bahamas, remembering it as "horrible in its intensity and duration."[103] This sense of time stalled and distended evokes Glissant's notion of the alluvial traces of the Middle Passage that live on long past conscious memory. The hurricane reactivates the crisis of the life and death aboard the slave ship. It turns the joyous fungibility of Black sociality on the muck inside out, replacing love and creation with terror and death, and dissolving the liminal Black diasporic geography into the cosmic uncaring of the sea. Nonetheless, because the hurricane is focalized mostly through Tea Cake and Janie, I read these two spaces as entangled with one another. Black aliveness and love mix together with an aesthetics of turbulence that places the human subject in crisis.

Janie first learns of the impending hurricane when she asks groups of departing Seminoles where they are going. They reply with a reading of the landscape, "Going to high ground. Saw-grass bloom. Hurricane coming."[104] The next day, the community sees rabbits, possums, and snakes scurrying and slithering east. By nighttime, the nonhuman world is abuzz: "Several times during the night Janie heard the snort of big animals like deer. Once the muted voice of a panther. Going east and east. That night the palm and banana trees began that long distance talk with rain. . . . A thousand buzzards held a flying meet and then went above the clouds and stayed."[105] Janie's matriarchal lineage of Black flesh grants her a sentience toward the nonhuman that is already manifest in the language of her sexual awakening under a pear tree. Here, Hurston shows her relationality with the nonhuman world that "talks" and otherwise signifies the hurricane. We see that such creatures—palm and banana trees and buzzards—relate to weather scales that far exceed the nation. Far from anthropomorphizing them, Hurston gives them a world of their own, only partially discernable by Janie. Joshua Bennett, in his reading of *Their Eyes Were Watching God*, puts this relation thus: "Here and elsewhere, Hurston's foremost commitment is not to cleanliness but to murk, to the dirty, difficult labor of giving language to the historically fraught proximity between black flesh and the beasts of the field. Rather than evade this adjacency, Hurston elaborates on it, giving musculature and music to the cut, making a world from what is widely known as nothingness."[106] At the advent of the hurricane, Janie's proximate relations extend from beasts of burden to wild animals in a conjunction that mirrors the wildness—and disposability—of the people who live on the muck. Hurston's language reveals, Bennett writes, "the briefest glimpse into the multitudes [the animals] contain."[107] Even more, the hurricane occasions glimpses of mutable geographies and weather as both terrorizing and creative actants.

The nomadic but linear exodus made by the animals is only a foretaste of a world turned upside down during the storm itself: "Sometime that night the winds came back. Everything in the world had a strong rattle, sharp and short like Stew Beef vibrating the drum head near the edge with his fingers. . . . It woke up old Okechobee [sic] and the monster began to roll in his bed. Began to roll and complain like a peevish world on a grumble. . . . Night was striking across nothingness with the whole round world in his hands."[108] Hurston's description of the storm connects Black cultural practices to the unbounded and threatening forces of the nonhuman. The wind sounds like drumming, fingers on the edge of the head. Dilating and extending this event as Hurston describes her personal experience of a hurricane in the Bahamas, Stew Beef's drumming evokes Kossula's memory at sea, where the wind vibrates the ship mercilessly, as discussed in chapter 1. The sense of the world suspended in "nothingness" recalls Kossula's void of being during his disorientation at sea. In the exigency of these dire conditions, life and death mingle together in language that echoes the blurred conditions of existence on board the slave ship: "The wind and water had given life to lots of things that folks think of as dead and given death to so much that had been living things."[109] Finally, Okeechobee becomes a monstrous sea that joins the wind in a "multiplied roar . . . and a wail," a sonic cry that resembles the description Kossula gave to Hurston in *Barracoon* of the most terrifying aspect of the Middle Passage.[110] Language breaks down into pure sound, but it also suggests the animation of the lake into a force resembling Black insurgency. The chains of the "monstropolous beast" had been loosed by the wind, allowing him to "seiz[e] hold of his dikes and run forward," to uproot the migrants' quarters and then to "rush[] on after his supposed-to-be conquerors."[111] This beast overturns the white world. In the midst of this activity, the land becomes a sea, rolling the dikes, houses, and the people. White settler geography—fixed and gridded—is flooded and tossed by an unbounded force that is figured as Black rage: "The sea was walking the earth with a heavy heel."[112] In its wake, all hierarchies are overturned. When fleeing the water, Janie and Tea Cake "passed a dead man in a sitting position on a hummock, entirely surrounded by wild animals and snakes. Common danger made common friends. Nothing sought a conquest over the other."[113] Life and death blur: the dead man resembles someone alive and deadly snakes ignore humans due to a far greater danger. In this moment when white domination falters under the superior force of the storm figured as Black rebellion, relations with the nonhuman world are assembled laterally through an ethics of shared danger and mutual need. It even becomes possible for Janie's and Tea Cake's sensitivity to the nonhuman world to metamorphosize into their becoming animal. In the midst of Janie's near drowning, the cow to which she clings for life thinks she's an alligator; Tea Cake, diving into the water to rescue her, becomes an otter. In the water, humans and beasts are equivalent in desperate survival.

After the storm, as if a mighty battle were waged, "Bodies had to be searched out, carried to certain gathering places and buried. Corpses were not just found in wrecked houses. They were under houses, tangled in shrubbery, floating in water, hanging in trees, drifting under wreckage.... Death had found them watching, trying to see beyond seeing."[114] This description, as Posmentier argues, comments on the disposability of Black bodies in both Jim Crow lynchings and forced transport across the ocean.[115] It suggests that the violence of the storm is equivalent in devastation to the racism of modernity/coloniality. The victims' haunted eyes strain even in death to locate a cause beyond the visible for their suffering. Although the novel explicitly suggests that this entity is God, the long durational history referenced—of slavery and segregation—indicates structural racism. It is not until after the storm that racial and geographical order is reimposed. Black men, including Tea Cake, are forcibly conscripted to bury the dead in absurdly segregated burial grounds. This endeavor is absurd, as the novel explains, because white bodies turn black in death and white lime is sprinkled over all bodies causing racial differences to be indistinguishable. Nonetheless, it effectively reorders social relations in a manner that reimposes white supremacy. Meanwhile, Tea

Cake's and Janie's becoming animal goes horribly awry. When Janie is forced to shoot Tea Cake, who from rabies has turned into "some mad dog," their experiment in riotous living ends.[116] From segregation and anti-Black racism to the casual enactment and acceptance of domestic violence by Tea Cake and his male friends, the novel can only sustain brief moments of sexual and collective freedom, or being human otherwise than European Man. But the possibility of living otherwise, joyously and collectively through Afro-diasporic practices, has been briefly realized.

CLAUDE MCKAY'S ALLUVIAL ENTANGLEMENTS

> All this was like an unknown tongue to Lafala, but interesting to hear. His civilized contacts had been limited to the flotsam and jetsam of port life, people who went with the drift like the scum and froth of the tides breaking on the shore, their thinking confined to the immediate needs of a day's work down the docks or a trip on the boat or any other means of procuring money for flopping, feeding, loving.[117]

In this quotation from Claude McKay's circa 1929–1933 novel, *Romance in Marseille*, the protagonist Lafala refers to Black and red internationalism as "an unknown tongue." It widens his conceptual horizon, but only to a certain extent. Rather than dwell on the abstractions of the Marxist theory of world revolution that render his presence at the Seaman's Club "symbolic," he reflects on the "flotsam and jetsam of port life" who had heretofore comprised his "civilized contacts." The metaphor of dockside denizens with flotsam and jetsam associates these people with debris from ships, whether deliberately discarded (jetsam) or accidently lost (flotsam). This section argues that McKay's figure of the "flotsam and jetsam of port life," conjures a Middle Passage history of abyssal loss and human commodification.[118] What other people have been deliberately discarded en masse into the sea? Who else have lost themselves through suicide among the waves?[119] Granted, one might take flotsam and jetsam to be just a metaphor; however, this section will demonstrate that McKay's novel interrogates the social logic and history of racialized disposability alluded to by these terms. Paradoxically, the novel also suggests that this long history of expendability contains the seeds of a transformation of Black life via lateral and reciprocal relations with humans and nonhumans alike.[120] In the quotation above, the flotsam and jetsam "went with the drift like scum and froth of the tides breaking on the shore." McKay figures the Quayside population as intimately affected by surrounding pressures. These forces move them and they, in turn, affect their environment. Described in terms of unwanted microscopic plant life and overlooked spume (a froth caused by dissolved organic matter churned up by the sea), McKay casts these drifting "civilized contacts" in terms of nonhuman thingness.[121] In so doing, the figures turn abjection and disposability into dynamic self-creation by embodying a living, mixing, mobile force: "flopping, feeding, loving." By presenting the mutable, shifting collective of transients and day laborers in transitive, unanchored terms, the novel experiments with envisioning the human in terms other than those of the liberal subject.

Unlike autonomous liberal subjects who are held to act unilaterally upon the world in which they find themselves, "flotsam and jetsam" evokes the legacy of slavery whereby captive peoples are stripped of agency and autonomy. Because slaves were never autonomous, they and their descendants, as McKay shows, reinvent subjectivity as malleable and permeable to others and to their surroundings. They revalue and recast the very fungibility to which they were subjected. Such reinvention enacts a nonnormative, resistant relation to racial supremacy. In the quotation above, the same fungibility also describes a motley crew who embrace their designation as disposable and unwanted to transform that exclusion into an ongoing experiment of living otherwise.[122] They act in concert with their surroundings, "feeding, flopping, loving," to produce what Hartman calls, "a complete program of disorder . . . tumult, upheaval, open rebellion."[123] These transversal relations produce a radical Black collectivity: queer, interracial, international, embodied, sensual, and resistant.[124] Finally, by situating Lafala's "civilized contacts" on the shore, the novel insists on a mobile geography: shifting, unstable, porous, and sedimented with layers of historical accumulation. McKay shows how the shoreline is both a zone of pleasure and sexual freedom and a tightly patrolled border where the state regulates the influx of danger: from disease, immorality, sedition, unwanted peoples, contraband cargoes, and more.[125] This final chapter segment explores how the shoreline in *Romance in Marseille* provides a fecund location for sifting through the residues of slavery to salvage possibilities for living otherwise than the racist state demands.

From the shoreline, *Romance in Marseille* reconfigures its drifters as being liminal to national, racial, gender, and sexual normative categories that attach to territorializing societies. And so, despite its emphasis on Blackness formed through the legacy of slavery, Lafala's "civilized contacts" are multiracial and multinational. The character Étienne St. Dominique says, "we're all divided, all have a dual personality, Black, brown, yellow, white."[126] Given the port setting of these comments, we can think of this conflicted state of being through an oceanic frame. On the one hand, the violence of racial capitalism aims to imprison humans within clearly defined and enforced categories of racial supremacy and gender normativity. On the other hand, the chaos of the sea, with its endless drawing toward and away from the shore, emphasizes what Hester Blum calls the "unfixed, ungraspable contours" of the sensuous, plurivocal, nonlinear aquatic realm.[127] The sea, in this lens, is agential. Water is "an active participant in mediating intimacies and creating pleasure."[128] These twin forces, the centripetal order of state-sanctioned violence and the unmaking of those categories through centrifugal shoreline mixing and oceanic erotics produce in the characters who populate *Romance in Marseille* dual personalities who are either at war with the normative state apparatus or succumb to its power.

McKay already recognizes this complexity in the quotation above as he encodes slave history within the resolute contingency of the day laborers. Lafala represents the drifters' temporal horizon as being strictly limited to "the immediate needs of a day's work," achieved via improvised, flexible labor and exchange. Soon after, he admits that he had never considered "such toilers achieving anything different or changing the way of life that seemed as eternal as the rhythm of the waves alongside Quayside which they so much resembled."[129] Putting these two temporalities together, it becomes clear that the grinding everyday poverty and insecurity of the dockside inhabitants seems insurmountable because these people seem as "eternal as the rhythm of the waves." They seem to be outside of history because they are associated with the waves by means of the slave abyss.

In contrast to its foreclosure in European thought, abyssal history animates the narrative of *Romance in Marseille*. The flotsam and jetsam enact an upheaval against the omnipresence of state-sponsored violence, confinement, deportation, and harassment. McKay's novel upends the geography of reason in order to disclose a poetics of relation—lateral, reciprocal, and creative—between the human and nonhuman. In so doing, it attempts to disturb the smooth unfolding of narrative and the conventional assumptions of literary form in favor of the nonlinear, entangled, and disposable.[130] By foregrounding the abyssal history of the slave past, McKay's novel explores the ongoing afterlife of slavery and locates a poetics of relation from within the inherited structures of slavery, especially the commodification and mutilation of disposable persons. This section asks, how does McKay transform the biologically inferior status of human "refuse" that is Black life within racialized capitalism from waste to the alluvial entanglements of Black life lived otherwise?

More than any of McKay's other works, *Romance in Marseille* directly interrogates the afterlife of slavery in early twentieth-century Afrodiasporic cultures. Lafala's stowaway passage from Marseille to New York City results in his captivity and loss of legs at the hands of the crew. The settlement he receives from the shipping company for his double amputation exchanges his body parts for money. The announcements in the Black press resonate uncomfortably with slave auction catalogs and plantation account books, for instance, "AFRICAN LEGS BRING ONE HUNDRED THOUSAND DOLLARS."[131] Moreover, Lafala appears to accept his passive, objectified role within the system that has not only mutilated him but has also subjected him to manipulations by his multiple handlers: Black Angel who finds the appropriate lawyer for the case; the Jewish lawyer who defends him and wants half of the settlement money; the Company; and the official who represents Lafala's colonial status. And this manipulation continues in Marseille by the shipping company, his agent, friends, and enemies. Finally, Lafala's background, while not the complete natal alienation of slavery, nonetheless implies a fundamental rootlessness due to colonial cultural reprogramming. Colonial missionaries removed Lafala from his present-day Nigerian village at a young age so that he could be educated in a mission school in a larger town, thereby destroying Lafala's belonging to his ethnic community. The statelessness and familial homelessness, as well as his physical mutilation, is remarked on through his lawyer's third-person account of how Lafala's abject status will appear before a New York judge: "Poor African boy without any relatives taken away from his people when he was so young he did not even remember them, without family, without country even, without legs."[132] The resultant effect is that Lafala declares, "You are a good lawyer; this gentleman is a big official. I am nothing."[133] Swallowed up by a white world, Lafala drifts along, buffeted by the whims of others.

Lafala's love interest, Aslima, also exhibits a constrained sense of agency that can be attributed to her status as a sex slave in Morocco and as a prostitute in Marseille. Aslima was born a slave in North Africa. Her mother was "a robust Sudanese who was sold a slave to the Moors," of whom Aslima has only "a shadowy remembrance."[134] It's important to note that the terms "Sudanese" and "Moors" are both shorthand, anachronistic, and nongeographically specific terms used by English-speaking non-Muslims to denote Arabs. While Aslima's mother may have lived in Sudan, this term can also indicate her North African and Arab background more generally.[135] Aslima's childhood was short: at an early age, she was kidnapped to serve "as a decorative thing in the house of a wise old courtesan" until she could fetch a large price as a virgin sex slave.[136] Next, a French West Indian soldier bought her to be his concubine in Casablanca and later moved her to Algeria. Finally, a Corsican "tout" took her to Marseille as her protector until he sold her to a "loving house."[137] Aslima drifted from house to house until she struck out on her own, with the protection of her pimp, Titin. In Marseille, Aslima becomes Lafala's lover, steals his money, and prompts his disastrous return voyage to New York after which he loses his legs to frostbite. Lafala, enthralled once again with Aslima on his return to Marseille, invites her to go "Back to Africa" with him.[138] Such an invitation echoes Marcus Garvey's rallying cry of a popular Black internationalism and identifies both Lafala and Aslima as products of slavery and members of an extended Black diaspora. Here, McKay acknowledges the diasporic aftereffects of slavery in Africa and Europe. Caribbean creolization extends its project into the "old" world. Even more, Aslima combines pan-Africanism with Orientalism given her association with the Islamic and animist cultures of North Africa where she grew up. Such racial blending works to displace a Black/white binary into a multiracial and multinational continuum of diasporic identities.[139] Here, McKay prefigures Glissant's creolizing account of Afro-diasporic multiplicity extended into the "tout-monde." Further, the Asiatic dimension of Aslima's character provides a sensuous and exotic eroticism that at times allows her to escape her commodified sexuality.

The question of whether to live otherwise than the white world demands, to exert however constrained an agency, drives the plot: Will Lafala take Aslima with him back to Africa? Who will double-cross whom or will true love win? The motivation of each character is opaque. Each is faced with the choice between money and love. The uncertainty of the outcome drives the plot and confronts readers with the unknowability of human actions. This difficulty is particularly clear in Lafala's case. After he is released from the Marseille prison where he was held by the shipping company for the earlier crime of stowing away, his agent advises him to abandon Aslima and "leave Marseille at once to avoid further complications."[140] The agent speaks out of shock after learning that Aslima "was just a colored creature of the dives of Quayside."[141] The agent's racist misogyny accords with Lafala's practical impulse to protect his money and outweighs "the sensual" aspect of his character in the "clear and sobering daylight" on the morning that Lafala is to leave Marseille.[142] Lafala's friends also cast doubt on Aslima's motivations by warning him that she intends to steal his money again. Despite the fact that Lafala is "overwhelmed in love" with Aslima, he takes action to preserve his newfound wealth and status by abandoning Aslima and leaving her money to salve his guilty conscience.[143] His choice speaks to the "dual personality" of living in a white world: namely, the conflict between the prizes offered under racialized capitalism, on the one hand, and the precarious possibility of living otherwise, on the other. Meanwhile, Aslima's motivations also remain murky until the denouement. While this opacity mimics the hardboiled detective novel, when we account for the Middle Passage history and disposable status of the Quayside population that subtends this plot, the possibilities of living otherwise—fleeting, ephemeral, excessive—are far more subversive than a potboiler whodunit can convey. These "experiments in freedom," as Hartman calls it, that include riotous conduct, queer sexuality, and gaming the system, form a "beautiful [counter]plot against the plantation."[144] The counterplot depends upon embracing contingent, lateral relations with human "refuse"—the queer, the stranger, and the sex worker—to succeed.

Besides the prizes offered under racialized capitalism for accepting the system, there are also coercive constraints to achieve obeisance. The absent presence of slavery in *Romance in Marseille* occurs through the racial state: frequent, unanticipated arrests; the condemnation of the drifting unemployed for attempting to live outside the racist structures of labor; the criminalization of prostitutes, communist organizers, and queer subjects; and the policing of national boundaries that entails the deportation of those without the necessary papers. These efforts halt movement, inject uncertainty, and devalue the community's experiments in living. In addition, the fugitive memory of the Middle Passage haunts Lafala's double amputation. The palimpsest of suffering, both past and present, has the effect of collapsing time frames and disrupting chronological history. It draws upon an alluvium that sediments both Black suffering and collective rejuvenation. The point is underscored when Lafala attends a reception at the Tout-va-Bien to celebrate his release from jail: "Everybody was close together in a thick juice melted by wine and music."[145] The beguine was playing, "always living [sic] this heady Martinique dance, blood cousin to the other West Indian folk dances, the Aframerican shuffle and the African swaying."[146] Time and space are collapsed into one heady celebration where music and dancing evoke both African and Afro-diasporic practices. The crowd merges into a potent being-in-common, dissolving into one another, while the music evokes a Black Atlantic mobility that through music expresses a dispersed "blood" kinship and shared racial memory.[147]

Lafala is literally carried off by the current of erotic, sensual energy: "The beguine rhythm caught him by the middle, drop by drop. The music swelled up and down with a sweep and rushed him off his feet."[148] Ironically, it is the pull of the music that propels Lafala *to* his feet as he attempts to dance for the first time since his amputations. But he can only do so by relying on the force of the music and crowd and on his dependence on Aslima: "He found it was not so difficult after all with Aslima carrying him along."[149] The pun on beguine, as both a dance and slang for sexual attraction, transforms Aslima into a bulwark for Lafala as she "stiffened her breast to bear him up."[150] The scene underscores Lafala's physical dependence upon the Quayside community, and Aslima in particular, to rejuvenate him. After all, he seems to walk without assistance elsewhere in the novel. The dance displays the necessity of Aslima's Black femininity to transform the valuation of Lafala's vulnerable and dependent masculinity. So, too, the festivity renders him a full participant in the multiracial collective. The celebration at Tout-va-Bien is an entanglement of bodies, energies, and elemental rhythms: music without, wine within, that allow subjects to become porous and slippery against one another in a living, mixing, mobile force. The alluvial scene occurs in spite of and within the ever-present racist structures that seek to eliminate such defiant activity and compel the servitude of menial labor and sexual commodification.

A crucial alluvial entanglement in *Romance in Marseille* occurs through the resignification and revaluation of the term "pig." During their first sexual encounter upon Lafala's return to Marseille, Aslima remarks, "I've been a pig all my life.... But with you I don't feel that it's just a mud bath. I feel like we're clean pigs."[151] Their racial association with animality and filth interrogates the human as it is defined by the West. Aslima scrubs Black sexuality clean from its association with dirt, immorality, and licentiousness while maintaining its relation to animality. Together, Lafala and Aslima "reconstruct intimate life" from the racialized confines begun on the slave ship and the plantation. Hartman says of these sexually revolutionary practices: "The bedroom was a domain of thought in deed and a site of enacting, exceeding, undoing, and remaking relations of power."[152] Aslima, in particular, reinvents herself as a creative, loving human entangled joyfully with another in a manner that negates her social position as a disposable, vilified prostitute of color. Yet she does not mimic a white autonomous subject who claims to have full agency over their surrounds. Aslima configures herself and Lafala in lateral, mutual terms. Neither condemns the other for their Blackness, disability, or profession. Their partial agency, arising out of their confinement within raced and gendered systems of power, finds freedom only by embracing and exploring the very derogatory terms with which they are associated. Such metaphorical and historical proximity to dirt and animality emphasizes the resistant fungibility of their Black bodies as they momentarily escape the fixity of raced and gendered hierarchies. By affirming this designation rather than condemning it, the novel proposes a scandalous liaison that wallows in its sensual, pleasurable, and liberating force. This reconsideration of sexuality is especially important for Aslima, as we'll see below.

In more general terms, McKay's novels occasion a broad rethinking of the human through the very process of dehumanization. Jennifer F. Wang argues that McKay's association in the earlier 1928 novel *Home to Harlem* of working-class Black subjects with animals is a "racial-form-of-life [in which] . . . revitalization emerges out of the revisioning of biological and organic life ('living itself')."[153] The suggestion that Black reimagining of the human proceeds by revisioning its relation to biological and organic life makes Aslima's declaration to Lafala, "I want to convince you that I am human at bottom," resonate with the long history of Black dehumanization.[154] Her assertion revalues and reimagines the alluvial location to which Black life has been consigned. *At bottom, as refuse, as flesh, I am human*. To grasp the revolutionary potential of this alluvial reinvention of the human, it's important to keep in mind the racial chasm, as Hartman stresses:

> the Negress occupied a different rung of existence than the mistress and the lady of the house, the very term signaled a break or caesura in species life, a variant in the human, an antagonism or dimorphism more fundamental than man and woman. Yet, was there an opportunity . . . in the refusal to emulate and mimic the standards of who and what you were directed and commanded to be (but never would be)? It was difficult to put this visceral and abiding sense of existing otherwise, at odds with the given, into words.[155]

It is McKay's genius that he did put the revolutionary potential of alluvial entanglements—sexual, fungible, human and nonhuman, shifting and open—into words in his novels. *Romance in Marseille* goes further than his other novels in taking seriously how Black femininity, as it exists otherwise, must be central to a Black reinvention of the human. I turn next to consider how Aslima is the fulcrum around which the novel's "experiments in freedom that unfolded within slavery's shadow" take place.[156]

To return to the conversation in *Romance in Marseille* that opened this section, when St. Dominique informs Lafala that "[His] race represented the very lowest level of humanity, biologically and spiritually speaking,"

we can certainly read his words as chiming with evolutionary history and racist science.[157] St. Dominique's statement associates Blackness with biology and immanence, a failure of the Black race to transcend their so-called barbaric conditions. Reading against the grain, as I believe the novel's irony in this scene suggests, I argue that it is precisely the revaluation of the association of Blackness with biology and immanence that provides the basis for McKay's Black liberatory aesthetics. Lafala, after all, rejects the Seaman's Club and the hierarchical structure of its Marxist world-historical narrative that is represented by St. Dominique. Crucially, McKay's aesthetics center around Aslima and Black feminine sexuality.

That Glissant does not explicitly address sexual violence is symptomatic of the afterlife of slavery, namely, that sexual violence against Black women remains profoundly widespread and unspoken, that is, accepted with impunity (or disavowed) throughout most of the twentieth century. Hartman writes, "the repression and negation of this act of violence are central not only to the pained constitution of Blackness but also to the figuration and the deployment of sexuality in the context of captivity."[158] While no longer a de facto enslaved person, Aslima's seamless transition from slavery to sexual slavery allows McKay to comment on the violence and domination that she continues to face in her sex work in Marseille. Her status as "a stranger" and her profession of lending her body for impersonal sexual congress reflects the extreme precariousness of her social position.[159] Such precariousness shows itself when Aslima suggests to her pimp, Titin, that they marry. Titin reflects to himself, "It was an unthinkable thing—the idea of marrying a whore, a woman whose card of identity was the yellow one of prostitution, a woman without family, without home, without name."[160] Permanently labeled adversely by the state and existing in a state of natal alienation, Aslima cannot escape her status as a commodity. She exists solely to be the vessel for the projection of others' desires for possession and domination until she is rejected for even this role. Thinking about Aslima's suggestion of marriage, Titin reflects (via free indirect narration), "There were certain Quaysiders who were married to professional prostitutes but they were creatures of brothels and allied places of the same status as the inmates. Titin referred to such men as degenerates and perverts. He felt sick in the guts from the suggestion at his becoming a member of that class of men."[161] Titin's categorization of those who love prostitutes queers Lafala and relegates both he and Aslima to the lowest ranks of society. Lafala becomes viscerally abhorrent and morally outrageous in the view of those who uphold the social order, including those, like Titin, who are parasitical on the very women whom they condemn.

The effect of this abuse is to render Aslima barely legible. The fungibility to which she is reduced produces a countercharge that is erotic and transformative, but unspoken. Although the slave system and its afterlife project Black women's perceived constant sexual availability onto Black feminine (and other) bodies, their domination was and is never total. King argues that "fungibility is, in fact, a product of White anxiety and representation, an attempt to 'get in front of' or anticipate Black fugitive movement."[162] The system of turning people into property depended on deploying physical and social violence that was ongoing, inventive, excessive, and repeated. In response to white violence, "Black struggle's resistance to and maneuvering within fungibility is as unpredictable and uncontainable."[163] King continues, "Black fungibility can denote and connote pure flux, process, and potential. To be rendered Black and fungible under conquest is to be rendered porous, undulating, fluttering, sensuous, and in a space and state at-the-edge and outside of normative configurations of sex, gender, sexuality, space, and time to stabilize and fix the human category."[164] Aslima offers resistance by means of her body and its connection to nonhuman life. She elicits a sensuous and ecstatic, erotic state in Lafala who remarks, "Under her coarse and hard exterior there was always that rare green and fruity quality which had so intoxicated him when they first met."[165] Together, Aslima and Lafala reinvent the human as coterminous with the nonhuman world, "rare green and fruity." They enact a nonnormative sexuality that transports them elsewhere, through the deprivations of the absent memory of the Middle Passage and through the alluvium of their disposable and degraded status, to a refiguration of Black life. Audre Lorde speaks of the erotic as an overlooked resource that has been "vilified, abused, and devalued within western society."[166] The word, she states, "comes from the Greek word eros, the personification of love in all its aspects—born of Chaos, and personifying creative power and harmony.[167] Lorde calls eros a "lifeforce" and associates it with women, although it can be easily broadened to account for many forms of embodied resistance to Cartesian dualism.[168] Eros evokes a wider reality than Enlightenment thought allows. Its formlessness joins together with sensual, spiritual, physical, emotional and creative energies across individuals and beyond the limit of the spoken. Aslima enacts an erotic fungibility of flux and potentiality even as she suspects that she'll be sacrificed to the dominant order that confines her.

In presenting the setting for Aslima's vision of her sacrifice, McKay transposes Caribbean creolization onto North African Islamic and animist cultures so as to render time and space nonlinear and nonplanar. The geographic lamination of Africa, the Caribbean, and the East render disparate places and times simultaneous and overdetermined. The multiplied setting is exemplified by the fact that McKay drafted much of *Romance in Marseille* while living in Morocco. It renders a sense of diasporic mobility that is nearly as shifting and mutable as the sea itself. East and West, past and present, mingle sharply in Aslima's hallucinatory nocturnal vision on the Marseille wharf. As she sits near the shoreline, overlooking the bay, enveloped in darkness and obscurity:

> A red light appeared in the horizon revealing to her a different scene. She was in the heart of an antique white-washed city. And there was loud mounting music of voices as if a thousand golden-throated muezzins were calling in one mighty chorus. . . . There followed a loving feast. . . .
> When the feasting was finished the belly-moving beat of the drum roused the people again after an interval of rest to dancing and chanting over and over again repeating and reiterating from pattern to pattern unraveling the threads of life from the most intricate to the simplest to the naked bottom as if in evocation of the first gods who emerged out of the ancient unfathomed womb of Africa to procreate and spread over the vast surface of the land.[169]

Although the simile in the first sentence, "as if a thousand golden-throated muezzins were calling," suggests an Islamic religious celebration and the feast of Iftar during the holy month of Ramadan, we learn instead that the crowds, some enslaved and some free, gather together to worship "the Sword of Life." Animism and Islam meet, conjoin, and creolize through the mixing of slaves and freepersons from within and beyond the Islamic world. The vision is overwrought, as the crowd worships "a flaming sword suspended from the center for the dome," but it serves two functions. The first is to assert an African life force, a shared "racial memory" of the "threads of life."[170] These threads are unraveled to the "naked bottom," the facts of reproduction and death. The second is to foreshadow the novel's ending.

The passage insists on both its sensuous and erotic features in the present moment and a sedimentation of deep time and the now. "As if in evocation of the first gods" both invokes a prehistorical time and cancels it in favor of a lurid description in the present. As the participants dance and chant, their civilized façade is stripped away to reveal their elemental selves: naked, spontaneous, and uninhibited, as McKay avails himself of the discourse of primitivism. Similarly, "the naked bottom" is compared to the gods emerging from "the ancient unfathomable womb of Africa." The comparison is structurally similar to Glissant's alluvium that sediments the "unconscious memory" of the Middle Passage, although Glissant is marking the aftereffects of the historical event of transatlantic passage. This is so especially when Glissant figures the slave ship as a "womb abyss" in birthing African captives as enslaved people.[171] Significantly, both McKay and Glissant convert nonhuman sites into gendered ones to link materiality—the landscape of Africa; the infrastructure of the slave ship—with feminized Blackness. This assemblage then allows for the reclamation of flesh in the vision above and when Aslima repeatedly insists, as discussed earlier, that she and Lafala are pigs wallowing in the mud. The alluvial, figured as mud, silt, the womb, and sea-born detritus, in North Africa as well as the Caribbean and Marseille, refers to life stripped to its most basic elements and celebrated as such: a collective, creative, embodied energy that strengthens the Afro-Orientalist liaison, an alliance that would reach its apex at the 1955 Bandung Conference. The second function of this vision is to preordain the plot twists to come. Aslima's vision is her fate. In the hallucination, she is among the group who would be offered up "body and soul as a sacrifice."[172] The vision foreshadows the plot denouement when Aslima, after learning that Lafala left for Africa without her, attacks her pimp with a knife because he threatens to kill Lafala. Titin riddles her body with bullets, thereby making Aslima into a sacrificial offering to Lafala's altar of monied prestige.

Aslima shows the limits of Black femininity in the face of racialized capitalism. She remains in the chaos of oceanic eros and reveals the "unfixed, ungraspable contours" of fluid sensuality and self-abnegating love. Hartman underscores the potentiality of Aslima's life experience that cannot yet be realized. She writes, "The most significant absence of all in the dramaturgy of struggle, in the cosmic shattered history of Black life, in the unfolding plot of the wretched, was that of [the Black] woman. . . . If the text of the human was written over and against [the Black man], she fell out of the order of representation all together. Neither subject nor object, but a mute silenced thing, like an impossible metaphor or a beached whale or as a form yet to be named."[173] Hartman's metaphor of a "beached whale" is apposite. Aslima's location on the alluvial portside, attempting to live otherwise than the racist state demands, is an impossible place. It cannot be mapped or read. She is out of place and slowly suffocating. McKay cannot fully represent her. She remains opaque, her physical presence—erotic, sensual, alluvial—hints at the form "yet to be named" of Black humanity. Her last moments, riddled by bullets from Titin's gun, exemplify the "unanchored, malleable, and open signs" of Black fungibility: "She threw up her hands like a bird of prey about to swoop down upon a victim and pitched headlong to the door."[174] Aslima is reduced to flesh—torn and bleeding—and she simultaneously refers to another way of being. She appears as an avenging animal, fluttering, porous, and beyond the racist categories to which she is assigned. She signifies both racist confinement and the possibility of transforming that confinement into an alluvial entanglement with human and nonhuman alike.

Revaluing Black femininity whose flesh has been written over by colonial masters, Lafala links Aslima's body to the fecund earth in an alluvial form that gives shape to Black as well as Afro-Oriental freedom and futurity. On their final night together, Lafala marvels: "It was as if Aslima had all the time reserved a secret cell in her being and had unlocked it now for him alone to enter. And how like a rare tropical garden it was where every fruit was delicious to taste."[175] Her body and soul are figuratively linked to "a rare tropical garden," not, I think, to simply link Black femininity with nature, but to assemble the human and nonhuman in a coterminous and transformative relation. McKay inverts colonial fantasies of the female captive body, associated with the domination of the land, into the mutual enjoyment of self and land in an affirming, creative, intimate sharing. Aslima, after all, must make herself vulnerable—unlock her being—for this experience to occur. However, this mutuality is not to last. As Aslima's body is torn apart by bullets, it returns to mere flesh and its association with waste. McKay's novel implies that Black alluvial life is precarious under conditions of racial capitalism. But, as Aslima shows, it must be attempted against all odds.

    This chapter on alluvium has focused on life along the shifting, unstable ecotone of land and water and the detritus that washes into the docks and onto the shore. It argues that Black lives are also treated as sea-born refuse, but that Hughes's *The Big Sea*, Hurston's *Their Eyes Were Watching God*, and McKay's *Romance in Marseille* revalue this aftereffect of the Middle Passage by reimagining Blackness as produced through ecological interdependence and oceanic mobility, eros, and connection. Rather than follow a linear narrative path from race-blind white modernists to the inventive ways in which Black modernists revalue Blackness, geography, and the human itself, I begin with Black modernism's overlooked engagement with the Middle Passage to demonstrate to readers how they remember and transform received myths about the event. Next, I take a step backward to address the violent legacies of colonization, slavery, and the Great War as they occur in texts by white modernists. During the interlude that follows, I explore how white modernists both engaged and disavowed connections to the slave trade. Chiefly, I argue that white femininity is intimately tied to racializing conquest and slavery. Critiques of gender and race must attend to the longue durée of racializing and sexualizing violence in order to discern the shared structures and statist violence that can reduce unruly white women and Black men and women to flesh.

(INTERLUDE)

An interlude is a pause between acts in a play. It serves as a source of connection as well as differentiation between two acts, or, in music, two parts of a song. As it bridges discontinuous parts, an interlude provides a perilous passage across the formlessness that separates and subtends aesthetic works of art. It slows the reader or listener down and suspends them in unanchored time and space. The interlude on these pages resonates with literary modernist interludes, including those in W. E. B. Du Bois's *The Souls of Black Folk* (1903) where musical excerpts of "The Sorrow Songs" serve as interludes between each essay. They provide, as Du Bois says, "a haunting echo of these weird old songs in which the soul of the black slave spoke to men."[1] They sound from everywhere and nowhere at once, in an uncanny sense of the return of the dead. As collective, anonymous soundings, they register the undocumented but lingering, felt memories of slavery's past. Du Bois asserts, "The songs are indeed the siftings of centuries; the music is far more ancient than the words."[2] While Du Bois subsumes this African survival into a narrative of Black uplift, charting Afro-diasporic people's transition from atavism to aspiring citizens of the United States, might we stay with the song itself? As an interlude, it marks the threshold of the dead: its formlessness lends itself to expressing the longue durée of constitutive violence and formless materiality that delimits representational thought. Du Bois's interludes also signal Afro-diasporic living on and metamorphosing chiefly through remembered ties to kin. He offers as evidence of slavery's past his grandfather's grandmother who, "seized by an evil Dutch trader two centuries ago" and carried to exile in the Hudson Valley, crooned a "heathen" melody to her child. Du Bois's family passed down this untranslated and misremembered melody (since its words resemble no actual African language), "Do ba-na co-ba, ge-ne me, ge-ne me!"[3] The nonreferential lullaby marks Black maternity as it crossed the water from Africa to the Americas and resonates as what Julie Beth Napolin calls, "a song of survival, of living on.... [It] survives the Middle Passage and reopens it as a primary channel of listening and receiving."[4] The lullaby sounds Afro-diasporic mother-child relations, a primary connection and reciprocal interaction that sustains the passage between Africa and the "new" world as break and continuity; reinvention and remembrance.

Other modernists use interludes to capture a world beyond human intention. These include Virginia Woolf's impersonal seaside interludes in *The Waves*; the "Time Passes" section in *To the Lighthouse* where the violence of World War One dwarfs the domestic realm; and William Faulkner's interludes in *The Big Woods* (1955) that describe the physical transformation of the Mississippi wilderness through deep time in which human agency appears miniscule but devastating. In these interludes, modernists adapted and radicalized the boundary-blurring method of free indirect discourse. This technique, as is well-known, allows an impersonal narrator to have access to an individual character's inner thoughts and feelings, thereby blending personal and social perspectives undecideably in what Anna Kornbluh defines as a "representation of unattributed mental action."[5] Free indirect discourse highlights the otherness of language. Without direct attribution of speech, language indexes a collective sensibility honed through a society's long accumulation of sedimented meaning. Its impersonality, too, can be extended to the nonhuman world in a manner that dissolves subject/object distinctions. Of particular interest to us here, modernists including Joseph Conrad, Faulkner, Langston Hughes, Zora Neale Hurston, and Woolf began to use the technique to represent nonhuman perspectives and the agency of nonliving objects. Kelly Sultzbach argues:

> Experiments with modern interiority delve into perceived realities that are difficult to articulate, more felt than understood, and subject to

change.... The surrounding environment gains a new presence as modernism explores the boundaries of language and the possibilities of nonhuman lives that operate outside of human control.... Although the modernist reactions to these new understandings of nature and nonhuman varied—horror, hostility, and humility among them—the subjective force of the nonhuman consistently asserts itself in distinctly new representations.[6]

While Sultzbach usefully draws attention to modernists' felt responses to more-than-human aliveness, their ecological consciousness appears disembodied. It floats free of the materiality of bodies and the violent histories that produced them.

Instead, let us consider the interlude in Woolf's *To the Lighthouse* (1927), "Time Passes," that hinges the more conventional narratives of Parts 1 and 3 by experimentally giving voice to the inhuman otherness of death. The interlude's impersonal address opens with:

> So with the lamps all put out, the moon sunk, and a thin rain drumming on the roof a downpouring of immense darkness began. Nothing, it seemed, could survive the flood, the profusion of darkness which, creeping in at keyholes and crevices, stole round window blinds, came into bedrooms, swallowed up here a jug and basin, there a bowl of red and yellow dahlias, there the sharp edges and firm bulk of a chest of drawers. Not only was furniture confounded; there was scarcely anything left of body or mind by which one could say, "This is he," or "This is she." Sometimes a hand was raised as if to clutch something or ward off something, or somebody groaned, or somebody laughed aloud as if sharing a joke with nothingness.[7]

Darkness and water are conflated in this passage. The darkness is a "downpouring," a "flood," formless and immense. It is figured as both sleep and death. The agency of this nonhuman matter is indirect and fugitive. It creeps, steals, and swallows. It dissolves both objects and visitors to the summer home, "scarcely anything was left of body or mind," along with the gender difference and individuality of "he" and "she." Instead, bodies are fragmented—a hand is raised—and signification is reduced to nonreferential groaning and laughter that is "shared" with the cosmic scale of the fluid shadows that remain impervious to such sounds. Woolf's free indirect discourse may well indicate the individualized existential "horror" that Sultzbach suggests above, but there is also a specific historical and figurative repertoire at work here. That history is the violence and mass deaths of World War One and the personal losses that Woolf sustained in childhood and young adult life.

I argue that the free indirect narration in *To the Lighthouse* holds together World War One, the individual deaths that Woolf's family had sustained, as well as the longer historical lexicon of the slave trade. As the darkness in "Time Passes" dissolves all markers of human-scaled space, temporal registers shift as well. As the airs nudge and darkness prevails, "there was time at their disposal."[8] While the passage above refers to one night in diegetic time, the darkness in "Time Passes" lasts the duration of the Great War and beyond. The free indirect discourse toggles between human-scale, cosmic immensity, and "flesh turned to atoms."[9] It figures heterotemporalities chafing against one another. This effect makes one pause by opening the present to its ungrounding. Free indirect discourse unsettles human-centered knowledge and scale by rendering them contingent through the dissolution of their boundaries. It negates individual focalization to encompass the formless chaos of violence and death. More terrifying still, the interlude shifts momentarily to human scale to present the chaos of unmeaning in ordinary, domestic space. It states, "The stillness and the brightness of the day were as strange as the chaos and tumult of night, with the trees standing there, and the flowers standing there, looking before them, looking up, yet beholding nothing, eyeless, and so terrible."[10] Rather than sentimentalizing nature as picturesque, a projection that objectifies and subordinates the landscape to human-centered needs, the trees and flowers become things with a horrific inhuman drive that threatens to swallow whole the summer house. The sensibility of alien nature and unbounded, cosmic uncaring dissolves categories of knowledge that shield the subject from finitude.

This impersonality finds a resonance in the previous five-hundred-year-long slave abyss. Kidnapped, marched, and forcibly deported from anything familiar, the African captives were, as Hortense J. Spillers influentially argues, "nowhere at all":

Those African persons in "Middle Passage" were literally suspended in the "oceanic," if we think of the latter in its Freudian orientation as an analogy for undifferentiated identity: removed from the Indigenous land and culture, and not-yet "American" either, these captive persons, without names that their captors would recognize, were in movement across the Atlantic, but they were also nowhere at all. Inasmuch as, on any given day, we might imagine, the captive personality did not know where s/he was, we could say that they were culturally "unmade," thrown in the midst of a figurative darkness that "exposed" their destinies to an unknown course.[11]

On board the slave ship, ways of marking time and space disappeared. A figurative darkness enveloped the bondspersons and dissolved identity, gender, and the boundedness of human scale. I'm not arguing that Woolf is explicitly thinking about the Middle Passage in her interlude. However, as her free indirect discourse captures a sensibility of mass death along with non-human-centered life, it allows a hiatus—an interlude—in which we might hear other traumas and open imaginative space for other possibilities to arise. Namely, both "Time Passes" and Spillers's reimagination of the Middle Passage make visible and audible the material substrate of the liberal subject and its technology, the novel. Returning to the "Time Passes" quote above, and this time with Spillers's intervention in mind, the immensity of the fluid darkness echoes the ocean that swallows objects and bodies whole, a swirling nonplace on which the slave ship floats that "confounds" bodies into flesh, disintegrates human subjects, genders, languages, and ethnic affiliations, and gives rise to horrific groans, absurdist laughter, and inhuman indifference. Finally, Woolf's and Spillers's experimental/theoretical efforts to represent mass trauma counters Western forms of subjectivity, geography, time, and space and shows the contingency of such forms.

In case the reader is skeptical of my linking "Time Passes" to the slave abyss, let me turn next to another work that explicitly associates the Great War with the slave trade. In J. M. Coetzee's novel *Foe* (1986), Part IV takes us outside the diegetic space of the novel to probe the limits of novelistic discourse. In a postcolonial rewriting of the first Anglophone novel, William Defoe's *Robinson Crusoe* (1719), Coetzee's novel meditates on the centrality of slavery and colonization to the rise of fiction, specifically through the function of Friday's otherness. In Part IV, we enter Friday's world. Focalized through an "I" that both is and is not the protagonist, Susan Barton, the figure dives down to a shipwreck in which "The timbers are black, the hole even blacker that gives entry. If the kraken lurks anywhere, it lurks here, watching out of its stony hooded undersea eyes."[12] Crawling into the hole on hands and knees, the speaker reflects, "I had not thought the sea could be dirty. But the sand under my hands is soft, dank, slimy, outside the circulation of the waters. It is like the mud of Flanders, in which generations of grenadiers now lie dead, trampled in the postures of sleep. If I am still for more than a moment I begin to sink, inch by inch."[13] Time has stopped. The historically particular reference to "the mud of Flanders" layers biographical, imperial, geophysical, and catastrophic times in a heterotemporal now. It suggests that time does not pass but rather accumulates, stacking European mass death on top of the slave trade in a manner that connects to Woolf's interlude. This is not the sensationalism of gothic horror; instead, it presents the mind-numbing fact of mass death and engineered, rationalized suffering to derealize the present. It brings the centuries-past of slavery and colonization to bear on twentieth-century mass-killing machines and, in Coetzee's case, to the South African anti-Apartheid struggle. The speaker says, "In the black space of this cabin the water is still and dead, the same water as yesterday, as last year, as three hundred years ago."[14] Rather than suturing together parts of a narrative as an interlude might, Coetzee's writing undoes the novel altogether. As the narrator passes through one enclosed space after another, they finger decaying corpses, crumbling manuscripts, dirt, and ruins. In so doing, they make sensible the novel's greatest fear: the formlessness of "being subsumed and disintegrated" by watery darkness and death.[15] This is a place without words: "Each syllable, as it comes out [of Friday's mouth] is caught and filled with water and diffused."[16] Coetzee figures the ungrounded space of the antinovel—of terror, boundlessness, and death—that marks the limits of the liberal subject and his narratives.

Interludes connect, as I've shown above, but they also divide. The two ellipses, figured as a wave of water, in this interlude enact the void above which the interlude perilously bridges. I've discussed the formal qualities of interludes and now I turn to historical content. Woolf and Jean Rhys, considered in the next two chapters, describe the ocean as expressing a void of being and portray an impersonal, often hostile, land- and seascape emptied of humans. They only fleetingly acknowledge slavery and the Middle Passage. Why was this Atlantic history disavowed by white modernists? As discussed in chapter 1, the ocean was a key mechanism for denying the constitutive connections between modernity and coloniality. The maritime mobility of the hold ensured that the founding connection between Blackness and modernity would be forgotten. The "free seas" were shielded from oversight, set apart from national laws, and disavowed by means of the oceanic element that Europeans imagined as nothingness. Not only was the Atlantic Ocean forgotten, but it served as the means by which to forget. Geographically unstable, the ocean made the events on the slave ships exceptional and, until the Abolition Movement, mostly undocumented. It was a wilderness where subjectivity is unmade and reason founders. Terrifying watery depths, storms, and the omnipresent possibility of death by drowning made the Atlantic, for European subjects, a nonplace to be crossed as quickly as possible on route to wealth and adventure. This interlude expresses the disconnect between Black and white modernisms that were separated by means of the Middle Passage that established a metaphysics of race and the human. As a mobile bridge between Africa and the Americas, it manufactured both Blackness and European Man by means of the unremitting, excessive violence aboard the floating dungeon, torture chamber, and seasoning ground. Modernity, as Stefano Harney and Fred Moten write, "is sutured by the hold."[17] The two parts, Blackness and modernity, are both continuous and discontinuous with one another. The sutures of the hold both join and separate the two forces: the social death of the African captives and the exponential growth of a global system of trade and accumulation powered by Man.[18]

The forgetting of the violence at sea was loosening its repressive hold in the early twentieth century. The experimental aesthetics that characterizes modernism as well as the extremist politics of the early to mid-twentieth century offered intensified critiques of modernity that, at times, invoked the slave trade. Nonetheless, Woolf's and Rhys's cosmopolitan stances, while articulating world-spanning affiliations and advocating a plurality of voices and perspectives, are blind to histories that are not European. For them, the political modernity of the European nation-state system was the only means by which to make history. The modernity/coloniality divide continued to structure what was visible as civilization, even if these modernists could understand the culpability of civilized nations in producing barbarism. If anything, they recognized racial otherness in order to appropriate slavery's history to express their heroine's suffering (as it does for Woolf's Rhoda) and Creole otherness (in the case of Rhys's Anna and Antoinette). European modernist cosmopolitanism and the liberal subjectivity that informs it do not recognize Afro-diasporic poetics of relation.

In the August 2007 edition of *The Caribbean Review of Books*, Jamaican novelist Marlon James hazards an explanation for Rhys's and Woolf's historical and racial blindness. He writes that Rhys:

> understood the worthless woman in the most literal state of the word, a gift (or curse) she shared with Faulkner, [Tennessee] Williams, and Flannery O'Connor. Her women, like Julia Martin in After Leaving Mr. Mckenzie [sic], can be wildly self-destructive—their own worst enemies, to use another cliché—but they stand in striking contrast to Henry James's or Edith Wharton's or (to a lesser extent) Virginia Woolf's heroines in that they are willful players in their own fall.... Rhys knew her position was indefensible—the unwronged white woman—but to enter the twentieth century, as so many Southern women did, with the skin of privilege but not the wealth or class, was to prove a devastating tragedy.... Maybe this sense of dislocation was what allowed her, along with Woolf, to create the first true twentieth century women, too late for the Victorian world but too early for the postcolonial one.[19]

Writing in the interregnum, as modernists who feel their end is near, Woolf and Rhys peel away the puny European human world to reveal the implacable, impersonal forces of the nonhuman. For Woolf, this attention to the nonhuman produces a queer ecology in which the marginal character, Rhoda, in *The Waves* aligns with the nonhuman. In contrast, Rhys finds the more-than-human in the Caribbean and associates it with Afro-diasporic culture. Tragically, her female protagonists, thoroughly conditioned by white privilege, cannot dwell there. James suggests that it was social movements that dislocated Rhys and Woolf from the West's previous position of unquestioned dominance. While Woolf, James says, created heroines "beautifully depressed and doomed" who were "of the right class for such epic demise," Rhys's protagonists "scratch and bleed and scream and burn houses."[20] They refuse their fate even as it consumes them. Despite their class and geographical differences, both Rhys's and Woolf's protagonists—especially Antoinette, Anna Morgan, Rachel Vinrace, and Rhoda—share a sense of historical displacement that James identifies as "white women coming out on the wrong side of slavery's legacy."[21] A few decades later, these attitudes became obsolete as civil rights and anti-colonial movements demonstrated the humanity and history-making abilities of Global South peoples to form independent nations and to become citizens.

The next two chapters consider the aporia between white modernism and the legacy of slavery and colonization as well as the critical possibilities of reading them through the very history they deny. Some of this restorative work, as I discuss, has been accomplished by Woolf's and Rhys's literary interlocutors, the performance artist Kabe Wilson (for Woolf) and Marlon James and Jamaica Kincaid (for Rhys). To conclude this interlude, I provide an instance of what we may gain from exploring the disavowed historical connection between white feminist writers and the legacy of the Middle Passage. I bring the racial longue durée to bear on white feminist modernist discourse to show how attention to disavowed relations across modernity/coloniality, center and periphery, land and water, Black and white, past and present foregrounds uneven circulations, the commodification of humans and art, and the disciplining of white women that have been sedimented through the centuries.

Elizabeth DeLoughrey traces the term "Middle Passage" to twentieth-century mass politics. She notes that there are no cognate terms for "Middle Passage" in languages other than English:

> "Middle Passage" comes from abolitionist discourse where Thomas Clarkson's often-reproduced plan of the HMS Brookes, depicting the terrors of spatial and bodily compression, became synonymous with the

Middle Passage experience.... The invocation of the unhealthy "flesh" of the contained slaves and the hold's unhygienic stench reflected not only abolitionist humanism but also a particularly modern dilemma about the contaminating effluvia of the masses.[22]

We can see a linkage between slavery and the threatening phenomenon of the masses when Virginia Woolf, Jean Rhys, and others describe situations in which white women are reduced to flesh through violent suppression. This connection is not direct; that is, white feminist modernists seldom engage directly with the legacy of slavery, with Caribbean-born Rhys being an exception. However, if we consider British women's mass political protest for the vote and, specifically, their political tactic of hunger striking in prison to achieve status as a political prisoner, we find a crucial and overlooked connection to the hunger striking captives on board the slave ships. In formulating this connection, let us consider Orlando Patterson's *Slavery and Social Death* where he reconfigures Hegel's master-slave dialectic through the biopolitical term parasitism.[23] Rather than use Hegel's notion of the master's "recognition" of his dependence upon enslaved persons, a term that implies the master's benevolent paternalism, Patterson argues that the dependence of the master upon his bondsperson is better conceptualized as parasitism. Discussing his choice of the term, Patterson says, "Domination and its companion exploitation ... focus upon the dominator or exploiter as the active agent in the relationship and place upon the exploited the further burden of passivity."[24] In contrast, he says, "Parasitism emphasizes the asymmetry of all such unequal relations" whereby the host may be the more active of the two.[25] The parasite and host enter into a symbiotic relationship in which the host may or may not be affected adversely by the parasite. Further, the term suggests how the sovereign master consumes the bare life (life reduced to flesh) of the bondsperson in a manner that reveals "the unstable dependence of power on bare life."[26] Stressing the radical implications of conceptualizing the dependence of sovereign power on bare life, Ewa Płonowska Ziarek writes, "Like a reversed figure of the vampire sucking the blood of the living, the parasitical side of absolute power suggests that perhaps sovereignty is one of the most powerful political fantasies, masking power's dependence on bare life, which, although socially 'dead,' continues to threaten and provide sexual satisfaction [as the recipient of brutal sadism]."²⁷ Patterson's biosocial term calls attention to what Ziarek terms "a corporeal challenge to discursive practices of power."²⁸ One might recall how the slave trade abolitionist archive discussed in chapter 1 reveals instances where captives, hovering between life and certain death by means of a hunger strike or jumping overboard, appear to experience a moment of elation or peace. The flicker of freedom, a turning of uneven power relations by snatching away their host bodies from the master's teeth, demonstrates the symbiosis between bare life and sovereign power and therefore a means of contesting this divide.

Returning to white modernist women writers, it's important to remember the early twentieth-century shock of white women's militancy in the streets and, in the United Kingdom, in prison through the drama of the state's forcible feeding of hunger striking inmates. Ziarek argues that "by willing to destroy their bodies for political freedom, hunger striking suffragettes put bare life at the center of the struggle for human rights."²⁹ More, this struggle "acquire[d] a bodily and materialist turn that goes beyond both symbolic recognition [the right to vote] and the materialist politics of redistribution."³⁰ While Ziarek connects forcible feeding of hunger striking suffragettes with the fungibility of slavery, her emphasis on the early twentieth century misses the fact that forcible feeding was a common practice on slave ships where captives frequently refused sustenance to protest their kidnapping. This fact is never included in histories of hunger striking, the omission of which maintains the disciplinary divide between races, geographies, and centuries. Ziarek examines white women in the United Kingdom and Black women in the United States without connecting the two via the transatlantic slave passage, the crucible of biopolitical gendered and racialized struggle.

An emphasis on the long history of forcible feeding makes palpable the hidden connections between anti-Black racism and white women's gender struggles. For example, in September 1914, American novelist and journalist Djuna Barnes staged her own forcible feeding in solidarity with hunger striking British women's suffrage activists. Writing in *The World Magazine*, Barnes conveys her terror of the procedure as it brings her to the verge of choking to death in what is today classified as a form of torture. The semiotics of the procedure enforces her liminal state at the cusp of death: she is wrapped in a long white straitjacket and resembles a corpse. Barnes's staged experience of torture makes visible the occluded horror of what Ziarek calls, the British government's "seemingly 'apolitical' violence of rape masquerading as 'medical' treatment" upon women suffragists demanding status as political prisoners.[31] The tactic of hunger striking is itself ambiguous: inflicted upon the self, Ziarek writes, "as a substitute for political power, [it] acts by refusing to act: it collapses clear distinctions between passivity and activity, victim and enemy."[32] Although Barnes neither participates in the hunger strike nor in militant suffrage activism, the forcible feeding underscores the ease by which she becomes flesh. White women participate in the social symbolics of patriarchy only to the extent that they hide the flip side: the irreducible materiality and vulnerability of their reproductive and sexualized bodies. Forcible feeding reveals this underside. Barnes likens her ordeal to expulsion from patriarchal kinship: "This, at least, is one picture that will never go into the family album."[33] Years seem to pass as she hovers between life and death by suffocation: "There was no progress on this pilgrimage. Now I abandoned myself.... I had lapsed into a physical mechanism without power to oppose or resent the outrage to my will."[34] She is reduced to bare life. As the forcible feeding continues, Barnes begins to hallucinate an underwater nightmare:

> Unbidden visions of remote horrors danced madly through my mind. There arose the hideous thought of being gripped in the tentacles of some monster devil fish in the depths of a tropic sea, as the liquid slowly sensed its way along innumerable endless passages that seemed to traverse my nose, my ears, the inner interstices of my throbbing head. Unsuspected nerves thrilled pain tidings that racked the area of my face and bosom. They seared along my spine. They set my heart at catapultic plunging.[35]

Barnes imagines herself at the bottom of a "tropic sea," in the grips of "the tentacles of some monster devil fish." The imagery is prodigious, damned, and underwater. The giant squid confines her as the water slowly drowns her, entwining her inside and outside in an unbreathable atmosphere of liquid violence. She momentarily presents herself as malleable and permeable. Does Barnes's passive resistance in the figurative depths of the sea, entwined with a sea monster, anticipate Coetzee's kraken? What is submerged in the sea depths refuses to stay put. It's darkly alive; its tentacles entwine those who dare to enter. Barnes's passive resistance—her embodied struggle—entangles her momentarily with the devil fish. Her physical autonomy is negated; enemy without becomes enemy within; and any action she takes threatens her life. The "unbidden" images are "remote," located as they are in the tropics, but they are nonetheless conjoined in Barnes's solidarity with feminist struggles in the North Atlantic.

While Barnes walks away from her ordeal relatively unscathed, she not only draws attention to state violence against politically unruly white women in the United Kingdom, but she triangulates this violence through the tropical seas that evoke the slave trade. The policing of white femininity overlaps with the history of racializing conquest. Readers miss an important critique of gender and race when this history is severed. In relating white modernist feminism to the slave trade by means of the shared political tactic of the hunger strike, one sees in stark terms how the extremity of statist repression transforms humans from subjects to flesh, imaged here as an entangled, monstrous configuration with the nonhuman and elemental. Although, to be sure, white women seldom endure natal alienation or the permanence of being flesh as enslaved and imprisoned Black people have and still do endure. Barnes's exposé figures the sea monster as the hands of the state, showing how its desperate, repressive measures function to keep bare life submissive so that it can continue to suck its blood.

Chapter 3 examines how Woolf addresses the long history of violence against white women in her novel *The Waves* (1931). She explores this violence in terms of abolitionist discourse and Middle Passage imagery, but the connection between patriarchal violence toward white women and African-descended peoples is then reburied with the drowning suicide of Rhoda. I call Woolf's experimental aesthetics a queer ecology that, while ultimately disavowing racializing histories, nevertheless challenges the form/materiality divide between the human and nonhuman.

3

WAVES

Virginia Woolf and Kabe Wilson

WAVE:

*A movement in the sea or other collection of water, by which a portion of the water rises above the normal level and then subsides, at the same time traveling a greater or smaller distance over the surface; a moving ridge or swell of water between two depressions or "troughs"; one of the long ridges or rollers which, in the shallower parts of the sea, follow each other at regular intervals, assuming an arched form, and successively break on the shore. Sometimes the word is applied to the ridge and the accompanying trough taken together, and occasionally to the concave curve of the surface between the crest of one ridge and that of the next.
 *Used in collective singular for "water," "sea."
 *A forward movement of a large body of persons (chiefly invaders or immigrants overrunning a country, or soldiers advancing to an attack), or of military vehicles or aircraft, which either recedes and returns after an interval, or is followed after a time by another body repeating the same movement.
 *Rough, stormy, or fluctuating conditions.
 *A swelling, onward movement and subsidence (of feeling, thought, opinion, a custom, condition, etc.); a movement (of common sentiment, opinion, excitement) sweeping over a community, and not easily resisted. Also, a sharp increase in the extent or degree of some phenomenon.

The wave of the future: the inevitable future fashion or trend; the coming thing.

Physics: Each of those rhythmic alternations of disturbance and recovery of configuration in successively contiguous portions of a fluid or solid mass, by which a state of motion travels in some direction without corresponding progressive movement of the particles successively affected. Examples are the waves in the surface of water, the waves of the air which convey sound, and the (hypothetical) waves of the ether which are concerned in the transmission of light, heat, and electricity.

As Hester Blum reminds us, "The sea is not a metaphor."[1] Nor are its waves. Rather, in the excerpted *Oxford English Dictionary (OED)* definition above, the meaning of waves shifts from physical description to the historico-political sense of repeated attacks and retreats on the part of human collectives, to atmospheric, affective, attitudinal, and futural forces, and to wave theories of water and air that explain how waves convey sound, light, heat, and electricity. The waves, in their irreducible materiality and dynamic energy, produce meanings and exert agency. Matter, as new materialist thinkers argue, is neither inert nor immutable, but, rather, as Karen Barad demonstrates, it is "a doing, a congealing of agency."[2] The waves, therefore, are not simply produced by external forces acting upon them—the gravitational pull of the moon upon the tides, for instance—they also generate the matter and meanings around them. Barad writes, "Matter is produced and productive, generated and generative."[3] Through this framework and taking the *OED*'s shape-shifting definitions as a cue, this chapter understands the waves as "material-formal entities" that produce and are produced by other matter, bodies, and spatio-temporal frameworks.[4] As the varied meanings of *wave* capture both the physical properties of fluid (and airborne) matter and the human world of struggle and desire, they point to how matter is intimately entwined, indeed co-constitutive, with the human and its social meanings.

This chapter engages with the work of new materialist thinkers who include Barad, Rosi Braidotti, Jane Bennett, Stacy Alaimo, and Susan Hekman, but critically, insofar as they fail to recognize or account for racializing structures.[5] New materialism emphasizes the lively and often wayward forcefulness of matter, especially in the Anthropocene era when weather patterns, geologic formations, and climatic zones are changing quickly and unpredictably. In addition, this critical school arose in response to the poststructuralist emphasis on social constructionism, the view that there is no outside the text because the empirical world is always mediated through language. Social constructivism challenges societies' normative scripts, but its cultural and linguistic turn renders matter passive, a blank slate upon which cultures construct meaning. New materialists borrow from Spinoza, Nietzsche, Bergson, and Deleuze the paradigm of an imminent plane on which all things are vital matter. Their attention to scientific data and empirical investigations as well as to seemingly less mediated affective and aesthetic encounters with things promise a more empirical account of "life" than attention to the symbolic register alone can provide. New materialism is important for bringing to critical attention the effects of geography, the elements, affect, and other material forces on humans and, conversely, human entanglements with the nonhuman world.

However, as Diana Leong argues, "the very aspects that would make matter more 'real' than language or culture are the same aspects that restrict its ethical potential and facilitate a conceptual rejection of race."[6] Stated more bluntly, Leong posits that "[new materialist] reduction [of race to identity politics] and disavowal of race . . . is something of a structural necessity for the new materialisms."[7] In occupying the virtual plane of matter, the new materialist critic adopts a presentist sensibility, one that is unable to account for the long history of sedimented structures that continue to endanger racialized peoples. To illustrate, in *The Posthuman*, Braidotti explicitly rejects an accounting of persistent anti-Black and racist history when she writes:

> [A new pan-humanity] expresses the affirmative, ethical dimension of becoming-posthuman as a gesture of collective self-styling. It actualizes a community that is not bound negatively by shared vulnerability, the guilt of ancestral communal violence, or the melancholia of unpayable ontological debts, but rather by the compassionate acknowledgement of their interdependence with multiple others most of which, in the age of the anthropocene, are quite simply not anthropomorphic.[8]

Because this "pan-humanity" includes a majority of nonhuman others, it absolves one from needing to account for white privilege or racist exclusion. Braidotti's passage also partakes of European Man's universalizing impulse. Anyone seemingly from anywhere can affirm their belonging in this "collective self-styling" that performatively conjures a group identity as a break from the past and into the nowness of postmodernity. Leong writes that the new materialisms' racial disavowal "untethers non-, in-, and post-human from their historically proper site of production."[9] This universalism is entirely unlike Glissant's particular location at the alluvial shoreline that memorializes the transatlantic slave trade even though his poetics of relation potentially extends to the "tout-monde," as discussed in chapter 2.

In a manner akin to Glissant, Hortense J. Spillers specifies the historical particularity and location of Black female flesh on the slave ship to argue that it structures global modernity from below. In "Mama's Baby, Papa's Maybe: An American Grammar Book," she distinguishes between the body, so central to new materialist theories, and "flesh." She states, "Before the 'body' there is the 'flesh,' that zero degree of social conceptualization that does not escape concealment under the brush of discourse, or the reflexes of iconography."[10] Leong glosses her statement as follows: "Unlike the socially legible and historically-given 'body,' the material conditions of captive and ungendered 'flesh' cannot be altered by either the symbolic—'the brush of discourse'—or the imaginary—'the reflexes of iconography.' Flesh instead serves as a structuring dynamic for the coherence of both registers, and as such, must be eternally reproduced."[11] Black female flesh remains the material substrate for white national subjects who reproduce themselves through bourgeois domesticity. Their fleshly existence, Leong states, "remains a structural vulnerability to violence, a condition that is also a 'grammar'—an unconscious system of rules—that marks black women as the 'zero degree of social conceptualization.'"[12] It is also the place from where new political and social imaginaries arise. Spillers calls "the female stand[ing] in the flesh ... [a] different social subject."[13] By claiming *"the insurgent ground"* for this different sociality and "zero degree of social conceptualization," one necessarily reimagines the whole because Black death is structurally necessary for the benefit of white life.[14] Tiffany Lethabo King puts it thus: "To become or 'ascend' to Whiteness is to enact a self—or self-actualize—in a way that requires the death of others. The position of the conquistador is tethered to the process of 'ascending to whiteness,' or becoming human under the terms required by multiple versions of the human that keeps the category an exclusive and privileged site of unfettered self-actualization."[15] Black unfreedoms are needed to produce white freedoms.

It is my contention in this chapter that Virginia Woolf shares new materialist thinkers' racial disavowals, but for reasons of history as well as of philosophical affiliation. My reading of Woolf situates her as part of the women's suffrage struggle and, in so doing, connects her historically to the many images, cartoons, and posters that document the movement in the United States and the United Kingdom. I turn next to a newspaper cartoon of the US women's suffrage movement. As the image presents the specter of unruly women agitating for the vote, it unconsciously reveals the material substrate of Black flesh that also structures Woolf's novel. In a 1914 political cartoon on behalf of the US women's suffrage campaign (not shown), we might discern the unconscious of Western colonization and slavery.[16] While the image assures its viewers that women's suffrage is an inexorable outcome of the "tides" of history (the natural progress of civilization), it also inadvertently unleashes fears of women's sexuality and revolt that it seeks to contain. The association of undulating waters with unruly feminine forces has a long history in Western art. The sea has been figured as the motherly waters of birth, the fluid fecundity of life, the sexual lure of female seduction, and the dangerous threat of women in revolt. This overdetermination of meaning condenses into the paradoxical sense of water as both purifying and life-giving as well as contaminating and life-threatening. Visually, this doubled rhetoric appears as the water itself: the white women appealing for the vote are depicted as crests of the waves where the dark water turns into white foam. This lightness and whiteness suggests an idealized white femininity emerging from the waters, an image with a long history in Western art, from Sandro Botticelli's *The Birth of Venus* (1485) and Titian's *Venus Anadyomene* (1520) to the early twentieth-century woodcut by English author and artist W. G. Collingwood that depicts the Icelandic god *Heimdal and His Nine Mothers* as dazzling white figures floating on the crest of a wave.[17] By contrast, the water's depths are inscrutable and without figuration. In the depths, representation breaks down, as do bodies. It is here that racial difference is both produced and disavowed. Spillers, as discussed in the interlude, argues that the ocean is where Blackness is made: "African persons in the 'Middle Passage' were literally suspended in the 'oceanic,' captured in an 'undifferentiated identity' that made of them 'ungendered flesh.'"[18] Buried below, in the deep time of the ocean, are the chemical traces of African bodies and "balls and chains gone green."[19] This racial longue durée, I will show, subtends the experimental aesthetics and feminist and queer politics of Woolf's modernist aesthetics. My claim will be substantiated as we follow Woolf into the waves in a manner that makes palpable and nearly present what's hidden in the depths, namely, the occluded histories of slavery as the material substrate of modernist aesthetics. After my discussion of Woolf, the British-born performance artist, Kabe Wilson, has the final word on Woolf's racial blind spots in his 2014 performance art, "Of One Woman or So."

In what follows, the turbulent, swirling energies of the waves reveal the aesthetic and political possibilities that Woolf herself saw in natural phenomena. From *To the Lighthouse* and "Thunder at Wembley" to *The Waves*, Woolf used impersonal, nonhuman phenomena to reveal new possibilities for relating otherwise, with none more far-ranging than *The Waves*. I slow my pace with this text to examine in detail how the waves, as more-than-human configurations, reveal submerged and disavowed histories that connect marginalized peoples then and now, a connection that the text fails to make explicit. Woolf's ecological sensibility instead captures the agency of the waves, especially their nonlinearity and three-dimensional turbulence, to critique the institution of art. The waves unmoor aesthetic and political norms by foregrounding embodiment and materiality as shaping determinants of aesthetic form. The shift in viewpoint—from ideal abstraction to mobile materiality—emphasizes aesthetic *forming*, a performative encounter that dissolves, even if only momentarily, subjects into their surroundings. An attention to waves as a generative, co-constitutive force disrupts Western aesthetics' form-matter distinction and alerts us to how Woolf experimented with dynamic form: new modes of narration and figuration that take the materiality of the seas and shoreline as its cue. Like the new materialists, however, Woolf fails to recognize how Black flesh continues to structure white freedoms.

READING *THE WAVES*

Virginia Woolf composed *The Waves*, as Gillian Beer reminds us, over the course of four years of "intense emotional, political, and social involvement."[20] These years encompassed Woolf's work with the Co-operative Women's Guild and the writing of the introduction to their anthology, *Life as We Have Known It* (published by the Hogarth Press in 1931); the peak of her love affair with Vita Sackville-West; Woolf's publication of the mock-biography *Orlando* (1928) that playfully exceeds the limits of gender binaries, death, and the nation; and the publication of her first major feminist polemic, *A Room of One's Own* (1929). Concluding *A Room* with a reminder of the suicide of Shakespeare's sister, Judith, Woolf promises that "If we have the habit of freedom and the courage to write exactly what we think; if we escape a little from the common sitting-room and see human beings not always in their relation to each other but in relation to reality; and the sky, too, and the trees or whatever it may be in themselves ... then the opportunity will come and the dead poet who was Shakespeare's sister will put on the body which she has so often laid down."[21]

The dead poet, laid to rest in an unmarked grave "at some cross-roads where the omnibuses now stop outside the Elephant and Castle," haunts Woolf's essay with both the violence of Judith's demise and the promise of her future creativity and brilliance.[22] Woolf's sketch of an impregnated and suicided anonymous woman poet, drawn "from the lives of the unknown who were her forerunners," allows us to think through the relation of past and present that Woolf is arguing for.[23] The violent, depersonalizing force of misogyny, felt over centuries, haunts Woolf's writing, but it is overwritten by the promise that "if we worked for her," this abandoned and gifted woman would find it possible to live and write her poetry.[24] To live on and to write, freely and courageously, concerning not only human relations, but also relations to the sky, the trees, or "whatever it may be in themselves" is Woolf's inauguration of a feminist and a queer ecology to counter the gender hierarchies that ensure gifted women's erasure.[25] And this ecology is alive and active: Woolf's novel *The Waves* teaches its readers how to relate to the "in themselves" through a mode of queer ecological reading and writing. A queer ecology, as I am presenting it, encompasses the content, form, and practice of *The Waves*.

This reading departs from Nicole Rizzuto's assertion that Woolf's repeated reference to "the waste of water" in the novel and her diary refer strictly to the unconscious and silence as well as to menacing anti-colonial resistance.[26] To my mind, Rizzuto places Woolf's references to "waste" strictly within an imperialist context, and hence misses what I argue is Woolf's queer and feminist reclaiming of women deemed expendable, as I will show through a reading of Rhoda's death by drowning. My interpretation situates *The Waves* as a feminist sea memorial that draws on the language of slavery to connect the disposability of queer women to the expendability of African-descended peoples. These references (chains, bondage) problematically appropriate this history for white feminism, but reading today after anti-colonial and anti-racist achievements, they suggest the counter-history of the Middle Passage and centuries-long struggle against dehumanization.[27] That Woolf fails to reference anti-colonial and anti-racist struggles (beyond fleeting symbolic images) underway during the writing of *The Waves* underscores the persistence of the "racial longue durée."[28] The British Empire may be ending, but the structure of racial difference continues to foreclose the majority of colonial and minority subjects from full personhood and history.

This reading of *The Waves* extends previous critical work by Jane Marcus, Jessica Berman, and others who analyze the novel's critique of imperialism and the stultifying gender roles available to the British ruling class.[29] Drawing on, yet going beyond these critiques to questions of embodiment and relationality, I argue for the transformative potential of the novel's experimental aesthetics. While the novel mourns the lonely, limited white female lives that empire and patriarchy produce, it counters those losses with a queer ecological aesthetics that suggests a mode of being and relating otherwise. The novel conjoins aesthetic perception with the rhythmic materiality of the sea to create a lateral, nonhierarchical relationality between subjects and the nonhuman world, a decentering that opens the present to multiple temporalities. As I will show, this lateral relationality problematizes boundaries between self, others, and world. I argue that this practice is similar to what new materialists advocate, but both fail to consider how Blackness structures their ecologies.

In the sections to come, I first develop what I mean by Woolf's queer ecology, then I consider how Woolf's queer ecology cannot be understood apart from the innovative feminist politics from which it emerged. This is necessary to prevent Woolf's aesthetics from being separated from its historical and political contexts and rendered static and universal. Next, I turn to that which Woolf is writing against—the imperial mappings of the sea and how the structures of empire and patriarchy violently exclude Rhoda, the queer female character in *The Waves*, from its normative framework. Last, I conclude by widening my critical purview to the larger circuits of the novel's queer ecology: the contingency and virtuality of reading the novel and its dissolution back into the turbulent matter from whence it came.

QUEER ECOLOGY

Queer ecology is a mode of relating to the nonhuman that is erotic, pleasurable, multiple, and shot through with world-making potentialities as well as with memories of trauma, violence, and loss. Thinking both world-making *and* loss simultaneously deconstructs the aporia of modernity/coloniality and opens the subject to its co-constitution with the more-than-human. Woolf would not have defined herself or her writing as participating in a queer ecology, because, as Bonnie Kime Scott reminds us, ecofeminism—not to mention its later offshoot, queer ecology—has only been around since the mid-1970s.[30] However, as I will show, Woolf's aesthetic and compositional practices in *The Waves* weave the six characters with nonhuman, vital forces of water, air, and light into an open-ended ecological whole. I claim that Woolf's ability to incorporate the nonhuman into her vision of aesthetic wholeness stems from her feminism, i.e., the consciousness of female devaluation. Going further, Woolf, the author of *Orlando* and the defender of Radclyffe Hall's *The Well of Loneliness*, was aware of the unnaturalness of gender norms and heterosexual binaries. She sought in *The Waves* to envision how women (and others) might relate to nonhuman organisms and materialities in a nonhierarchical manner that imagines and ethically enacts a future world without the instrumental, violent appropriation of women's bodies and the natural world. Rather than reproduce gender norms, a queer sensibility interrupts the reified "naturalness" of heteronormativity.

Instead, a queer sensibility opens the present to multiple temporalities that connote not only past loss but future potentials. Ecology concerns the relationships between living organisms and their environment. The modifier, "queer," opens the term to a variegated history of loss, struggle, and creative transformation. The semantic history of the term queer shifts from the use of the term to inflict injury and exclude—its principle meaning during Woolf's lifetime—to its reclamation and revaluation as a badge of resistance and inclusion in the late twentieth century. Although the value of queer has altered dramatically, it cannot be said that its prior derogatory inflections have been simply overcome. Judith Butler argues that the term queer must always open the present moment to both a long history and possible futures: "If the term queer is to be a site of collective contestation, the point of departure for a set of historical reflections and futural imaginings, it will have to remain that which is, in the present, never fully owned, but always and only redeployed, twisted, queered from a prior usage and in the direction of urgent and expanding political purposes."[31] Butler underscores the constant troping demanded by the term queer itself and the fact that it has been partially rehabilitated. The meaning of queer is never fixed or fully present because the term is perpetually in contest between its pejorative and transformative meanings. Through this struggle, queer opens the present to the past in a form of temporal and spatial warping and connotes the transverse, oblique, crosswise, and obstructive.[32] Queer slows the experience of time down, pinning subjects to their bodies and to the materiality of their surroundings.[33] It insists on the imminence of matter and meaning, bodies and words: how subjects are able to manifest themselves in the world, given the long misogynist, racist, and homophobic history that accretes social constraints, even as it materializes bodies.[34] Queer is a sensibility and orientation toward the world that makes it possible, as Dana Luciano and Mel Y. Chen have convincingly argued, to imagine an "inhuman intimacy" with stone, sky, trees, and waves and with "the presence of these pasts."[35]

An instance of how Woolf evokes an inhuman intimacy in *The Waves* occurs via the nine interludes that begin, end, and interrupt the soliloquies of the six characters.[36] The interludes narrate the sun's rising and setting above a seaside littoral. Rather than encapsulating the social world in which characters interact, the unbounded seaside is empty of people. The impersonal narration that describes the coast alternately faces the vast ocean horizon and the shore that includes empty beach houses. This shoreline ecotone is one in which, as Meg Samuelson puts it, "elements of earth and water ceaselessly overlap and draw apart."[37] This gathering and dispersal marks the rhythm of the novel: the monologues of six characters' embodied intensities are diffused by the impersonal interludes. Although the interludes are deserted of people, the language describing this world is tactile, sensual, and erotic: "*The sun sharpened the walls of the house, and rested like the tip of a fan upon a white blind and made a blue fingerprint of shadow under the leaf by the bedroom window.*"[38] Like a lover who beckons with a fan and leaves an imprint of their fleeting presence, this unpeopled world seethes with vitality, desire, and yearning. Woolf's call in *A Room* for a turn to "things in themselves" effectively displaces the human-centered world, yet a human-infused desire saturates this scene.

Certainly, this desire cannot be conceptualized as sexual in terms of the binary categories of hetero/homosexuality. But the scene's "tactile erotics," yearning affect, and sensual description suggest the capaciousness of queer sensibility and orientation that goes beyond intrahuman relations.[39] This sensibility of pleasure, as I will show, is mixed with dark images of violence, death, and loss. How might we understand this combination of past losses and possible pleasures as it relates to ecology? In defining queer ecological practice, Catriona Mortimer-Sandilands and Bruce Erikson write:

> The task of a queer ecology is to probe the intersections of sex and nature with an eye to developing a sexual politics that more clearly includes considerations of the natural world and its biosocial constitution, and an environmental politics that demonstrates an understanding of the ways in which sexual relations organize and influence both the material world of nature and our perceptions, experiences, and constitutions of that world.[40]

In other words, nature is saturated with sexual and gendered meanings and, conversely, the ways in which social institutions regulate sexualities and genders shape how subjects perceive, move within, and intra-act with, nature. Queer ecology seeks to intervene in those meanings, perceptions, embodied experiences, and actions to challenge normative understandings of sexuality and genders and to transform how humans relate with and perceive nature. Greta Gaard summarizes these mutually constitutive ends as follows: "Dominant Western culture's devaluation of the erotic parallels its devaluations of women and of nature. It becomes clear that liberating women requires liberating nature, the erotic, and queers."[41] Queer ecology, then, is an offshoot of feminism insofar as feminism is concerned with sameness (equal access to work, education, legal status, housing, and more) as well as with sex and gender differences. Queer ecology emphasizes these differences when it explores nonnormative relations with the material world. By changing relations with and perceptions of nature, valuations of human differences will also shift.

Writing on contemporary queer ecology, Luciano and Chen argue for a widened purview of sexuality that they define as "the constitutive pleasure and potentiality of forms of corporeal communing."[42] Further, they say, if there is no "nature" prior to and other than that given through human relations, then nature cannot be used to regulate sexuality.[43] Given that homosexual and queer sexual practices are frequently vilified as "unnatural," Luciano and Chen argue, "lifting that prohibition [against the unnatural], in turn, multiplies not only the possibilities for intrahuman connection but also our ability to imagine other kinds of trans/material attachments."[44] Transmateriality, according to Barad, refers to how matter "wanders" and enters into "promiscuous" relations that are "inventive . . . even . . . imaginative."[45] For instance, water—a source of life, death, and the erotic, as mermaids, sirens, Venus, and other bathers in Western art history testify—constantly crosses the membranes of bodies. It slides, buoys, and tumbles living beings within it. *The Waves* experiments with water's transmaterial interaction with bodies and art's interaction with water to reconfigure how the hydrosphere is imagined. More than merely representing the cultural sedimentations that help us imagine the seas, *The Waves*, by thematizing and self-consciously performing its writing and reading practices mediated by the aquatic, creates a world of transmaterial affective and sensuous relationality.[46]

Moreover, *The Waves* both produces and dissolves empire: it names its violence and imagines its undoing.

The sea in *The Waves*, as Rizzuto argues, "stimulates readers' imaginations using something in 'common' but which is not 'ground'—the global free sea."[47] Unlike Euclidean space that abstracts the seas by means of longitude and latitude, and unlike the sublime excess of the seas—beyond representation, inscrutable, and wildly other—the sea in *The Waves* is a living form. It is, as marine geographers Philip Steinberg and Kimberley Peters write, "indisputably voluminous, stubbornly material, and unmistakably undergoing continual reformation."[48] And it is also boundless. Woolf, in her diary, writes that in *The Waves*, she "wants to saturate every atom . . . to give the moment whole; whatever it includes. Say that the moment is a combination of thought; sensation; the voice of the sea."[49] The sea is mobile, shifting ground that in combination with thought and sensation problematizes the fundamental grounds upon which material existence is actualized. The sea's fluid "grounds" do not exclude, but instead incorporate life and nonlife into a sensual, aesthetic relationality. The novel reconfigures the sea as participating in a queer intrarelationality, rather than serving as a backdrop for imperial and military adventure. Most importantly, Woolf wishes to exclude nothing in her evocation of the whole that is captured in a single moment, what she calls "moments of being."[50]

Let us return to Woolf's exhortation in *A Room* to relate to the sky and the trees or whatever it may be "in themselves" to understand this relation as enacting a queer ecological mode of reading and writing that transforms human relations with one another and to their surroundings. Benjamin Hagen uses the term "sensuous pedagogy" to describe Woolf's method of relating to the nonhuman in "A Sketch of the Past," where she elaborates on moments of being. He writes, " 'A Sketch' is a rich account of Woolf's learning to intuit this aesthetic ontology [in which, as she says, "the whole world is a work of art"], to treasure its shocking moments, to respond to them with vivid compositions of her own, and to assign herself and her readers reflective tasks related to thinking the self as a dispersion rather than a coherent identity or narrative."[51] This dispersal occurs because the moment is "uncanny and untimely" and entangles one "in a vibrant field. One becomes part of a differential ongoingness."[52] This ongoingness includes past and present losses as well as possible pleasures.

Woolf elaborates on how these moments are mediated through writing: "[This] shock-receiving capacity is what makes me a writer. It is a token of some real thing behind appearances; and I make it real by putting it into words . . . behind the cotton wool is hidden a pattern; that we—I mean all human beings—are connected with this; that the whole world is a work of art; that we are parts of the work of art . . . we are the words; we are the music; we are the thing itself."[53]

If humans are included in "the thing itself," then the natural world is not a metaphysical category, outside of culture, but is integral to the aesthetic whole of which humans are part. One sees this formal experiment most explicitly as the interludes of emptied shoreline blur into the character soliloquies, infusing the human drama of everyday life with ecological impersonality.

The effect of framing and unframing and the undoing of time and the self is to problematize categories of inside and outside. It renders the novel into a Möbius strip in which the book as a material object and narrative technique quite literally returns to inchoate matter. For instance, *The Waves* insistently refuses the sea as backdrop, figuring it instead as text and medium. Consider the novel's opening interlude: "*The sun had not yet risen. The sea was indistinguishable from the sky, except that the sea was slightly creased as if a cloth had wrinkles on it. Gradually as the sky whitened a dark line lay on the horizon dividing the sea from the sky and the grey cloth became barred with thick strokes moving, one after another, beneath the surface, following each other, pursuing each other, perpetually.*"[54]

This unpeopled setting is not one of pristine nature "out there," but of writing, and doubly mediated, writing in the genre of ekphrasis, a description of a painting. The sea is a textile, with tiny folds. Sea and sky, light and water at first appear indistinguishable, as unremarked matter, but then a dark line divides it. One sees objectification (sea versus sky) being produced *as if* (a figuration) someone has drawn a line at the horizon. The writer performatively intervenes, rather than reflects, to create the distinction of sea and sky. Woolf emphasizes the act of drawing, of co-creating sea and sky. "Grey cloth," the sea, is then written on, as it becomes "barred with thick strokes moving." This writing plunges "beneath the surface" into the materiality of the sea, "with thick strokes . . . following each other, pursuing each other, perpetually." Writing here is desire: the desire to know, to order, and to make sense of. Bernard, the writer-figure in *The Waves*, foregrounds this ceaseless becoming when he is described as a dangling wire, who senses, absorbs, and invents without end. But more than a vector moving perpetually forward, the temporality of this opening interlude folds, as it names the future anterior tense that is a perpetual "not yet," ever-changing, merging, and pursuing beneath the surface as inchoate matter. It is this latent, queer desire below and inside that gathers into forms only to have them dissolve soon after. The rhythm of the waves is a cresting, an intensification and assembling, followed by a dispersion and relaxation, without temporal or spatial progression. Waves seldom move forward; they stay in one place.

More than this, the opening of *The Waves* alludes to the biblical myth of Genesis, the scene of ex nihilo creation, with the difference that Woolf's language, as Melba Cuddy-Keane argues, "reaches back to the previously observed: a wrinkled cloth, a breathing sleeper, sediment clearing in wine, or the arm of a woman raising a lamp . . . a slowly emerging landscape is recorded, notated, and doubled in the mind. Perception in this guise merely apprehends what has preceded, in its existence, the sensory act."[55] The woman raising a lamp self-reflexively suggests Woolf as creator who composes (in the sense of "placing with") multiple sources to disidentify from the myth of the author as an originator of meaning. By means of this collage form, time is unhinged from the present moment. The woman artist occupies the beginning of the world, recent history, present, and future, anticipated by the rising sun. She is creator, composer, and medium, entangled in the scene she witnesses.

Woolf's queer ecology not only appears in the text of *The Waves*, but it also characterizes her process of writing the novel. She refers in her diary to composting her novel, akin to how the sea (and earth) recycles and recombines elements, minerals, and organic material in an endless process of life, death, and decay. She highlights her nondominant or weak agency by rejecting the notion of originality and highlighting instead her activity of rearranging, recycling, recombining that which already exists. She describes writing *The Waves* as follows:

> I am stuck fast in that book [*The Waves*]—I mean, glued to it, like a fly on gummed paper. Sometimes I am out of touch; but go on; then again feel that I have at least, by violent measures—like breaking through gorse—set my hands on something central. . . . But how to pull it together,

how to compost it—press it into one—I do not know; nor can I guess the end—it might be a gigantic conversation. The interludes are very difficult, yet I think essential; so as to bridge & also give a background—the sea; insensitive nature—I don't know. But I think, when I feel this sudden directness, that it must be right: anyhow no other form of fiction suggests itself except as a repetition at the moment.[56]

This model of writing as compost precludes detachment: Woolf is "glued" to her text. It is "beside" her. She "set[s] her hands on something central" and, by means of the interludes that "give a background," she hopes to "press it into one." The mechanism by which the novel is composted suggests the intra-action of matter and form. Woolf allows the material itself to both act and be acted upon by herself. Composting as a writing method, as Steve Mentz writes, "recognizes multiple presences in multiple states of decay."[57] Rather than representing nature as pristine, in Woolf's treatment, it rots, repulses, and mixes with the brief lives of her characters. Woolf touches her material, breaks through it, and lives with it in proximity—a relationship that emphasizes the materiality of her body, her manuscript, and creative energies that are compositional, i.e., lateral and mutually constitutive. Taken together, these proximities work to disrupt what Woolf calls in "A Sketch of the Past" the "cotton wool" of "nonbeing" by breaking into multiple states of being and decay.[58] Woolf's composting practice allows the remixing and realignment of the past with the present. It emphasizes what Braidotti calls the "vitality of [these materials'] bond" and the ability of nonhuman entities to intrarelate with the agency of the writer herself.[59] This ethics of suspended agency informs Woolf's writing process, in which she imagines herself serving as a medium who gathers, shepherds, and orchestrates a conversation between nonhuman and human, nature and culture, deep time with the embodied rhythms of the present moment. Woolf's composition of *The Waves* follows a queer ecological practice *avant la lettre*.[60]

The rhythmic energies of Woolf's experimental aesthetic emerged from the feminist and working-class political gatherings of women's suffrage and labor organizing. The place of women and children, associated with the fecundity of nature and the amorphous flux of embodiment, assumed new political significance in the early twentieth century. The collective contestation of women for their autonomy and difference in the public sphere necessitated that they occupy both sides of the nature/culture divide. This liminal position is vital for understanding *The Waves'* experimental aesthetics: the way in which, for instance, Bernard imagines that he and Susan float above the trees and how the impersonal seaside interludes intrude into character soliloquies, and vice versa. It revalues bodies and the material world and imagines modes of being otherwise together.

The militant women's suffrage struggle transformed both art and politics through its reformulation of political discourse and revaluation of women's lives. Ewa Płonowska Ziarek argues that militant suffrage feminism, because it struggled for both women's equality within the universal rights discourse of liberal democracy and for the difference of their sexed particularity, produces a performative contradiction, or "abyss," between the two aims that exceeds the right to vote. Instead, the contradiction between equality and difference in women's public and political struggle becomes "the right to revolt." Ziarek states, "In other words, the crucial implication of suffrage militancy is the redefinition of the logical contradiction between universality and difference in terms of the creative novelty of positive freedom."[61] Drawing on Woolf's discussion of innovative art and feminist politics in *A Room of One's Own*, Ziarek summarizes how the fraught political relationship between difference and equality gives rise to creative freedom: "The militant struggle for the vote, economic opportunities, and women's rights is one of the preconditions of women's political and intellectual freedom, which transforms impossibility and the destruction of female art into its future possibility."[62]

The "abyss," then, is the creative and indeterminate zone of political and aesthetic reformulation. It is predicated on no single event and simultaneously transforms both past and future. For instance, *The Waves* imagines the lost life of Rhoda as a means of registering both the past violence and possible future freedom of women. Because women have been rendered mute, the feminist writer cannot simply recover women's lives. Ziarek argues, "Women's experimental writing shifts the emphasis from the representation of the ideological 'fact' to the exploration of what is excluded from history and the creation of new possibilities in 'fiction.'"[63] *The Waves*, in this reading, not only mourns the damage to women under patriarchy, especially through the character Rhoda, but it also envisions an experimental feminist aesthetics of possibility, a counterfactual potentiality that I am calling a queer ecology, an orientation toward the natural world that is erotic, pleasurable, and nonhierarchical.

This experimental aesthetics in *The Waves* reconfigures relations across the nature/culture and equality/difference divide and takes its cue from the women's suffrage movement. For example, let us consider a women's suffrage postcard, Ernestine Mills's "The New Mrs Partington (of the Anti Suffrage Society)" with its slogan, "Somehow the Tide Keeps Rising!" [see Figure 3.1]. Mills was a jewelry maker and member of the militant suffrage group the Women's Social and Political Union (WSPU). She created this postcard in 1910 when the militant campaign for women's suffrage was at its peak. The postcard represents the heterogeneity of women (mothers, working women, medical women, liberal women, taxpayers, civil servants, factory workers, writers, professional women, conservative women, unionist women) as the many peaks of waves, while racial difference is conspicuously absent yet analogous to the inchoate depths of the sea, as I discussed previously in terms of the US women's suffrage political

FIGURE 3.1 Artist Ernestine Mills, image "The New Mrs Partington," created 1910

London Museum ref 50.82/864; copyright permission artist's estate cartoon. The waves of women inundate the shore while Mrs. Partington furiously and ineffectively tries to sweep them back. But the postcard conveys more than the association of women with water: in political terms, the waves conjoin unity and difference; geophysical surrounds and individual bodies and groups. It figures the watery "abyss," or performative contradiction, between two categories, a move that displaces women from their normative gender roles: wife, mother, prostitute. Yet it leaves racial difference intact, offshore from the white nation. The image reformulates the right to vote as the right to revolt, a transformation that includes the possibility of feminist experimental aesthetics. I use the poster to periodize Woolf's work and to emphasize the claim that the militant women's suffrage movement—and the queer desire, feminist militancy, and institutional transformation it unleashed—allowed Woolf to dramatically recast the novel form.

The Waves moves from representing women as water (an object or symbol) to performatively producing—and inhabiting—modes of being otherwise together. In an early draft of *The Waves*, Woolf imagines the sea as containing "labour, self-loss, origins prolonged beyond memory: the anonymity of child birth."[64] The swampy soup of fecundity is lost to recollection as are women's unrecorded lives, but this memory nonetheless persists in symbolic and presymbolic associations of water with women and reproduction. She fails to remark on the more recent history of the slave trade and its transformation of women into ungendered monstrosities. Instead, she reaches back into evolutionary time where women's relation to the sea is more than symbolic: it is biological. The sea holds evidence of the deep time of evolution that renders contingent the gender relations of the present time, as Woolf knew well from her avid reading of Darwin. For instance, Darwin, concluding a letter to Charles Lyell in 1860, remarked, "our ancestor was an animal which breathed water, had a swim bladder, a great swimming tail, an imperfect skull, and undoubtedly was a hermaphrodite! Here is a pleasant genealogy for mankind."[65] By reaching back into deep evolutionary time, Darwin tracks an occluded, intraspecies, pansexual genealogy for humankind.

This latent queerness in Darwin's evolutionary formulations contributes to the queer ecology of *The Waves*, as Woolf likewise emphasizes human entanglement with this watery environment.[66] Bodies are conjoined with deep history, bodily inside with environmental outside, and foreground with background. The sea is the fluid, erotic medium through which the six characters of the novel speak, and which—rather than act as a backdrop, as it is usually read—serves as a nonhuman agent that permeates the characters through its unrelenting, perpetual force. Bernard establishes this fluid, impersonal agency when he says, "but when we sit together, close . . . we melt into one another with phrases. We are edged with mist. We make an unsubstantial territory."[67] The characters "melt," or overlap, into each other, resembling the formless, nationless sea. Taking her cue from the churning ocean, Woolf transforms the socially oriented, conventional novel form into an embodied, intimate, and performatively produced, unbounded, and nonlinear (co-constituted) queer sea fiction. This mode of being otherwise is manifold in its temporalities as it tracks the convergence and divergence of the evolutionary time of the sea with human time. I turn next to the tides of history in *The Waves*: the waning empire and the waxing creative possibilities of the world to come.

EMPIRE AND THE SEA

In Woolf's 1925 novel *Mrs. Dalloway*, the eponymous character says to herself: "We are a doomed race, chained to a sinking ship."[68] Her bleak outlook figures what may have been unconscious to her contemporary readers: namely, the violence of slavery and colonization as an apocalyptic endgame for the British. By contrast, Bernard in *The Waves* offers a childhood fantasy in which waves of light, air, and water intermingle so that runners swim above the trees: "We shall sink like swimmers just touching the ground with the tips of their toes. We shall sink through the green air of the leaves. . . . We sink as we run. The waves close over us. . . . Now we have fallen through tree-tops to the earth. The air no longer rolls its long, unhappy purple waves over us. We touch earth; we tread ground."[69] Although Mrs. Dalloway's ominous view persists in *The Waves*, the children's sea-infused play counters the stranglehold of empire and patriarchy and registers an imaginative and affective zeal for an intra-active relation with comingling elemental forces. *The Waves* offers not only an anatomy of how the forces of empire "chain" its ruling-class subjects to suffocating social roles, but how it also, contrapuntally, proposes a queer ecology, a way of relating to others and to one's surrounds laterally, intimately, and creatively.

Bernard's childhood fantasy in *The Waves* rejects even the division of air and sea. In his monologue, Bernard enjoins his nursery school companion, Susan, to participate in his fantasy. Together, they hover over and then sink into the utopian world of Elvedon, in which a lady "sits between two long windows, writing. The gardeners sweep the lawn with giant brooms."[70] Bernard's mesmeric spoken rhythm, insistent in the present-time urgency of make-believe, merges Susan and he into a shared, private, queer world. Queer, in this context, denotes the propensity of children to revel in make-believe, disorientation, and, as Jack Halberstam puts it, "a total indifference to adult conceptions of success and failure," premised on the heteronormative disciplining of mind and body in schools and society.[71] I am not saying that these children are queer, but that the style of their make-believe allows for a more capacious imagining of their affective and physical relations to the world than a strictly rationalized and heteronormative worldview allows. As they mature, such wild imaginings are curbed. Woolf presents the children's undisciplined imaginations and desires through the atmospherics of air and water: their bodies defy gravity and refuse fixity: they both float and sink, suspend and move. In addition, their fantastical Elvedon evades fixed spatial or temporal coordinates.

Bernard and Susan, children of empire, approach their pretend world as foreign conquerors, "discoverers of an unknown land," under threat of violent reprisal: "We are in a hostile country!"[72] They flee in terror. Juxtaposed to this imperial fantasy, their imagined encounter with this bucolic scene suggests a momentary brush with a mode of being and imagining otherwise in a watery world. The fantastical merging of land and sea, air and water in Bernard's make-believe: "We shall sink through the green air of the leaves. . . . We touch earth; we tread ground," suggests a queer conviviality in which, as José Muñoz puts it, "meaning does not properly 'line up.'"[73] Swimming, walking, flying merge together and alter the possibilities of inhabiting one's body and moving through space. Rather than fixing themselves within the geometrical logics of time and space, Bernard's characters pose alternative ways of being in the world.[74] Meaning in this make-believe world refuses normative familial roles, heterosexuality and reproduction. Drawing from Sara Ahmed's queer phenomenology, we can say that Bernard's turbulent, wavy disorientation allows him to revel in seeing the world "slantwise" as opposed to the overcoming of queer moments, repressing them, and pulling oneself "upright."[75] Bernard's imagined sense of three-dimensionality, liquid solidity, force, and mass of the waves of light and air disorient normative modes of perception and "upright" embodiment.

The Waves also demonstrates that by not attending to the disorienting, fluid medium of the sea, subjects become encapsulated in social norms. These conflicting forces—fluid and dissolving versus rigid and ossified—weave together the tensions and textures of the novel. As discussed in chapter 1, the sea has been mapped in fixed, knowable coordinates that allowed the British to dominate the seas. The Australian expatriate businessman, Louis, in *The Waves* registers this source of power when he says, "[w]e have laced the world together with our ships. The globe is strung with our lines."[76] This mapping was politically motivated and instrumental in producing the great wealth of empire. The Cartesian cartographies also helped to build the normative hierarchies of the British Empire. The abstract spatial and temporal coordinates produce racial, geographical, gendered, and sexed divisions that support this system and disallow other modes of being to have legitimacy. While ships sailed the oceans by means of latitude and longitude, the actual sea was imagined to be a free space—devoid of the rule of law and national markers—and associated with waste, dirt, and pollution.[77] Nonnormative bodies were aligned with that waste.

The narrative trajectory of *The Waves* loosely follows history. When the sun has risen in the interludes, implying the ascendancy of empire, the binaries of culture/nature are most pronounced. We see how at the horizon of empire—with its good schools, fine cuisine, and abundant lifestyle—lurk threats, savagery, and oozing, rotten excretions. These imperial imaginings of danger and pollution on the peripheries seep into the impersonal seascapes of the interlude: "*The skin of rotten fruit broke, and matter oozed too thick to run. Yellow excretions were exuded by slugs and now and again an amorphous body with a head at either end swayed slowly from side to side.... The waves drummed on the shore, like turbaned warriors, like turbaned men with poisoned assegais who, whirling their arms on high, advance upon the feeding flocks, the white sheep.*"[78]

Woolf places colonized subjects, "turbaned men whirling their arms on high," alongside nature, locking them into a threatening otherness and a "tide" of history. Rizzuto contextualizes this image for the reader:

> by placing "poisoned assegais" in the[] hands [of Mawlawi whirling dervishes who perform the Sufi dance to praise Allah] Woolf disfigures this Muslim art that begins in the thirteenth century, transforming the ritual of glorifying god that occurs in central Islamic regions into a practice of warfare in Africa, and confuses the Mawlawi with different historical actors. Assegais were deployed throughout the African continent in inter-tribal conflicts as well as anti-colonial revolt . . . [made through] guerilla tactics.[79]

This description of the sea poses it as carrying a foreign peril, not merely at the time that Woolf was writing *The Waves*, but through the longue durée of empire. The poisoned weapons and anti-colonial hatred of empire carried by the advancing guerilla fighters invade the serene English littoral and suggest the fragility of maritime and colonial dominance and the permeability of imperial borders. It figures the English as "white sheep" and hence easy prey for an invading force. This rhetoric anticipates Faulkner's false victimization of white plantation families at the hands of rebelling Black enslaved and free peoples that I discuss in chapter 5. In addition, Louis, the character most associated with the rise and fall of empires, repeatedly hears the threat of subjugated nations in the pounding surf: "A great beast's foot is chained. It stamps, and stamps, and stamps."[80] Accompanying this civilized/barbaric binary, nature as formless and grotesque serves as the opposite of culture and art. It also poses a vague threat to the children of empire as it is described as abject matter preyed upon by birds who "plunged the tips of their beaks savagely into the sticky mixture."[81] The binaries that produce the "civilized" world of empire and its opposing "barbarism" also police the heteronormative roles performed by the six characters. It is here that Rhoda's marginality—her inability to fulfil her heteronormative role and subsequent exclusion from the social formation of empire—links her to what is foreclosed from empire: anti-colonial and imperial violence *and* the drowned at the bottom of the sea. The exigencies of social reproduction render Rhoda's life disposable, a precarity I'm tracing that is both similar and different to the biopolitics of slavery, as discussed in the interlude.

Woolf's evocation of the nonhuman agency of the seas and their deep time eclipses human history. Only the detritus in the seas shows the effects of humans' puny efforts: the shipwrecks, bones, and chains that circulate through the novel are composted into an ambivalent elegy for empire. The sea churns up a history of violent conquest and death that marks the dark underside of Britain's maritime dominance.[82] Chains, especially, drifting slowly to the bottom of the sea and soon to be joined by Rhoda's suicided body, evokes for the reader the lexicon of slavery although the novel declines to address this history head-on. In refusing to treat abolition history, Woolf problematically appropriates this history for white unfreedoms, namely, Rhoda's inability to live as she desires. The text itself acknowledges its blind spots when Bernard obliquely recognizes the annihilation of peoples to forge an empire. He remarks, "We have destroyed something by our presence, a world perhaps."[83] Woolf's anatomy of the six children of empire encompasses them in a bubble of privilege and imperial imagery, one that Bernard intuitively recognizes depends upon the obliteration of other worlds. When Rhoda drowns herself, her body indexes the history of violence and loss that subtends both patriarchy and the British Empire. *The Waves* presents the sea as graveyard: the drifting flotsam and jetsam of ship parts and chains. To see how sources of this detritus were erased from history, I build upon my discussion of European maritime empires in chapter 1 to remind readers of how European empires divided and distributed the globe by means of the geometrical lines of longitude and latitude. This division abstracted from the fluid materiality of the seas.

When the British, Dutch, and French began their bids for empire following the earlier colonizing path of the Spanish and Portuguese, they supplanted the older religious rationale of the divine right to rule with a nationalist and later, a racialist, sense of their dominance of the seas and other lands. As discussed in chapter 1, Atlantic, Indian, and Pacific Ocean voyages of discovery and conquest erased Indigenous histories and Europe's own prior Mediterranean history in favor of the "new."[84] They also depended upon scientific technologies of time and space to navigate across the great expanses of water. What emerges from this global grid of longitude and latitude is the time-space compression of the seafaring ship.[85] The time-space condensation, or Paul Gilroy's chronotope of the ship, became the source for the invention of narrative prose fiction.

The ship is a metonym for heroic captaincy, the male leader who navigates through the hostile environment of the sea. His voyage becomes a narrative of time elapsed and obstacles overcome. In this way, the chronotope of the ship obscures the experiences of those in the hold, and it necessitates the disavowal of the material nature of the sea. The cognitive mapping required by Western maritime navigation reduces the sea to its perception as waste, a term that is etymologically related to the Latin *vastus* and "signifies uninhabited or uncultivated space."[86] The sea resists inscription and fixed determination. Its formlessness connects its material waste to the bodies of women, bondspersons, and the sick and injured. Although white women were essential to settler colonial dominance and to empire more generally, their gendered bodies could just as easily become part of the "contaminating effluvia of the masses."[87] Gillian Beer makes the subordinate place of white women at sea quite clear: "Initiation into society for women involves initiation into descent. They will become vehicles of descent, not borne aloft by the boat that carries them, but themselves bearing and carrying: childbearing."[88] They cannot steer the ship: they are the ship in their own sea of waters.[89] *The Waves* is that submarine world, Beer writes, in which "the language of the book covers every space."[90] The dissolving form immerses the reader and characters in a sea of writing that breaks the frame of inside and outside the text.[91] The sea allows Woolf the conceit of including the boundlessness of space and time in her novel. In place of the ship's chronotope, the submarine narrative of *The Waves* stalls the forward movement of plot—except for the rising and setting of the sun and the duration of life—so that a disorienting flux ensues. The sea's perpetual movement, its immense, voluminous materiality—its depth, its force and mass, as Elizabeth DeLoughrey writes, "diffracts the accumulation of narrative."[92]

I turn next to Rhoda to argue that, through her, Woolf mourns the violence of patriarchy and empire that destroys women's lives, including the fictional Judith Shakespeare. Although Rhoda is a child of empire who playacts the Armada, loves Percival (the colonizer-hero), and has a clandestine affair with Louis (the reclusive global businessman), she misrecognizes herself in these ties. The novel demonstrates how meaning does not properly line up for her. Rhoda is oriented in relation to society in a manner that is "slantwise": she turns, twists, and queers social forms simply by her inability to inhabit and reproduce them with a seemingly natural effortlessness.[93] She shows their unnaturalness. This "slantwise" orientation, as indicated earlier, is disorienting as it contradicts the abstract logic of heteronormative time and space (i.e., clock time, longitude, and latitude). In early drafts of *The Waves*, Rhoda is explicitly lesbian. She fantasizes "day and night" about kissing a girl named Alice.[94] Denied the ability to pursue her desire and live outright with a homosexual orientation, she is rendered invisible, "faceless," and without a recognized identity.[95] In what follows, I emphasize Rhoda's alignment with the disorienting flux of the sea as opposed to the other six characters (including Percival) who reproduce the structures of empire. I trace how Woolf associates Rhoda's queer orientation with the sea, a state of being suspended by water, where "all is soft, and bending."[96] I connect this unanchored disorientation, following Ahmed, to queer moments in phenomenology. These moments, as Maurice Merleau-Ponty observes, "involve not only the intellectual experience of disorder, but the vital experience of giddiness and nausea, which is the awareness of our contingency, and the horror with which it fills us."[97] Ahmed suggests that to be disoriented is to feel queered because temporality becomes unhinged and nonlinear: it intermingles deep time, an association with the sea and rocks, with nontime (e.g., the facelessness or existential crisis that Rhoda experiences), which is unformed and without narrative progression. By contrast, heteronormative orientation is a straightening of bodily experience, a Cartesian fixing of one's location, and a single-minded attention to the present moment alone: "to become vertical, to pull one's self 'upright,' would mean that the queer effect is being overcome and objects in the world no longer appear off-centre or slantwise."[98] Heteronormativity forecloses the queerness of the world and the indeterminacy of matter.

In order to maintain heteronormative structures, nonconforming subjects must be excluded because they demonstrate the contingency, or unnaturalness, of those structures. In her lonely marginality, Rhoda does not transcend her body; she remains stubbornly attached to the painful materiality of her disoriented existence. In nursery school, she stays in from recess to complete her math problems. Terrified of the sums she cannot solve, she imagines a loop of a figure "is beginning to fill with time; it holds the world in it. I begin to draw a figure and the world is looped in it, and I myself am outside the loop [of time]."[99] Rhoda figures herself as the latency undeveloped by the history-making, world-making British Empire. Excluded from this historical narrative, she hangs in bed "suspended," mired in dreams described as watery.[100] She is "turned" and "tumbled" in a matrix of unfulfilled desire.[101] "To whom shall I give all that now flows through me, from my warm, my porous body? Oh, to whom?"[102] Never allowed to pursue who and what she longs for, she briefly has a clandestine and alienated, possibly abject, sexual relationship with Louis.[103] Louis says of Rhoda, "We wake her. We torture her. She dreads us, she despises us, yet comes cringing to our sides."[104] The sedimentation of history embeds her as sheer matter; she does not transcend it through narrative: "An immense pressure is on me. I cannot move without dislodging the weight of centuries."[105] Heteronormative structures threaten to capture her in a rigid order that terrorizes her. Woolf gives Rhoda her own memory of being unable to traverse a puddle that Rhoda describes as "cadaverous," "awful," and "grey": "I could not cross it. Identity failed me. We are nothing, I said, and fell. I was blown like a feather. I was wafted down tunnels."[106] Rhoda merges with elemental nature and the chaos of matter.

Just prior to her suicide, Rhoda climbs a mountain in Spain from the top of which she sees across the Straits of Gibraltar to Africa, the continent where Britain's naked greed and imperial incompetence were most starkly revealed.[107] Gibraltar is one of the two pillars of Hercules, beyond which, according to Plato and subsequent Renaissance writers, is the unknown and monstrous Atlantic. That Rhoda's last appearance occurs at this geographically liminal site between north and south, and between the Mediterranean and global world systems, metonymically associates her with the emergence of the triangle trade that spawned industrialization. Moreover, Rhoda's failure to occupy a heteronormative position—wife, mother, socialite—links patriarchal violence to that of empire. As she climbs, Rhoda accuses "life" of staining and corrupting her: "What dissolution of the soul you demanded in order to get through one day, what lies, bowings, scrapings, fluency, and servility! How you chained me to one spot, one hour, one chair, and sat yourself down opposite! How you snatched me from the white spaces that lie between hour and hour and rolled them into dirty pellets and tossed them into the wastepaper basket with your greasy paws."[108] The reference to unfreedom—"chained"—symptomatically connects homophobic and misogynist structures within the metropole to the wider racism of empire.[109] Rhoda's chains associate her with Louis's repeated reference to the threat of uprising by the colonized: "a great beast's foot is chained. It stamps, and stamps, and stamps."[110] These references to the restive, threatening masses are aligned with the great power of the surf, the tides of anti-colonial history that will not be stopped: *"The waves fell; withdrew and fell again, like the thud of a great beast stamping"* and with persistent allusions to the sea's "drumming."[111] Rhoda's reference to the "white spaces ... tossed into the wastepaper basket" devalues queer and "untimely" orientation—existing between hour and hour. "Life" within empire forecloses the margins, but these unwritten zones are required to produce the prevailing structures of heteronormativity. The "white spaces" rolled into "dirty pellets" align Rhoda with the materiality and contaminated "waste" of the sea which merge with her suicide by drowning. This death is shown obliquely; she first imagines it:

> Now the bed gives under me. The sheets spotted with yellow holes let me fall through. ... We [Rhoda addresses her flowers] launch now over the precipice. Beneath us lie the lights of the herring fleet. The cliffs vanish. Rippling small, rippling grey, innumerable waves spread beneath us. I touch nothing. I see nothing. We may sink and settle on the waves. The sea will drum in my ears. The white petals will be darkened with sea water. They will float for a moment and then sink. Rolling me over the waves will shoulder me under. Everything falls in a tremendous shower, dissolving me.[112]

Rhoda imagines her future death in the present tense: how the order and solidity of the world disappear, whiteness "darkens," and vertigo and "drumming" of the sea ensues. She will enter the sea as waste, as another addition to the bottom of the sea. This is not liberation but defeat, another wasted, silent life that is sacrificed to empire. The suspended temporality of Rhoda's "slantwise" world informs her description of the future that becomes yet one more "moment" laminated onto the present in a static tableau vivant. Moreover, the event of her death lacks climax—in contradistinction to Percival's—and remains unmourned and unspoken. Because she is ambiguous, both part of and excluded from empire, Rhoda is expendable. Her death is almost entirely unremarked—Bernard flatly informs us of Rhoda's actual suicide seventy-five pages after she envisions her death. Between Rhoda's futural imaginings and Bernard's recollection of her suicide, Rhoda's death escapes signification and unhinges—suspends in the white spaces—the forward flowing of time. Like compost, however, this death is both loss and future fecundity. Rhoda's suicide echoes Woolf's promise in *A Room*, that "if we work for her," Judith's successors might have fulfilling lives.[113]

Although Woolf mourns the subjugation of women, and especially queer women, in empire through Rhoda, the novel's experimental aesthetics suggests possible ways of relating that are not premised on violent exclusions or instrumentalities. To conclude, I consider briefly how *The Waves* comments on the material practice of reading, writing, and producing the book in a manner that is in line with a queer ecology. Toward the novel's end, Woolf unframes her fictional world and dissolves the novel as a material object back into the chaos of matter. At the conclusion of the novel, Bernard states: "[My being] lies deep, tideless, immune, now that he is dead, the man I called 'Bernard,' the man who kept a book in his pocket in which he made notes."[114] Bernard may be proleptically remarking on his own death, or he may be commenting on the dissolution of his own identity, gathered under the sign of "Bernard." Bernard claims responsibility for having represented all the characters when he says to his unnamed interlocutor: "And now I ask, 'Who am I?' I have been talking of Bernard, Neville, Jinny, Susan, Rhoda and Louis. Am I all of them? Am I one and distinct?"[115] The answer is both: Woolf dissolves character into the narrative waves that reemerge periodically as individuals. Alternatively, Woolf may be turning the book inside out to comment self-reflexively on her own character's death. Who, after all, called this man "Bernard"? Is Bernard announcing his impending death, imagining the cessation of his identity as a writer, or is Woolf breaking the spell of fiction to remark self-reflexively on the cessation of her character, Bernard, the writer-figure of the novel? Is she also announcing the death of the author? The voice is indeterminate, but this very indeterminacy is telling; it is both author and character, and more. Soon after, Bernard's physical book drops to the ground: "My book, stuffed with phrases, has dropped to the floor. It lies under the table to be swept up by the charwoman when she comes wearily at dawn looking for scrapes of paper, old tram tickets, and here and there a note screwed into a ball and left with the litter to be swept up."[116] This scene announces the virtuality of the scene of reading, an imagined connection between the reader and the fictional narrative. The book is "at once Woolf's and Bernard's and ours."[117] Laura Doyle notes that the reference to the "charwoman" (one on whom both Bernard and Woolf depend) suggests the class-bound nature of empire: "As a woman writer, Woolf lets us know that she speaks a doubled voice, standing at the edge of but not outside the circle of an imperialist sublimity. She reveals that her writing moves along, not beyond, its circumference."[118] The physical gesture of dropping the book to the floor, as a decomposing object, suggests that the novel, too, is a contingent encounter with the indeterminacy of matter. Moreover, it suggests that as empire dissolves, Woolf's writing will become a remnant of empire—as subjects from beyond the imperial center will rewrite the novel. It also suggests how culture is intimately related to impersonal matter—as it is shaped into a virtual reality and then decomposes into rubbish.

The scene also extends its contingency to the scene of reading. The reader inhabits its world temporarily which then fades away when they move on, closing the book and selecting another to read. *The Waves* teaches its readers to attend to the allegory of writing and reading—deferred, evanescent, forming, then dissolving—akin to the medium of waves of light and water. Through the dissolution and overlapping nature of the character soliloquies and the waves, one can perceive an untimely convergence of deep time with the present that extends forward to a queer, postimperial world to come. But it also makes the violent, death-bound logic of empire, with its racism, misogyny, and homophobia equally present. It is an open question as to whether humanity will remain chained to a sinking ship or reimagine its being, as the younger Bernard delights in. The novel shows its readers how to write and read provisionally to hold open a space for being with humans, nonhumans, and the elemental alike.

Woolf gives the waves the last word in the novel: "*The waves broke upon the shore.*"[119] The novel ends with an empty, dark stage in which the elements have the last wordless words and foreground and background merge into a singular sense of the aesthetic whole. The waves continue past Bernard's demise and gesture toward future openings of the novel. These include alternative genealogies of Black Power and Afro-diasporic texts that Kabe Wilson invokes as he recodes and recycles Woolf's writings.

KABE WILSON'S "OF ONE WOMAN OR SO"

The British-Nigerian performance artist Kabe Wilson's rewriting of Woolf refuses to leave the problem of race in Woolf's writing as a historically regrettable entwinement of modernism with empire. Unlike new materialist critics, Wilson recognizes that the sedimented structures of racial difference must be confronted in order to move past them. The idea for Wilson's project centers around the inexcusable racial damage caused by Woolf's statement in *A Room of One's Own*: "It is one of the great advantages of being a woman that one can pass even a very fine negress without wishing to make an Englishwoman of her."[120] Wilson asks, "How does a contemporary mixed race person connect with *A Room*?"[121] In 2009, at the "Rooms of Our Own" exhibit held at Lucy Cavendish College of Cambridge University, Wilson viewed the manuscript of Woolf's famous essay and arrived at the nucleus of his project: he would recycle *A Room of One's Own*. This undertaking involved rearranging the essay's 37,971 words and using only those words in the precise number of times that Woolf uses them, a feat only made possible by means of digital technologies.[122]

On May 19, 2014, Wilson presented "The Dreadlocks Hoax" in the drawing room of Woolf's Bloomsbury home. Dressed as a middle-aged Woolf and sporting greying dreadlocks, Wilson parodied Woolf's participation in the 1910 "Dreadnought Hoax." In that prank, Woolf posed cross-dressed and blacked up as an Ethiopian diplomat seeking a tour of a British "dreadnought" battleship, along with her brother and four male friends. Wilson's recycling of Woolf's seriocomic stunt imparts a scathing critique without eliminating the wound of racism and colonization. His physical presence mocks Woolf's earlier blacking up with the difference that Wilson's physical presence also indexes a five-hundred-year legacy of slavery and colonization. Wilson delivered a speech (that was itself a reordering of Woolf's 1937 essay "Craftsmanship") as a way of introducing his textual rearrangement of *A Room of One's Own*.[123] He titled the latter work, "Of One Woman or So" by Olivia N'Gowfri, an anagrammatic spelling of both Woolf's essay title and her name. The text took the form of a single scroll of paper on which every word from *A Room* had been glued, emphasizing the materiality and recirculation of the words themselves.

"Of One Woman or So" emphasizes the power of Woolf's words to constrain the possibilities of writers who succeed her. The text tells of a mixed-race, queer Cambridge scholarship student, Olivia N'Gowfri, who at first feels lonely in her new elite surroundings, then alienated, and then outraged. The narrative reaches a climax when she decides to set fire to five university libraries in a farcical but pointed reenactment of a 1960s race riot that took place in Cambridge, Maryland, an event N'Gowfri learns about as she reads works by Stokely Carmichael (a recycling of Woolf's Mary Carmichael) and H. Rap Brown to educate herself about racism. The play on Cambridge (both the British university and the name of several towns in the United States) simultaneously points to various geographical locations in a fluid formulation referred to throughout the text as "(t)here." Furthermore, Wilson's remixing of Woolf's essay presents *A Room of One's Own* as a "porous," leaky text that affords metamorphic connections through time.[124] He rearranges Woolf's essay into a composite work (i.e., one that transforms its content through rearrangement) that combines Woolf's densely allusive essay with Black Power and other African American texts by C. L. R. James, Stokely Carmichael, H. Rap Brown, bell hooks, Toni Morrison, Zadie Smith, and others. In so doing, Wilson offers a powerful detour from Woolf's center of empire through an Afro-diasporic tradition and back again to transform the meaning of Woolf's original text.

N'Gowfri's decision to burn the libraries occurs after she attempts to gain entrance to the highly selective and secret Cambridge Shakespeare Society. The society invites her to attend a party; and, after hesitating, she accepts. There, the attendees trade literary witticisms and puns in a manner that N'Gowfri likens to playing the dozens, an African American game of exchanging insults. She parries successfully until a young man, Oscar, puts forth: "Come on, calm down. Or do you need grass, negress?"[125] The outdated racial term rearranged from Woolf's essay punctures the party's veneer of social acceptance and racial equality. No one comes to her defense. She is rendered speechless by the insult, and, as the contest is also a frat house-style drinking game, her opponent indicates that she must drink. N'Gowfri takes the bottle, flings it violently at a wine glass, and leaves the party.

From there, N'Gowfri becomes increasingly attuned to questions of sexual and racial subordination at the university, the absence of writers of color in the English curriculum, and issues of internal colonization created by institutions of higher learning, including through the study of literature. She decides that setting fire to the libraries is the only appropriate response to these overwhelming issues. Moving to throw the manuscript copy of *A Room of One's Own* into the flames, an echo of Woolf's account in *A Room* of being unable to consult Milton's manuscript because she is an unaccompanied woman, she stops: "*Something about the physical presence of the letters on the precious yellowing paper brought back all that had gone through her mind when reading it, and it became abundantly clear that it had had a far greater effect than it had lately seemed.*"[126] Following this realization, the ending self-reflexively refers back to Wilson's own endeavor to reorder Woolf's text. Olivia asks herself, "if we were to begin mending the world by rewriting it. . . . By the Book. . . . One book used well can do whatever you want it to."[127] She cuts the words up, counts them all, and adds her own commas. She muses, "[a] composite, and I must compose it. An elemental craft. And write 'by Miss A. Grammar.'"[128] Wilson's method emphasizes spatial rearrangement as his sentences pull apart various syntactical and semantic structures, for instance, the shift from "composite" to "I must compose it." The noun becomes a verb as N'Gowfri expresses both an action and how the future text is already a preordained thing, as it is solely dependent on the words Woolf uses in her essay. The agency of the work is both determined and determining: it is something acted upon even as it constrains other possibilities for action. The "elemental craft" that succeeds this thought alludes both to the basic technique of writing and a boat in the elements, tossed about and constrained by their force, but also exerting its own counterforce of navigation. Through this mixture of agency and passivity, N'Gowfri alters the grammar of race, from a predicated object of a racial mathematics (captains' log books, slave auction catalogs, and plantation accounting books) to a reordering of the world so that the ethics of the speaking subject no longer depend upon excluding other peoples and the nonhuman.[129] This ethics is open-ended because the human becomes a doing, an ongoing discovery and reinvention of relations with humans and nonhumans alike. Through this grammatical rearrangement, subjects and their surrounding are revealed as co-constituted. Racialized groups are shaped and acted upon as much as they act in the world. By contrast, colonizing narratives depend upon subordinating racialized groups by dehumanizing them. They are excluded from the civilized category of the human, as Woolf's arch statement about refusing to make a "negress" into an Englishwoman suggests. N'Gowfri's "elemental craft" pulls this normative understanding of the human offshore and into the swirl of composite recombination. No longer grounded by a national and racially superior narrative, Woolf's essay is recoded by means of later anti-colonial and anti-racist movements to provide a place from which these formerly excluded subjects can occupy speaking positions that refuse to subordinate others.

This remixing equally refuses to disavow the past. N'Gowfri's concluding decision to reorder Woolf's essay to begin to mend the world follows the injurious use of the epithet "negress" at the literary society. The outdated term still stings. In a 2019 interview with Susan Stanford Friedman, Wilson comments on the inability of "negress" to be fully resignified: "It retains its older meaning even as you recycle it into something new."[130] Building on the ecological metaphor of recycling, Wilson continues: "'Negress' for me reads more like a chunk of plastic than a decomposing leaf."[131] Floating on the sea and endangering sea life, plastic blocks the fluidity and life-giving force of the sea. It also interrupts European assumptions of human domination of the physical world and its normative epistemology. Plastic reveals the fatal shortsightedness of scientific and industrial hubris that destroys the very planetary system on which it depends for life. Woolf's toxic racial epithet also arrests the universalization of her prose. One can't read past "negress" without pausing at the racial blindness of its author or the violent history that produced the masquerade of an Englishwoman as the beacon of civilization. Wilson states, "Negress wasn't going to be life giving for [Olivia]. It refuses to break down."[132] The word indexes five hundred years of violent conquest that, in 2014 and now, still excludes and wounds. Wilson combines N'Gowfri's racialized embodiment with literature's centuries-old alibi for slavery and colonization when he says, "[N'Gowfri's] narrative would have to bear that scar."[133] This healed, although still visible, wound thickens and swirls literary history. It reveals the violent conquest that underwrites European aesthetic accomplishments and insists on a dynamic interplay across the deep past, recent past, present, and future. It drags at the global circulation of world literature that flows across languages by means of their digestible and easily translated aesthetic form.[134] And it challenges the limitations of formal analysis by insisting on a material, embodied relation to the text.

Wilson's recoding of Woolf's essay does not exist as a published text: it was presented as an art object and delivered as a performance. This multimedia and genre-bending production opens literature to what exists beyond its frame: the ontology of being Black in Britain and an elemental destabilization of what might count as literature and how we read it. We can see this ontological subversion at the text's conclusion when the pseudo-author metamorphosizes into a literary object and a political statement: Olivia N'Gowfri reveals her name to be a micropoem: "I-*live*-here, an'-*go*-free-."[135] The proper noun becomes an action and an ontological statement of political purpose. N'Gowfri affirms her place and dedication to escaping the binds of racial and national exclusion.

Wilson's disidentification with Woolf injects incommensurability into literary history. It delineates the ways in which the past impacts women, nonnormative persons, and racialized people differently from its victors. It does so, however, without denying a relation to that written history. His engagement with the canon withholds an easy acceptance of *A Room of One's Own* and instead lingers on the political and ethical effects of not only Woolf's text, but also of the institutions of literature and higher education that too often foreclose an alternative genealogy of subaltern and minority critique as a counterforce to the canon. This political and ethical critique, however, had already begun with Woolf. N'Gowfri concludes, "[*A Room of One's Own*] had asked questions that she had had to answer herself, as those of the writer had been inadequate. Its value was its inquiry, not its conclusions."[136] Woolf's writing opens the institutions of art and politics to questions of difference. She challenges future writers to build upon her work by bringing new currents of thought and experience to an all too narrowly conceived notion of the literary.

Chapter 4, "Archipelago," centers around the writings of Jean Rhys that more thoroughly unsettles the time of the nation. It brings the history of slavery and colonization front and center into metropolitan modernism. This presence eviscerates the bildungsroman of the white, colonial woman and allows us to glimpse decolonial and anti-racist ways of being human otherwise.

4

ARCHIPELAGO

Jean Rhys, Marlon James, and Jamaica Kincaid

What is the Caribbean in fact? A multiple series of relationships. We all feel it, we express it in all kinds of hidden or twisted ways, or we fiercely deny it. But we sense that this sea exists within us with its weight of now revealed islands. . . . In the Caribbean each island embodies openness. The dialectic between inside and outside is reflected in the relationship of land and sea. It is only those who are tied to the European continent who see insularity as confining. A Caribbean imagination liberates us from being smothered.

—ÉDOUARD GLISSANT, *CARIBBEAN DISCOURSE*

Glissant, in the epigraph above, describes the Caribbean as an archipelago, a turbulent and dynamic series of land and water both within and around the islanders. To read and write the Caribbean as archipelago pushes back against the colonial notion of the islands as insular spots of paradise—gardens of Eden—that allow for control and surveillance of the land, Indigenous inhabitants, and imported laborers who work the plantation.[1] The presumed transparency and knowability of the insular islands afford Europeans the ability to exercise domination and control over their workforce by imposing a panoptic structure of social hierarchies based on racial and gender difference.[2] Jettisoning this colonial mentality, Glissant instead configures the islands and sea as a "dialectic between inside and outside." The sea exists within Caribbean peoples as affect and submerged unity forged through relation.[3] This relationship turns the cartography of islands and sea inside out, with the sea opening the islands to unbounded connection and unspeakable loss. Anticipating Oceanian writer Epeli Hau'ofa's inversion of islands scattered in the sea as a "sea of islands," Glissant shifts the land-water relation from a floating island paradise seemingly disconnected from its marine surroundings to a gush of seawater bearing heavy knots of unwished-for colonial history.[4] His focus on the elemental nature of Caribbean life postulates expressive cultures arising from the material substrate of the Caribbean archipelago. For him, an archipelagic aesthetic is both material and metaphorical, contingent and deeply structured by histories of slavery and colonization. Glissant names this aesthetic a poetics of relation, defined as a desire for interconnection *despite* the opacity of the other.[5] Relation is a problematic collision of difference. Joshua Bennett vividly describes it as "exemplified not by the lifelong bond or the unbreakable phalanx but by strangers screaming in disparate tongues across the void."[6] Before I turn to how this geographic and aesthetic grouping of land and sea will allow me to read Jean Rhys's novels with an attention to the Middle Passage, it is necessary to discuss the method and form of reading the archipelago as laid out by scholars of the Caribbean. I claim that the Caribbean's repeating arc of islands, shoreline, and water ungrounds narratives of modernity and reveals a multitemporal "now" constituted by the violence and loss of the Middle Passage. I show this through a reading of Rhys's novels that demonstrates how their fragmentation, multivocality, dead ends, and melancholy registers this long history. I also posit that, at times, Rhys's work momentarily envisions Black Creole culture as affirming Caribbean cultures and futurity. I conclude the chapter with novelists Marlon James and Jamaica Kincaid who rewrite Rhys to strengthen this sense.

The term *archipelago*, as Brian Russell Roberts and Michelle Ann Stephens argue, denotes a geographical form that is culturally contingent. While the commonsense notion of archipelagos rely on "coherence through proximity," that is, through a cartographically visible grouping of islands, a closer examination of the Caribbean archipelago (although any archipelago would do) reveals discrepancies.[7] Of more than seven hundred Caribbean islands, islets, and cays only about half are situated on the Caribbean tectonic plate. Further complicating its boundaries, the archipelago extends to the Central and South American continental mainland, including Belize, Nicaragua, the Caribbean region of Colombia, Cozumel, the Yucatán Peninsula, Margarita Island, and the Guianas (Guiana, Suriname, French Guiana, the Guiana region in Venezuela, and Amapá in Brazil). These continental regions are often included within the archipelago due to shared historical, political, and cultural ties. The coastal islands and other regions of the United States South also share an ambiguous affiliation with the archipelago. In addition, there are lesser archipelagos, such as the Bahama archipelago, which technically does not border the Caribbean Sea, but is nonetheless said to be contained within the greater Caribbean archipelago. A detailed investigation of what is meant by this geological formation, as Roberts and Stephens note, "functions to undercut a view of the archipelago as a naturally coherent entity, pushing the archipelagic form toward what for some may feel like an uncomfortably tropological or metaphorical model."[8] They add, however, that the term has always carried a sense of metaphoricity and unpredictability, despite its ostensibly empirical aims to express human relations to a specific geophysical formation.

    Roberts and Stephens argue that the term *archipelago* etymologically descends from "the Italian term *archipélago* (with *arci-* signifying "principle" or "chief," and *-pélago* signifying "pool" or "abyss"), which arose during the thirteenth century."[9] In a metonymic slippage, the term came to refer to the islands scattered within the Aegean Sea rather than to the sea itself. During the Age of Discovery, Western explorers used the term to denote any region that exhibited "an uncanny and formal recognition of the Aegean in the island-studded zones they now beheld and wrote about. Consequently, the term 'archipelago' ceased to name a specific sea and began structuring and describing a formal and indeed tropological human relation to material geographies that span the planet."[10] It is precisely the notion that the archipelago repeats itself around the globe that prompts Antonio Benítez-Rojo to frame the Caribbean archipelago as exemplifying what scientists and mathematicians call Chaos, a term that he defines as "dynamic states or regularities [in Nature] that repeat themselves globally."[11] The repeating archipelago is chaotic in how it "reproduces, grows, decays, unfolds, flows, spins, vibrates, seethes."[12] This dynamic and unpredictable material and signifying brew is characterized by a "discontinuous conjunction (of what?): unstable condensations, turbulences, whirlpools, clumps of bubbles, frayed seaweed, sunken galleons, crashing breakers, flying fish, seagull squawks, downpours, nighttime phosphorescence, eddies and pools, uncertain voyages of signification."[13] Benítez-Rojo's list dwells on the physically perceptible heterogeneity of what he calls the "flow and interruption" that comprise the Caribbean.[14]

Benítez-Rojo's ebullient use of Chaos theory to depict the Caribbean is generative for framing the region as a central hub of transatlantic trade and a harbinger of the global plantation system and postcolonial multiracialism rather than as a backwater. This euphoria is tempered by the element that Roberts and Stephens trace in the etymology of the archipelago, namely, the abyss. For Roberts and Stephens, the uncanny repetitions of the archipelago formation around the planet break down mimesis and reveal the metaphoricity of their designation and the fundamental unknowability (mise-en-abyme) of the repeating pattern. The discontinuity and repetition of the archipelago disrupts the smooth flow of signification, revealing "a space of reality that cannot be measured and has not been integrated into the symbolic orders of language and knowledge."[15] Unlike Roberts and Stephens who conceptualize the abyss as a global Lacanian Real, Benítez-Rojo locates a specifically Caribbean history in the unknowability of the archipelagic formation that surfaces when writers take up the pen. He states, "the Caribbean poem and novel are not only projects for ironizing a set of values taken as universal; they are, also, projects that communicate their own turbulence, their own clash, and their own void, the swirling black hole of social violence, produced by the *encomienda* and the plantation, that is, their otherness, their peripheral asymmetry with regard to the West."[16] Crucially, Benítez-Rojo joins the racial longue durée of colonization and slavery to the archipelagic assemblage. "The swirling black hole of social violence" adds otherness, asymmetry, and multiple, conflicting temporalties into the repeating island that emerges around the globe.[17] The effect of this emphasis on racial and genocidal violence is to disrupt the global flow of literature. The slave abyss breaks down signification, fragments narrative, and suffuses form with melancholy as well as with Black Creole creativity. It articulates the effects of global modernity while also positing the clash of temporalities and spaces resistant to such flows.[18] Rhys's novels exemplify this contested terrain, as her work is claimed for modernist, postcolonial, and Caribbean literatures alike, but always uneasily. They never fully occupy a single category.[19] Part of the difficulty stems from the fact that Rhys, like Woolf, expressed views on racial difference that are abhorrent.[20] She insists on the racial divide while also bringing into literary representation Black Creole culture. While this chapter addresses her attitudes and appropriations, it does so through the larger geomorphology of the land- and seascape. It reads Rhys as an archipelagic writer who attends to the "swirling black hole of social violence" not only in the Caribbean but also in the North Atlantic archipelago of the British Isles.[21] The ripple effect of the Caribbean on other regions, Benítez-Rojo maintains, is due to the status of the Caribbean archipelago as a meta-archipelago in that it is both physical and metaphorical. It "has the virtue of having neither a boundary nor a center."[22]

Unlike the unending rhythm and mobility of the waves in the chapter 3, Rhys's peripheral location as a Caribbean writer necessitated that her novels grapple with both fluidity and blockage that inheres in the Caribbean archipelago. Moreover, this repeating pattern of chaos, Benítez-Rojo argues, displaces European literary form: "For the reader who is attuned to Chaos, there will be an opening upon unexpected corridors allowing passage from one point to another in the labyrinth."[23] The reader finds "an opening of unexpected corridors" in Caribbean literature due to the tendency of writers to move beyond literary form's "generic ambit" by means of "metonymic displacement toward scenic, ritual, and mythological forms."[24] For Rhys, this "generic ambit" is undoubtedly the bildungsroman. She obsessively wrote and rewrote the bildungsroman across her long career, inverting its plot of social integration into one of dissolution, death, and despair. From *Postures* (1929), titled *Quartet* in the United States, to *Wide Sargasso Sea* (1966), Rhys's female protagonists fail to learn from their mistakes, find their place in society, or achieve happiness. And, of course, *Wide Sargasso Sea* rewrites the Victorian ur-bildungsroman *Jane Eyre* that assimilates the English white woman into fictions of nation and empire. Reading Rhys's bildungsromane through the archipelago, I focus less on what Jed Esty calls the developmental passage to maturity than on the "unexpected corridors."[25] I examine the metonymic displacements in Rhys's novels that repeat various Caribbean scenes: flashbacks and digressions to the plantation, beaches, gardens, carnival, ocean-going ships, obeah rituals, and hallucinations. I argue that the extended temporality of racial and colonial violence prompts the frequent interruptions, swerves, and lateral movements onto densely textured, static tableaus that express the labyrinthine chaos of the Caribbean. These "unexpected corridors" multiply locations and epistemologies in a manner that creolizes (reproduces, grows, spins, decays) the novel. Creolization of the novel, as I read it in Rhys, dissolves the liberal subject into archipelagic chaos.

SLAVE ABYSS

Sometime during the 1920s, in what is referred to by Rhys scholars as the black exercise book, Rhys reflected on her childhood in Dominica and how she became a writer. I paraphrase her exact language: Sometimes I'd seem to understand the language the ocean speaks—It felt so awful this yearning and sadness of the mountains and the sound of the rain after sunset. Then I realized that the worst of these feelings would dissipate when I wrote poems and I became peaceful. There's an atmosphere of violence and pain in the West Indies.[26] The melancholic, yearning atmosphere of the Caribbean landscape, "the sadness of the mountains," and the "sound of rain" merges with the pervasiveness in the West Indies of enduring violence and pain. Elsewhere in her notebook, also paraphrased, Rhys recalls how she would feel ashamed of and sickened by the stories of slavery told without regard for the enslaved people, including how descendants of slaveowners would lightheartedly recollect torture, including the practice of rubbing salt into wounds made through punishment.[27] For Rhys, the proximity to the terror and violence of slavery—the salt of the sea mixed with blood—lingers in the atmosphere as well as in the archipelagic mixture of land and sea. She senses that the geography of the island is filled with its own sensations, affect, and ways of knowing that dilate the present into the longue durée of slavery and colonization. It speaks to her in a manner that, as Katherine McKittrick puts it, "disclose[s] that geography is always human and that humanness is always geographic—blood, bones, hands, lips, wrists, this is your land, your planet, your road, your sea."[28] This geography refuses the static grid of Cartesian geometry that territorializes land and sea to better navigate and control the seething vitality of life-forms and the elements. In its place, human geography holds that the environment and humans intra-act to mutually constitute one another. The dynamic relation produces space that includes landscape, seascape, infrastructure, and human communities. In human geography, space is not a background or container for human activity. Instead, it is actively produced through human struggle and imagination and, conversely, it exerts a material and affective force on humans and nonhumans who inhabit that space.

The human geography of the Caribbean that made Rhys a writer is informed by the damages of the slave abyss. Especially in *Wide Sargasso Sea,* Rhys explores how the slave trade and slavery produced the utter dependency of white colonial women on the patriarchy through their alienating idealization of Europe. This exploration has direct lines to Rhys's family biography. As third- and fourth-generation descendants of slave owners, Rhys's family epitomizes failure, stagnation, and an unwanted presence on the island in which, during Rhys's childhood, Blacks outnumbered whites by a ratio of a hundred to one. While she notes that "I realized that the worst of these feelings would dissipate when I wrote poems," melancholy nonetheless suffuses her writing. This affect is not purely negative, however. The haunting violence and pain that the waters speak—its archipelagic turbulence, clash, and void—motivates Rhys to write; and they prompt her to imagine the world otherwise than the hierarchies of empire had trained her. She transforms the destructive muteness of colonial women's voices represented as narrative impasse and suffocation into a mechanism for breaking the frame of the bildungsroman.[29] She does this by foregrounding abyssal time and space as part of the Caribbean archipelagic imaginary. Rhys represents white and Black Creole women through silence, opacity, and relation, all elements, Glissant argues, that reflect the absent presence of the Middle Passage in the archipelago. Writing from this perspective dissolves the novel's boundaries, renders its time uncertain, and questions its ontology by mixing water, land, and people in the racial longue durée. My analysis of the slave abyss in Rhys's work builds upon an early assessment of *Wide Sargasso Sea* by the West Indian critic Wally Look Lai. He wrote in the Trinidad-based *New Beacon* in 1968 that:

the real greatness of this novel lies . . . in the way [Rhys] made use of this theme [of rejected womanhood] in order to convey a totally different reading of experience. . . . It is with this more fundamental reading that we are concerned, for this is what constitutes the essentially West Indian nature of the novel. The West Indian setting, far from being incidental, is central to the novel: it is not that it provides a mere background to the theme of rejected womanhood, but rather that the theme of rejected womanhood is utilized symbolically in order to make an artistic statement about West Indian society, and about an aspect of West Indian experience.[30]

What Lai casts as "rejected womanhood" owes its melancholy, I'm arguing, to the very West Indian setting that he identifies as central to Rhys's final novel.[31] But rather than characterize the West Indies as a "setting," or passive backdrop, I read the turbulent archipelago as "central to the novel[s]."

As an instance of this reading, I hold that the melancholy that Rhys discerns in the land and water that surrounds her is neither individual neurosis nor empathy for others' suffering, but an impersonal affect of the slave abyss, a mixing of atmosphere, land- and seascape, and bodily moods. In making this claim, I draw from work on melancholy by M. Jacqui Alexander, Anne Anlin Cheng, Ann Cvetkovich, Saidiya Hartman, and Ewa Płonowska Ziarek. These critics see women's and Afro-diasporic melancholy as both deeply personal *and* unavoidably social and political. In addition, it is difficult to represent because the long-term legacies of slavery—dispossession, displacement, genocide—cannot be located directly through archival evidence.[32] The object of this melancholy has been lost: the archival record of men's and women's lives during the forced marches to the West African coast, the Middle Passage, slavery and post-slavery, and on the Caribbean plantation do not exist. But what cannot be seen or read is nonetheless felt. For example, Hartman calls the "slippery and elusive" search for her ancestors and homeland, "a story about an encounter with nothing."[33] Even so, the violence that was instituted during the slave trade and slavery live on through "a complex continuity" with the present.[34] In this regard, the absent presence of the Middle Passage has been sedimented and diffused into everyday, ordinary geographies of racism and sexism.[35] It is at this level that Rhys's melancholy finds itself: the rain, the water, the mountains; it is atmosphere, hovering nowhere yet everywhere and, even in a segregated colonial society, it crosses the color line. In the US context, Cheng argues that, "even as we recognize how deeply uncomfortable it is to talk about the ways the racialized minority is as bound to racial melancholia as the dominant subject, we must also see how urgent it is that we start to look at the historical, cultural, and cross-racial consequences of racial wounding and to situate these effects as crucial, formative elements of individual, national, and cultural identities."[36] Cheng draws attention to how racial wounding is asymmetrical across the color line, with persons of color bearing the brunt of its effects. Nevertheless, the effects of racism, she argues, extend far beyond individual instances, racial groups, and single generations. Affect resides both as an interior sensation and externally as an effect of alienation, displacement, and everyday acts of exclusion. As such, it undoes the Western dualism between mind and body, offering in its stead the possibility of reinventing aesthetic form that can mediate between the institution of art (inherited literary form) and the experience and embodied location of the melancholic female writer.

Before I explore where and how the slave abyss appears in Rhys's novels, I want to differentiate historically, following Glissant, between the voluntary transplantation of white colonizer immigrants "who continue to survive elsewhere" and the transfer via the slave trade "of a population to another place where they change into something different, into a new set of possibilities. It is in this metamorphosis that we must try to detect one of the best kept secrets of creolization. Through it we can see that the mingling of experiences is at work, there for us to know and producing the process of being."[37] The forcibly transported African captives began the creative process of creolization in the slave ship hold. Their cultural metamorphosis, catalyzed by terror, soon spread throughout the archipelago and affected all inhabitants. According to Françoise Lionnet, creolization refers to "a mode of belonging that connects one to a history of coerced contact that produced unpredictable cultural formations and linguistic variations."[38] Arising from forced migrations across maritime economies, especially the Atlantic and Indian Oceans, Creole cultures are primarily oral and denigrated by the colonizing class. Further, the Creole subject "continues to index a racial, cultural, economic, and linguistic *deficit* embodied by the illiterate manual or indentured laborer, slave, or economic migrant whose position is ipso facto that of a subject devoid of civilizational quotient and depth."[39] Even white Creoles, who usually benefit from privileged racial, economic, cultural, and educational status on the islands, occupy in Europe the category of "contaminated and strange," a judgment that Rhys frequently stresses.[40] Rhys's ancestors did not experience the slave abyss, but the metamorphosis produced by this horrific experience began the process of creolization—a vital element of the archipelago—that repeats, seethes, reproduces, grows, and decays.

The time and space of the slave abyss appear in Rhys's fiction when they animate a "tortured sense of time" and a perpetual, unlocatable movement across the ocean.[41] These disturbances in the ontological fabric of the novel include many drowning and suiciding scenes, walking underwater, "walking as though I were flying," descriptions of "time [that] has no meaning," the "vastness of space," a lack of solidity and fixed background, shadows rather than substances.[42] Her protagonists' melancholic affect and uncertain ontology that hovers between life and death has the effect of ungrounding narrative and referring back to the void of the slave abyss. There is no origin in the slave abyss: the absence of bodies and historical markers collapses space and time and de-links from colonial reason. Abyssal history has no ground upon which to anchor thought. It begins with trauma, loss of memory, melancholy, violence, and deracination that results in a radical loss of language, kinship, and humanity. In the Caribbean, modernity begins through a disorientating dislocation, a "painful negation."[43] In writing from this nonlocation, where "movement is geography," Rhys dissolves static territorial demarcations that posit violence and abjection in one zone (the "free seas" and islands) and civilization (Europe) in another.[44] The resultant displacement is neither beholden to linear temporality, nor to the boundary between the colonies and the metropole. It is indeterminate and groundless, what John E. Drabinski calls a "drowned archeological non-site" in which the event of the Middle Passage ramifies across time and space.[45] Given this swirl of darkness, horror, and loss, a narrative of development becomes impossible.

For example, in *Voyage in the Dark* (published in 1934 as Rhys's second novel, but drafted around 1911–1912) Anna Morgan, Rhys's most autobiographical protagonist, who, after experiencing perpetual nonrecognition of her West Indianness in England by her former lover, Walter Jeffries, decides to give up. She accepts her extreme marginality and the melancholic burden of a collective history of Caribbean people's muteness, erasure, and dehumanization: "It was like letting go and falling back into water and seeing yourself grinning up through the water, your face like a mask, and seeing the bubbles coming up as if you were trying to speak from under the water. And how do you know what it's like to try to speak from under water when you're drowned?"[46] In this passage, Rhys comments on the problem of the Caribbean woman writer: the form and language of the European novel simply cannot account for her creolized and feminized subjectivity. Not only that, but the temporal logic of Anna's question also suggests the mutually reinforcing nature of white women's and Afro-diasporic men's and women's exclusion from representation: without a written archive and literary forebears, there are no voices to testify to their previous and current foreclosure from representation. If they're already silenced, how can they convey their experiences? Nor can Western literary form represent Anna's shifting location and felt sense of the ongoing afterlife of slavery and the slave abyss. By contrast, European and other Western writers, including Woolf, often maintain the structure of static geography, including the center and periphery divide. As Anna succumbs to despair and melancholic muteness, she is reduced to a floating, drowned corpse whose ghostly presence testifies to her negated subjectivity. She bears witness to legions of silenced Caribbean peoples by enacting a self-forgetting through extreme duress. She figures a paralysis of aesthetic and social praxis.[47] The next line is a remembered remark by her father regarding Englishmen: "And I've met a lot of them who were monkeys too."[48] It particularizes the scene and places Anna's extreme alienation within a colonial lens by othering the English. Rhys reroutes plantation history and culture across the Atlantic in a chaotic repetition of the archipelago that intertwines the relation of past and present, here and there, metropole and periphery, subject and her watery surroundings. The ongoing effects of the slave abyss account for this dilation of time and simultaneity of geographies. In addition, the melancholy of the abyss provides an important counterweight to creolization theories that emphasize the mixing of cultures and languages without necessarily acknowledging the ongoing racial and gendered asymmetries of power, knowledge, and space. While Rhys problematically conflates white Creole and Afro-diasporic suffering and erasure, she also insists on the racial longue durée as a rejoinder to the modernist emphasis on the present.

Adding to the alteration of the temporal and geographical parameters of the novel, Rhys encodes her protagonists' narratives with an often deathly antagonism between the novel of development and the occluded history of raced and sexed subjects. The excised ending of *Voyage in the Dark* is a case in point. The novel was rejected by three publishers before Constable & Co. agreed to publish it with the proviso that Rhys rewrite the ending, what she referred to as the novel's "mutilation."[49] In the original ending, Anna's interior monologue expresses her extreme duress as she lays in a hotel room in Paris, hemorrhaging from a botched abortion. Intercut with this scene are memories of Anna's childhood on an unnamed Caribbean island. Watching an Afro-Caribbean masquerade from behind the window jalousies of her family's home, Anna sees "the masks the women wore . . . were flesh-coloured [white] and over the slits for the eyes mild blue eyes were painted and then there was a small straight nose and a little red heart-shaped mouth and under the mouth another slit so that they could put their tongues out at you."[50] While Anna's father reads the protruding tongues as demonstrating "the idea of a malevolent idiot at the back of everything," a nothingness or void, Anna understands that the women are "singing defiance" and laughing "at the idea that anybody black would want to be white."[51] For Anna, the women's tongues that protrude from their masks of whiteness give fleshy reality to an expansive and resistant sexuality as well as to the possibility of Black women's speech. Rather than a nothingness or void, the tongues testify to an embodied and communal counter-history of resistance to white domination. Their collective energy—colorful costumes, music of the chak-chak, triangle, and concertina, dancing and singing *Charlie Lulu* and *There's a Brown Girl in the Ring*—in conjunction with the women's mockery of whiteness allows the young Anna to join them imaginatively: "I knew and so I was dancing and the concertina was going."[52]

However, Anna's momentary freedom is sharply curtailed by an unnamed man, possibly her Uncle Bo, who responds to Anna's newly found sexual energies by attempting to seduce her. Liberation mixes with what for Anna is the threat and reality of sexual servitude. Meanwhile, her present-time dizziness from blood loss merges with the remembered "rhythm of seeds of seed."[53] The chak-chak derives from Caribbean plant life; Anna's giddiness stems from the result of male fertility. As she begins to lose consciousness, she connects her physical sensations to a remembered fall from a horse near the sea. "Now he's galloping beside a precipice and far beneath I can see dead rotting leaves and soft earth that soft red earth I shall fall on."[54] She feels "waves of pain going through me like the sea [sic] I always knew it was like waves and like the sea [sic] Now I'm beyond the trees and beyond the stones."[55] The suspension of temporality is rendered by the empty spaces between fragments of thought and registers the inadequacy of language to encompass the suffering and dissolution of her body. Her sense of being "beyond the stones" suggests that she imagines being at sea. Rhys represents consciousness beyond death to show exactly what the form of the novel disavows: the abjection and death of those deemed expendable to colonial systems of power. Rhys inverts the novel's formal logic by dissolving her heroine back into the shapeless materiality of damaged bodies and uncultivated landscapes, "dead rotting leaves and soft earth," that are excluded from the narrative of development.[56] This omission repeats when Rhys's publisher "mutilates" the novel by removing references to the Caribbean landscape to which Anna imagines she returns when she dies.[57] Instead, the published ending simply extends into what Esty calls, an inconclusive, endless youth in which the protagonist recovers from her abortion and is pronounced, "ready to start all over again in no time."[58]

The novel's original version turns the novel inside out to dissolve the heroine into an archipelagic chaos that Benítez-Rojo calls, "a (dis)order that swarms around what we already know of as Nature."[59] Sexual and racial violence in the metropole repeat colonial and plantation violence, a connection that Rhys makes plain when Anna, having just been seduced for the first time by Walter, tells him about "an old slave-list" she viewed at her family's estate house.[60] She thinks, "Maillotte Boyd, aged 18, mulatto, house servant. The sins of the fathers Hester said are visited upon the children unto the third and fourth generation."[61] Anna's stepmother's warning suggests the continuation of the sexual and racial violence begun generations ago. Both Anna and Hester believe that the family descends from Black as well as European ancestors, and Anna implies that she, too, has been made into a sexualized commodity. Moreover, the fragmented snippets and ellipses throughout the novel produce a turbulent rhythm and clash of memories, cultures, and the void that express archipelagic chaos. Melancholia extends the past into the present and suggests the impossibility of extricating oneself from the horrors of slavery and colonization. These "repeating regularities" find their resting place in the Caribbean as Anna loses consciousness. We see Anna's soon-to-be decomposing body joining the red earth, rotting leaves and the sea.[62] It is precisely this chaotic materiality against which the novel typically asserts order: the bildungsroman narrates the sovereign rational subject who governs an unruly nature. The original version of *Voyage in the Dark*, however, incorporates Anna's demise indifferently into its chaos by dissolving the protagonist's inert body into its alluvial surroundings.

The excised ending also provides a glimpse of relation, a poetic that provides Anna—too late, of course, since she's dying—with an alternative to her silence and narrative impasse. Anna's memories of the Caribbean imaginatively grasp the creativity of Black women's double-talk and collective life mixed with the dangers of feminine sexuality that Anna thinks she shares with the women.[63] The Black women are surrogates for Anna's desire for sexual and racial freedom.[64] In this, they are made familiar and allow for Anna's disidentification from whiteness. Beyond the identity categories offered in this scene, however, the poetics of relation breaks the frame of the bildungsroman and enacts a nonhierarchical mixing of carnival, land- and seascape, resistant life and death, blood and salt. Relation mixes Anna's memories with an imaginative return to her Caribbean home as a repeating presence (sea, stones, leaves, earth, blood, and loss of life). Rather than remain solely within the bildungsroman's biographical time, Rhys's novel expresses long durational time in which the accumulated presence of the past—the deep time of the ocean and its abyssal history of wasted, stolen lives—lives on and on. But from the abyss comes the creative rerooting in the Caribbean archipelago, a world of cross-cultural contact and syncretic belief. This world, however, is still ungraspable as a political possibility for Rhys in the 1920s. Words fail as Anna lapses into unconsciousness and death.

But the ending that Rhys was forced to cut from her second novel haunts her other work as she refuses to self-censor the abjection of Caribbean women from the novel's field of representation. In the next section, I consider the relation between European aesthetics and the Caribbean archipelago. Literary form, in Rhys's treatment, reveals the disavowed history of European economic and political domination whose effects include destroyed bodies, the exploitation of natural resources, and alienation.

MODERNIST AESTHETICS AND RACIALIZED ABJECTION

To better understand how abjection, as in Anna Morgan's fatal hemorrhage above, affords Rhys the ability to confront the colonizing imaginary of the bildungsroman, it is important to remember how the ocean voyage shaped the novel of development. For Western writers, the transatlantic crossing was a paradigm of uninterrupted mobility and flow that translated into personal freedom. Margaret Cohen writes, "Travel was a value in modernity, one that is as important to acknowledge as political enfranchisement or enlightenment. Novels about seafaring certainly consecrated mobility, despite their critics' efforts to reduce their plots to the scales of land [as in *Robinson Crusoe*.]"[65] The ability to move freely corresponded to personal freedoms and the capacity to reach one's highest potential, as the novel of development made clear. By contrast, writers from the Caribbean who are attuned to slavery's history recast the Atlantic crossing by altering the chronotope of the ship that speedily navigates across the wasted space of the waters. Considered from the perspective of captive Africans packed into the hold, the ship produces instead a chronotope of immobility that condenses time and space into a thick knot of stasis, disorientation, and waste. As I've shown in previous chapters, the reduction to flesh un-gendered the captives and, by the eighteenth century, racialized them as Black. This abject state of racialization, in which the captives were stripped of personhood and had their physical boundaries violated in an abject dissolution, metonymically extends to the slave ship itself.

To understand how the materiality of the slave ship parallels the experience of the captives, a connection that will allow me to show how Rhys both invokes the hold and displaces it, I turn briefly to Jamaican novelist John Hearne's *The Sure Salvation* (1981) that rewrites an earlier tale of a drifting slave ship, Herman Melville's novella *Benito Cereno* (1855). Elizabeth DeLoughrey describes Hearne's text as instituting "a model of diaspora [that] inscribes extreme immobility, stasis, and timelessness, a literal waste of feces, blood, vomit, and sperm that envelops both the ship and the middle passage experience."[66] Becalmed on a tropical sea for weeks, the ship intends to arrive in Brazil with a load of illegally transported Africans gathered from the Congo to Angola. Its opening chapter, "The

Poop," begins: "By the tenth day, the barque was ringed by the unbroken crust of its own garbage. And the refuse itself had discharged a contour of dully iridescent grease which seemed to have been painted onto the sea with one stroke of a broad brush."[67] In this scene, time accumulates, rather than passes, concretized by means of the image of waste piling up. Moreover, the sea is completely still and refuses to swallow the effluvia emanating from the ship. The horrors of the slave ship remain floating and evident rather than conveniently disappeared into the depths. Such a slow-moving, abject tale contests narratives of global trade and oceanic flow and reveals the occluded, material underside of those narratives. Fetishized objects (the bondsperson as commodity) depend upon the disavowal of the human and environmental waste that are the flip side of the fetishized object. Caribbean writers, such as Rhys, refuse to overlook the effluvia of the sea and the disposable nature of chattel slavery. Instead, they show how abstraction and abject materiality are twin components of the Atlantic system of chattel slavery. Paradoxically, dwelling on the abjection of captive bodies leads to the possibility of contesting the commodification of bodies and other materialities, including art and nature. As I'll show, Rhys's repeating treatment of the Caribbean archipelago extends its watery history into the North Atlantic metropole to contest its arid compartmentalism.

In Rhys's penultimate novel, *Good Morning, Midnight* (1939), the protagonist, Sasha Jensen, reflects on a rich patron who hired her to ghostwrite fairy stories. She's shrewd, "hard as a nail, and with what sense of property!"[68] She expects certain skills (shorthand), vocabulary (long words), and feeds Sasha storylines. Sasha thinks, "[t]hey explain people like that by saying that their minds are in water-tight compartments, but it never seemed so to me. It's all washing about, like the bilge in the hold of a ship, all washing around in the same hold—no water-tight compartments."[69] The patron's cold distance, demanding nature (she had after all paid for Sasha's writerly services to be available around the clock), and vigorous enforcement of property relations alienates Sasha from her labor. This social structure is similar, but not reducible, to the ownership of slaves since Sasha has full personhood. Nonetheless, Sasha's emphasis on her employer's sense of property targets her whiteness, which is legally defined as being free to own property, including, under slavery, persons codified as Black. In commodifying persons and things, white people abstract lively (and living) material entities into exchange value, a relation of equivalence. As a result, an interconnected, open, embodied, ethical relation is foreclosed.[70] It is within this context that Sasha rejects the idea that rich white people have minds "in water-tight compartments." The imagery here suggests a reified, arid consciousness, which is, at surface level, true. Sasha concedes that such people "haven't the slightest idea how to spend their money; they haven't the slightest idea how to enjoy themselves. Either they have no taste at all, or, if they have any taste, it's like a mausoleum and they're shut up in it."[71] Art as property is reduced to a dead object, sealed off from life and frozen in time at the moment of purchase.[72] This view of art represents a monetary equivalent and static form rather than serving as the means by which the viewer can access aesthetic pleasure and render a materialist critique.[73]

However, Sasha's simile that rich white people have minds "like the bilge in the hold of a ship" is far more damning than claiming that rich people are self-enclosed and therefore sterile and joyless. To be compared with the filthy, liquified waste sloshing around in the hold of a transoceanic ship marks the bourgeoisie as a far more nefarious force than a hoarder of art ever could be. The simile connects whiteness, gender normativity, and property to its constitutive outside, a zone of the unintelligible materiality of waste and abject bodies. While Rhys does not explicitly connect her patron with the Middle Passage, the reference to transoceanic travel and racialized abjection that haunts her novels marks its disavowed presence. The absent reference to human bodies in the hold is metonymically connected to bilge water. The captives' inability to access sanitary means of evacuation meant that the hold was literally turned into a container for bilge water. Sasha's simile displaces the actual cargo of abducted Africans onto a less threatening marker of filth, but one that is nonetheless also located in the belowdecks of a ship. What occurs on the sea, in the depths of the hold, produces whiteness (the ability to own property), generates great wealth, and is simultaneously foreclosed, erased and disconnected from the beauty and ease of privileged European life.[74] Sasha cannily places her own position, as a paid producer of aesthetic form, midway between the production of wealth and the violence and abjection of captive Africans. She occupies the vestibule between universalized European forms, on the one hand, and the particularity of slavery, on the other.

Sasha's reflection disrupts the "water-tight container" of reified thought and demonstrates how the violence of economic and racial privilege began in the roaming crucible of the slave ship on the "free" seas. The slave ship factories rendered African captives unintelligible and associated with filth and formlessness.[75] Meanwhile white privilege could not attain its property (its right to possess *and* its own whiteness as property in a mutually constitutive loop of naturalized acquisition) without fomenting and then disavowing the chaos they sowed. Simon Gikandi demonstrates how wealthy beneficiaries of slavery erased their connection to this violence and fetishized art in its place. He writes, "At the heart of this ideology [of an autonomous aesthetic] was the belief that the realm of the aesthetic represented an alternative sphere of experience separated from the vulgarity of the everyday . . . [and] a way out of the materiality of life that was his [Codrington's] legacy and inheritance [as a plantation owner]."[76] Rhys, in effect, shows that race and modernism (autonomous art) are not merely entwined at the level of identity (modern versus primitive), but are also structurally and materially co-constitutive.

Rhys insists upon an archipelagic geography that opens the imperial metropolis to the world-system as she describes the art patron above. Rather than occupying the crypt-like sterility of a mausoleum, filled with objects canonized by the art market, Sasha sends the patron on a figurative transoceanic voyage that makes visible through bilge water the relation between high European culture and abject bodies. Writing and thinking from the Caribbean archipelago in which there is "neither a boundary nor a center" allows Rhys to trouble the geographical divisions between European center and colonial periphery and between aesthetics and racial violence.[77] At the heart of this confrontation between European form and racialized abjection lies the archipelago, a mode of geographical thinking that posits the Atlantic as a shifting, unfixed origin of modernity constituted by exorbitant violence and loss. The watery abyss ungrounds narratives and suspends time and space. This geography is expressed by Sasha, who descends from white slave owners but, as a Creole, is excluded from European privilege. She claims, "I have no pride—no pride, no name, no face, no country. I don't belong anywhere. Too sad, too sad. . . . It doesn't matter, there I am, like one of those straws which floats round the edge of a whirlpool and is gradually sucked into the centre, the dead centre, where everything is stagnant, everything is calm."[78] This stasis prevents Sasha's social integration. Rather than contribute to a narrative of development, the abyss is a "dead centre" around which Sasha floats without aim, already marked for death and already excluded from the social. This blocked future is a central formal element in all of Rhys's novels: Sasha's seedy Parisian hotel is located at an "impasse" in the street, forbidding forward movement; *Wide Sargasso Sea* opens with the deadpan report that the neighbor, Mr. Luttrell, had been "the first who got tired of waiting. . . . One calm evening he shot his dog, swam out to sea and was gone for always."[79] Marya, in *Quartet*, and Anna, in the original ending of *Voyage in the Dark,* die young. Mr. Mackenzie, assessing Julia Martin's future, "foresaw that the final stage of her descent in the social scale was inevitable, and not far off."[80] These narrative impasses block character development. Excluded from the social landscape due to their lack of background and hence from filial narratives of growth, continuation, and development, Rhys's protagonists drift, suffused with melancholy, imbued with physical unease (numbness, disassociation, coldness, loss of will and direction), and act "without a sense for self-preservation."[81] Marya, in *Quartet,* fights "wildly, with tears, with futile rages, with extravagant abandon—all bad weapons."[82] Their self-undoing exhibits the felt impossibility of giving literary form to Caribbean history while, at the same time, asserts a longing for a radical reformulation of the structures of social life and new possibilities for agency and personhood.[83]

THE WILD SARGASSO SEA

In the preceding section, I focused on how an archipelagic lens opens the local to the global. I highlighted the oceanic passages between colony and metropole that make visible how the archipelago has "neither a boundary nor a center."[84] I deployed the term archipelago to account for what Rhys as well as Benítez-Rojo indicate as the absent presence of the Middle Passage in the Caribbean, the violence and pain that the waters speak. The void of history disrupts connective vision and instead furthers the chaos, the turbulence, and unpredictability of the archipelagic relation. In turning to *Wide Sargasso Sea,* that unpredictability is heightened. Rhys drafted much of the novel when Anglophone-speaking Caribbean islands and coastal nations, including Dominica and Jamaica, belonged to the short-lived Caribbean Federation (1958–1962), an archipelagic geopolitical entity that declared independence from the British Empire. Speaking to this event in 1958, Trinidadian novelist, theorist, and historian C. L. R. James gave a lecture in British Guiana on the challenges and opportunities of the Caribbean Federation. In order for the federation to be a success, he said, its citizens must break free of colonial mentality and forge "new human relations" to establish multinational and multiracial ties.[85] This transformation, he argued, is as much cultural as it is political. The Caribbean novelist must not limit the possibilities of Caribbean self-expression because it is crucial to adapt the English language and its imaginary to the experience of formerly colonized inhabitants. James concluded his lecture by turning to the merits of Caribbean novelists Sam Selvon and V. S. Naipaul, whom he saw as articulating postcolonial Caribbean relations in their writing. Despite James's optimistic pronouncements, the federation foundered upon internal political divisions only four years later. The "new human relations" could not withstand the complexity of governing a formerly colonized and enslaved archipelagic region. Against this failed backdrop, Rhys's final novel discloses something overlooked by James: the relations of the archipelago that are affective, embodied, sensual, and interwoven with the racial longue durée.

In order to attend to the novel's neglected material, geographical, and affectual relations, I underscore its polyvocality. Specifically, I show how the novel produces meanings often contrary to the author's intention. In her private writings, Rhys makes plain her negative attitude toward Black people. But her last novel produced perspectives with which Rhys was not particularly comfortable. In a letter to her editor, Diana Anthill, Rhys admitted, "[t]he most seriously wrong thing with Part II is that I've made the obeah woman, the nurse, too articulate. I thought of cutting it a bit, I will if you like, but after all no one will notice. Besides there's no reason why one particular negro woman shouldn't be articulate enough, especially if she's spent most of her life in a white household."[86] What Rhys deemed expendable, namely Christophine's point of view, becomes an opening through which fragments of Black Creole culture pass into literary representation. These fragments provide a crucial mechanism for discerning how Black Creole culture reimagines the human, mediated by land, sea, and loss.

I argue that reading modernism after postcolonial and anti-racist revaluations of Black cultures and history allows us to find resistance to modernity/coloniality through Glissant's materialist poetics. This is so because it keeps the Middle Passage in the foreground and allows for an analysis of how creolization rethinks human and more-than-human relations. As introduced in chapter 2, a poetics of relation is shared knowledge and creativity based on the unknown coordinates and haunting of the slave abyss. It refuses metaphysics (a nonhistorical value system) and instead generates knowledge collectively and in relation to the melancholic land- and seascape. Because relation is based on unknowing and loss, it figures lack and an openness to other perspectives. It is not grounded on a foundational story, historical figure, or god, but upon a scattering, a collapse, and a vital remaking. Relation is based upon a rerooting in the Caribbean landscape. Glissant writes, "The relationship with the land...becomes so fundamental in this [Caribbean] discourse that landscape in the work stops being merely decorative or supportive and emerges as a full character. Describing landscape is not enough. The individual, the community, the land are inextricable in the process of creating history. Landscape is a character in this process. Its deepest meanings need to be understood."[87] Reading the landscape as agential posits the human subject as an intra-active participant in the larger, longer archipelagic poetics. Glissant's abyssal history combines the landscape with the sea to signal that this rerooting is contingent upon the larger unknowability of the archipelago and ocean. Specifically, traces of the abyss wash up on shore and mix with the "new" world landscape to produce both melancholic affect and postcolonial resistance alike. This poetics is not hybridity but a dispersed series of parts that interact.

In calling this section the *wild* Sargasso Sea, I highlight the chaotic specificity of the Caribbean archipelago: the weed-entangled Sargasso Sea, the human geographies comprised of intra-acting bodies, land, and sea, and the "swirling black hole of social violence" that is the still-present legacy of slavery and colonization.[88] Wildness calls attention to what is untamable, unknown, and disorderly, akin to what Benítez-Rojo calls—in an equally materialist register—chaos. As Michael Taussig extensively documents, the colonial imaginary projects wildness onto the Indigenous other and uses rationality, the law, and violence to tame and control it, but always with incomplete results. Rhys, in her final book, captures the quality of wildness and unpredictability of the West Indian archipelago. The novel conveys this chaos by means of a surreal, hallucinatory quality of competing modes of being and knowing on the islands.[89] Rhys renders the Caribbean in *Wide Sargasso Sea* archipelagic through its multilingualism (French, English, Carib, and Francophone and Anglophone Creole); its intercolonial histories and territories (French, British, and Spanish empires); its Caribbean regional cosmopolitanism (where, for instance, Antoinette refers proudly to St. Pierre, Martinique, as "the Paris of the West Indies"); its mixture of racial identities and island populations from Martinique, Jamaica, and Dominica; its equivocations of Afro-Caribbean fetishes (obeah packets) and European fetishes (books); and its intra-active relations between Creole persons and their surroundings.[90] Moreover, the text's restless shuttling between Caribbean and English locations, between the perspectives of Antoinette and her unnamed husband (who will be hereafter called by his name in *Jane Eyre*, Rochester), and between *Jane Eyre* (1847) and Rhys's rewriting of Bertha's narrative, evokes a contradictory state of suspension and a hallucinatory unreal space that I am reading as the murky realm of wildness that disrupts the colonial order of things.

Wide Sargasso Sea begins just after 1834 when slavery was abolished in the British colonies. Its opening describes two hardly auspicious events: the family horse is poisoned and the neighbor, Mr. Luttrell, tired of waiting for compensation for his freed bondspeople, shoots his dog, swims out to sea, and "was gone for always."[91] The littoral setting introduces two important contexts for the novel: the association of the sea with death and the botanical knowledge that informs the obeah practiced by enslaved people and freed Black inhabitants on the island that can either harm or heal. When Antoinette's mother, Annette, learns that her horse has been poisoned, she announces, "[n]ow we are marooned," a Spanish-derived term which means "wild and untamed" and refers to the sovereignty of rebel communities of escaped bondspersons[92] The term also signifies being abandoned on a deserted island which aptly describes the Cosway family as they are forsaken by Jamaican white Creoles after Antoinette's father's death. The descriptor places them within the wildness of the Jamaican rural landscape as castaways, and it also evokes the refusal of the Maroon communities to accept the authority of colonial governance.

This assemblage of death, abandonment, and violence on an edge of the Caribbean archipelago enfolds the Cosways and Antoinette, in particular, in a landscape of terror and opacity. The novel's opening lines combine the rumor-laden, impersonal "they" with the proverbial: "They say when trouble comes close ranks, and so the white people did. But we were not in their ranks."[93] The beginning of the quotation is probably spoken by the Black community, "they," who objectify the white people. Midway through the sentence the pronoun shifts to "we" to situate the Cosway family, ambiguously and dangerously, between both groups. Further marginalizing the hapless family, Christophine, the Martinican enslaved person turned servant following Emancipation, has the first directly attributed speech in the novel: "The Jamaican ladies never approved of my mother, 'because she pretty like pretty self.'"[94] But it is Antoinette, in the singular, who refers to "my mother" and therefore embeds Christophine's speech within her own. Christophine's creolized words situate the Cosways in a world quite different from the English culture they are expected to idealize. Overall, the effect of such turns and twists is to disorient both reader and protagonist. Antoinette is buffeted by a turbulent and bitterly divided land and culture; she rides the waves of social disorder and division. Soon after this dismal opening, Antoinette seeks refuge from the cruelties of Jamaica's postslavery divisions in the garden that surrounds her semi-abandoned plantation estate named Coulibri:[95]

> Our garden was large and beautiful as that garden in the Bible—the tree of life grew there. But it had gone wild. The paths were overgrown and a smell of dead flowers mixed with the fresh living smell. Underneath the tree ferns, tall as forest tree ferns, the light was green. Orchids flourished out of reach or for some reason not to be touched. One was snaky looking, another like an octopus with long thin brown tentacles bare of leaves hanging from a twisted root. Twice a year the octopus orchid flowered—then not an inch of tentacle showed.[96]

Referring to the Caribbean as a paradise, or Eden, "gone wild," we see nature, not the devil, provoking the ruination of paradise, a figure for Rhys's plantation nostalgia. Because the formerly enslaved people no longer maintain the garden, the plants have overtaken their cultivated form and grown sinister. In its threatening atmosphere lurks the colonizer's fear of freed Black people's revolt (as happened in Rhys's own history when her family's Geneva plantation was burned to the ground in 1844 and again in 1932) and of sexual predation. In the garden, life and death mingle; the light, as if underwater, is green. The octopus orchid further lends to the undersea otherworldliness of the setting. Nature has gone awry, overcoming human structures and systems. Background and figure, island and sea merge. The orchids are phallic and "snaky-looking." Although flowers are hermaphroditic and blur sexual difference, in this scenario, they are ominous and vaguely threatening to Antoinette who maintains throughout the novel that nature is cruel and indifferent to humans. The scene also prefigures Antoinette's recurring dream of enduring sexual violence in a ruined garden.

Like the sadness the water speaks and the yearning, pain, and violence of the island that Rhys discerns in her notebook, in her novel she portrays the overgrown garden in affective terms that bespeak past and present, land- and seascape at once, and mingle terror with violence. The setting's atmosphere conveys the surreal "ordinariness of the extraordinary atrocities" of slavery and settler colonialism.[97] Its uncanniness, whereby the disavowed savagery of colonialism and plantation slavery is displaced onto the landscape as a return of the repressed, unsettles the empirically given. Jack Halberstam calls wildness "an inscription that seeks not to be read but to leave its mark as evidence of absence, loss, and death."[98] He draws from Taussig who argues that colonizing forces project terror onto the landscape, a potent mixture of truth and illusion. Colonization and plantation slavery justified their brutality and genocide through myths and realities of threatening slave rebellions and hostile Indigenous groups. Conversely, the terror of the colonization and slavery enter into Afro-Caribbean and Amerindian counter-mythologies. This imaginary produces uncanny, threatening stories, such as those told to the young Rhys by her Black nurse, Meta, filled with "zombies, soucriants, and loups-garoux (werewolves)."[99] The effect of the colonial unconscious is to produce an uncertain reality, menacing and murky.[100]

Despite the death that lurks, the emphasis in this garden is on the Tree of Life rather than of the Tree of Knowledge of Good and Evil. The shift highlights the biological, as well as mythic, aspects of the garden, as it is a foundational concept in Darwin's *Origin of Species*.[101] Its "wildness" provides a locus and movement of, as Halberstam puts it, "the unknown and disorderly.... It describes the space and modes of knowing and unknowing that emerge in the encounter between capital [here, plantation colonialism] and chaos, privilege and struggle, myth and counter myth."[102] The overgrown plantation garden is at once foundational and liminal space—the mythic origin of European colonization and plantation settlement, as well as the ruin of whiteness and the site of abandon. As Halberstam points out, wildness paradoxically becomes a space of resistance that is nonetheless fraught with danger: it risks collapsing into primitivism and exoticization (if one denies its agency). It often looks like madness or a drug-induced hallucination because wildness is neither sovereign nor rational. It is a life force that undoes fixed meanings and static materialities, including those of marked bodies. In the garden, Antoinette finds refuge from both Black and white communities. She becomes momentarily a liminal and unclaimed body. I suggest that wildness introduces and mediates Antoinette's attraction to the counter-archive of obeah and eventually allows Antoinette to reject the colonial system that results in her imprisonment in Thornfield Hall.

Rhys's unwriting of the bildungsroman depends upon the wildness of the archipelago to serve as a counter-myth to Enlightenment thought. It injects a space of unmeaning and chaos into the symbolic order of signification, which falters and sometimes collapses, as when Rochester succumbs to hallucinatory echoes in Part 2 of the novel. This indeterminacy throws the liberal subject into a state of chaos that blurs the boundaries between subject and object, white and Black, land- and seascape. Wildness, such as that which attaches to Antoinette, is the in-between, disruptive, and the liminal to the colonial order. It merges self with surroundings, especially the melancholic water and the uncultivated postslavery landscape. Wildness is an environmental and anti-colonial relation between material surroundings and the self.[103] This relation becomes apparent through Rhys's engagement with obeah, the outlawed spiritual and botanical practice of Afro-diasporic peoples in Jamaica and elsewhere.

In the spring of 1964, a few years prior to the publication of *Wide Sargasso Sea*, Rhys wrote to fellow writer Francis Wyndham to report on the novel's progress. After struggling for years with drafting the novel, Rhys described a creative breakthrough that would see the novel to completion. She included in the letter a poem that she had written from the point of view of Rochester called "Obeah Night." In it, Rochester wonders whether he could have "tamed and changed a wild girl" and if so:

> Perhaps Love would have smiled then
> > Shown us the way
>
> Across that sea. They say it's strewn with wrecks
> > And weed-infested
>
> Few dare it, fewer still escape
> But *we*, led by smiling Love
> *We* could have sailed
> > Reached a safe harbor
>
> Found a sweet, brief heaven
> > Lived our short lives.[104]

Rhys's poem refers to the treacherous Sargasso Sea. Its vast morass of algae, roughly the size of Australia, has flummoxed Europeans seeking the Americas, from Christopher Columbus onward.[105] The Sargasso Sea is the only sea in the world that has no land-based borders, a fact that points to the contingency of archipelagic and sea geographies. The deeper, colder Atlantic spins counterclockwise around this "interior" and floating sea. The sea was called "The Horse Latitudes" by Spanish sailors because, becalmed on the waters and entangled in the weeds, the crew was often forced to throw their horses overboard to conserve drinking water or to slaughter them for food. This action echoes, infamously, how slavers would jettison their human cargo into the ocean when they were dangerously low on water supplies, seeking to outrun other ships, or, as in the infamous case of the *Zong*, trying to collect insurance money. The morass of weed hovers over an oceanic abyss of loss and murder, "strewn with wrecks." What's more, the vegetal profusion of the sea blocks the colonial desire to sail unimpeded to and from the Americas. Because the vegetation obscures a clear view into the depths, the sea aligns with what DeGuzman calls *Wide Sargasso Sea*'s "narrative[] impenetrability."[106] An entangled stew of plant growth figures the gulf that separates Rochester from Antoinette. It disrupts linear development and challenges individual autonomy within a chaotic geography that exerts its own agency and history. Rather than allowing for an unimpeded crossing of the waters and a smooth, untroubled connection between Europe and the Caribbean, the Sargasso Sea prevents such attachments. Rhys's poem wishes for a romantic, ideal love between colonizer and colonial, but the material reality of plantation history—figured as a nearly impassable, weedy gulf—announces its tragic denouement. Antoinette remains wild, an unassimilable product of Creole culture.

It was this poem, Rhys recounts, that enabled her breakthrough in drafting the novel: "Only when I wrote this poem—then it clicked—and all was there and always had been. The first clue is Obeah."[107] The brief honeymoon interlude between Antoinette and Rochester in which "she *magic* with him" produces the tension between colonial romance and its creolizing unraveling.[108] Its title, "Obeah Night," links Afro-diasporic healing practices with the vine-strewn morass of the Sargasso Sea. Rochester's violent response to Antoinette's love-potion not only points to the impassable gulf between Europe and the Caribbean but the presence of obeah in their bedroom also brings the archipelago into domestic, intimate, and embodied space. Both sea and potion are archipelagic: they mix interior and exterior, environments and bodies, memory and desire. Obeah, as I'll explore next, is a Black Creole aesthetic practice, a poetics of relation, which is diametrically in opposition to the liberal subject of the bildungsroman.

Obeah does not involve communal rituals; instead, its knowledge is passed down only through secret initiation, especially once the practice was outlawed in 1760.[109] It is a fundamentally opaque practice. Therefore, Anglophone colonial officials in Jamaica and elsewhere could only prohibit the practice by targeting "the material objects that possessed ritual and spiritual significance to slaves and free blacks. When the first law was enacted against Obeah in the Caribbean, possession of blood [human and animal], feathers, parrot's beaks, alligator's teeth, dog's teeth, broken bottles, grave dirt, rum and egg shells were specifically proscribed."[110] These objects, bound together into a potion or packet, speak of an indexical relation to the living world.[111] They point to both natural and supernatural contexts at once and "express continuity with circumstances to which they remain in relation."[112] Further, they articulate an uneven geography and nonlinear time insofar as the dirt and bones of the dead, the prehistorical (of, say, a Carib stone axe), seawater millions of years in the making, and contemporary objects and substances comingle.[113] They also indicate futurity insofar as the potions or packets express desires for a forthcoming occurrence. These objects are not abstracted from their contexts and rendered equivalent as a market exchange model would demand. Rather, their material differences work together to invoke the spiritual forces of the ancestors and duppies (malevolent spirits) and to harness natural powers. For example, feathers index birds' ability to fly above any difficulties; cemetery earth conveys the spirit of the buried person; and powdered camwood exhibits "the reddish color of which traditionally signals transition and mediation"[114] Together, these materials, held in close proximity of a bundle or elixir, exert a collective capacity to act on humans: to poison, protect, or cure spiritual and physical ailments, including a fading of love or sexual attraction. Reading the relation of disparate substances in this manner, obeah practices reference a wider African-descended understanding of ecology. Stephen Haymes writes, "Slave ecologies ... [are] relational ecologies: they do not accord final moral value to nature, the ecosystem, or the environment. Such a view is analogous to kin relationships, in which each individual part—humans, soil, plants, lands, waters—is cared for and nurtured by the community or family."[115] Furthermore, they express a "commitment to the security and material and emotional well-being of living others in the family ... [that] implies not just acknowledging an interdependence, illustrative of Western holism, but also obligation to communal relations."[116] Importantly, this obligation "refuses to firmly prioritize either the interests of individuals or the interest of the community."[117] As an assemblage of human, animal, land, and water, no particular element is valued more highly than any other. Their relations are lateral and dispersed, as with the archipelago. They bespeak of "place" insofar as there is a milieu in which these elements temporarily cohere.

Caribbean colonizers both feared and desired obeah medicines. As Antoinette's marriage begins to disintegrate, she visits her former nurse, Christophine, an obeah practitioner, on the rural, unnamed island where she honeymoons. Antoinette arrives at the former slave's two-room house, sits at her feet, and smells the "clean cotton, starched and ironed" of her dress. She thinks, "[t]his is my place and this is where I belong and this is where I wish to stay," but then quickly distracts herself with other thoughts including her "soft silk cotton mattress and fine sheets."[118] After she tells Christophine about her marriage difficulties, Christophine advises her to leave her husband. But Antoinette still idealizes England and counters that "[she] wish[es] to see England."[119] Rejecting Christophine's advice, Antoinette instead asks for a love-potion to preserve her marriage. Christophine reluctantly agrees and gives her a potion. As Antoinette leaves, she reflects, "I can remember every second of that morning, if I shut my eyes I can see the deep blue colour of the sky and the mango leaves, the pink and red hibiscus, the yellow handkerchief [Christophine] wore round her head, tied in the Martinique fashion with the sharp points in front, but now I see everything still, fixed for ever like the colours in a stained-glass window. Only the clouds move. It was wrapped in a leaf, what she had given me, and I felt it cool and smooth against my skin."[120] This scene is aestheticized in memory and rendered sacred, "like the colours in a stained-glass window," suggesting an Afro-diasporic cosmology wherein spirits inhabit the landscape and render it hallowed. The leaf-wrapped potion is soothing as it rests next to Antoinette's skin, joining her physically to this scene and especially to Christophine and obeah. The smells, sounds, and sensations hold her suspended in time and place. Nothing moves but the clouds. Of course, this is a memory and thus a fragment, but it also suggests how Antoinette is momentarily held in the web of her material surrounds, with the packet nestled against her body. Her desire is amplified by the obeah potion; her participation in the practice joins her fleetingly to the landscape and Black Creole culture. The potion, as a fetish, "mediates the relations between inside and out," as relations between self and agential material surroundings subvert the autonomy of the liberal subject. This remembered scene situates Antoinette's subjectivity in the archipelagic crucible where radically heterogenous worlds—European, Caribbean, and African—mediate historical void, opacity, and difference.[121] In this counter-aesthetic, the fetish is not a representation; rather, it combines material elements intra-actively. The potion's effectivity occurs "by making a new relation of forces in the present."[122] The vision flattens hierarchies and acts upon Antoinette by means of an assemblage with agential, even supernatural, powers. It produces a moment of communal recognition that temporarily undoes the colonial structure of Antoinette's thoughts and desires. It is the final goodbye to her authentic place before she administers the potion to Rochester who, the next morning, violently severs their union and eventually imprisons her in the attic in Thornfield.

After the disastrous obeah night, Antoinette is reduced to a zombified state, defined by the colonial ethnographic text that Rochester reads as "a dead person who seems to be alive or a living person who is dead. A zombie can also be the spirit of a place, usually malignant. . . .'They cry out in the wind that is their voice, they rage in the sea that is their anger.'"[123] A nonhuman figure, the zombie occupies a liminal state that is partially human and very much of the elements: the wind and the sea. The zombie's ontology is uncertain. Like the drowned Anna Morgan, it hovers between life and death, but unlike Anna's passive surrender, the zombie is a malignant force. As a Creole figure, it embodies the devasting absence of the Middle Passage, the violence and pain that lingers in the islands. In the letter to Wyndham previously mentioned, Rhys describes Antoinette's state of mind once her marriage is dissolved: "Now she is angry too. Like a hurricane. Like a Creole."[124] Creole history sediments land and sea with a history of dispossession and outrage. Body, affect, land, and sea conjoin in a manner that is both geo-elemental and particular to the Caribbean. On the voyage to England, Antoinette asks the sea to aid her revolt: "I smashed the glasses and plates against the porthole. I hoped it would break and the [still tropical] sea come in."[125] Antoinette's wildness looks like craziness from a colonial perspective: the ship's doctor gives her a sedative; the staff will not meet her gaze; her husband has confined her. As she appeals to the sea as an agent, she enters into relation with it, affirming the Afro-Caribbean sense of water as holding both life and death.

Once in England, held captive in Thornfield Hall's attic, an archipelagic sensibility awakens Antoinette from her catatonic state by means of the scent that still clings to a red dress brought from Jamaica. It smells of "vetivert and frangipani, of cinnamon and dust and lime trees when they are flowering. The smell of the sun and the smell of the rain."[126] The sensory proximity to her place in the rural Caribbean reanimates her memories. Once awakened, Antoinette dreams a recurrent dream, but now she sees the ending in which she asks Christophine again for help to escape from her husband. The temporality of the dreamlike state is recursive: she dreams of what will happen in the future by means of her past encounter with Christophine. It condenses past, present, and future into a now. Moreover, the dream state suggests that she remains wild. Her actions are distracted, accidental, and disastrous. She takes the keys and a candle from her sleeping caretaker. As she walks the halls of Thornfield, she knocks down other candles and sets the house on fire. She narrates:

> As I ran or perhaps floated or flew I called help me Christophine help me and looking behind me I saw that I had been helped. There was a wall of fire protecting me but it was too hot, it scorched me and I went away from it. . . . The wind caught my hair and it streamed out like wings. It might bear me up, I thought, if I jumped to those hard stones. But when I looked over the edge I saw the pool at Coulibri. Tia was there. She beckoned me and when I hesitated, she laughed. I heard her say, You frightened? . . . I called Tia! and jumped and woke.[127]

The wall of flame separates her from Rochester's attempt to rescue her, allowing Antoinette to dwell imaginatively within the Caribbean archipelago. Her vision encompasses both England and the Caribbean in a unlocatable imaginary fluidity that mimics the geography of the sea, and specifically, given her imagined interlocutors Christophine and Tia, a Black Atlantic geography. "Perhaps floated or flew" echoes slaves' belief that after death, the soul returns to the ancestral home over the waters. Her wildness—accidentally knocking over a candle, throwing herself off a roof—delivers her from the living death of the attic. Death and life comingle as one continuum. Obeah culture and Black Caribbean life, especially its ecological questioning of a distinct human ontology, merges with the death-dealing Sargasso Sea. The pool at Coulibri appears in her dream to which Tia, her Black childhood companion, urges Antoinette to plunge, an action that echoes the drowning suicides on board slave ships. Akin to history of the Sargasso Sea, disaster proliferates, the marriage is one more wreck in the tangled weeds of the Sargasso Sea, but through this disaster, a creolized relation to the world is glimpsed even as Antoinette plunges to her death. The vision of her watery death imaginatively allows Antoinette to reclaim her place in the Caribbean archipelago by reenacting the haunting presence—death in life and life in death—of the Middle Passage.

This dramatic ending, however, isn't quite final. Recall that when Antoinette narrates her experience in England that includes the dream of fire and suicide, she frames it as follows:

> When night comes, and [Grace Poole, her caretaker] has had several drinks and sleeps, it is easy to take the keys.... Then I open the door and walk into their world. It is, as I always knew, made of cardboard. I have seen it before somewhere, this cardboard world where everything is coloured brown or dark red or yellow that has no light in it. As I walk along the passages I wish I could see what is behind the cardboard. They tell me I am in England but I don't believe them.[128]

This cardboard world is the book as fetish. It references the strange, animating powers of literary technology.[129] In Part 3 of the novel, Antoinette enters into the intertextual world of *Jane Eyre* and revives it, but only to a certain extent. The book as fetish curtails reality; it renders the imagined world of Northern England in the mid-nineteenth century as hallucinatory and alien to Antoinette as the Caribbean had been unreal, hidden, and menacing for Rochester. Antoinette's emphasis on the book's materiality—its wood pulp—suggests, as in Afro-Caribbean fetishes, an intra-active relation of substances and human communities. In contrast to the vivid, life-giving nature of the obeah fetish earlier, Antoinette's investment in the European book as fetish is so overpowering that she loses her color and substance in the cardboard world. She's rendered spectral as she haunts the British canon. Both types of fetishes mediate the relation between inside and outside, and the subject and their surroundings. In the Thornfield Hall scene above, author, character, and readers share an intimate bond—a felt world—through the book's mediating force. But by making visible the outlines of the fetish—Antoinette's self-awareness that she inhabits the fiction of someone else's story and the reader's awareness that they are occupying the fictional worlds of *Wide Sargasso Sea* and *Jane Eyre* simultaneously—the boundaries of inside and outside start to crumble.[130] Antoinette's vision of her ending refers the reader to the conclusion of *Jane Eyre*. *Wide Sargasso Sea*, in effect, doesn't end definitively. It just trails off as literary form dissolves into the watery darkness of dreams.

Anna in *Voyage in the Dark* also instructs readers to become aware of the book as fetish. She describes her experience of reading Émile Zola's *Nana*: "The print was very small, and the endless procession of words gave me a curious feeling—sad, excited, and frightened. *It wasn't what I was reading, it was the look of the dark, blurred words going on endlessly that gave me that feeling.*"[131] The text trains us to follow Anna's cue. The materiality of words on the page, their image and their unbounded, "endless procession," gives both her and the reader a series of mixed feelings: sad, excited, and frightened. The words are dark and blurred, the print is very small, as if viewing the page through an unclear medium: underwater or in a dream. Anna reads not for content but for materiality: the look and feel of the page. The text provides her with an effect, not a meaning.[132] This "epistemic murk" of reading as feeling from outside a given interpretive framework presents ecological and social disorderliness as a means of "tripping up power."[133] This subversion is occasioned by the undoing of literary form: framing devices dissolve; meaning is affective, not discursive; opacity reigns. What is revealed is precisely the racial and gendered substrate, the ongoing structure of colonization and slavery, that is disavowed in order to produce European aesthetic form. In *Wide Sargasso Sea,* Antoinette's dream not only reveals the racial and gendered infrastructure of imperial fictions, but it also opens to a poetics of relation that Caribbean anti-colonialism made a lived reality by the 1960s. In so doing, Rhys's last novel transforms the Victorian novel through a creolizing synthesis in which the book and obeah fetish meet in the opacity of surreal vision. Together, they stage a crisis of intercultural representation, an archipelagic chaos, that challenges European ways of knowing.[134] In the final scene, Rhys exposes the fetish of colonial romance by dissolving it into a scene of Black collectivity and Antoinette's death.

BLACK REWRITINGS OF RHYS

In chapter 1, I considered the problem of how slavery and the transatlantic passage rendered Black maternity monstrous. This last section asks, as did chapter 2 when discussing Claude McKay's *Romance in Marseille*, how can the destruction of Black female bodies be rewritten in and through their monstrosity and formlessness rather than be denied? How would this aesthetic alter the liberal subject still in place in modernist cosmopolitan texts? I explore Black revisions of Rhys's *Voyage in the Dark* and *Wide Sargasso Sea*, especially Anna's monstrous pregnancy and abortion.[135]

Marlon James's novel *The Book of Night Women* (2009) takes place in the first decade of the nineteenth century in Jamaica. The novel rewrites aspects of Rhys's protagonists Anna Morgan and Antoinette Cosway through the character Isobel. It also interrogates the power dynamics and limited perspectives between whites and Blacks in the war zone of plantation culture. Isobel is the daughter of the French Creole Roget family who own and run the Coulibre [sic] plantation. James tells the tale of a women-led slave revolt in contemporary Kingston dialect, a stylistic choice that narrates the past event of a slave rebellion as continuous with ongoing postcolonial violence and misogyny in present-day Jamaica. Verb tenses are uniformly in the continuous present. The reader first meets Isobel as a child when she and her mother visit at the neighboring Montpelier plantation. There, Isobel plays with Rhys's character Francine who, in this novel, is recast as the protagonist Lilith:

> The white girl call her lank chicken and Lilith call her rank goat and they scream and laugh, and the girl take Lilith hand and neither think it uncanny. Then one day the girl come to the plantation dress up in bonnet like her mama and bawl out, Mama pray tell why is that nigger addressing me? Lilith get a slap for that from a thin house niggerwoman who smell of mint and lemongrass. Lilith don't go near the great house after that and the white girl stop coming to Montpelier altogether.[136]

In this scene, James echoes Edward Kamau Brathwaite's early assessment of *Wide Sargasso Sea* where he argues that a friendship between a white and Black child was impossible under slavery.[137] It is Isobel/Antoinette who reinforces the color line as she matures and adopts her mother's behavior, rather than Francine/Lilith who betrays Antoinette in *Wide Sargasso Sea*. Further, in James's novel, it is the older Lilith, rather than a group of Black people in revolt against the possible return of slavery, who single-handedly burns down Coulibre [sic], killing the entire Roget family except for Isobel.

More far-reaching than factual correctives from the historical record of slavery, James represents plantation life as a perpetual war that continues the excessive, ongoing, capricious atrocities begun on board the slave ship. He renders the metaphorical and real fungibility of Black flesh through Lilith's perspective: "She watch the [punishment of a captured fugitive] woman turn into nigger, then animal, then dirt, then nothing. Crow food."[138] Lilith's story is an elemental struggle of life in and against death, beginning with her monstrous birth. She is the offspring of the overseer's rape of a thirteen-year-old girl whose brother had nearly killed him in a nearby swamp. Her birth coincides with the novel's beginning and immediately eviscerates the possibility that an enslaved person could be a self-determined subject. In the brutal Caribbean plantation world, flesh partakes in elemental struggles of birth and death that are so ubiquitous that blood fails to signify. It blends in with "white or blue or black or nothing."[139] The interior of Black bodies turn inside out, porous and coterminous with the plantation setting:

> People think blood red, but blood don't got no colour. Not when blood wash the floor she lying on as she scream for that son of a bitch to come, the lone baby of 1785. Not when the baby wash in crimson and squealing like it just depart heaven to come to hell, another place of red. Not when the midwife know that the mother shed too much blood, and she who don't reach fourteen birthday yet speak curse 'pon the child and the papa, and then she drop down dead like old horse. Not when blood spurt from the skin, or spring from the axe, the cat-o'-nine, the whip, the cane, and the blackjack and every day in slave life is a day that colour red.[140]

Lilith's entrance into plantation hell is a place of chaotic generation where the intersubjectivity of mother and child becomes monstrous. Lilith's life is overwritten by a maternal curse and death. The pain of childbirth is indistinguishable from the ongoing brutality of sexualized violence.

Against this backdrop of physical and existential horror, Isobel deploys her white Creole knowledge of Black practices to expose the use of obeah on the Montpelier estate, rather than, in Rhys's white fantasy, to align with Blackness through obeah. On hearing of the demise of an enslaved woman who succumbed to symptoms similar to dysentery, Isobel identifies the cause as obeah. The master of Montpelier, an Englishman named Humphrey Wilson, swears, "Confound it that the age of reason should visit everywhere but the goddamn colonies. . . . Are there no ministers here, no priests? How in an age of Christ could so many be swayed by this . . . this darkness?"[141] Isobel replies, "It flows in them like blood. . . . I daresay it comes as natural to them as our lord and saviour is to us. I find the whole thing ungodly, but a wise master would do well to understand their ways. Even use them."[142] Both Humphrey and Isobel naturalize the division of European reason and Christian faith, on the one hand, and the darkness and evilness that "flows" from Black blood, a quality, Isobel assures Humphrey, that they took with them "from the dark continent, you know."[143] Her advice is to appropriate obeah practices and "Make your own Obeah seem greater."[144] Isobel's "intimate knowledge of [the slaves] every move" as a native informant paradoxically ungrounds her own adherence to white principles.[145] She becomes, as James says of Rhys and her heroines, a victim of fate, a white Creole who belongs nowhere. Expressing her outcast status, Isobel travels alone at night to Kingston opium dens after her family's death. And when she eventually seduces Humphrey, she initiates her downfall as an unmarried woman. Rather than assume responsibility for her own actions, she occupies a victim role when he refuses to marry her. Finally, Isobel's racial blindness is everywhere evident, despite her boasts to the contrary. She talks endlessly about herself to Lilith (who, once grown, becomes her personal maid), without recognizing the sexual and other violence to which Lilith is continually exposed. James makes clear that Isobel's power plays are conditioned by her white privilege and upon a mistaken and appropriative belief in her knowledge of Afro-diasporic culture.

Jamaica Kincaid's novel *The Autobiography of My Mother* (1996) does not dwell on plantation violence and fungible bodies. Instead, it lingers on the aftermath of slavery and Indigenous genocide in late twentieth-century Dominica. Kincaid's choice to set her novel on Rhys's natal island of Dominica alerts the reader that she, like James, is signifying on Rhys's *Voyage in the Dark* and *Wide Sargasso Sea*. She, too, opens her novel with the loss of a mother as she gives birth. The female protagonist, Xuela Claudette Richardson, describes the vexed nature of her being, born on the occasion of her Carib mother's death and abandoned by her Black and Scottish father:

> My mother died at the moment I was born, and so for my whole life there was nothing standing between myself and eternity; at my back was always a bleak, black wind. I could not have known at the beginning of my life that this would be so; I only came to know this in the middle of my life. . . . And this realization of loss and gain made me look backward and forward: at my beginning was this woman whose face I had never seen, but at my end was nothing, no one between me and the black room of the world. I came to feel that for my whole life I had been standing on a precipice, that my loss had made me vulnerable, hard, and helpless; on knowing this I became overwhelmed with sadness and shame and pity for myself.[146]

Xuela describes her existence as akin to nothingness, an external orientation that describes Blackness. It is the loss of maternity, kinship, and genealogy. "The black room of the world" suggests Xuela's vulnerability to the confinement in Blackness, a sense of being cast out of community and entirely subjected to the will of the master. Being Black and gendered feminine is to be a body of extraction for the pleasure of the master and to be devoid of self-determination. For Xuela, being Black is an existential state of being that occurs through removal from historical continuity, being thrown instead into the bleak sea and wind, and hence to be nowhere at all. The proximity to death—her sense of always standing on a precipice follows this hollowing out of being. But rather than rest in a Rhysian self-immolating stance of sadness, shame, and self-pity, Xuela resists her fate. Although she echoes Rhys's heroines' expression of duration, looking both forward and backward at once, with all dimensions inhabiting the present, she jams the colonial machinery of signification and thereby opens a space for Black futural imaginings.

Xuela disrupts colonial scripts of Blackness and Indigeneity by producing Black feminine difference in a manner that will not become useful, appropriable, or known to the colonizer, although at great cost to herself. She summarizes her life: "This account is an account of the person who was never allowed to be and an account of the person I did not allow myself to become."[147] This chiasmus of being is both similar to Rhys's heroines' predicaments and an important corrective to them. Rhys's Anna Morgan and Antoinette Cosway must become who they're fated to be: the scorned mistress and the doomed heiress. And their fantasies of belonging to an Afro-Caribbean community are fleeting and rejected in advance as impossible. Kincaid writes against Rhys's blindness to the realities of slavery and colonial conquest, tracing a Black and Indigenous archive written onto the land, the water, and Xuela's body. For instance, Xuela eventually goes to live with her father in Massacre, the small town near to which Antoinette and Rochester have their honeymoon. In *Wide Sargasso Sea,* when Rochester asks Antoinette the meaning of the name, she replies, "Something must have happened a long time ago. Nobody remembers now."[148] In contrast, Xuela tells readers, "It was at Massacre that Indian Warner, the illegitimate son of a Carib woman and a European man, was murdered by his half-brother, an Englishman named Philip Warner, because Philip Warner did not like having such a close relative whose mother was a Carib woman."[149] This event, unspoken by Rhys's protagonist, nevertheless casts a long historical shadow on the racial tragedy that unfolds in the novel. It is Antoinette's illegitimate kinship ties to African-descended peoples on the island that proves the undoing of her marriage and life. Kincaid's explicit description of the event has the effect of writing Caribs back into the historical record, but only as a fragile community facing certain extinction. They were, as Xuela says elsewhere, "defeated and then exterminated, thrown away like the weeds in a garden."[150] While the Caribs metaphorically and historically belong to the land, the Africans and their descendants are associated with water and, in Kincaid's novel, are a much stronger force of resistance.[151]

Kincaid comments directly on the presence of Middle Passage history among the African-descended people in Dominica. The enticement of the water, as a zone of fugitivity, freedom and promise, continues. Xuela recounts that when walking to school one day with a group of children:

> We saw a woman in the part of the river where the mouth met the sea. It was deep there and we could not tell if she was sitting or standing, but we knew she was naked. She was a beautiful woman, more beautiful than any woman we had ever seen, beautiful in a way that made sense to us, not a European way: she was dark brown in skin, her hair was black and shiny and twisted into small coils all around her head. Her face was like a moon, a soft, brown, glistening moon. She opened her mouth and a strange yet sweet sound came out. She was surrounded by fruit... and

they were all ripe, and those shades of red, pink, and yellow were tantalizing and mouth-watering. She beckoned to us to come to her."[152]

While all the children are tempted, only one boy heeds her call. He wears "the male mask of heedlessness and boastfulness" as he swims toward her. Soon after, he begins to sink from exhaustion. "And then the woman with her fruit vanished, too, as if she had never been there, as if the whole thing never happened."[153] But the boy, Xuela claims, although he was never seen again, wasn't dead. The unstated inference was that perhaps he lives underwater with the siren because his body was never found.[154] The children start to believe that they had imagined the entire scene, like "an act of faith, like the Virgin Birth for some people, or other such miracles."[155] The loss occurs without physical evidence and therefore gathers around it the shroud of faith and the status of myth: "That woman was not a woman; she was a something that took the shape of a woman. It was almost as if the reality of this terror was so overwhelming that it became a myth, as if it had happened a very long time ago and to other people, not us."[156] The myth may express the unmarked experience of death during the forced transportation across the Atlantic, even though the occurrence is narrated in Xuela's childhood present, marking duration. The colonial archive delegitimates the lived effects of the vanished past as unrealistic and without evidence. It is labeled a false myth occasioned by so-called primitive belief. As a result, the rest of the children began to doubt what they had seen. The protagonist remarks:

> Everything about us is held in doubt and we the defeated define all that is unreal, all that is not human, all that is without love, all that is without mercy. Our experience cannot be interpreted by us; we do not know the truth of it. Our God was not the correct one, our understanding of heaven and hell was not a respectable one. Belief in that apparition of a naked woman with outstretched arms beckoning a small boy to his death was the belief of the illegitimate, the poor, the low. I believed in that apparition then and I believe in it now.[157]

The racialized poor are alienated from their own experience and their own myths, in contrast to Christian myths that are granted legitimacy. Black myths define the hallucinatory, irrational, and superstitious. But

Xuela resists foreclosing from a people their own truth. She consciously wills a belief in the reality of water as freedom and life. Rather than figuring death and forgetfulness, the water offers beauty and a feminine sensuality of fluidity and abundance, a permeable interface comprised of bodies, gestation, and environment co-constituting one another. Elsewhere, Xuela imagines she can sense an Atlantis about to rise from the sea floor: "I could see the reflection of the sun's light on the surface of the seawater, and it always had the quality of an expectation just about to be fulfilled, as if at any moment a small city made out of that special light of the sun on the water would arise, and from it might flow a joy I had not yet imagined."[158] In this utopian underwater space lies freedom, the possibility of which occasions joy, heretofore unimaginable to the protagonist.

These moments of anticipating Black freedom are seldom, but they rewrite Rhys fundamentally in refusing her heroines' tragedy and self-destruction in favor of Black possibility and self-reinvention. In a fundamental instance, Kincaid rejects Anna Morgan's masochistic suffering in her botched abortion by acting out in extreme, provocative ways the monstrous nature of Black maternity. Xuela, too, suffers a brutal abortion procedure, but she survives and declares, "I had carried my own life in my own hands."[159] Like Anna, she refuses to serve as an instrument of reproduction for men. This will to repudiate her predetermined role as mother of unwanted children does not stop at her own silence and suffering, as Anna's does. Instead, Xuela externalizes the monstrosity of Black women's maternal role in society. This extraordinary passage is worth quoting in full:

> My life was beyond empty. I had never had a mother, I had just recently refused to become one, and I knew then that this refusal would be complete.... I would bear children, but I would never be a mother to them. I would bear them in abundance; they would emerge from my head, from my armpits, from between my legs; I would bear children, they would hang from me like fruit from a vine, but I would destroy them with the carelessness of a god. I would bear children in the morning, I would bathe them at noon in a water that came from myself, and I would eat them at night, swallowing them whole, all at once. They would live and they would not live, I would walk them to the edge of a precipice. I

would not push them over; I would not have to; the sweet voices of unusual pleasures would call to them from its bottom; they would not rest until they became one with these sounds. I would cover their bodies with diseases, embellish skins with thinly crusted sores, the sores sometimes oozing a thick pus for which they would thirst, a thirst that would never be quenched. I would condemn them to live in an empty space frozen in the same posture in which they had been born. I would throw them from a great height; every bone in their body would be broken and the bones would never properly be set, healing in the way they were broken, healing never at all. I would decorate them when they were only corpses and set each corpse in a polished wooden box, and place the polished wooden box in the earth and forget the part of the earth where I buried the box.[160]

Xuela refuses the modes of relating that were established through slavery and the Middle Passage.[161] Rather than disavow the monstrous role of Black women's maternity, she resignifies it in a manner that unsettles the foundation of Black fungibility upon which rests Man's overrepresentation as human. The metaphoricity of the pure exchangeability of Black bodies becomes the very means by which to reinvent the human in open and porous relationality with others, including the nonhuman. Zakiyyah Imam Jackson phrases this unsetting of the human through the Black women's maternity as "the latent symbolic-material capacities of black *mater*, as mater, as matter, to destabilize or even rupture the reigning order of representation that grounds the thought-world relation."[162] In the passage above, the maternal body refuses to remain abject. Instead, she speaks back and thereby disrupts the categories that produce Western forms of knowing and being: Man as a speaking subject who defines himself against the chaos of nature, including Black maternal reproduction. Xuela's monstrous maternity vitiates the boundary between life and death, interiority and exteriority, and human and nonhuman. She underscores the somatic plasticity demanded of Black people, especially of women, to serve as the ground for the sexualized violence of pornotroping.[163] But rather than accept that role, Xuela reinvents the fungibility of Black women as her body's own agentic capacity of monstrous, toxic maternity. Her body has multiple orifices for generation. The children are alive, dead, diseased, and mutilated. Blackness turns in on itself. She eats her children; her children drink emanations of their own disease. Their skin is porous; their bodies are broken, disjointed, and deformed. Their corpses are consigned to the earth but instantly forgotten. This passage repudiates formal coherence and instead spawns a surplus of meaning induced by Black fungibility. In so doing, Xuela's resistant maternity interrupts the colonizer's categories that had previously disempowered Black women and posits instead the intimacy of life and death, reproduction and decay. Western structures of thought disavow Black women's embodied agency in order to control and contain the proliferating, generative chaos of bodies and nature. By placing life and death on a continuum of open-ended amphibious meaning, Kincaid's as well as Rhys's novels decolonize capitalist land and labor use that extracts value while rendering the remainder waste.

The next chapter, "Delta," returns to the circumscribed agency of enslaved persons that results, at times, in a turn toward death. In chapter 1, I discussed how the extreme circumstances of the Middle Passage induced some captives to prefer suicide, with its brief triumph before death and a return to the ancestors, over their ongoing bondage in chattel slavery. In chapter 5, I consider the turn toward death in the context of extractive industries in the Mississippi and Niger Deltas. I trace the long history of resource withdrawal from the colonies: first gold, then people conscripted to work in the mines and on plantations, the export agriculture itself, and finally, oil. In these modes of production, the division of labor mirrors the colonizer's dividing line between life and nonlife, with enslaved and colonized people falling into the latter category of the inert. Then, I follow how William Faulkner in the 1930s and 1940s and Amos Tutuola in the 1950s trouble these categories by envisioning Black characters whose turn toward death paradoxically asserts agency amid the inhuman matter of the delta: the fluvial, decaying mixture of water, soil, and plant and animal life. Life and death, in these instances, are cyclical and continuous. Here, the resistant turn toward death upends the colonizer's and settler's certainties regarding Blackness as well as resource extraction.

5

DELTA

William Faulkner and Amos Tutuola

And this country shouted for centuries that we are brute beasts; that the pulsing of humanity stops at the entrance of the slave-compound; that we are walking manure a hideous forerunner of tender cane and silky cotton.

—AIMÉ CÉSAIRE, *NOTEBOOK OF A RETURN TO MY NATIVE LAND*

The geographical term "delta" derives from the uppercase Greek letter D and first denoted the triangle-shaped tracts of land that emerge from accumulating silt and shifting, multitudinous channels and wetlands formed by the Nile River's cycle of flooding. As with the term "archipelago" examined in chapter 4, explorers named similar formations they encountered around the world "delta" although the land and water interactions may be quite different from the Nile's. Despite its various manifestations around the world, "delta" consistently names an ecological edge zone, a fertile and dynamic combination of silt, marsh land, and water that, to varying extents, produces a rich diversity of flora and fauna. And its rich, alluvial soil is the basis of exceptional harvests. As its Greek symbol suggests, it is predicated on change: seasonal flooding, shifting land masses, and erosion that constantly alter delta plains and water pathways. During the era of Western exploration, the lure of extracting "natural resources" from these fertile regions, first in Africa and then in the "new" world, drew explorers and, later, colonizers and settlers to these far-flung regions. The explorers first sought gold and silver, then rich deposits of nitrogen, phosphorous, and other minerals in delta soils through export agriculture, and more recently, oil. In the early to mid-twentieth century, geologists discovered that buried beneath many deltas are fossil fuels: the remains of marine animals and plants that millions of years ago became covered by layers of sand, silt, and rock. The heat and pressure of these layers compacted these remains into oil.[1] Sharad Chari says, "Oil is literally rot. As biomass decomposing over millions of years, oil is the rot of ages, and yet it has become the fuel we cannot live without. This dialectic of protracted ruination and fatal promise crystallizes the ethos of our times."[2] We see an instance of this dialectic when, in the 1930s and 1940s, the petroleum industry promised that oil would liberate capitalist ventures from the problems associated with other resource extraction projects: soil depletion and flooding in delta agriculture and an organized working class that demanded better pay and working conditions. At the dawn of the oil age, as Stephanie LeMenager puts it, "Oil literally was conceived as a replacement for slave labor."[3]

That race and geological extraction in the deltas were thought together should come as no surprise. Geological science, Kathryn Yusoff claims, rather than being an objective study of the earth's physical structure and transformation, went hand-in-hand with colonization to function as "a racialized optic razed on the earth."[4] She reminds us that colonizers first purchased and forcibly transported African bondspeople to the Americas to work the gold and silver mines in South America because the Indigenous population had been decimated through violence and disease by upward of 90 percent. The Africans were selected because they could be transmuted into property via the slave trade already existing in Africa and because the colonizers believed Africans to embody valuable properties that could be extracted to build an empire in the Americas, including the propensity for hard work, the need for "civilizing" direction, and resistance to tropical diseases. The agentic European Man holds property—the captive Africans who become subjugated objects of exchange—and extracts their life force to achieve maximum surplus value. Yusoff argues, "Racialization belongs to a material categorization of the division of matter (corporeal and mineralogical) into active and inert. Extractable matter must be both passive (awaiting extraction and possessing valuable properties) and able to be activated through the mastery of white men."[5] The colonizer's association of Blackness with inert materiality ensures that their lives are precariously proximate to the razed earth, with its instabilities and poisoning that are a by-product of colonial land use. Once extraction takes place, the waste products—polluted earth, exhausted and mutilated bodies—occupy the same zone, a rift in the land, defined by Yusoff as "a temporal scene and a material experience of shattered grounds."[6] As such, Blackness is, Yusoff says, "a historically constituted and intentionally enacted deformation in the formation of subjectivity, a deformation that presses an inhuman categorization and an inhuman earth into intimacy."[7] Importantly, the bondspersons refashioned this intimacy with the earth, Yusoff continues, "for survival and formed [this intimacy] into a praxis for remaking other selves that were built in the harshest of conditions."[8] This praxis, as we'll see, involves Black subjects' reinvention of relationality with the land in resistance to the colonizer's coercion of their labor to rob the earth of its resources.

Yusoff underscores an aspect of colonization that involves geopolitics, rather than the oft-trod discourse of biopolitics. The category of the inhuman central to geology directs us toward ecologies of harm and the need for the restoration of intimate ties between humans, land, and water. In this chapter, Afro-diasporic reconnection to fluvial planes, that I show in Faulkner, is a form of rerooting in the Americas and, for Tutuola, a warning to West Africans to stay connected to the land and to acknowledge colonial traumas, including the slave trade, in the midst of West African modernization on the eve of Nigeria's national independence. In the Americas, displaced bondspersons' reattachment to land functioned to re-Indigenize, or transplant, their cultures, as Sylvia Wynter argues, a transformation that does not claim the position of the already existing Indigenous in the "new" world, but rather reinvents Black relationality to the land, often in dialogue with Amerindian practices and beliefs.[9] Next, this rerooting in the delta provides agency to bondspeople through the turn toward death, a willingness to die for freedom when confronting the slave regime, as I detail below. Finally, in reading Faulkner in the 1930s and 1940s and Tutuola in the 1950s, I explore how each author rewrites the geological grammar of extraction. They track how the category of Blackness as inhuman slides—i.e., fails to remain fixed and inert—to reveal Black agency that reorders and rehumanizes relations between themselves and the earth. This altered grammar also fashions a particular narrative form. I argue that both writers challenge extraction processes on the deltas by crafting narratives of ruination. Rather than a linear plotting of obstacles overcome, Faulkner and Tutuola sediment their stories, layering one situation on top of the other, to express both continuity and rupture. Narratives of ruination excavate the accumulated toll of extractive economies as well as locate ruptures in that gravitational accretion where the colonized and enslaved people fought back, often by means of a turn toward death. In the sections to come, I show how Faulkner provides a deep history of the land whereas Tutuola presents the continuous now of colonial resource extraction, including oil. For both writers, the force of gravity, pressing down on layers of colonized subjugation, expresses the overwhelming power of colonization. Yet, in digging down through layers, they expose corpses hidden below (Faulkner's plantation secrets) as well as moments of victorious resistance (Tutuola). Their work also suggests that the polluted, low-lying areas consigned to Africans, Afro-diasporic peoples, and American Indigenous peoples, are never fully tamed. A rupture from colonial continuity occurs in these rifts, especially, for my book's purposes, in the subterranean and submarine Black zones of resistance. In effect, Faulkner's and Tutuola's novels express a dialectic of ruination and the fatal promise of colonial wealth, decades before the oil industry had fully taken over the Mississippi and Niger deltas.

Pairing these two writers defies expected groupings based on shared location and race. However, when organized around deltas, they speak to each other through ecological and decolonizing commonalities and important differences. Specifically, my comparison of Tutuola and Faulkner is motivated by the following: 1) I seek to avoid furthering US exceptionalism that functions to marginalize and even erase Africa from considerations of modernity/coloniality. This erasure has been the case as well in Black Atlantic studies. I discussed in chapter 1 how Paul Gilroy's work often fails to consider Africa when discussing the European slave trade and I work to rectify that absence; 2) My critical lens in each chapter concerns a specific metaphoric and material geography. By focusing on the agentic capacities of land and water, new commonalities arise. In this case, deltas tell of extraction, dispossession, and Black rifts in the earth; and 3) I seek to understand the planetary process of racialization. Although racial categories operate very differently in the United States and Nigeria—the former being a settler colony; the latter, a zone of imperial resource extraction—extractive industries in both locations render Blackness an inhuman category that legitimates mining, drilling, and industrial agriculture. I ask: How can attention to Black rifts in the earth rewrite geological relations and chart a planetary post-petrofuture different from ongoing resource extraction? The climate emergency is shaped by settler colonial and imperial practices. Hence, understanding differential power relations and circulations is vital to combating the ongoing catastrophe. One last methodological note: in this final chapter, the geographic formation of deltas, as I use it, assembles the hydro-critical terms organizing the previous chapters. Deltas—in particular, the Mississippi and Niger Deltas—shape the alluvia that, as chapter 2 argues, carries the felt traumas of slavery and the Middle Passage. Deltas' dynamic qualities are slower and more cyclical than the rhythm of waves but still invite an intra-active understanding of bodies in relation to their nonhuman surroundings, as explored in chapter 3. Last, deltas function on a smaller scale than archipelagos, but their chaotic, shifting, and flooding geographies contest the colonial fixity of space and reveal Black social and ecological relations that challenge the racialized land use practices of settler colonial and imperialist regimes.

Because this chapter broadens the geographical purview of transatlantic slavery to West Africa and the south-central United States, I detour in significant ways from Glissant's Caribbean. As discussed in chapters 2 and 4, Glissant theorizes a poetics of relation that depends upon Afro-diasporicpeoples' transgenerational trauma that he calls the slave abyss. In West Africa, unlike the Caribbean, the atrocities of the transatlantic slave trade emanate from the interior of the continent and flow outward toward the Atlantic. Hence, alluvium is less about the Middle Passage than about the kidnapping, forced marches, and terror in West Africa that led up to the embarkation of captives on the transatlantic slave ships. In the United States, the Mississippi Delta was a switch point in the transatlantic slave trade. Its hub, New Orleans, received enslaved African and Caribbean persons from abroad as well as bondspeople from the North American interior who were transported down the Mississippi River, usually to work the delta's cotton fields. Unlike archipelagos discussed in chapter 4, the Mississippi and Niger deltas are bottomlands that are today among the most environmentally polluted regions in the world, largely due to the petroleum industry.[10] This environmental devastation, however acute today, has a long history in both regions. In the Mississippi Delta, slavery and Jim Crow violence resulted in disease, malnutrition, and environmental destruction (logging, draining wetlands, building railways, industrial agriculture, etc.) that wreaked havoc on its Black population. In the Niger Delta, colonial and neocolonial extractive industries (first gold and ivory, followed by the slave trade, then palm oil, and now petroleum) adopted a scorched-earth policy with no regard for the land or its peoples. Mbembe terms this policy *necropolitics*, a state of perpetual war in which a sovereign power dictates who may live and who must die. In Africa, necropolitics initially took the form of colonial conquest. Mbembe writes, "That colonies might be ruled over in absolute lawlessness stems from the racial denial of any common bond between the conqueror and the native. In the eyes of the conqueror, *savage life* is just another form of *animal life,* a horrifying experience, something alien beyond imagination or comprehension."[11] Their alterity was such that, as Hannah Arendt remarks, "when European men massacred them they somehow were not aware they had committed murder."[12] The Indigenous, the colonizers believed, behaved like part of nature so that clearing the bush—asserting sovereignty over the territory—necessitated killing its inhabitants with impunity in order to control it. Mbembe continues, "*Colonial occupation* itself was a matter of seizing, delimiting, and asserting control over a physical geographic area—of writing on the ground a new set of social and spatial relations. The writing of new spatial relations (territorialization) was, ultimately, tantamount to the production of boundaries and hierarchies, zones and enclaves."[13] This rewriting of space includes "the new geography of resource extraction" that considers expendable Indigenous communities and the biospheres in which they live.[14] By contrast, deltas routinely overwrite territorial boundaries by means of the flux of land and water. Both Faulkner and Tutuola foreground colonizing hubris over the deltas and enslaved and colonized people through their narratives of ruination. The violent, corrupt, and toxic afterlife of slavery and colonization is plain to see in both regions.

This chapter first investigates Faulkner's conflation of Afro-diasporic bondspersons with the land as dependent, unimaginative appendages of the plantation. I read *Absalom, Absalom!* (1936) as well as his screenplay

The Last Slaver (1936) in this manner. Then, I extend the argument by leading Faulkner scholar Jay Watson that Faulkner, especially by 1940 when *Go Down, Moses* was published, did imagine Black resistance by means of the turn toward death. I discuss resistant aspects of *Absalom*, the short story "Red Leaves," and *Go Down, Moses* through this lens while connecting the turn toward death with the geology of racialized extraction and Black rewritings of that geological grammar. This chapter then discusses Tutuola's reassessment of the slave trade. I argue that his first two novels, *The Palm-Wine Drinkard* and *My Life in the Bush of Ghosts* (1952, 1954), offer a narrative of ruination that begins with the long history of the slave trade and other forms of resource extraction. *The Palm-Wine Drinkard* opens in a palm plantation and follows the protagonist, the son of the plantation owner, into the land of the "deads" to retrieve his tapster who has fallen to his death while tapping palm wine. *My Life in the Bush of Ghosts* begins with a slave raid and the main character, a young boy, hides in the evil forest to escape the raiders. While it is well-known that Tutuola relied on Yoruba oral folktales from his youth as well as D. O. Fagunwa's folkloric novel *Forest of Thousand Daemons* (1949), written in Yoruba, he does not simply translate these stories into his novels. Instead, he inventories both literary and oral techniques for usable tools, including frame narratives, episodic tales, and commentary on modern technologies. Here, my reading of Tutuola is vastly different from the naïve Yoruba folklorist that the British literary elite made him out to be when he was first published by Faber and Faber.[15]

THE MISSISSIPPI DELTA

Faulkner's apocryphal Yoknapatawpha County is loosely based on Lafayette County, Mississippi, where he lived, but the actual county does not overlap with the Mississippi Delta. Faulkner signaled the delta's importance to the history of the region by adding it to his mythic territory. He derived the county's name from the Chickasaw compound word "yocona" and "petopha" meaning "split land" or "water flows slow through flat land."[16] The name thus emphasizes the flood-prone, swampy region. Philip Gordon writes, "[Faulkner] placed deep in its [Yoknapatawpha's] history an image of the Delta, moving, shifting, always on the edge of man's teetering existence, but always ever-so-slightly perilous and uncontrollable, beyond man's ability to tame it into submission even as he clears a patch of land within it to live on and try to make something for himself bigger than what he started with."[17] Critics who attend to Faulkner's geography, however, have not considered how this wetland is racialized and how Faulkner connects the delta's sedimented history of resistance to settler colonial extractive practices.[18] I consider the glittering promise of wealth through resource extraction in the delta that spurred settler colonial expansion and increased demand for bondspeople via the transatlantic slave trade.[19] In his geographic imagination, the delta is the locus of Black insurgent geographies: swamp, creek, wilderness.

Faulkner engaged overtly with the Middle Passage in only two written works: the first is the short story "Red Leaves," published in 1930 in the *Saturday Evening Post*; the second is a screenplay that he cowrote in Hollywood in 1936 called *The Last Slaver* that was adapted from George S. King's novel by the same name, published in 1933. Twentieth-Century Fox released the film, now titled *Slave Ship,* in 1937. King's novel describes the slave ship hold, Congo coastal forts, irons, captives, and their illegal sale in morally outraged terms. For instance, "The newly fettered slaves were forced into the black hold, some never to see the light of day again; others, less fortunate, to be brought out again, after a terrible voyage of suffering, to a life of toil and torture beyond description."[20] The novel includes a diagram of the hold, an unattributed replica of the slave trade abolitionist drawing of the HMS *Brookes*. The plot centers around the protagonist Kane, a Yankee sailor who was tricked into signing on to *The Wanderer*, and who learns to his horror that he is part of the illegal slave trade. With the help of the loyal African cook, Kalva, who acts as translator to the captives, some Northern European sailors, and the captives themselves, he successfully leads a mutiny to rescue the captives and return them to Africa. In Faulkner's screenplay, the captives are reduced to the background and never seen in armed revolt. Further, the only African to speak is a small boy who delivers a letter to a shipmate and says, "White man gimme this to give you."[21] Faulkner made other sweeping changes, working from a prior version of the screenplay. He eliminated the West Indies (the intended destination of *The Wanderer's* cargo of bondspeople) and had a Yankee captain, renamed Lovett, purchase the ship from someone sailing out of the "Potomac Yacht Club." This geographical switch underscores the role that Washington and the North played in the slave trade and their complicity in the wealth that it generated. Faulkner's targeting of Washington, D.C. statesmen and military brass was later deleted by the film studio producers. Finally, Lovett's new wife, Nancy, who accompanies him on his voyage to Africa, discovers that a bracelet he has gifted her is a replica of one worn by an African woman captive newly arrived on the slave ship. The screenplay provides the following stage directions: "Approaching her are several female slaves. As they draw nearer, Nancy's eyes are caught by the bracelet on a woman's arm. She gasps. It is a duplicate of the one on her own arm. Wresting the bracelet from her arm, she throws it into the sea, and then runs from the deck, unable to bear the sight of any more."[22] Jeff Karem says of the doubling and contamination that exists between a white Northern woman and an abducted African woman, "Much that Nancy has valued—beauty, wealth, her husband—is revealed to be an outgrowth of injustice, of victimhood, and of Africa itself."[23] The commodity in this scene is defetishized and its circulation through the triangle trade revealed in all its horrific violence. As in the novel, the mutiny is successful and the captives are repatriated to West Africa, although Lovett dies in the effort, thereby (the plot wants to say) at least partly redeeming himself for his role in the slave trade.

That Faulkner eliminates scenes of Black revolt, speaking roles for Africans, references to the Caribbean, and expands historical guilt for slavery to the entire nation, including its white women, suggests, as Jeff Karem argues, his fear of creolization.[24] This fear is more deeply explored in the novel Faulkner had just completed when he began work on the screenplay: *Absalom, Absalom!*. The novel presents Faulkner's fullest engagement with Black Atlantic history, especially the Haitian Revolution, even if only tendentiously. In the novel, Haiti is the deeply buried source of racial mixing for the protagonist, Thomas Sutpen. Sutpen's possible involvement in the illegal slave trade, his indispensable, although anachronistic, role in subduing a Black uprising on a Haitian plantation, and his marriage to the plantation owner's daughter provide the wealth he needs to establish himself as a Mississippi plantation owner. It also proves to be his downfall as he belatedly discovers his first wife's mixed-race origins, a contamination that eventually results in murder, incest, and ruin. The novel's gothic plot of downfall metaphorically and literally occurs in the myriad channels and the muddy flats of the Mississippi Delta. While the island republic of Haiti could be quarantined historically and socially, it nonetheless "seeps" into the Southern United States via the port of New Orleans. It is from New Orleans that Sutpen's disavowed mixed-race family, Charles Bon and his mother Eulalia, gradually destroy his plans to establish a Mississippi plantation dynasty. Creolization, like the waters themselves, proliferates and overflows. Commenting on William Faulkner's depiction of the Mississippi River, Glissant writes, "The grand Old Man [the Mississippi River] . . . [is] a channel of life and death leading from the continent's Nordic heart to its Creole delta."[25] This description encapsulates the antagonism between white life and Black death that occurs on the water and in the marshy land formations that guard the river's pathway and exit. White life is figured as central—indeed, the primary motor of continental flows—while the Creole delta is the bottomland, the impure, and death-bound. Glissant imagines creolization as a force isomorphic to the Mississippi's flood-prone delta. He calls it, "the unstoppable conjunction despite misery, oppression, and lynching. The conjunction that unleashes torrents of unpredictable results; (like a tumultuous and boundless Mississippi)."[26] While the "Nordic heart" built great houses, levees, flood walls, and reclaimed land as a means to control the watershed and deepen the class and race divides of the plantation system, creolization joins together peoples, geographies, and imaginaries "with torrents of unpredictable results."[27]

That such unpredictability should be *Absalom's* worst nightmare is an understatement. Instead, the novel presents time as accumulating slowly, sedimenting itself in a never-changing same of cursed fatalism. Here is Quentin Compson's description of historical change made during in his dead-of-night, stream of consciousness confession to Shrevelin McCannon, a fellow student at Harvard University:

Maybe nothing ever happens once and is finished. Maybe happen is never once but like ripples maybe on water after the pebble sinks, the ripples moving on, spreading, the pool attached by a narrow umbilical water-cord to the next pool which the first pool feeds, has fed, did feed, let this second pool contain a different temperature of water, a different molecularity of having seen, felt, remembered, reflect in a different tone the infinite unchanging sky, it didn't matter: that pebble's watery echo whose fall it did not even see moves across the surface too at the original ripple-space, to the old ineradicable rhythm.[28]

History changes tone, temperature, and ambience but still reflects the same "infinite unchanging sky." While in *Absalom* there exists founding events—massacre, war, swindling Indigenous peoples of their land, enslaving others—the slow, structural violence ripples outward, spreading, taking on new tones and forms that echo the old. The analogy of water uncannily recalls the now-time of Middle Passage trauma that lingers in the Atlantic waters, as discussed in chapter 1. But rather than carrying the material trace of transgenerational trauma, what fails to change in *Absalom*'s waters and history is white supremacy. Change, for Quentin, Rosa Coldfield, and Faulkner himself, is seemingly impossible.[29] Miss Rosa, telling her tale to Quentin, puts it thus, "Yes, fatality and curse on the South and on our family as though because some ancestor of ours had elected to establish his descent in a land primed for fatality and already cursed with it, even if it had not been our family, our father's progenitors, who had incurred the curse long years before and had been coerced by Heaven into establishing itself in the land and the time already cursed."[30] Rosa places blame on Heaven and time "already cursed" for inducing white Southerners to acquire land. Further, it is the land itself that enacts vengeance while human culpability and resistance are elided. She prophesizes, "What is it to me that the land or the earth or whatever it was got tired of [Sutpen] at last and turned and destroyed him? . . . It's going to turn and destroy us all someday, whether our name happens to be Sutpen or Coldfield or not?"[31] The land enacts a cumulative geophysical force. Like the alluvial soil of the delta, its deep time supplants the narrow vision and ephemeral presence of humans, akin to what Faulkner's interludes in *The Big Woods* describe: "The wild Algonquian, Chickasaw and Choctaw and Natchez and Pascagoula, . . . had barely time to whirl and look behind him at ten and then a hundred and then a thousand Spaniards come overland from the Atlantic Ocean: a tide, a wash, a thrice flux-and-ebb of motion so rapid and quick across the land's slow alluvial chronical as to resemble the limber flicking of the magician's one hand before the other holding the deck of inconstant cards."[32] As vital and prescient for environmental thought as Faulkner's sedimentary consciousness may be, it disavows white crimes, figured above as a magician's card trick, as well as Black revolt and historicity. As I've argued throughout this book, ecological criticism needs to be supplemented with histories of racial subordination or else it whitewashes ecological thought.

Where time does pass in Quentin's rumination above, it does so via "a narrow umbilical water-cord," a maternal image that suggests Clytemnestra's role in the novel. Clytie, the child of rape between Sutpen and an enslaved woman on his Mississippi plantation, serves as a primary instance of this "old ineradicable rhythm." She bridges the old and new and ensures that little changes. She represents to her white half-siblings, "the threatful portent of the old."[33] This threat is repeated when Confederate soldiers return from war, as Clytie's half-sibling Henry recounts: "Not the same men who had marched away but transformed—and this the worst, the ultimate degradation to which war brings the spirit, the soul—into the likeness of that man who abuses from very despair and pity the beloved wife or mistress who in his absence was raped. We were afraid."[34] Violence begets more violence, this time, in a manner that victimizes white people. *Absalom* buries white culpability in the sedimented soil, transforming racializing sexual violence into white suffering. Meanwhile, Henry, Thomas Sutpen's white, legitimate son, describes Clytie as "perverse, inscrutable and paradox: free, yet incapable of freedom who had never once called herself a slave."[35] In effect, she figures a continuity with Haiti, whose postindependence developments were followed closely by Southern plantation owners. Ryan Heryford writes that Southern whites "distorted and manipulated post-independence Haiti to reaffirm their beliefs regarding distinctions between the races.... Southerners looked to Haiti more than to the Northern states to evaluate what freedom meant to blacks."[36] We'll see below how the novel describes Haiti as mired in the traumas of the past. Similarly, Clytie, although freed, remains on the plantation and represents how the past will not be transcended, least of all by freed bondspeople who, Henry suggests, didn't even register their enslaved condition. Clytie slowly shrinks, becoming grotesque and unthreatening in her aging body. Quentin describes her as a "tiny gnomelike creature.... Not much more than five feet tall and looking like a little bundle of clean rags so that you went and took her arm and helped her up and her arm felt like a stick, as light and dry and brittle as a stick."[37] Recalling Faulkner's favorite book, *The Nigger of 'The Narcissus,'* she resembles James Wait in his desiccated, confined, and unthreatening otherness.[38] Clytie hides the worst secrets of the plantation: unbeknownst to the wider community, she cares for the dying Henry Sutpen, thereby saving him from being convicted of the murder of his half-brother, Charles Bon. Once Henry is discovered, Clytie sets fire to the Great House, an act that kills both herself and Henry and prevents the murder from coming to justice. Her self-abnegating defense of white supremacy culminates in the fiery purification of the Mississippi plantation as it kills the last of the legitimate Sutpens and rids the family of its Creole excess. The lone family survivor, the mentally disabled "Negro," Jim Bond, becomes a fugitive. Clytie's self-immolation returns her to the land, dissolving Black agency into the neutral, impersonal force of the earth. She is one with the delta: impure and death-bound.

That Clytie recapitulates Haiti becomes more palpable as Quentin's midnight ramble at Harvard takes on an increasingly macabre and hallucinatory tone, making his words ambiguously blur the reported speech of his grandfather. Here is part of his free association of Haiti, lengthy but well worth quoting:

> but where high mortality was concomitant with the money and the sheen on the dollars was not from gold but from blood—a spot of earth which might have been created and set aside by Heaven itself, Grandfather said, as a theatre for violence and injustice and bloodshed and all the satanic lusts of human greed and cruelty, for the last despairing fury of all the pariah-interdict and all the doomed—a little island set in a smiling and fury-lurked and incredible indigo sea, which was the halfway point between what we call the jungle and what we call civilization, halfway between the dark inscrutable continent from which the black blood, the black bones and flesh and thinking and remembering and hopes and desires, was ravished by violence and the cold known land to which it was doomed, the civilised land and people which had expelled some of its own blood and thinking and desires that had become too crass to be faced and borne longer, and set it homeless and desperate on the lonely ocean—a little lost island in a latitude which would require ten thousand years of equatorial heritage to bear its climate, a soil manured with black blood from two hundred years of oppression and exploitation until it sprang with an incredible paradox of peaceful greenery

and crimson flowers and sugar cane sapling size and three times the height of a man and a little bulkier of course but valuable pound for pound almost with silver ore, as if nature held a balance and kept a book and offered a recompense for the torn limbs and outraged hearts even if man did not, the planting of nature and man too watered not only by the wasted blood but breathed over by the winds in which the doomed ships had fled in vain, out of which the last tatter of sail had sunk into the blue sea, along which the last vain despairing cry of women or child had blown away;—the planting of men too: the yet intact bones and brains in which the old unsleeping blood that had vanished into the earth they trod still cried out for vengeance.[39]

Quentin's stream of consciousness sediments past and present, in an unchanging, nightmarish same. According to Quentin's memories of his grandfather's thoughts (an alluviation of memory and of present and past voices mingling together), causation slips between white and Black blood, nature and flesh, the Middle Passage and the drowning deaths of white women and children. Heaven itself quarantines Haiti and it is the land, not the Haitian people, who remember and seek to avenge the past. Haiti's isolated geography, according to Quentin and his grandfather, "served as a theatre of violence and injustice and bloodshed and all the satanic lusts of human greed and cruelty." Such cruelty produces cane as valuable as "silver ore," an equation that erases the violent mining of energy from Black bondspeople, the depletion of the soil, and the destruction of the biosphere. The island serves as a staged laboratory of violence, a pariah state, and a forbidden island.[40] The passage reflects not only on the Haitian Revolution and its aftermath but also on the recent occupation of Haiti by US marines (1915–1934) that secured US imperialist hegemony in the Western hemisphere and united North and South for the first time since the Civil War.[41] Quentin, ventriloquizing his grandfather, imagines that when the planters' actions on the island "had become too crass to be faced and borne longer," they evacuated the island "and set it homeless and desperate on a lonely ocean." In a reversal of the Middle Passage, the passage depicts planter-class white women and children fleeing the doomed island in ships that sank, possibly from mutiny or else from an unaccounted-for displacement of Black revolution into the "fury-lurked ... indigo sea." If the former, they become victims of the specter of Black violence and their own colonial excesses. The image of Haiti as drifting "homeless and desperate on the lonely ocean" recalls the conclusion of Joseph Conrad's *The Nigger of the 'Narcissus'* where England, as a "ship of state," provides an anchor of stability in a storm-tossed sea, as discussed in chapter 1. Haiti, unlike anchored England, drifts midway between the "dark continent" and "civilization." In revising the above passage concerning Haiti, as Karem has noted, Faulkner rewrites Black hands and arms into blood and flesh, turning Black political agency into abjection.[42] Black blood "manures" and "waters" the land, as Césaire underscores in the epigraph. Faulkner transmutes Black revolutionary slaughter of the plantation-owning class into nature's revenge. In the final version of *Absalom*, it is the land that remembers past atrocities: "Nature held a balance and kept a book and offered recompense for the torn limbs and outraged hearts even if man did not." Bondspeople merge with the soil as a disposable supplement so that land, rather than organized collectivities, takes its revenge. The novel sees Black people, like Clytie, as part of the delta: creolized, impure, and one with nature. A version of Mbembe's necropolitics animates Faulkner's imagination and racializes his geography.[43]

But is this all that can be said for Clytie's actions and Faulkner's perception of Black subjects? Watson argues that Clytie's arson, rather than protecting the Sutpen family secret, is her long-awaited opportunity to seal the family's doom. He writes, "Perhaps Clytie has been the closeted one all along, a black Jacobin masquerading as a loyal Sutpen, biding her time until the moment is right to negate the plantation design."[44] To build the case for this reading, Watson claims for Clytie the bondspersons' turn toward death. To do so, he draws upon Hegel's "Lord and Bondsman" dialectic. In Hegel, the bondsman submits to the master because he is not willing to risk his own death. The slaveholder gains honor and absolute authority over his bondsperson, and, conversely, he becomes dependent upon the labor and existence of his subordinate. Watson summarizes, "[The bondsman] bows to the superior physical force, the uncompromising will and *worldview* of his adversary, and becomes his slave. In the crucible of deadly struggle, then, what defines the bondsman is his preference for 'his conqueror's version of reality' over his own death."[45] But Hegel's schema of the victorious Western conqueror hardly does justice to the historical actuality of bondspersons' resistance to new world slavery. Marshaling evidence from Hegel's historical milieu, Susan Buck-Morss argues that he deliberately censored the victorious Haitian Revolution from his account of the Lord and Bondsman struggle. She stresses how the Haitian victory did not merely reverse the position of master and bondsperson: "The goal of this liberation out of slavery cannot be subjugation of the master in turn, which would be merely to repeat the master's 'existential' impasse [of dependency on the bondsperson] but, rather, elimination of the institution of slavery altogether."[46] The Haitian Revolution challenged the entire structure of modernity/coloniality and panicked slaveholders for generations in the US South. In this era, even individual acts of self-destruction could shake the self-certainties of slave masters and lead to widening abolitionist views. Terri L. Synder writes, "the contradictions posed by slave suicide led to fundamental changes in the way that Americans and Europeans viewed slavery. Every choice to die by suicide could be politically construed as fundamentally, even if unintentionally, an antislavery act, a resounding criticism of the institution. . . . Like resistance to sale or running away, slave suicide created a heightened public awareness of the violence and power of slavery."[47] In addition, as Watson shows, Faulkner's views on Black resistance sharpened in the 1930s and 1940s in response to New Deal federal reforms in the South that ended sharecropping and instituted waged labor; African American mass migration to the North; and his exposure to New Negro writers' accounts of Black life in the United States. George Hutchinson argues that Richard Wright's *Native Son* (1940) was particularly influential on Faulkner's outlook on race relations in the South.[48] Watson concludes that such influences produced in Faulkner the ability to "dare to imagine otherwise" than ongoing Black defeat.[49] I agree and add that the turn toward death in Faulkner's 1930s and 1940s fiction rejects the settler's extractive regime and asserts instead a resistant grammar of intimacy with the more-than-human.

In reinterpreting Clytie's actions, we begin with her name. In Aeschylus's *Oresteia*, Clytemnestra murders her husband, Agamemnon, to end his domination. The intentionality of her name suggests that she acts not out of self-abnegation but toward redemptive violence. Second, Faulkner sets Sutpen's Hundred in the delta wilderness, in the northwest corner of Yoknapatawpha County. Sutpen adds to the outpost a crew of "wild Negroes" from Haiti who build the biggest plantation house in the region and "conjure more cotton per acre from the soil than any tame ones had ever done."⁵⁰ He works side by side with his bondsmen, raising the mansion out of the swamp, all of them naked and "plastered over with mud against the mosquitoes and . . . distinguishable one from another only by [Sutpen's] beard and eyes alone."⁵¹ More, Sutpen pits his "Negroes" against one another in fights and "participated now and then himself."⁵² Sutpen reveals his dirt-poor background and proximity to Blackness as he feels required to repeatedly conquer his bondsmen through violent matches. And he lacks a moral compass: slaveholding has degraded him. Rosa speculates that he quite possibly sired a child from Clytie, his own daughter, an outrage that could easily motivate Clytie to bide her time and wreak vengeance on his dynasty.⁵³ Finally, Rosa relates how "[Sutpen's] presence alone compelled the house to accept and retain human life; as though houses actually possess a sentience, a personality and character . . . inherent in the wood and brick or begotten upon the wood and brick by the man or men who conceived and built them."⁵⁴ Built atop the flood-prone, fecund delta, the moribund house takes on human qualities and mirrors Sutpen's own decay.⁵⁵ In a 1934 letter to Harrison Smith, Faulkner conveys the kernel of *Absalom*'s plot: "Roughly, the theme is a man who outraged the land, and the land then turned and destroyed the man's family."⁵⁶ The delta and the house ensure a narrative of ruination despite Sutpen's grand plans to the contrary.

While we can fault Faulkner for once again erasing Black agency in favor of the land's naturalized revolt, attention to the descriptive detail of the novel's climax places Sutpen's bondspersons in the very timbers of the ruin; they hollow out the false promise that Sutpen's dynasty will reign supreme. The climax begins with Quentin's and Rosa Coldfield's visit to the plantation big house, Sutpen's Hundred, determined to uncover whatever secrets lurk there. When the mansion comes into view, "Quentin saw completely through it a ragged segment of sky with three hot stars in it as if the house were of one dimension, painted on a canvas curtain in which there was a tear; now, almost beneath it, the dead furnace-breath of air in which they moved seemed to reek in slow and protracted violence with a smell of desolation and decay as if the wood of which it was built were flesh."⁵⁷ The scene announces that it will not reproduce seamlessly the plantation big house as settler colonial ideology teaches us to read it. Instead, its boundaries are torn; inside and outside mingle; domestic space and the prolific vegetal life and Black flesh that dwells in the delta merge. Rotting wood—part of the waste material after labor and energy are extracted—breaks open plantation ideology and restores the land to cosmic proportions rather than secular valuation. The language anticipates the house's fiery demise: the stars are hot, the air is a "dead furnace-breath." And the rotting fetid air merges wood with flesh: it anticipates Rosa and Quentin's discovery of Henry Sutpen's decaying (but still alive) body shut up inside the crumbling walls that recapitulate the flesh of the Haitian bondsmen whose labor metabolized the wood into house. Their physical trace composts with the wood in a manner that situates bondsmen on an inanimate (death-in-life) continuum with the area's extractable resources. Further, Clytie's description also conflates flesh with wood. Once inside the house, Quentin lifts Clytie from the ground after Rosa strikes her: "When he raised her it was like picking up a handful of sticks concealed in a rag bundle."[58] This description repeats, or sediments, the earlier one given above (when Quentin says, "her arm felt like a stick, as light and dry and brittle as a stick"). The built structure and the bodies will combust and their ashy remains return to the soil.

What they find upstairs is the heir to the plantation, Henry Sutpen who has been on the run from the law since killing his half-brother, Charles Bon, for intending to marry his sister. Unbeknownst to the community, four years ago, Henry secretly returned home to wait for death. He appears to have become contaminated and diseased, perhaps through the murder of and proximity to his father's Haitian son. He has a "wasted yellow face ... [and] wasted hands crossed on the breast as if he were already a corpse."[59] He's entombed within the house, with all the shutters closed, in which, "waking or sleeping it was the same and would be the same forever as long as he lived."[60] Both he and Clytie are death-bound. But Clytie plans for their ending. She instructs Jim Bond, Charles's grandson and the last of the Sutpens, to fill a room with tinder and trash, laced with kerosene. When Rosa and Quentin return to Sutpen's Hundred three months later with an ambulance for Henry, Clytie is ready for them. The house is instantly set on fire and—"maybe"—they see Clytie's face looking down at them from the window. Quentin recalls, "perhaps not even now with triumph and no more of despair than it had ever worn, possibly even serene above the melting clapboards before the smoke swirled across it again."[61] Clytie is as insubstantial as a ghost as she merges with the smoke. Neither panic nor revenge motivates her. Her turn toward death is a strong, long-standing statement of condemnation. Prefiguring Jean Rhys's Antoinette Mason, she burns to the ground the "monstrous tinder-dry rotten shell" that was Sutpen's Hundred so as to wipe out the "mausoleum" to the patriarch's glittering ambitions.[62] Clytie destroys the plantation's extractive regime by producing instead a Black rift in the earth, where wood and flesh turned to ash mingle intimately with the delta's soil. She destroys the enclosure of property and propriety begun by the already fraying big house. Last, Jim Bond flees the scene, "howling with human reason," a final commentary on the conflagration that reverberates across the centuries and across the waters, echoing the terrified and mournful cries of the saltwater slaves.[63]

The demise of Sutpen's Hundred occurs in the first decade of the twentieth century. In Quentin's narrative recalled from his grandfather, Sutpen recounts how he purchased one hundred square miles of delta land from the Indian Chief Issetibeha in 1833. In Faulkner's sedimented history of the region, the earliest account of the delta occurs after just this sale in the astonishing short story "Red Leaves" published in 1930. We learn there that Issetibeha's father, Doom (a mispronunciation of d'homme), influenced by the West Indian woman he meets and marries in New Orleans, purchases bondspeople and begins a small plantation in the delta sometime in the first decade of the nineteenth century. Hence, this is no origin story: the "Indians" wear snuff boxes and build neat western-style brick and whitewashed cabins for their bonded labor. The two focalized "Indian" characters, Three Basket and Louis Berry, wax nostalgic for the "old days" when they had more free time and no bondspeople to coerce, i.e., before their people's corruption by Western ways. For Faulkner, colonial mimicry evinces the "Indian's" inferiority: they are poor slaveholders and even worse plantation owners. The story begins with Issetibeha's death that occasions Basket and Berry to search for his manservant who must be ritually sacrificed, along with his horse and dog, to serve the Chief in the afterlife. The unnamed manservant, we soon learn, is a saltwater slave: "He was forty, a Guinea man.... He had been taken at fourteen by a trader off Kamerun, before his teeth had been filed. He had been Issetibbeha's body servant for twenty-three years."[64] Further, the story implies that the majority of the bondspeople held by the "Indians" are directly from Africa and, given the mismanagement of the plantation, they continue their African practices, "In utter idleness the majority of them led lives transplanted whole out of African jungles."[65]

The bondspeople know that the manservant will be put to death and that he has fled, and their fear is palpable. As the two "Indians" enter the darkened slave quarters to look for the servant, "The smell of them [their fear], seemed to ebb and flux in the still hot air. They seemed to be musing as one upon something remote, inscrutable. They were like a single octopus. They were like the roots of a huge tree uncovered, the earth broken momentarily upon the writhen, thick, fetid tangle of its lightless and outraged life."[66] Here is another Black rift in the earth. The captives are not described as individuals, but as a collective that holds itself in lateral relation to the earth. The subterranean (roots) and submarine (octopus) elements break the "plateau" of the plantation economy, defined by its instrumental use of the earth as a mineralogical resource for growing export crops and of Afro-diasporic persons as energy. This description also connotes the hold: both underwater and under the deck, in a rank, atrocious, mangle of limbs where the air is suffocating and the captives' cosmologies and languages appear to non-Africans as remote and inscrutable. The story enforces this likeness to the slave ship hold given that the "Indians" have dragged an abandoned river steamboat twelve miles overland on cypress rollers to serve as their big house. Watson argues that the steamboat, "may be the text's way of suggesting that the manservant has never really left the slave ship."[67] I concur, but add that the displaced steamboat also underscores the terraqueous nature of the delta where extensive wetlands serve as a Black zone of insurgent geography and in which the manservant will discover a poetics that rewrites the grammar of slavery and extraction. More, the rift (both wetlands and slave ship hold) produces what Yusoff calls, "an abysmal divide between human and inhuman . . . [that] launched a space in which a new language was born to speak otherwise of this inhuman condition."[68] As we'll see, the Guinea man's flight is one in which he finds language and actions with which to redescribe and revalue these inhuman conditions.

After Basket and Berry ask unsuccessfully after the manservant's whereabouts, they condemn the group because, "They do not like to die. . . . They cling. It makes trouble for us, always. A people without honor and without decorum."[69] The story turns next to the manservant who we discover is indeed acting without honor by clinging to life. He has thus far refrained from fleeing the plantation and hides instead in a nearby barn where he can watch the events unfold surrounding the Chief's death. Reminiscent of Harriet Jacob's hiding place in her grandmother's attic, the manservant refrains from running and crafts instead "a loophole of retreat" where his thoughts wander freely even if he cannot. For the first time in his writing, Faulkner allows a Black character an interior monologue that provides access to his thoughts, feelings, and, eventually, self-transformation. The monologue begins with the manservant's double consciousness, first he hears an exterior voice from the perspective of the "Indians" say, "You are dead," and next he expresses his inner desire for freedom and mobility to participate in his community's African-derived practices: "He imagined himself springing out of the bushes, leaping among the drums on his bare, lean, greasy, invisible limbs."[70] Given that the manservant, in clinging to life, must adopt his master's will and worldview, this interior access is revolutionary in acknowledging how submission is never total. His double consciousness perceives his death in life and this problem, as Watson notes, following Gilroy, "must be traced to the black Atlantic."[71] And so it is that the manservant next remembers his transatlantic voyage: "He was a boy then, but just come to America. They had lived ninety days in a three-foot-high 'tween deck in tropic latitudes, hearing from topside the drunken New England captain intoning aloud from a book which he did not recognize for ten years afterward to be the Bible."[72] This passage evokes Olaudah Equiano's trope of the Talking Book that functions to relativize Christianity by means of defamiliarizing its sacred text, and it comments on Christianity's hypocritical participation in the slave trade.

The manservant's desire to engage in communal practices motivates him to flee. He first visits the creek bottom where the bondspeople hold drumming ceremonies. The drums were "hidden in the creek bottom . . . buried in the mud on the bank of a slough; a lad of fourteen guarded them. He was undersized, and a mute; he squatted in the mud there all day, clouded over with mosquitoes, naked save for the mud which he coated himself against the mosquitoes."[73] We might recall Thomas Sutpen, who, just a few years later, will occupy the same creek bottom, naked and coated with mud, making bricks for the big house alongside his bondsmen. But here, rather than promoting resource extraction, the bondspersons hold their ceremonies that mingle bodies, spirits, and the earth in sacred, proximate relations. Next, the manservant continues his flight until he arrives at a wetland, where, likewise covered in mud, he confronts fully his impending death: "At sunset, creeping along the creek bank toward where he had spotted a frog, a cottonmouth moccasin slashed him suddenly across the forearm with a thick, sluggish blow. It struck clumsily, leaving two long slashes across his arm like two razor slashes."[74] Rather than ward off the blows, the manservant greets the snake, possibly in the tradition of his African ancestry, with "Olé, grandfather." Robert Farris Thompson claims that the ceremonial address, "resembles words for authority, protection, and honor in several West African languages."[75] Only when faced with this attack does the bondsman's desire to live become fully articulated: "He touched [the snake's] head and watched it slash him again across his arm, and again, with thick, raking, awkward blows. 'It's that I do not wish to die," he said. Then he said it again—'It's that I do not wish to die'—in a quiet tone, of slow and low amaze, as though it were something that, until the words said themselves, he found that he had not known, or had not known the depth and extent of his desire."[76] The Guinea man, in facing the snake's attack, comes face-to-face with his will to live and, at the same time, a way to confront death on his own terms. As Watson says, the bondsman "transforms [the accidental strike] into a product of conscious volition, solemnized with words that suggest a ritual element."[77] This ritual element transplants African practices into the Americas in a manner that creates a poetics of Black resistance that reorders earth, sacred animal, and water and refuses the animate/inanimate dichotomy at work in extractive economies. More, the manservant has at last silenced the external master's voice that declares his life ended. He repeats his desire not to die with certainty, a clear connection to his interiority. But he can do this, Watson notes, "only by going all the way. To cheat death, the Guinea man must embrace it."[78] The swamp animal paralyzes the fugitive's arm, lowering his value as a laborer in this world and the next. In letting the snake bite him again and again, the manservant's will to die paradoxically allows him to live. The story closes as Basket and Berry find the manservant chanting in his native language, "his face lifted to the rising sun. His voice was clear, full, with a quality wild and sad.... [The manservant] watched them quietly until one touched him on the maimed arm. 'Come,' the Indian said. 'You ran well. Do not be ashamed.'"[79] The manservant restores his nonextractive, mutual relation to the nonhuman world. In so doing, he becomes honorable, even in the eyes of slaveholders. He has altered the grammar of geology by turning his subjection into a revalued self-consciousness. Now, his transplantation is complete: he is a "new" world subject.

Go Down, Moses (1941) is the only of Faulkner's novels to take its title from Black culture and is dedicated to Faulkner's "mammy," Caroline Barr, who had recently died. *Go Down, Moses* is Faulkner's greatest expression of Black rewritings of the grammar of extraction. The novel, as I'll show, is explicitly a sedimented form with corpses and plantation loot buried below in a manner that destabilizes settler colonial extraction schemes. Written as seven discontinuous short stories that Faulkner insisted comprised a novel, each story links to one another through genealogy or location. Together, they span a duration of 144 years, from 1807 to the time of the novel's writing, and shuttle between the McCaslin plantation and its environs to the delta's last remaining wilds, the Big Woods, where hunters gather in an old lodge that had been Sutpen's overseer's house. Sutpen's Hundred is, of course, no more. The novel's second story, "The Fire in the Hearth," thematically as well as formally incorporates the area's sedimented history. The story's protagonist, Lucas Beauchamp, is a descendant of the McCaslin plantation founder, Q. D. C. McCaslin, and his Black concubine, Eunice. By means of his interior monologue, we learn that Lucas harbors a resentment that the plantation has been inherited by Q. D. C.'s grandnephew, Carothers "Roth" Edmonds, because Lucas, as a direct but mixed-race descendent, cannot inherit it. The story opens in the middle of the night when Lucas hides his bootleg whiskey distillery equipment in an "Indian mound" at the creek bottom. While he is digging, the mound collapses: "It was probably only a sigh but it sounded to him louder than an avalanche, as though the whole mound had stooped roaring down at him—the entire overhang sloughed. It drummed on the hollow kettle, covering it and the worm, and boiled about his feet ... hurling clods and dirt at him, striking him a final blow squarely in the face ... a sort of final admonitory pat from the spirit of darkness and solitude, the old earth, perhaps the old ancestors themselves."[80] The earth is animated: it sighs, roars, drums, and strikes. And it "sloughs," reminding us of the delta's ecotonal qualities of transition from solid to liquid. When the movement stops, the clod of earth that hits him in the face turns out to be a fragment of an earthenware vessel that disintegrates to reveal a single gold coin. The coin distracts Lucas from the lively earth and "perhaps" the ancestors in favor of extractive cuts of commodities from the land. Although not suffering from financial want, Lucas becomes obsessed with finding more buried gold. Together, his fixation with buried gold and plantation ownership underscores how he has marginalized Afro-diasporic ways of rerooting in the land. Instead, Lucas's attention is directed toward revenge against slaveholding by means of the extractive economy. What Lucas finds buried in the creek bottom (unlike the Africans' drums in "Red Leaves") came from the Civil War era when, as Watson argues, "enslaved African American labor turns into value that the slaveholding class converts into precious minerals, silver and gold, which, in order to prevent their confiscation by invading Union Army troops, must be buried in the earth."[81] Local lore has kept this fact alive, and Lucas, upon finding the coin, "his brain boiling with all the images of buried money he had ever listened to or heard of," becomes possessed with the desire to find more.[82] The discovery of a thousand-dollar gold piece buried in the earth conflates Black enslaved labor extraction with precious mineral extraction, or "black gold." Perhaps Lucas is propelled by fantasies of revenge against his white overlords, nonetheless his actions align himself with those selfsame plantation owners among whom he wishes he could number.

His wife, Molly, however, has other views. Motivated by Christian values, she approaches Roth Edmunds, the plantation owner, to ask for a divorce from Lucas. She explains her wish: "He's bad sick, marster. He's done a thing the Lord aint meant for folks to do." Molly then quotes from the Bible where "God say, 'What's rendered to My earth, it belong to Me unto I resurrect it. And let him or her touch it, and beware.' And I'm afraid. I got to go. I got to be free of him."[83] Roth advises Molly to give Lucas a dose of his own medicine by staying out all night with his "divining-machine" hunting for the treasure. Then, he tries to convince Lucas to give up his quest, but fails. Soon after, Molly disappears, becoming, like the Guinea man before her, a fugitive who must be hunted in the muddy flats of the creek bottom. The trackers, who include Lucas, "followed . . . the faint, light prints of the old woman's feet as they seemed to wander without purpose among the jungle of brier and rotted logs along the creek. It was almost noon when they found her, lying on her face, the once immaculate apron and the clean faded skirts stained and torn, one hand still grasping the handle of the divining-machine as she had fallen with it. She was not dead."[84] Molly refuses the extractive economy that Lucas has embraced. For her, the creek bottom was never a place to bury secrets or recover them. It's a Black rift in the earth. Rather than following the telos of extracted value, she wanders among the jungle of tangled vines and rotted logs, pointing our attention toward the wasted by-product of extraction that includes uncultivated "waste" and her own aging body. Like Clytie, Molly is ancient and wizened; she, too, whether intentional or not, mingles intimately with the earth. She lies face down, mud-stained, and still holding the divining-machine. The story ends well when Lucas gives up his quest and the pair reconciles. Their love and mutual bond overcomes Lucas's desire for revenge that is a mere reversal of master/servant relations rather than its supersession.

Molly's actions unwittingly repeat those of Lucas's grandmother Eunice. We have no direct access to Eunice. Her life is buried near the end of *Go Down, Moses,* in Part IV of "The Bear," the longest story in the novel and set in the delta. In Part IV, however, the narrative returns to the "tamed" and "ordered" McCaslin plantation.[85] As is so often the case with subaltern history, Eunice's life inadvertently appears in a few lines written by slave owners, encased in layers of text. Ike McCaslin, the grandson of Q. D. C. McCaslin, obliquely embeds her story in his explanation to his cousin Roth Edmunds as to why, at age twenty-one, he has decided to renounce his inheritance of the McCaslin plantation. He tells Roth how five years ago, while idly reading his father Buck's plantation ledgers, he came across his semiliterate entry, "*Eunice Bought by Father in New Orleans 1807 $650. dolars. Marrid to Thucydus 1809 Drowd in Crick Cristmas Day 1832* [sic throughout]"[86] Ike's suspicions are triggered when his Uncle Buddy's handwriting appears in the ledger for the first time and in direct contradiction of Buck's account of Eunice's death, "*June 21th 1833 Drownd* [sic] *herself.*"[87] Two days later, Buck retorts, "*23 Jun 1833 Who in hell ever heard of a niger drowning him self* [sic throughout]"[88] This exchange, on the one hand, vanishes Eunice more completely as her death becomes the circumstance for the brothers' disagreement. On the other hand, the argument attests to how the bondswoman's possible act of self-destruction upends slaveholder certainty, as expressed by Buck's "who in hell" comment. From this heated exchange, Ike guesses the source of the conflict: that his grandfather purchased Eunice to be his concubine in New Orleans in 1807 and that he begot a child with her, Tomasina, who "dide in Child bed June 1833 and Burd."[89] Ike speculates that Eunice may have learned of Tomasina's pregnancy at Christmas and believed Tomey's father, L. D. Q., to have also fathered this child. This possibility echoes the rumored knowledge that Thomas Sutpen compounded the rape of Clytie's mother with incest with her daughter, a monstrous crime designed to destroy kinship relations. In Ike's estimation, L. D. Q. likewise becomes a monster. Once Tomasina (Tomey) gives birth to the light-skinned child, Terrel (Turl), in June, Buddy retroactively ascribes to Eunice her motivation six months earlier to drown herself.

Given the sedimentation of the region's geography, across novels and stories, Eunice's possible suicide occurs in the very creek where Molly collapses with the divining-machine. The creek's unstable terrain, where the drums and gold were buried, marks the zone where the grammar of extraction is overturned in favor of Black insurgency through the turn toward death. Ike imagines Eunice's last moment, "he seemed to see her actually walking into the icy creek on that Christmas day six months before her daughter's . . . child was born, solitary, inflexible, griefless, ceremonial, in formal and succinct repudiation of grief and despair who had already had to repudiate belief and hope."[90] Eunice's actions are purportedly "ceremonial," an agency formed in intimate proximity to the ancestors, land, and water. She refuses the gravitational accretion that presses her to serve as the material strata for white mastery and extraction. Suicide reorders Black life in death mandated by slavery into a rift in the ground that destabilizes geological categories. Her agency revalues the earth, in its untamable, sacred relationality with the human.

I conclude my discussion of Faulkner's work with a description of Ike's approach to the delta wilderness to hunt with Sam Fathers:

> The surrey moving through the skeleton stalks of cotton and corn in the last of open country, the last trace of man's puny gnawing at the immemorial flank, until dwarfed by that perspective into an almost ridiculous diminishment, the surrey itself seemed to have ceased to move (this too to be completed later, years later, after he had grown to a man and had seen the sea) as a solitary small boat hangs in lonely immobility, merely tossing up and down, in the infinite waste of the ocean while the water

and then the apparently impenetrable land which it nears without appreciable progress, swings lowly and opens the widening inlet which is the anchorage.[91]

The novel describes the delta as an abyss of groundlessness that anticipates a post-petrofuture. The passage echoes Joseph Conrad's description of the *Narcissus* as it decenters human intentions in favor of the planetary, as discussed in chapter 1. It expands the scale of the delta to an "infinite waste" that emphasizes how the more-than-human upends anthropomorphic certainty. Instead, it envisions a planetary delta, a universalization of "inhuman intimacy" with the broken earth. It also comments upon the extractive economy by means of "skeleton stalks of cotton and corn." In harvesting bondspeople's energy, lives, and future generations as well as the selectively valued resources of the earth, it produces death; it will not last. As Faulkner shows, the delta will have the last word on human greed. That Eunice, Molly, and Clytie are foremost in this struggle points to unpredictability of Black female flesh and their primacy in ending extraction economies.

THE NIGER DELTA

Moving from the Mississippi River Delta to the Niger Delta demands recognition of convergences as well as crucial divergences in Africanist and Afro-diasporic thought. Chief among these differences is the discrepancy between the settler colonies and plantation logics of the West and the extractive practices of resource-hungry multinational corporations that feed on Africa. Newly arrived from Nigeria to the United States for study, the environmental scholar Cajetan Iheka recounts his surprise at the spectacular media coverage of the 2010 Deepwater Horizon oil spill in the Gulf of Mexico as well as the government's and British Petroleum's response to the crisis: "As I followed the disaster in America, the contrast with the Nigerian scenario where oil companies and government at different levels ignore damage caused by frequent oil spills, gas flaring, and other forms of environmental degradation became even more glaring and disturbing."[92] He references an estimated 5,000 oil spills in the Niger

Delta between 1976 and 1996 for an approximate total of 2,369,470 barrels of oil leaked into the environment. The sheer scale of the devastation wrought by negligence makes the Niger Delta one of the most polluted regions in the world. And while Royal Dutch Shell's first exports of oil from the Niger Delta did not occur until 1958, oil exploration and other extractivist activities have a much longer history in the region. In 1914, the British occupiers cobbled together the state of Nigeria *and* promulgated the Colonial Mineral Ordinance. The ordinance gave the British monopoly control with ownership rights to all petroleum found in the territory. In 1937, this monopoly power was transferred to Shell who gained "exclusive exploration and prospecting rights in the country."[93] Already in the 1930s, Shell's prospecting activities included explosives used in seismic operations as well as extensive drilling. These activities resulted in massive damage to mangrove swamps and forests; they dispersed or destroyed flora and fauna and dredged organic matter from rivers and canals and heaped it alongside the waters in harmful piles of waste material.[94]

Reading Tutuola's novels as petrofiction that comment on the long history of colonialist resource extraction goes against the grain of the novels' initial reception. Revising this history, both Jennifer Wenzel and Vaclav Paris have argued that Tutuola was self-aware of his positionality as an African Anglophone writer. They show how the writer comments on the colonizing dialectic between local raw materials (folklore, palm oil, and fossil fuel) and Western technologies (print culture, mass culture, including television, music, dance halls, and photography) within his early novels. As Wenzel puts it, the activity of "tapping" palm wine in Tutuola's first novel refers to: 1) the extraction of African natural resources; 2) the ways in which Tutuola "taps into" Yoruba folklore in order to export his novel as a global commodity and how his novels were initially received as natural resources by the West; and 3) the uneven geopolitical relations between the West and Africa.[95] In working through this dialectic, Tutuola creates "a dynamic, palimpsestic site of both internal and external conflict."[96] I deepen the palimpsest to include not only the textual world of Tutuola's imagination but also his poetics of the material and animative force of the more-than-human that resists internal and external extractive forces. The bush is both magical and "independently alive," filled with spirits and agentive creatures, including animals, magic canoes, and trees.[97] In sum, I argue that Tutuola interrogates Nigeria's process of modernization as it was poised to become an independent nation. His novels, I show, are a warning against the forgetfulness of modernity by countering it with the trauma of the slave trade and highlighting West African cosmologies where life and death exist on a continuum and where the forest seethes with spirits, animals, and plants that exist on the same plane as its human visitors.

To support this claim, I draw from recent postcolonial readings of Tutuola's work that presents modernity as the Janus-face of coloniality. New readings of the novels by Matthew Omelsky, Laura Murphy, and Iheka find environmental, historical, and commodity critiques in Tutuola's work that situate him as a foe of modernity/coloniality. I show how his first two novels comment on the extractivist violence in the delta, the trauma of the transatlantic slave trade, and posit anti-colonial liberation through animist ontologies and agencies that reorder an extractivist grammar and narrate a continuous now of accumulated disaster. Tutuola's novels foreground folkloric oral traditions that, while embedded in a frame narrative, are not subsumed within the developmental time and the hierarchical privileging of the individual against all else. Instead, the land takes center stage and is animated by spirits, magic, and shape-shifting transformations. These strange and wonderous possibilities sit next to the protagonists' various disasters and emerge in an episodic format that, as Ato Quayson argues, provides a "sense of the presence of an abundance of stories" that resists closure.[98] Tutuola's novels convey the richness and generative fecundity of the land that belongs collectively to everyone and no one, as expressed by the novelist's endlessly inventive, animist storytelling.

To begin, Omelsky reads the novels as partaking in a "creaturely modernism." Rather than see in the novels an anxiety toward modernity as traditions dissolve in favor of new alienated ways of life, Omelsky argues that Tutuola's early work melds together "the fantastical aesthetic tradition of West African folklore" with creatures that "are literally composed of commodities, technologies, and tropes of exchange ... [that] give life to the global flows of capital."[99] The novels are populated by gold, silver, and copperish ghosts, a television-handed ghostess, airplanes, radios, cinematography, a dance hall, petrol, electricity, slaves, palm tree plantations (that not only produce palm wine but also palm oil for export). These manifestations of global trade and technology, Omelsky argues, function to reenchant the world: "[Tutuola's] modernism collapses these figures [of contradiction, freakishness, and mutation] to create a new sort of enchantment, embracing the tainted, messy, transfigured forms that tradition has become in modern Africa."[100] This conclusion, while convincingly arguing for Tutuola's modernist aesthetic, sits uncomfortably next to the landscape of terror, torture, and mass death, that Mbembe argues in his reading of the novels, comprise *"extreme forms of human life, death-worlds, forms of social existence in which vast populations are subjected to conditions of life that confer upon them the status of living dead (ghosts)."*[101] To be sure, Omelsky acknowledges the dark side of the novels. He writes that the creatures "live in a world of seemingly inescapable terror, exploitation, and surveillance. The aesthetics and materiality of the creaturely body cannot be separated from the politics of modernity in which populations are controlled, ordered, and put to work."[102] But in the end, he folds terror into enchantment. Coloniality and enslavement are subsumed by the promises of global modernity as the creatures' alternative ontologies are absorbed into a syncretic modernism that breaks from the past.

Murphy, by contrast, examines Tutuola's *My Life in the Bush of Ghosts* from the perspective of how he novelizes—and hence modernizes—Yoruba oral traditions. Rather than break from the past, Murphy's reading demonstrates how novelization sediments oral traditions via print culture to transmit the legacy of the slave trade as it has been passed down for generations through oral storytelling. She argues, "Reading *My Life* as a *cautionary novel* (as opposed to a series of cautionary tales) calls attention to the more specific narrative setting and its historic implications, as well as to the use of literary figurative language and novelistic structures.... It is precisely through the migration of these stories from the world of the oral to the world of the written that Tutuola underlines the memory of the ghosts of slavery that is indeed alive in the West African imagination of the bush."[103] This narrative structure articulates the past in the present, rather than positing its overcoming. The young protagonist in *My Life* explains that the warfare that caused him and his brother to flee their village was due to "the slave trade [that] was then still existing."[104] When the narrator's older brother is captured, the younger boy flees into the haunted, forbidden bush where his macabre, nightmarish, cautionary story unfolds. Time becomes a continuous now in which terror, cannibalism, human sacrifice, mutilation, murder, rape, torture, hunger, and physical metamorphosis sit side by side with the enchantments of modernity. Murphy reads this continuous present as an effect of the historical trauma of the slave trade on the Yoruba.

In Yorubaland, she writes, the height of the slave wars occurred relatively late, after 1790, and extended well into the nineteenth century, "making Lagos West Africa's leading slave port in the transatlantic trade following abolition."[105] This history informs the cautionary folktales told to children, especially in the city of Abeokuta, where Tutuola was born. Refugees of the Yoruba territorial wars, Murphy tells us, founded the city by populating it with those "who sought a safe haven in which they could hide from battles as well as slave raiders."[106] Although protected, the new inhabitants, as well as the thousands more affected by the slave raids, were changed by their ordeals: "Raiders terrorized villages all throughout West Africa to feed the insatiable European trade. In response, the fear of random attack and captivity changed the way the people of the interior lived their lives and understood their environment. The threat of capture inscribed itself upon work habits, trade negotiations, even child-rearing. The terror inflicted by slave raiders impacted not only the traditions and habits of the people affected, but also the psychic lives of generations to come."[107] The haunting legacy of the slave trade makes itself felt in the protagonist's twenty-six-year sojourn in the bush of ghosts where he reels from one instance of captivity and violence to the next. Adding to his hallucinatory experience is the layering of time in which slavery and modern life exist simultaneously. This palimpsest allows Murphy to read the novel as a moral tale as the novel concludes: "This is what hatred did."[108] More than merely remarking on the rivalry between the co-wives in the protagonist's family that resulted in the two boys being left alone during a slave raid, Murphy argues that "the novel is an admonition against the kind of anger that produces slave masters and slaves," not only during the slave trade but in the present moment at the dawn of Nigerian independence.[109] Murphy's work is foundational to a postcolonial reading of the novel, but her attention to the protagonist's moral and psychic development, a feature that distinguishes the novel from the folktale, sidesteps the animist and other-than-human ontologies that are integral to the text and that challenge the narrative of development. Given that Tutuola's imaginary stretches across the Atlantic to the dreaded fate of the slave raiders' victims, I hold that his narrative refuses to be confined by notions of individual or national development.[110] Moral development is minimal while the nightmarish logic of the bush assembles people, landscapes, insects, animals, things, elements, and technologies into an African futurity: at once the postcolonial nation in the world; modernism in times of terror; and African surrealism.

To think together these simultaneous aspects of the novels, it's important to consider how they convey multiplicity through unruly excess and disorder. Take, for instance, the trope of "the body in the bag" that Murphy argues represents the sensations of captivity, suffocation, and the forced mobility of the slave trade. She traces the figure back to Equiano's autobiography (1789) to argue for the trope's direct descendance from slavery to the mid-twentieth century. But far from Equiano's realist depiction of captivity, the protagonist describes his bagging in fantastical terms. The Smelling-Ghost "put me into the big bag . . . but when he threw me into the bag I was totally covered with the rotten blood of the animals which he was killing in the bush. This bag was so smelling and full of mosquitoes, small snakes with centipedes which did not let me rest for a moment."[111] On another occasion, in *The Palm-Wine Drinkard*, a "very huge man" places the protagonist and his wife into a bag that was large enough to hold forty-five persons: "We were afraid of touching the other creatures that we met inside that bag, because every part of their bodies was as cold as ice and hairy and sharp as sand-paper. The air of their noses and mouths was hot as steam, none of them talked inside the bag."[112] The reader, I hold, can interpret these passages along the lines of Murphy's argument, as conveying slavery's unsanitary, pestilential conditions as well as the unreality of slavery itself. But what of "the rotten blood of animals," and the small snakes, mosquitoes, and centipedes in the bag? What of the exaggerated proportions of the giant man and his enormous bag, and the creatures, at once both hairy and sharp, "cold as ice" and giving off air "hot as steam"? I claim that the novels ask the reader to think about the horrors of slavery and, *at the same time*, to animate such memories with endlessly inventive, exuberant aliveness. After all, the Smelling-Ghost cares for the snakes who live all over his body by feeding them with the half-dead game that he manages to capture. (He smells so badly that his prey is forewarned that he is near, making him a very poor hunter.) And while the protagonist complains about the horrible smells and disgusting symbiosis of human life with insects, maggots, and other crawling horrors as well as excreta (feces, urine, rotted blood), he ultimately takes it all in stride.[113] In the second instance, the proportions of the huge man and his bag that holds forty-five people stretches credibility. It asks readers to imagine a fantastical world where time, space, and phenomena do not follow empirical rules of scientific observation. Finally, the "faux-naif" uneducated English language deployed in the novel effects a jolting, fractured rhythm that destabilizes grammatical and syntactical order and meaning. In one sentence from above, "This bag was so smelling," an adjective become a present participle, "smelling" and a dependent clause, "small snakes with centipedes" fails to modify the meaning of the main clause. The language of displacement, disjunction, and (elsewhere) malapropism assert a "rotten" English that refuses to be properly Westernized.

Scaling up from scrambled grammar, the Grove Press double-volume set of *The Palm-Wine Drinkard* and *My Life in the Bush of Ghosts* is out of order, with the second novel *My Life* placed first and *Palm-Wine Drinkard* second. More confusing, when the protagonist makes an intertextual reference in *Palm-Wine Drinkard* to "the bush of ghosts," he is referring to the previously published short story, "The Wild Hunter in the Bush of Ghosts." When referring to *The Palm-Wine Drinkard* in *My Life*, the reader may not yet have read the first novel that is positioned after the second in the volume. In *My Life*, plot sequence is meaningless: the protagonist visits the 7th, 9th, 20th, and 10th town of ghosts interspersed with the nameless town, the town of short ghosts, the hopeless town, and other episodes. Spatial relations, too, are altered. In *Palm-Wine Drinkard*, the protagonist catches a red bird in the river and a red fish in the bush. Water and land are inverted and fauna is displaced. In *My Life*, the narrator has his head cut off and a ghost's head mistakenly put on his neck: "Whether I was talking or not it would be talking out the words which I did not mean in my mind and was telling out all my secret aims which I was planning in mind.... All these secret thoughts were speaking out by this inferior head ... and also telling lies against me."[114] The human subject is scrambled. Inner thoughts and spoken words are mingled without regard for appropriateness or even truth. The protagonist loses control over his presentation of self. He turns inside out and is ventriloquized by an evil foe. Finally, animism is attributed to land, trees, and ghosts. All can talk and sing; and ghosts are embodied: they eat, get dirty, and can be killed. In sum, the fantastical bush mingles together spirits, animals, land, water, and air with unborn, living, and dead human beings in what the third critic I discuss, Iheka, argues is an aesthetics of proximity. This aesthetics enables thinking multispecies (and, I add, heterotemporalities and elements) simultaneously.[115] Iheka contextualizes the novels' ecological vision within the burgeoning national independence movement of the 1950s. He argues, "Tutuola is invoking a Yoruba cosmology consisting of the worlds of the living, the dead, the unborn, and the transitional abyss. By taking on the vision of his Yoruba pluriverse, Tutuola challenges the human-centricity of his time. One great achievement of Tutuola's narrative is that it reinstates an ecosystem receding in the secular imagination of the Enlightenment-inspired modernity that colonialism brought to Africa."[116] Tutuola's novels envision an anti-colonial liberation where life and death are conjoined and impossible for the extractivist state to control fully. The novels express a mutual dependence and permeability between humans and their more-than-human surrounds.

While Iheka's engagement with Tutuola's animist thought is a crucial ecocritical intervention, I hold that, even more importantly, Tutuola braids together animist thought with the legacy of the slave trade and the continuing extractive, polluting logics of contemporary neocoloniality, especially in the Niger Delta. Combining ongoing trauma with alternative categories of time, space, and the human itself, Tutuola tempers the dangers of animist enchantment with a critical, ongoing response to colonization. Consider the episode of the full-bodied gentleman in *The Palm-Wine Drinkard*. The dandified gentleman, who is followed by a lady enchanted with his beautiful appearance, steadily returns his rented appendages in the bush to reveal himself to be nothing but a skull. When the lady tries to flee, he imprisons her in a hole in the ground. Managing to escape the hole, the lady finds to her horror that the entire skull community is chasing her: All the skulls "were rushing out, they were rolling on the ground as if a thousand petrol drums were pushing along a hard road."[117] Here, captivity, death, and petrol drums are hideously conflated in a cautionary tale for the delta's (and Nigeria's) future. A Yoruba woman becomes captive and then fugitive to death heads who are likened to Nigeria's petrofuture: remember that Shell had not yet begun its commercial export of oil from the delta when the novels were published. Yet Tutuola applies similar extractive logics to both the slave past and petrofuture as they are laminated onto one another.

To counter these terrors, Tutola's novels imagine an animist world that vies against a pollutive extractivist past and future. The unruly exuberance of the narrator's adventures emerges from an anti-colonial landscape and cosmology. He is not an autonomous hero; rather, he is a fugal, multiple, plastic being. He's at times a god, a human, air, a horse, cow, camel, half ghost, wrapped in a spider's web, swallowed by a boa constrictor, swelled up like a pregnant woman, and more. This multispecies and animist relationality refuses colonial and metaphysical dichotomies by means of an inventive liveliness that contests the worldview of the colonizer. The narrative proceeds by an inventive parataxis that accumulates stories and adventures rather than overcoming them. The bush and dead's town are unmappable spaces that also blend temporalities of past, present, and future. Like the delta, these spaces are bottomlands, filled with death and spirits. They are ontologically multiple edge zones that change drastically and with great fecundity. These geographies are impure, syncretic, and enfolded into the death space of extractive logics. Life and death mingle together, with animist vitality camouflaged by a façade of death. Finally, it is song—cultural inventiveness—that saves the narrator in each novel, a testimony to creative expression in the face of dehumanization. Tutuola presents conflicting imaginaries that reveal animism not to be an enchantment of modernity—as Wenzel worries that an animist argument might convey—but a necessary anti-colonial response to violence, terror, and ecocide.[118]

To conclude my argument that Tutuola's novels not only remember slave trade atrocities and debilitating colonial resource extraction but that they simultaneously enact exuberant, creative, boundless African creativity and aliveness derived from Yoruban traditions rather than Western modernism, I turn to the episode in *The Palm-Wine Drinkard* in which the narrator and his wife encounter a white tree "one thousand and fifty feet in length and about two hundred feet in diameter."[119] This scene comments on the limits of Western-derived modern life. The couple is surveilled by someone in the tree and commanded to stop. When they refuse, the talking tree stretches its hands out to draw them inside its magical space. Once inside, they sell their death and lend their fear with interest and find that they are in "the largest dancing hall" with over three hundred people dancing together. The couple is photographed and their images, along with those of many others, are placed on "technicolor" lit walls that changed "colours at five minutes intervals" and that are lavishly "decorated with about one million pounds."[120] There are over twenty stages and "uncountable orchestras, musicians, dancers and tappers" and "about three hundred and forty cooks."[121] Omelsky links the "cacophonous sound, color and movement" of the dance hall to "Josephine Baker's *La Revue Negre* in 1920s Paris, Duke Ellington's orchestra at Harlem's Cotton Club, and the Highlife clubs in Nigeria and Ghana in the first decades of the twentieth century."[122] The couple gamble, drink, eat, and dance. They run out of money. The protagonist says, "We had forgotten all our past torments" and "I had forgotten that one day, we should leave there and need money to spend."[123] While they are eventually allowed to leave, having gambled away their money, after a period of one year and two weeks, they cannot recover their death, having sold it, although they regain their fear. In effect, Tutuola comments on the allures of the modernist dance hall. Power, pleasure, and amnesia pervades its culture. At the same time, the couple's future adventures in the bush—unleashed from the biological finitude of death—threaten to extend into the seemingly boundless, uncountable, "bad infinity" of capitalist accumulation.[124] They will not die. Tutuola rebukes Western modernism because it forgets the past and fails to consider death as an aspect of life. It eliminates old ways and cautionary tales and leaves its participants stripped of an awareness of limitations that allow for meaningful relationality. In contrast, life mingled with death is regenerative, courageous, and lived to the full. Tutuola's vision of African sociality, drawing on its Indigenist traditions but transforming them in the present, insists on remembering the slave trade and showing its continuity with contemporary resource extraction. Despite—or perhaps because of—dwelling on the dark underside of modernity, the novels' visions are exuberant, unruly, and situated in the fecund, shifting setting of the bottomlands. Storytelling from this location, where humans and nonhumans shapeshift with ease, anticipate a vibrant postcolonial future for Nigeria.

CODA

The cover image of this book, a photograph included in Emma Langdon Roche's *Historic Sketches of the South* (1914) of what was then believed to be the half-submerged ruins of the *Clotilda*, underscores the swirling temporalities of reading with the sea that have animated these pages. This ship brought what was probably the very last cargo of African captives to the American South in 1860 as memorialized in both *Historic Sketches of the South* and Zora Neale Hurston's *Barracoon*. After disembarking its human cargo, the owners set fire to the schooner in order to hide the evidence of their egregious crime. The shipwreck in Roche's photograph, upon further investigation, turned out not to be the *Clotilda*. Over one hundred years later, in January 2018, a bomb cyclone further north and east exposed another ship's remains in the extreme low tide of the Mobile River amid the swampy wetlands of the Mobile-Tensaw Delta.[1] Marine archeologists, upon inspecting the artifacts, again determined that it was not the vestiges of the *Clotilda*. But the excitement generated by local and national news reports revived the quest to locate the slave ship's remnants. And, sure enough, within the next year, another ship's detritus was recovered and confirmed to belong to the *Clotilda*.[2] The long history of enslavement, the early twentieth-century interest in that past, and twenty-first-century climate change-induced storms come together to tell this tale of loss, recovery, and celebration.[3] In like manner, the temporal swirl of my analysis began with Kara Walker's

"Daughter of the Waters," then swerved back to the slave trade archive and forward to early and mid-twentieth-century modernism. In modernist literature, I've traced momentary openings that enact the human in lateral, mutually constitutive relations to the nonhuman. I've argued that modernist experimental texts are often engaged with the submerged histories of the slave trade and slavery as a means of excavating the basis for alternative futures.

To glimpse these practices and ways of being that flicker momentarily in modernist writing before being blotted out from the written record, I've drawn attention to modernist experimental form. I've shown how attention to ways of being human otherwise than that of European Man appears through the modernist technique of free indirect narration, the recognition of the agency of the more-than-human world (hurricanes, storms at sea, and the shoreline ecotones), the critique of the commodity structure, the zoning up and down of scale to include the cosmic, oceanic, and microscopic, and being human in relation to the nonhuman. Together, these experimental aesthetic techniques articulate far-reaching, inventive human, animist, and geographical possibilities that glimmer through ongoing violence. By locating modernity on the sea, I've removed the territorial fixity that shores up citizenship and have shown how the narrative structure of the modernist novel at sea becomes unmoored. Background becomes central; impasses, detours, flotsam, and jetsam accumulate. Temporalities proliferate to reach back into the past to speculate on counter-futures that emerge from denigrated locations. And these temporal swirls continue into the present so as to fold modernist works and the longer Afro-diasporic past into the contemporary. For instance, Zadie Smith's *On Beauty* (2005) rewrites E. M. Forster's *Howard's End* (1911) by placing the Haitian Iwa of the sea, Erzulie, at the center of aesthetic debates regarding Black art and the differences of race and class in the institution of higher education. Erna Brodber's *Louisiana* (1994) rewrites the life and work of Zora Neale Hurston and imagines a Black Atlantic world that stretches from postreconstruction labor organizing in the deep South, women Garveyite organizers in Chicago, West Indian communities in New York City and Jamaica, and Black sailors and hoodoo priestesses in New Orleans. Jesmyn Ward's *Salvage the Bones* (2011) rewrites William Faulkner and Hurston by addressing the fallout of Hurricane Katrina in a rural, impoverished Black community in the deep South and figures the protagonist, Esch, through a land- and water-based, embodied praxis accompanied by an interior monologue on interspecies maternity. In the Caribbean, Edward Kamau Brathwaite's *DS: Dream Stories (2)* (2007), Edwidge Danticat's "Children of the Sea" from *Krik? Krak!* (1996), Ana-Maurine Lara's *Erzulie's Skirt* (2006), Paule Marshall's *Praisesong for the Widow* (1983), and Derek Walcott's *Omeros* (1990) make reverse ocean crossings and comment on intra-Caribbean migrations to relate the Middle Passage to current refugee crises.

As important as it is to recover an overlooked engagement with slave trade history in modernism, scholars of Afro-diasporic history and literature have argued that there are multiple problems with emphasizing the Middle Passage, or, as Gilroy terms it, the "slave sublime," as the primary locus of Afro-diasporic history and identity.[4] The first is that it limits Afro-diasporic belonging to descendants of enslaved people in the Western hemisphere, a qualification that enforces the gulf between Africans and Afro-diasporic peoples in the West and excludes recent African immigrants to the West from US Afro-diasporic belonging, as Chimamanda Ngozi Adichie's novel *Americanah* explores. Conversely, it maintains the impasse between Afro-diasporic subjects in Africa who seek to recover a lost history and homeland and the Africans they encounter for whom slave history is not uppermost in their minds, as Saidiya Hartman's *Lose Your Mother* emphasizes. Second, it makes exceptional the Atlantic Ocean circuit that ignores the far longer histories of Indian Ocean slavery and forced and voluntary migrations in that region, and neglects relations between slavery, indenture, and colonization that occurred worldwide and that mingled migrant Asians, Africans, and the Indigenous everywhere. This closed Western circuit, "across the pond," has been powerfully challenged by critics and writers working on Indian Ocean, South Atlantic, Antarctic Convergence, and Pacific Ocean circulations. Scholarly interventions by Kerry Bystrom and Joseph R. Slaughter, Elizabeth DeLoughrey, Epeli Hau'ofa, Isabel Hofmeyr, Charne Lavery and Meg Samuelson, Maebh Long and Matthew Hayward, Françoise Lionnet, Sarah Nuttall, Alice Te Punga Somerville and others have drawn attention to the millennia-long history of Indian Ocean exchanges between Africa, the Arabian peninsula, the Indian subcontinent, and East Asia and Pacific Ocean histories.[5] Their readings highlight postcolonial reimaginings and interventions in continually unfolding imperialism, colonization, and environmental crisis in those waters by writers including J. M. Coetzee, Mia Couto, Amitav Ghosh, Abdulrazak Gurnah, Zakes Mda, Briohny Doyle, Keri Hulme, Witi Ihimaera, Craig Santos Perez, and others. Another objection to Middle Passage genealogies is that an emphasis on the trauma of slavery reinforces the perception of Afro-diasporic peoples as still suffering and disempowered by their hostile environments so as to be incapable of assimilating into dominant society.

In light of these objections, is there another modernist genealogy of submerged histories and alternative futures that avoids the pitfalls of Middle Passage history? Absolutely: W. E. B. Du Bois's genealogy that begins with World War One articulates the "dark world's" long history of imperialist and colonizing wars along with manifold potentials for grappling with contemporary issues of mass migrations, ongoing wars, and the problem of statelessness. His multigeneric *Darkwater* (1920), written just after the deadly 1919 race riots in the United States, condemns Western imperialism, US racism, and the mass violence unleashed in the Great War. Comparing the white world's suffering in the Great War with its ongoing history of racist and colonial atrocities, he writes:

> War is horrible! This the dark world knows to its awful cost. But has it just become horrible, in these last days, when under essentially equal conditions and equipment, with equal waste of wealth white men are fighting white men with surgeons and nurses hovering near? . . . Think of the wars through which we have lived in the last decade: in German Africa, in British Nigeria, in French and Spanish Morocco, in China, in Persia, in the Balkans, in Tripoli, in Mexico, and in a dozen lesser places—were not these horrible, too? Mind you, there were for most of these wars no Red Cross funds. . . . As we saw the dead dimly through rifts of battle-smoke and heard faintly the cursings and accusations of blood brothers, we darker men said: This is not Europe gone mad; this is not aberration nor insanity; this *is* Europe; this seeming Terrible is the real soul of white culture—back of all culture,—stripped and visible today. This is where the world has arrived,—these dark and awful depths and not the shining and ineffable heights of which it boasted.[6]

In this passage, Du Bois anticipates both Hannah Arendt's analysis of the rise of totalitarianism in Europe as intimately linked to imperialism (1950) and Aimé Césaire's *Discourse on Colonialism* (1955) where he writes: "And then one fine day the bourgeoisie is awakened by a terrific boomerang effect: the gestapos are busy, the prisons fill up, the torturers standing around the racks invent, refine, discuss . . . that it is Nazism, yes, but that before they were its victims, they were its accomplices; . . . until then, it had been applied only to non-European peoples."[7] The longue durée of violence in the colonies arrives at last in the imperial center to unleash chaos there. Not only that, but the geopolitical aftermath of the Great War compounded this disarray. Arendt characterizes the postwar period as one in which, "Civil wars which ushered in and spread over the twenty years of uncertain peace were not only bloodier and more cruel than all their predecessors; they were followed by migrations of groups who, unlike their happier predecessors in the religious wars, were welcomed nowhere and could be assimilated nowhere. Once they had left their homeland they remained homeless, once they had left their state they become stateless."[8] She warns against the securement of human rights through recourse to national citizenship.

The recognition and protections afforded to those with national belonging functions to delegitimize what Neferti X. M. Tadiar calls "remaindered life," those who live in the interstices of global capitalism and insist on decolonial forms of sociality: nomadic, Indigenous, fugitive, and more. In my efforts to delineate ways of living otherwise than modernity/coloniality demands, it is essential to remember that these practices are located within capitalism and are not a version of romanticized primitivism. These social groups struggle continually against dominant practices intent on removing them from their land and other communal resources that sustain their creative social capacities. It is no accident that, in "The Souls of White Folk," an essay included in *Darkwater,* Du Bois defines whiteness as "the ownership of the earth forever and ever."[9] While I have drawn attention to the long history of slavery and colonization in these pages, we can follow Du Bois's lead and uncover other colonizing genealogies that have negated decolonial ways of living and being. For instance, Tadiar's work on remaindered life draws attention to "other, longer antecedents for the present [longer than capitalist labor] which have been operating in creatively persistent ways through the time of capital."[10] Such understandings underscore heterotemporalities of the present and uneven, actively formed geographies around the planet. These locations produce what Tadiar characterizes as "hidden transmissions of other terms of humanity, bearing elements of the pasts that created a ground in the making of another lineage of living and invention."[11]

I bookend the cover photograph of ruin and loss with a life-affirming visual image of Afrofuturism: African American artist Ellen Gallagher's 2005 painting/collage, "Watery Ecstatic" [see Figure con.1]. The painting is part of an extended series of films, sculpture, and mixed-media works that comprise the ongoing *Watery Ecstatic* project (2001–present). The painting features a fantastical jellyfish floating in underwater currents, edged by lacy carvings cut into the white paper. Its underside houses a mass of egg- or seedlike shapes. Pink tentacles emerge from its round body and fronds of green seaweed seem to be either grafted onto or woven into the tentacles. Along the fronds are dark nodes, resembling knots in wood, but upon closer inspection (not possible in the printed reproduction) these nodes turn out to be human faces accompanied by tiny magazine cutouts of e's and o's. Within this book's purview, the e's circle back to Hurston's attribution to her ethnographic subject, Oluale Kossula, of a voicing of resonant ee's to describe his passage from Africa on the *Clotilda*. Unlike Hurston, Gallagher locates her soundings in the tracks of the Detroit-based techno band Drexciya. The band, she explains in an interview, "channel[s] oral hallucinations from the Middle Passage. They imagined this black Atlantis made up of women and children who went overboard during the Middle Passage. And it's this kind [of] militarized zone of this underwater sea world."[12] In the liner notes to their CD *The Quest*, Drexciya asks:

> Could it be possible for humans to breathe underwater? A fetus in its mother's womb is certainly alive in an aquatic environment. Is it possible that they could have given birth at sea to babies that never needed air? Recent experiments have shown mice able to breathe liquid oxygen, a premature human infant saved from certain death by breathing liquid oxygen through its underdeveloped lungs. These facts combined with reported sightings of Gillmen and Swamp Monsters in the coastal

swamps of the South Eastern United States make the slave trade theory startlingly feasible.[13]

The amphibious mutants of the transatlantic passage can be heard in Gallagher's moaning, ghostly o's and resonate with M. NourbeSe Philip's Middle Passage poem *Zong!*. Philip rearranges the cut-up transcript of the *Zong* legal case that exonerated the captain of the murder of an estimated 130 captives, tossed alive into the sea. Philip explains, "*Zong!* bears witness to the resurfacing of the drowned and the oppressed and transforms the desiccated, legal report into a cacophony of voices—wails, cries, moans, and shouts that had earlier been banned from the [legal] text."[14] Philip's poem puns the moaning o's with the Latin word "os" meaning bone or mouth. And this pun resounds in Gallagher's method of etching or cutting into paper, especially the lacing fringes along the jellyfish's perimeter. The artist connects this activity to scrimshaw, the intricate carvings into bone made by sailors during long whaling voyages. The art of scrimshaw, she says, "in this overwhelming, scary [oceanic] expanse [gave the sailors a] kind of focus that would give you a sense of control."[15] Here, the act of signification is one of absence, a taking away from the shape, that signals the presence of the unknown and foregrounds the materiality of the paper. And it points to a shifting of scale from the gigantic realm of the oceanic to the miniature carving that signals a hunkering down to make meaning from death's physical remains. More, the round shape of a mouthed "o" reveals a passage or opening onto an "aquafuturist" world.[16]

Although Gallagher's mixed-media painting references the all-male society of sailing, it is merely a point of passage. Unlike Drexciya's masculine, warlike aqua-zone or the sailors' homosocial environs, Gallagher's figure affirms the monstrous maternity of Black women, "on the threshold of knowability."[17] The central maternal image is a colorful, life-giving assemblage of human, plant, and animal and floats unmoored underwater. Rather than speculate on a dark and unknowable lost archive of the Middle Passage, Gallagher moves fearlessly underwater to imagine an aquafuture where Black maternity births something akin to an intraspecies and vegetal mode of being human. The futurist jellyfish figure reveals the mutability of the human in its proximate, mutually dependent relation to the more-than-human. This image, moreover, is decidedly queer. Suzanna Chan associates the nodal faces to queer

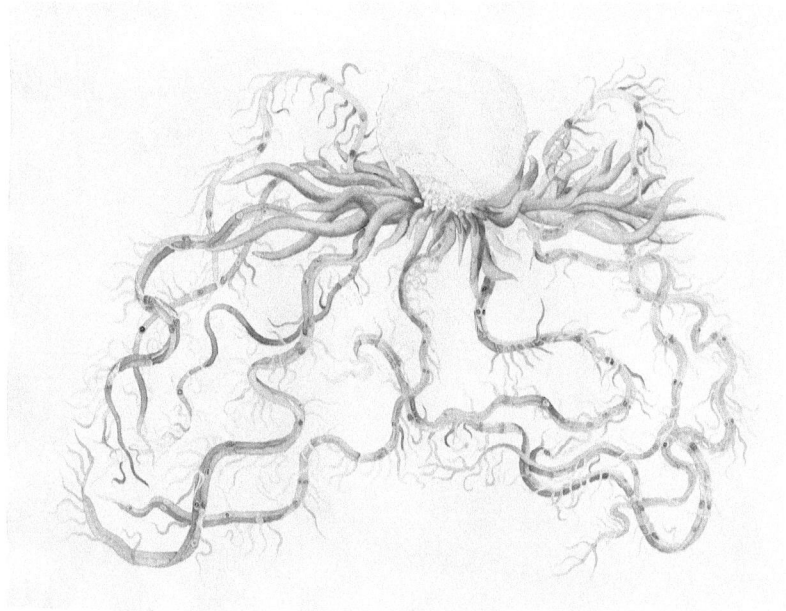

FIGURE CON.1 Ellen Gallagher, *Watery Ecstatic*, 2005. Watercolor, ink, oil, varnish, collage, and cut paper on paper. 32 1/2 × 42 1/4 inches (83 × 107.6 cm)

© Ellen Gallagher. Courtesy the artist and Gagosian. Photo: Mike Bruce.

sailors, calling them "exquisite cabin creatures," a formation that echoes the queer scene in the sailors' quarters described in Langston Hughes's *The Big Sea* discussed in chapter 2. She says, "These exquisite cabin creatures, sustained by a marine maternity, are the speculative offspring of murdered, enslaved pregnant African women. They are reborn in a *Drexciya* reimagined as a fatherless realm awash with oppositions to the white patriarchal familial formation. Sexual difference is reworked toward open possibilities that resonate with queer black futurity."[18] This is an aquatic zone of gender shifts and creative multiplicity. Rather than posit a threatening encounter with a tentacled squid or kraken at the bottom of the ocean that Djuna Barnes and J. M. Coetzee imagine, as discussed in the interlude, the ocean is filled with light and the tentacles are life-giving, perhaps referencing Octavia E. Butler's tentacled ship in *Lilith's Brood*.[19] The tentacles promote connection and watery becomings whose future is an open and joyous question.

NOTES

OVERTURE

1. Tate Modern, "Look Closer: Kara Walker's Fons Americanus," accessed December 4, 2021, http://tate.org/whats-on/tate-modern/exhibition/hyundai-commission-kara-walker.
2. The definition of slavery as "social death" comes from Orlando Patterson's *Slavery and Social Death: A Comparative Study* (Cambridge, MA: Harvard University Press, 1982), where he writes: "The essence of slavery is that the slave, in his social death [his natal alienation in which he has no kin or ancestors], lives on the margin between community and chaos, life and death, the sacred and the secular," 51.
3. This myth inspired the Detroit-based techno band called Drexciya. See Katherine McKittrick, *Dear Science and Other Stories* (Durham, NC: Duke University Press, 2021), 50–57. Black visual artists from Romare Bearden to Ellen Gallagher have envisioned the underwater world of the Black Atlantic.
4. Alexander G. Weheliye, *Habeas Viscus: Racializing Assemblages, Biopolitics, and Black Feminist Theories of the Human* (Durham, NC: Duke University Press, 2014). Weheliye adapts the term assemblage from Deleuze and Guattari for rethinking the human from within a Black Studies framework. He writes, "Assemblages are inherently productive, entering into polyvalent becomings to produce and give expression to previously nonexistent realities, thoughts, bodies, affects, spaces, actions, ideas, and so on. The fecundity of these becomings, what Deleuze and Guattari term *machinic*, however, ought not be cognized as unavoidably positive or liberating, particularly when set against putatively rigid structures such as race and colonization, since assemblages transport potential territorializations as often if not more frequently than lines of flight" (46–47). He adds the caveat that, as Gayatri Spivak argued long ago, assemblages must

be supplemented with a critique of the subject who produces this knowledge. Because of the universalizing tendency of Eurocentrism, whiteness is too often left unmarked which "leads to a neglect of race as a critical category" (47). Second, the form-materiality divide I reference has a long history in Western philosophy. For Plato, forms are timeless, absolute, nonphysical essences or ideas. The material realm on Earth is changeable, particular, and only knowable through form. In terms of the novel, one can think of this division as how form shapes content, especially in terms of what can be narrated.

5. Empire and colonization have distinct but related meanings. Empire refers to a single political unit in which different territories—center and peripheries, either contiguous or widely scattered—are governed differently. Colonization is the practice by which one people or power controls another. In this process, the colonizer often imposes their religion, language, economies, and other practices. The imposition of racial categories is one way in which the colonizer maintains control over colonized groups of peoples. Racial difference attempts to naturalize power differentials between peoples.

6. Tate Modern, "Look Closer," http://tate.org/whats-on/tate-modern/exhibition/hyundai-commission-kara-walker.

7. Saidiya V. Hartman, *Lose Your Mother: A Journey Along the Atlantic Slave Route* (New York: Macmillan Press, 2008), 6.

8. Christina Sharpe, *In the Wake: On Blackness and Being* (Durham, NC: Duke University Press, 2016), 21.

9. Saidiya V. Hartman, "Venus in Two Acts," *Small Axe* 12, no. 2 (June 2008): 10–11. The contradiction of telling stories that are impossible to tell involve, Hartman argues, "advancing a series of speculative arguments and exploiting the capacities of the subjunctive (a grammatical mood that expresses doubts, wishes, and possibilities)" (11). It requires thinking both the scene of loss and "the matters absent, entangled and unavailable by [the methods of archival history]" (11).

10. Zora Neale Hurston, *Barracoon: The Story of the Last "Black Cargo,"* ed. Deborah G. Plant (New York: Amistad Press, 2018), 5.

11. Virginia Woolf, *The Waves* (New York: Harcourt Brace, 1931), 232; Jean Rhys, *Voyage in the Dark* (New York: Norton, 1982) 31; on empire's faltering, see Jed Esty, *Unseasonable Youth: Modernism, Colonialism, and the Fictions of Development* (New York: Oxford University Press, 2012); and John Marx, *The Modernist Novel and the Decline of Empire* (New York: Cambridge University Press, 2005).

12. Laura T. Murphy, *Metaphor and the Slave Trade in West African Literature* (Athens: Ohio University Press, 2012). Murphy argues that Tutuola's trope of "body in a bag" refers to the transatlantic slave trade. I draw on her argument here and in chapter 5.

13. See, for instance, Henry Louis Gates Jr., "The Trope of a New Negro and the Reconstruction of the Image of the Black," *Representations* 24 (Autumn 1988): 129–55.

14. Yogita Goyal, *Runaway Genres: The Global Afterlives of Slavery* (New York: New York University Press, 2019), 22.

15. In the first category is Jane Marcus, *Hearts of Darkness: White Women Write Race* (New Brunswick, NJ: Rutgers University Press, 2004); in the second are Anne Anlin Cheng,

Second Skin: Josephine Baker and the Modern Surface (New York: Oxford University Press, 2010); Ben Etherington, *Literary Primitivism* (Stanford, CA: Stanford University Press, 2018); Urmila Seshagiri, *Race and the Modernist Imagination* (Ithaca, NY: Cornell University Press, 2010); and Laura Winkiel, *Modernism, Race and Manifestos* (New York: Cambridge University Press, 2008).

16. Murphy, *Metaphor and the Slave Trade*, 1.
17. Hartman, *Lose Your Mother*, 32.
18. Maria Diedrich, Henry Louis Gates Jr., and Carl Pedersen, "The Middle Passage between History and Fiction," in *Black Imagination and the Middle Passage*, ed. Maria Diedrich, Henry Louis Gates Jr., and Carl Pedersen (New York: Oxford University Press, 1999), 8; see also Murphy, *Metaphor and the Slave Trade*, 129.
19. I take this formulation from Anna Kornbluh, *The Order of Forms: Realism, Formalism, and Social Space* (Chicago: University of Chicago Press, 2019), 6.
20. Frantz Fanon, *Black Skins, White Masks*, trans. Charles Lam Markmann (New York: Grove Press, 1967), 229.
21. This book engages with Afro-Pessimist thought that emphasizes the structural positionality of Black people in a white world. This apartness is starkly described by Frank B. Wilderson III in *Red, White & Black: Cinema and the Structure of U.S. Antagonisms* (Durham, NC: Duke University Press, 2010) where he draws on Orlando Patterson's *Slavery and Social Death*, to claim the Black in the present day is "anti-human: dishonored, perpetually open to gratuitous violence, and void of kinship structure, having no relations that need to be recognized, a being outside of relationality" (11). But many writers in the loosely affiliated Afro-Pessimist school, including Hartman, Tiffany Lethabo King, Katherine McKittrick, Fred Moten, Spillers, and Sylvia Wynter address slavery's afterlife as fundamental to Black formations of alternative kinship and community structures, experiments in wayward living, and nonhierarchical relations with the nonhuman world. It is from these latter writers and the possibility of other kinds of relations that I am primarily influenced.
22. I gloss Glissant's term in chapter 2; and Wynter's in chapter 1.
23. Cary Wolfe, *What is Posthumanism?* (Minneapolis: University of Minnesota Press, 2009), xi.
24. On the discourses of animalization and savagery through which Europeans initially made sense of their earliest encounters with Africans in West Africa, see Winthrop D. Jordan, *White Over Black: American Attitudes Toward the Negro, 1550–1812* (Chapel Hill: University of North Carolina Press, 1968), 24–40. See also Zakiyyah Iman Jackson's discussion of Jordan's text in *Becoming Human: Matter and Meaning in an Antiblack World* (New York: New York University Press, 2020), 7–9.
25. Weheliye, *Habeas Viscus*, 136. Weheliye is quoting from Walter Benjamin's 1934 article on the tenth anniversary of Franz Kafka's death.
26. Sylvia Wynter, "Beyond Miranda's Meanings: Un/Silencing the 'Demonic Ground' of Caliban's 'Woman,'" in *Out of the Kumbla: Caribbean Women and Literature*, ed. Carole Boyce Davies and Elaine Savory Fido (Trenton, NJ: Africa World Press, 1990). She defines demonic as "a frame of reference which parallels the 'demonic model' posited

by physicists who seek to conceive of a vantage point outside the space-time orientation of the humuncular [sic] observer," 364.

27. I adapt the phrase "dark underside of modernity" from Walter D. Mignolo, *The Darker Side of Western Modernity: Global Futures, Decolonial Options* (Durham, NC: Duke University Press, 2011), especially where he writes, "My focus [in this book] is the 'unity' of the colonial matrix of power, of which the rhetoric of modernity and the logic of coloniality are its two sides: one constantly named and celebrated (progress, development, growth) and the other silenced or named as problems to be solved by the former (poverty, misery, inequities, injustices, corruption, commodification, and dispensability of human life)" (xviii). Rather than objectifying coloniality as other from modernity, Mignolo insists on their co-constitution, with coloniality being the dark underside of modernity.

28. Houston A. Baker, *Modernism and the Harlem Renaissance* (Chicago: University of Chicago Press, 1987); Simon Gikandi, *Writing in Limbo: Modernism and Caribbean Literature* (Ithaca, NY: Cornell University Press, 1992); George Hutchinson, *The Harlem Renaissance in Black and White* (Cambridge, MA: Harvard University Press, 1995); Michael North, *The Dialect of Modernism: Race, Language and Twentieth-Century Literature* (New York: Oxford University Press, 1994); Jahan Ramzani, *A Transnational Poetics* (Chicago: University of Chicago Press, 2009).

29. Laura Doyle and Laura Winkiel, eds, *Geomodernisms: Race, Modernism, Modernity* (Bloomington: Indiana University Press, 2005), 3.

30. Fredric Jameson, "Modernism and Imperialism," in *Modernism, Colonialism, and Literature*, ed. Terry Eagleton, Fredric Jameson, and Edward Said (Minneapolis: University of Minnesota Press, 1990), 50–51.

31. Tiffany Lethabo King, *The Black Shoals: Offshore Formations of Black and Native Studies* (Durham, NC: Duke University Press, 2019), 23.

32. For a comparison of African and European modernisms along the lines I've sketched here, see Nicholas Brown, *Utopian Generations: The Political Horizon of Twentieth-Century Literature* (Princeton, NJ: Princeton University Press, 2005). A word here of caution: I use the term Black and African as shorthand for the process of racialization, knowing that, as Achille Mbembe writes, in *A Critique of Black Reason* (Durham, NC: Duke University Press, 2017), "Clearly not all Blacks are Africans, and not all Africans are Blacks" (12). Africanness may indicate a national or continental identity rather than a racial one.

33. Doyle and Winkiel, *Geomodernisms*, 4.

34. Jennifer Wenzel, *The Disposition of Nature: Environmental Crisis and World Literature* (New York: Fordham University Press, 2020), 2.

35. Wenzel, *The Disposition of Nature*, 9.

36. Wenzel, *The Disposition of Nature*, 9. On theorizing capitalism through the uneven circulation of contemporary literature, see the Warwick Research Collective (WReC), *Combined and Uneven Development: Towards a New Theory of World-Literature* (Liverpool: Liverpool University Press, 2015).

37. Aamir R. Mufti, *Forget English! Orientalisms and World Literatures* (Cambridge, MA: Harvard University Press, 2016), 16; See also Wenzel's extended discussion of Mufti, *The Disposition of Nature*, 27.
38. Paul Saint-Amour, "Weak Theory, Weak Modernism," *Modernism/modernity* 25, no. 3 (September 2018): 437.
39. Saint-Amour, "Weak Theory, Weak Modernism," 442.
40. Mufti, *Forget English!*, 9.
41. In the case of William Faulkner, the empire was the plantation system that enslaved Africans and African-descended peoples.
42. Mara de Gennaro, *Modernism After Postcolonialism: Toward a Nonterritorial Comparative Literature* (Baltimore, MD: Johns Hopkins University Press, 2020), 4.
43. De Gennaro, *Modernism After Postcolonialism*, 5.
44. De Gennaro, *Modernism After Postcolonialism*, 258; Wenzel, *The Disposition of Nature*, 9. De Gennaro compares Black, postcolonial, and white modernist texts. By attending to modernity's counter-history of slavery, this book addresses the formation of what Jennifer Wenzel calls, "traffic lines of power and modes of inequality" that determine which texts circulate globally, what counts as universal, what can be narrated, and what is cast off as refuse or inessential backdrop (2).
45. Simon Gikandi, "Afterword: Outside the Black Atlantic," *Research in African Literatures* 45, no. 3 (Fall 2014): 241; See also Yogita Goyal, "Africa and the Black Atlantic," *Research in African Literatures* 45, no. 3 (Fall 2014): v–xxv; Paul Gilroy, *The Black Atlantic: Modernity and Double Consciousness* (Cambridge, MA: Harvard University Press, 1993), 241.
46. Sharpe, *In the Wake*, 104.
47. Elizabeth DeLoughrey, "Heavy Waters: Waste and Atlantic Modernity," *PMLA* 125, no. 3 (2010): 704.
48. I use the term "decolonial" advisedly given the trenchant intervention of Eve Tuck and K. Wayne Yang's "Decolonization is not a Metaphor," *Decolonization: Indigeneity, Education & Society* 1, no. 1 (September 2012): 1–40. They argue that decolonization should be limited to the question of land-transfer and sovereignty of Indigenous peoples rather than settler colonial knowledge practices. However, I am persuaded by An Yountae's *The Coloniality of the Secular* (Durham, NC: Duke University Press, 2024), 13–17, that shows how the concept of sovereignty is itself a colonial term stemming from Christian politico-theological doctrine. Yountae draws on the decolonial Latin American scholarship of Enrique Dussel, Walter Mignolo, José Carlos Mariátegui, Anibal Quijano, and Sylvia Wynter.
49. Sylvia Wynter, "'No Humans Involved:' An Open Letter to My Colleagues," *Forum N.H.I.: Knowledge for the 21st Century*, "Knowledge on Trial," 1, no 1 (1994): 70. Quoted in Christina Sharpe, *In the Wake: On Blackness and Being* (Durham, NC: Duke University Press, 2016), 13.
50. Zakiyyah Iman Jackson, "Outer Worlds: The Persistence of Race in Movement 'Beyond the Human,'" *GLQ* 21, Nos. 2–3 (June 2015): 216.

51. Jackson, "Outer Worlds," 216.
52. Thank you to an anonymous reviewer for this restatement of my argument.
53. Dionne Brand, *A Map to the Door of No Return: Notes to Belonging* (Toronto: Vintage Canada, 2001), 4. Quoted in Daniel Barber, "On Black Negativity, Or The Affirmation of Nothing: Jared Sexton, Interviewed by Daniel Barber," *Society & Space* (September 18, 2017), n.p. (last accessed 05/15/2024).
54. Barber, "On Black Negativity," n.p.
55. Barber, "On Black Negativity," n.p.
56. Barber, "On Black Negativity," n.p.
57. Weheliye, in *Habeas Viscus*, writes, "Posthumanism and animal studies isomorphically yoke humanity to the limited possessive individualism of Man, because these discourses also presume that we have now entered a stage in human development where all subjects have been granted equal access to western humanity and that this is, indeed, what we all want to overcome" (10); Stacy Alaimo, *Bodily Natures: Science, Environment and the Material Self* (Bloomington: Indiana University Press, 2010); Jane Bennett, *Vibrant Matter: A Political Ecology of Things* (Durham, NC: Duke University Press, 2010); and Bruno Latour, *The Politics of Nature: How to Bring the Sciences into Democracy* (Cambridge, MA: Harvard University Press, 2004).
58. Esty, *Unseasonable Youth*. The term "intra-animated" refers to Karen Barad, *Meeting the Universe Halfway: Quantum Physics and the Entanglement of Matter and Meaning* (Durham, NC: Duke University Press, 2007). Barad uses the prefix "intra" to refer to how the social and the natural mutually constitute one another from a matrix of fluid potentialities.
59. Yan Tang, "The Politics of Naming," *Responses to the Special Issue on Weak Theory, Part 1* (blog), February 7, 2009, http://modernismmodernity.org/forums/posts/responses-special-issue-weak-theory-part-i. As part of the lively, six-part forum of responses to Saint-Amour's Modernism/modernity special issue on "Weak Theory, Weak Modernism," Tang writes, "I believe that the new modernist studies has been and will continue to be benefiting from this increasing attention to the affective-political weakening of modernism and our methodologies; more works in the vein of restructuring global modernism and decentering whiteness need to be done" (n.p.). My phrasing "breaking modernism open to the past and future," echoes my cowritten introduction with Laura Doyle to *Geomodernisms*, 3.

1. READING WITH THE SEA

1. For another instance of critical experimentation that foregrounds water's agency, see After Globalism Writing Group, "Water as Protagonist," *Social Text* 36, no. 1 (March 2018): 15–23.
2. Philip E. Steinberg and Kimberley Peters, "Wet Ontologies, Fluid Spaces: Giving Depth to Volume through Oceanic Thinking," *Environment and Planning D: Society and Space* 33, no. 2 (April 2015): 248.

3. Hester Blum, "Introduction: Oceanic Studies," *Atlantic Studies* 10, no. 2 (April 2013): 151.
4. Blum, "Introduction," 151; See also Philip E. Steinberg, "Of Other Seas," *Atlantic Studies* 10, no. 2 (April 2013): 157.
5. Steve Mentz, *Shipwreck Modernity: Ecologies of Globalization, 1550–1719* (Minneapolis: University of Minnesota Press, 2015), x.
6. This endeavor responds to critics including Michaela Bronstein, *Out of Context: The Uses of Modernist Fiction* (New York: Oxford University Press, 2020); Wai Chee Dimock, *Through Other Continents: American Literature across Deep Time* (Princeton, NJ: Princeton University Press, 2006); Rita Felski, *The Limits of Critique* (Chicago: University of Chicago Press, 2015); Susan Stanford Friedman, "Alternatives to Periodization: Literary History, Modernism, and the 'New' Temporalities," *Modern Language Quarterly* 80, no. 4 (December 2019): 379–402; and Eric Hayot, "Against Periodization; or, On Institutional Time," *New Literary History* 42, no. 4 (Autumn 2011): 739–56. In myriad ways, they call for reading modernist and other literatures through transhistorical frameworks that extend into the past and future. Friedman, who has long argued against the conventional periodization of modernism, asks, "Can we abandon the linear logic of periodization in favor of nonlinear notions of time to forge new methods of literary history that do not reproduce the limitation of conventional periodization?" (381). Periodization, she argues, depends upon the fixed boundaries of the time and territory of the nation that conventionally determine disciplinary units of history (385); See also Hayot, "Against Periodization," 151, 154. These units largely determine the context in which we read literature. Rejecting this narrow notion of time and space that pin the literary text to the site of authorship, Rita Felski, in *The Limits of Critique*, asserts that "standard ways of thinking about historical context are unable to explain how works of art move across time. We need models of textual mobility and transhistorical attachment that refuse to be browbeaten by the sacrosanct status of period boundaries" (154). Stating definitively that "History is not a box," Felski alerts us to how attention to the transhistorical circulation of literature reveal how texts function as "nonhuman actors" that are co-constituted with readers across a range of times and locations (154). By "nonhuman actors," she means that literature acts on its readers: they entangle readers in atmospheres, moods, rhythms, and affects that are physically felt. Literature draws the reader outside of themselves, enmeshes them in imagined landscapes, and exposes them to unfamiliar characters in other parts of the world.
7. Stephanie Smallwood, *Saltwater Slavery: A Middle Passage from Africa to American Diaspora* (Cambridge, MA: Harvard University Press, 2007), 7.
8. Smallwood, *Saltwater Slavery*, 2.
9. Smallwood, *Saltwater Slavery*, 34.
10. Smallwood, *Saltwater Slavery*, 35.
11. Smallwood, *Saltwater Slavery*, 35.
12. Smallwood, *Saltwater Slavery*, 5.
13. Hortense J. Spillers, "Mama's Baby, Papa's Maybe: An American Grammar Book," *Diacritics* 17, no. 2 (Summer 1987): 67.

14. Spillers, "Mama's Baby," 67.
15. Spillers, "Mama's Baby," 80; See also "'Whatcha Gonna Do?': Revisiting 'Mama's Baby, Papa's Maybe: An American Grammar Book:' A Conversation with Hortense Spillers, Saidiya Hartman, Farah Jasmine Griffin, Shelly Eversley, & Jennifer L. Morgan," *Women's Studies Quarterly* 35, no. 1–2 (Spring/Summer 2007), where Hartman says of Spillers's essay, "For me, part of the power of the essay is really about mobilizing black feminism and postcolonialism to do the work of interrogating the writing of the human" (303).
16. Spillers, "Mama's Baby," 72.
17. Frank B. Wilderson III, "The Position of the Unthought: An Interview with Saidiya V. Hartman," *Qui Parle* 13, no. 2 (Spring/Summer 2003): 184.
18. Wilderson III, "The Position of the Unthought," 185.
19. Wilderson III, "The Position of the Unthought," 187.
20. Saidiya V. Hartman, *Scenes of Subjection: Terror, Slavery, and Self-Making in Nineteenth-Century America* (New York: Oxford University Press, 1997), 21.
21. Hartman, *Scenes of Subjection*, 21.
22. Hartman, *Scenes of Subjection*, 7.
23. Tiffany Lethabo King, "The Labour of (Re)Reading Plantation Landscapes Fungible(ly)," *Antipode* 48, no. 4 (2016): 1025.
24. King, "Labor of (Re)Reading," 1025.
25. Jennifer L. Morgan, *Laboring Women: Reproduction and Gender in New World Slavery* (Philadelphia: University of Pennsylvania Press, 2004), 48; Richard Ligon, *A True and Exact History of the Island of Barbados* (London: St. Paul's Churchyard, 1657), 43–44.
26. Morgan, *Laboring Women*, 8; see also King, "Labor of (Re)reading," 1027.
27. King, "Labor of (Re)Reading," 1023.
28. King, "Labor of (Re)Reading," 1024.
29. C. Riley Snorton, *Black on Both Sides: A Racial History of Trans Identity* (Minneapolis: University of Minnesota Press, 2017), 84.
30. Karl Marx, *Capital: A Critique of Political Economy, Vol. 1* (New York: Vintage, 1977), 166.
31. Marx, in *Capital*, writes that "The commodity-form, and the value-relation of the products of labour within which it appears, have absolutely no connection with the physical nature of the commodity and the material [dinglich] relations arising out of this" (165).
32. Ewa Płonowska Ziarek, *Feminist Aesthetics and the Politics of Modernism* (New York: Columbia University Press, 2012). In particular, I draw on Part II, "Female Bodies, Violence and Form."
33. Fred Moten, *In the Break: The Aesthetics of the Black Radical Tradition* (Minneapolis: University of Minnesota Press, 2003), 2, 11.
34. Theodore W. Adorno, *Aesthetic Theory* (Minneapolis: University of Minnesota Press, 1997), 5.
35. Ziarek, *Feminist Aesthetics*, 12.
36. Ziarek, *Feminist Aesthetics*, 12.
37. Ziarek, *Feminist Aesthetics*, 12.

38. Ziarek, *Feminist Aesthetics*, 150. Ziarek is drawing from Orlando Patterson, *Slavery and Social Death: A Comparative Study*, rev. ed. (1982; repr., Cambridge, MA: Harvard University Press, 2018), 38, 46–48.
39. Ziarek, *Feminist Aesthetics*, 125.
40. Adorno, *Aesthetic Theory*, 23.
41. Katherine McKittrick, *Demonic Grounds: Black Women and the Cartographies of Struggle* (Minneapolis: University of Minnesota Press, 2006), xxii.
42. Édouard Glissant, *Caribbean Discourse: Selected Essays* (Charlottesville: University of Virginia Press, 1989), 150.
43. John E. Drabinski. *Glissant and the Middle Passage: Philosophy, Beginning, Abyss* (Minneapolis: University of Minnesota Press, 2019), 16.
44. Drabinski, *Glissant and the Middle Passage*, 140.
45. Jay Rajiva, *Towards an Animist Reading of Postcolonial Trauma Literature* (New York: Routledge, 2022), 11.
46. Rajiva, *Towards an Animist Reading*, 12–13.
47. The term "animism" has its own negative connotations. Graham Harvey, in *Animism: Respecting the Living World* (London: Hurst & Co., 2005), justifies its continued use as follows: "[Many academics] consider 'animism' irredeemably compromised by the dubious role it played in early anthropological theorising and religious polemic. I would agree with this assessment but for the fact that the term has escaped the constrictions imposed upon it by its colonial origins" (xviii).
48. Harry Garuba, "Explorations in Animist Materialism: Notes on Reading/Writing African Literature, Culture, and Society," *Public Culture* 15, no. 2 (2003): 270.
49. Rajiva, *Towards an Animist Reading*, 13.
50. Praxis denotes performativity and hence the fluidity and fungibility of the human. This notion differs fundamentally from the liberal humanist notion that Man establishes his supremacy by doing. For instance, Hannah Arendt in *The Human Condition* (Chicago: University of Chicago Press, 1998), writes "Labor assures not only individual survival, but the life of the species. Work and its product, the human artifact, bestow a measure of permanence and durability upon the futility of mortal life and the fleeting character of human time" (8).
51. Sylvia Wynter and Katherine McKittrick, "Unparalleled Catastrophe for Our Species? Or, to Give Humanness a Different Future: Conversations," in *Sylvia Wynter: On Being Human as Praxis*, ed. Katherine McKittrick (Durham, NC: Duke University Press, 2015), 33.
52. Alexander G. Weheliye, *Habeas Viscus: Racializing Assemblages, Biopolitics, and Black Feminist Theories of the Human* (Durham, NC: Duke University Press, 2014), 2.
53. Weheliye, *Habeas Viscus*, 2.
54. Jodi Byrd, *The Transit of Empire: Indigenous Critiques of Colonialism* (Minneapolis: University of Minnesota Press, 2011); Denise Ferreira Da Silva, *Towards a Global Idea of Race* (Minneapolis: University of Minnesota Press, 2007); Simon Gikandi, *Slavery and the Culture of Taste* (Princeton, NJ: Princeton University Press, 2011); Paul Gilroy, *The Black Atlantic: Modernity and Double Consciousness* (Cambridge, MA: Harvard

University Press, 1993); Hartman, *Scenes of Subjection*; Lisa Lowe, *The Intimacies of Four Continents* (Durham, NC: Duke University Press, 2015); Walter Mignolo, *The Darker Side of Western Modernity* (Durham, NC: Duke University Press, 2011); and Sylvia Wynter, "Unsettling the Coloniality of Being/Power/Truth/Freedom," *The New Centennial Review* 3, no 3 (Fall 2003).

55. Philip E. Steinberg, *The Social Construction of the Ocean* (New York: Cambridge University Press, 2001), contests the significance of this treaty: "There is little basis for the commonly held belief that these documents [The Treaty of Tordesillas] represent a parceling of foreign lands and even less basis for the belief that they represent a division of the world-ocean" (76). Instead, he says, "The 100-league line did not so much divide land-space or ocean-space between Spain and Portugal as it allocated to the two states exclusive vectors of exploration" (81). This point aligns with his larger argument that the seas cannot be mapped in the same manner that territory can. Rather, the ocean was constructed as an empty, voided space of passage. I return to this point later in the interlude. Nonetheless, I hold by Mignolo's emphasis on the epistemological importance of the documents, how they announce a universal, abstract scientific mapping of the globe, parceled out between two imperial nations. His reading follows that by Carl Schmitt, *The Nomos of the Earth in the International Law of the Jus Publicum Europaeum*, trans. G. L. Ulmen (New York: Telos Press, 2006); Elizabeth M. DeLoughrey, *Routes and Roots: Navigating Caribbean and Pacific Island Literature* (Honolulu: University of Hawai'i Press, 2007), also reads the Treaty along these lines (31). I thank marine historian Helen Rozwadowski for alerting me to this disagreement.

56. Schmitt, *Nomos*, 93. Glossing this point further, he says, "Everything that occurred 'beyond the line' remained outside the legal, moral, and political values recognized on this side of the line" (94). This geographical mapping designated "two types of 'open' spaces in which the activity of European nations proceeded unrestrained: first, an immeasurable space of free land—the New World, America, the land of freedom, i.e., land free for appropriation by Europeans—where the 'old' law was not in force; and second, the free *sea*—the newly discovered oceans conceived by the French, Dutch, and English to be a realm of freedom" (94).

57. Mignolo, *The Darker Side of Western Modernity*, 79.

58. See also Da Silva, *Towards a Global Idea of Race*, and Wynter, "Unsettling the Coloniality of Being/Power/Truth/Freedom," for concurrent genealogies of the modern.

59. Michelle Burnham, in *Transoceanic America: Risk, Writing, and Revolution in the Global Pacific* (New York: Oxford University Press, 2019), examines Pacific travel narratives of the eighteenth century and underscores how "the goals of disinterested scientific knowledge and self-interested commercial gains were always intricately entangled with one another; in most cases, the state-sponsored circumnavigations publicly announced goals of scientific discovery (such as tracking the transit of Venus, or locating the great southern continent, or charting new coastlines) while also secretly pursuing commercial goals (such as identifying new trade goods or locating sites for the establishment of trading posts, or competing in already established trade networks)" (33).

60. Mignolo, *The Darker Side of Western Modernity*, 80.

61. Two key figures in contesting the objectivity of scientific thought are Donna Haraway, "Situated Knowledges: the Science Question in Feminism and the Privilege of Partial Perspective," *Feminist Studies* 14, no. 3 (1988): 575–99, and Bruno Latour, *Politics of Nature: How to Bring the Sciences into Democracy* (Cambridge, MA: Harvard University Press, 2004).
62. Mignolo, *The Darker Side of Western Modernity*, 78.
63. See, for example, Simon Gikandi, *Slavery and the Culture of Taste* (Princeton, NJ: Princeton University Press, 2011).
64. Steinberg, *Social Construction*, 113.
65. Roland Barthes, *Mythologies*, trans. Jonathan Cape Ltd. (New York: Farrar, Straus and Giroux, 1972), 112.
66. Gaston Bachelard, *Water and Dreams: An Essay on the Imagination of Matter*, trans. Edith R. Farrell (Dallas, TX: The Dallas Institute Press, 1983), 12.
67. Burnham, *Transoceanic America*, 39.
68. Wynter, "Unsettling the Coloniality of Being/Power/Truth/Freedom," 265.
69. Wynter, "Unsettling the Coloniality of Being/Power/Truth/Freedom," 263; See also Mignolo, *The Darker Side of Western Modernity*, and Da Silva, *Towards a Global Idea of Race*.
70. Tiffany Lethabo King, *The Black Shoals: Offshore Formations of Black and Native Studies* (Durham, NC: Duke University Press, 2019), 76.
71. King, *The Black Shoals*, 79.
72. Lowe, *Intimacies of Four Continents*, 16.
73. Gilroy, in *Black Atlantic*, locates in the conflict between enslaved people and masters and mistresses the ungrounding of a metaphysics of meaning: Slavery, he writes, "was the product of circumstances where language lost something of its referentiality and its privileged relationship to concepts" (74). This crisis of representation finds itself well attuned toward finding formal expression through modernist experimentalism.
74. Simon Gikandi, in "Race and Cosmopolitanism," *American Literary History* 14, no. 3 (2002): 593–615, writes that "I want to use [Paul Gilroy's] *Against Race* to think through some of the conceptual and political problems that arise when the critique of race and racialism and other forms of identity rooted in a particular polity, nation, or region is brought face to face with the desire for a cosmopolitan identity" (594). The problem is, he says, "that the very institutions that were supposed to will into being universal and cosmopolitan identities were not simply corrupted by racialism, but were immanently racialist, if not racist" (599). Gilroy, he argues, "is acutely aware of the fatal linkage between race, nation, and cosmopolitanism in the genesis of modernity" but tries to redeem cosmopolitan thought by means of its purportedly democratic ethos that, as Gikandi argues, forcefully continues to exclude African and African-descended peoples from its inclusive vision (597, 599–601).
75. Douglas Mao and Rebecca L. Walkowitz, "The New Modernist Studies," *PMLA* 123, no. 3 (2008): 737–48. They argue that the new modernist studies that emerged around 1999 with the inauguration of the Modernist Studies Association possesses an "expansive tendency, the field is hardly unique: all period-centered areas of literary

scholarship have broadened in scope, and this is what we might think of as temporal, spatial, and vertical directions" (737). The new modernist studies reconfigures modernism as more inclusive of peripheral geographies, middlebrow and lowbrow cultural productions, and other media besides print cultures.

76. Zakiyyah Iman Jackson, *On Becoming Human: Matter and Meaning in an Antiblack World* (New York: New York University Press, 2020), 45.
77. Jackson, *On Becoming Human*, 45.
78. Joshua Bennett, *Being Property Once Myself: Blackness and the End of Man* (Cambridge, MA: Harvard University Press, 2020); Mara de Gennaro, *Modernism after Postcolonialism: Toward a Nonterritorial Comparative Literature* (Baltimore, MD: Johns Hopkins University Press, 2020); Nadia Nurhussein, *Black Land: Imperial Ethiopianism and African America* (Princeton, NJ: Princeton University Press, 2019); and Sonya Posmentier, *Cultivation and Catastrophe: The Lyric Ecology of Modern Black Literature* (Baltimore, MD: Johns Hopkins University Press, 2017).
79. Saidiya Hartman, "Venus in 2 Acts," *Small Axe* 26, vol. 12, no. 2 (June 2008): 2–3.
80. See *An Abstract of Evidence Delivered before a Select Committee of the House of Commons in the Years 1790, and 1791; On the Part of the Petitioners for the Abolition of the Slave-Trade* (London: James Philips, 1791), 102–3, for a description of so-called "refuse" bondspeople. See Dr. Falconbridge's testimony in the same abstract where he relates, "They had not so much room *as a man in his coffin either in length or breadth*" (85). The term "coffin ship" generally refers to the ships that brought Irish immigrants to the Americas during the Great Famine in the nineteenth century.
81. Smallwood, *Saltwater Slavery*, 125.
82. Marcus Rediker, *The Slave Ship: A Human History* (New York: Viking Penguin, 2007), 37–40. "The Greedy Robbers" section focuses on the sharks that trailed slave ships across the Atlantic.
83. Vincent Brown, "Social Death and Political Life in the Study of Slavery," *The American Historical Review* 114, no. 5 (December 2009): 1246.
84. Smallwood, *Saltwater Slavery*, 189, 191; also quoted in Brown, "Social Death," 1241.
85. Brown, "Social Death," 1246. Saidiya Hartman, in *Lose Your Mother: A Journey Along the Atlantic Slave Route* (New York: Macmillan Press, 2008), also comments on the omnipresence of death on board the slave ship. She writes, "It made it easier for a trader to countenance yet another dead black body or for a captain to dump a shipload of captives into the sea in order to collect the insurance, since it wasn't possible to kill cargo or to murder a thing already denied life. Death was simply part of the workings of the trade" (33).
86. See Toni Morrison, *Beloved* (New York: Vintage, 1987), where she writes, "All of it is now it is always now there will never be a time when I am not crouching and watching others who are crouching too" (210).
87. Kevin Dawson, *Undercurrents of Power: Aquatic Culture in the African Diaspora* (Philadelphia: University of Pennsylvania Press, 2021), 2; See also Ray Costello, *Black Salt: Seafarers of African Descent on British Ships* (Liverpool: Liverpool University Press,

2012), 76 and especially chapter 1 in which he describes the nautical and especially the navigational skills of coastal African sailors.
88. Dawson, *Undercurrents of Power*, 192, 194.
89. On slave ship melancholy, see Ramesh Mallipeddi, "'A Fixed Melancholy': Migration, Memory, and the Middle Passage," *The Eighteenth Century* 55, No. 2–3 (Summer/Fall 2014): 235–53.
90. *Abstract of Evidence Delivered*, 94.
91. Sowande' M. Mustakeem, *Slavery at Sea: Terror, Sex, and Sickness in the Middle Passage* (Urbana: University of Illinois Press, 2016), 117; see also Dawson, *Undercurrents of Power*, where he writes, "African cosmology provided a foundation for transmigration beliefs as people routinely integrated elements believed to facilitate this process into suicidal acts. Many Atlantic Africans believed water and wood linked the living to the world of the spirits, which was located either in or across a real or imagined body of water" (203).
92. *Abstract of Evidence Delivered*, 94.
93. *Abstract of Evidence Delivered*, 96.
94. Mustakeem, *Slavery at Sea*, 129.
95. Melody Jue, *Wild Blue Media: Thinking Through Seawater* (Durham, NC: Duke University Press, 2020). Jue writes that "When thinking through seawater, . . . processes of inscription and recording give way to watery processes of mediation involving residues and saturation. In all their ecological and spatial diversity, the oceans prompt a fundamental reexamination of the underlying environmental poetics and metaphorics of our concepts and theoretical positions" (163). These concepts include being human itself. Thinking through being human in the ocean depths, as Jue demonstrates, radically defamiliarizes humans' intra-actions with their environment at the level of oxygen saturation, proprioception, gravity, and atmospheric pressure.
96. Jackson, *On Becoming Human*, 57.
97. Fred D'Aguilar, *Feeding the Ghosts* (New York: HarperCollins, 1997), 41.
98. I am indebted to Christina Sharpe for her reading of this scene in D'Aguilar's novel at the University of Colorado, Boulder, on April 6, 2018.
99. D'Aguilar, *Feeding the Ghosts*, 207.
100. Hortense Spillers, "Mama's Baby, Papa's Maybe: An American Grammar Book," *Diacritics* 17, no. 2 (Summer 1987): 64–81. She defines flesh as "that zero degree of social conceptualization" (67). In *Scenes of Subjection*, Hartman calls it "existence defined at its most elemental level" (5).
101. King, *Black Shoals*, 24.
102. Zora Neale Hurston, *Barracoon: The Story of the Last "Black Cargo,"* ed. Deborah G. Plant (New York: Amistad Press, 2018), 5–6.
103. Hurston, *Barracoon*, 15.
104. The spelling of the ship *Clotilde* was common in the early twentieth century. Contemporary accounts prefer *Clotilda*.
105. Hurston, *Barracoon*, 55.

106. Kossula's account of the voyage states that it took seventy days, see Hurston, *Barracoon*, 56; Hannah Durkin's *The Survivors of the* Clotilda: *The Lost Stories of the Last Captives of the American Slave Trade* (New York: Amistad Press, 2024) claims that the voyage lasted just over six weeks (60). Thanks to Professor Miriam Thaggert for alerting me to Durkin's newly published text.
107. Hurston, *Barracoon*, 49.
108. Deborah G. Plant, afterword to *Barracoon*, by Zora Neale Hurston, 130.
109. Marissa, K. Lopéz, *Racial Immanence: Chicanx Bodies Beyond Representation* (New York: New York University Press, 2019), 6.
110. See Jue, *Wild Blue Media*, "Interface: Breathing Underwater," for a discussion of human proprioception when underwater.
111. Mel Y. Chen, *Animacies: Biopolitics, Racial Mattering, and Queer Affect* (Durham, NC: Duke University Press, 2012), 42.
112. It is significant that Kossula maintains that the passage was otherwise humane and uneventful: "Nobody ain' sick and nobody ain' dead. Cap'n Bill Foster a good man. He don't 'buse us and treat us mean on de ship," Hurston, *Barracoon*, 56. Despite their good treatment, the sea terrorizes and strips the captives of their sense of self.
113. Hurston, *Barracoon*, 74.
114. Olaudah Equiano, *Equiano's Travels*, ed. Paul Edwards (New York: Heineman Press, 1967), 25.
115. Admittedly, Hurston uses "skeered" in all of her renditions of African American dialect, but Kossula is the only speaker for whom the long e sound is attached to every verb as well as to some nonverbs: for example, "molassee" and "nexy" (next).
116. Julie Beth Napolin, *The Fact of Resonance: Modernist Acoustics and Narrative Form* (New York: Fordham University Press 2020), 5.
117. Napolin, *Fact of Resonance*. I am indebted to Napolin for this insight. She links the consolidated vision of empire with the consolidated voice, "soundless and implicitly neutral. The consolidated vision thus pushes out of view as much as (or perhaps more than) it presents for view. The acoustics of what is pushed out of view is what [Napolin's book draws attention to]" (3).
118. Hurston, *Barracoon*, 17, 88.
119. Hurston, *Barracoon*, 89.
120. Hurston, *Barracoon*, 98.
121. Hurston, *Barracoon*, 94. The notion that "we are being shown the wound," is taken from Alice Walker, forward to *Barracoon* by Zora Neale Hurston, xii.
122. I am drawing in part from Napolin, *Fact of Resonance*, chapter 2.
123. Joseph Conrad, *The Nigger of the 'Narcissus'* (New York: Penguin, 1989), 126.
124. Conrad, *Nigger of the 'Narcissus,'* 121.
125. Conrad, *Nigger of the 'Narcissus,'* 21.
126. Maxwell Uphaus, "Hurry Up and Wait: *The Nigger of the 'Narcissus'* and the Maritime in Modernism," *Modernist Cultures* 12, no. 2 (2017): 176.
127. Uphaus, "Hurry Up and Wait," 176.
128. Uphaus, "Hurry Up and Wait," 176.

129. Conrad, *Nigger of the 'Narcissus,'* 95.
130. Uphaus, "Hurry Up and Wait," 184.
131. Conrad, *Nigger of the 'Narcissus,'* 96.
132. Conrad, *Nigger of the 'Narcissus,'* 17, 52, 112.
133. Conrad, "To My Readers in America," *Nigger of the 'Narcissus,'* xlv.
134. Conrad, *Nigger of the 'Narcissus,'* 111, 113.
135. Conrad, *Nigger of the 'Narcissus,'* 76.
136. Conrad, *Nigger of the 'Narcissus,'* 77.
137. Michael North, *The Dialect of Modernism: Race, Language, and Twentieth-Century Literature* (New York: Oxford University Press, 1998), 54.
138. North, *Dialect of Modernism*, 55.
139. North, *Dialect of Modernism*, 56.
140. Conrad, *Nigger of the 'Narcissus,'* 128.
141. Conrad, *Nigger of the 'Narcissus,'* 83.
142. Conrad, *Nigger of the 'Narcissus,'* 83.

2. ALLUVIUM

1. Édouard Glissant, *Poetics of Relation* (Ann Arbor: University of Michigan Press, 1997), 7.
2. Sylvia Wynter, *Black Metamorphosis: New Natives in a New World* (Institute of the Black World Papers, Schomburg Center for Research in Black Culture), n.d. I take the figure of 1.8 million lost at sea from Marcus Rediker, *The Slave Ship: A Human History* (New York: Viking Penguin, 2007), 5. This number is also estimated at www.slavevoyages.org.
3. Glissant, *Poetics of Relation*, 111.
4. Glissant, *Poetics of Relation*, 111.
5. Glissant, *Poetics of Relation*, 7. While Glissant holds up the Caribbean as intensely creolized and therefore a vital source for studying the poetics of relation, he begins this book by invoking "all Africans who lived through the experience of deportation to the Americas" via the transatlantic slave trade (5). Hence, I also use the term "Black" to refer to Glissant's collectivity.
6. Glissant, *Poetics of Relation*, 7.
7. Glissant, *Poetics of Relation*, 8.
8. Rizvana Bradley and Damien-Adia Marassa, "Awakening to the World: Relation, Totality, and Writing from Below," *Discourse* 36, no. 1 (Winter 2014): 113.
9. Quoted in Valérie Loichot, *Water Graves: The Art of the Unritual in the Greater Caribbean* (Charlottesville: University of Virginia Press, 2020), 29.
10. Loichot, *Water Graves*, 28.
11. Loichot, *Water Graves*, 29.
12. Loichot, *Water Graves*, 28.
13. An Yountae, *The Coloniality of the Secular: Race, Religion, and Poetics of World Making* (Durham, NC: Duke University Press, 2024), 166. Yountae's work alerted me to Loichot's discussion of *entour*.

14. Yountae, *The Coloniality of the Secular*, 164.
15. Ewa Płonowska Ziarek, *Feminist Aesthetics and the Politics of Modernism* (New York: Columbia University Press, 2012), 176.
16. Theodor W. Adorno, *Aesthetic Theory* (Minneapolis: University of Minnesota Press, 1997), 7.
17. For histories of the Black Atlantic that foreground Black masculinity, see Paul Gilroy, *The Black Atlantic: Modernity and Double Consciousness* (Cambridge, MA: Harvard University Press, 1993); and Michelle Ann Stephens, *Black Empire: The Masculine Global Imaginary of Caribbean Intellectuals in the United States, 1914–1962* (Durham, NC: Duke University Press, 2005). Glissant uses the term "womb abyss" in *Poetics of Relation*, 6.
18. Édouard Glissant, *Caribbean Discourse: Selected Essays* (Charlottesville: University of Virginia Press, 1989), 66.
19. C. Riley Snorton, *Black on Both Sides: A Racial History of Trans Identities* (Minneapolis: University of Minnesota Press, 2017), 10.
20. Snorton, *Black on Both Sides*, 8.
21. Katherine McKittrick, *Demonic Grounds: Black Women and the Cartographies of Struggle* (Minneapolis: University of Minnesota Press, 2006), xi.
22. McKittrick, *Demonic Grounds*, xi.
23. McKittrick, *Demonic Grounds*, ix.
24. Critics who explore how geographies and bodies are malleable and porous, as detailed in chapter 1, include Alaimo, Bennett, Butler, Chen, King, McKittrick, Snorton, Wehiliye, and Sylvia Wynter, "Unsettling the Coloniality of Being/Power/Truth/Freedom: Toward the Human, After Man, Its Overrepresentation–An Argument," *The New Centennial Review* 3, no. 3 (Fall 2003): 257–337.
25. Robert F. Reid-Pharr, *Archives of Flesh: African America, Spain, and Post-Humanist Critique* (New York: New York University Press, 2016), 130.
26. Avery F. Gordon, *Ghostly Matters: Haunting and the Sociological Imagination* (Minneapolis: University of Minnesota Press, 1997), 195.
27. Langston Hughes, *The Big Sea: An Autobiography* (New York: Hill and Wang, 1993), 3. In this unburdening, Hughes echoes the long history of the colonizer's impulse to jettison books into the sea when embarking on or concluding a long voyage. Hakluyt's "A Discourse Concerning Western Planting" (1584) cautions that "Our men are driven to fling their Bibles and prayer books into the sea"; Shakespeare's Prospero throws his "book of magic spells deeper into the sea than any anchor ever sank" (Act 5, scene 1); and, travelers, in avoiding customs' censorship, often flung contraband books into the ports as they approached harbor, as Isabel Hofmeyr has traced. Later, Edwidge Danticat reinflects this trope as a silencing by means of the unspeakable loss of refugees drowned at sea. In "Children of the Sea," the Haitian refugees, fleeing the political violence of the Ton Ton Macoutes, throw their belongings, including the protagonist's journal that records his narrative, into the sea to postpone the capsizing of their boat.
28. Henry Louis Gates Jr., *The Signifying Monkey: A Theory of African-American Literary Criticism* (New York: Oxford University Press, 1988). The trope of the Talking Book "is the first repeated and revised trope of the [African American] tradition" (131). It

defines the African American's relationship to literacy, reason, and civilizational accomplishment. In Olaudah Equiano's *The Interesting Narrative of the Life of Olaudah Equiano, or Gustavus Vassa the African*, ed. Paul Edwards (1789; Portsmouth, NH: Heinemann, 1967), Equiano describes his initial encounter with the Talking Book: "I had often seen my master and Dick employed in reading; and I had a great curiosity to talk to the books, as I thought they did; and so to learn how all things had a beginning: for that purpose I have often taken up a book, and have talked to it, and then put my ears to it, when alone, in hopes that it would answer me; and I have remained very much concerned when it remained silent" (40). As the older, narrating Equiano comments on his younger, naïve African self, the shift in verb tense, Gates argues, "represent[s] the very movement that he is experiencing . . . as he transforms himself from African to Anglo-African, from slave to potential freedman, from an absence to a presence, and indeed from an object to a subject" (*The Signifying Monkey*, 157). Other slave narratives that feature the trope of the Talking Book include those by James Gronniosaw, John Marrat, John Jea, and Ottabah Cugoano. See also Yogita Goyal, *Runaway Genres: The Global Afterlives of Slavery* (New York: New York University Press, 2019), particularly chapter 4.

29. Hughes, *Big Sea*, 4.
30. Hughes, *Big Sea*, 98.
31. Saidiya V. Hartman, *Scenes of Subjection: Terror, Slavery, and Self-Making in Nineteenth-Century America* (New York: Oxford University Press, 1997), 117.
32. Hartman, *Scenes of Subjection*, 116.
33. Houston A. Baker, *Modernism and the Harlem Renaissance* (Chicago: University of Chicago Press, 1987), xvi.
34. Gates Jr., *Signifying Monkey*, 128.
35. Langston Hughes, "Sea Charm," *The Collected Poems of Langston Hughes*, ed. Arnold Rampersad (New York: Vintage, 1994), 44–45.
36. Hughes, "Caribbean Sunset," *The Collected Poems of Langston Hughes*, 98.
37. Hughes, "The Negro Mother," *The Collected Poems of Langston Hughes*, 155.
38. Shane Graham, *Cultural Entanglements: Langston Hughes and the Rise of African and Caribbean Literature* (Charlottesville: University of Virginia Press, 2020), 48.
39. Graham, *Cultural Entanglements*, 59.
40. Hughes, "To the Little Fort of San Lazaro on the Ocean Front, Havana," *The Collected Poems of Langston Hughes*, 136.
41. Graham, *Cultural Entanglements*, 65.
42. Graham, *Cultural Entanglements*, 65.
43. Hughes, "To the Little Fort," 137.
44. Hughes, *Big Sea*, 101.
45. Reid-Pharr, *Archives of Flesh*, 122.
46. Hughes, *Big Sea*, 91.
47. Hughes, *Big Sea*, 91. Planks, notoriously, were implemented during the slave trade. "Walking the plank" was a method of eliminating unwanted cargo. For Mr. Ecroyde Claxton's testimony, see "Minutes of the Evidence Taken before a Committee of the

House of Commons, Being a Select Committee, Appointed to take the Examination of Witnesses respecting the African SLAVE TRADE" (1791; reprinted New York: Cambridge University Press, 2007), 37.
48. Hughes, *Big Sea*, 91–92.
49. Hughes, *Big Sea*, 94–95.
50. See, Michael Rubenstein, Bruce Robbins, and Sophia Beal, "Infrastructuralism: An Introduction," in *Modern Fiction Studies* 61, no. 4 (Winter 2015): 576.
51. Hughes, *Big Sea*, 56.
52. Nadia Nurhussein, "Langston Hughes's Ship to Nowhere," a paper presented at the ACLA "Modernism's Working Waterfronts" seminar, April 2021. n.p. I am grateful to her for sharing with me her paper.
53. Hughes, *Big Sea*, 91.
54. Hughes, *Big Sea*, 90.
55. Hughes, *Big Sea*, 96.
56. Langston Hughes, "The Weary Blues," in *The Collected Poems of Langston Hughes*, ed. Arnold Rampersad and David Roessel (New York: Vintage, 1995), 50, line 35.
57. Nurhussein reads the ending of "The Weary Blues" as "echoing the suicidal end of the blues verse a few lines earlier, 'I wish that I had died.'" The choice between "sleeping like a rock," that she reads as healthy and "like a dead man," leaves the blues player, she writes, bound in a liminal state of suspended animation, borrowing the term from Rampersad (n.p.).
58. Arnold Rampersad, *The Life of Langston Hughes. Volume 1: 1902-1941* (New York: Oxford University Press, 2002), 61.
59. See, for instance, Graham, *Cultural Entanglements*, 11.
60. Hughes, in *Big Sea*, writes, "I realized that most dark Negroes in America do not like the word black at all. They prefer to be referred to as brownskin, or at the most as dark brownskin—no matter how dark they really are" (103-4). Hughes, however, due to his Native American and other ancestry, is called "white" by the Kru men he meets.
61. Hughes, *Big Sea*, 102.
62. Hughes, *Big Sea*, 112.
63. Hughes, *Big Sea*, 112.
64. Hughes, *Big Sea*, 112.
65. Eric Walrond, *Tropic Death* (New York: Liveright, 2013), 82.
66. Harris Feinsod, "Canal Zone Modernism: Cendrars, Walrond, and Stevens at the 'Suction Sea,'" *English Language Notes*, ed. Laura Winkiel, 57, no. 1 (April 2019): 123.
67. For more on this term, see Brett Clarke and John Bellamy Foster, "Ecological Imperialism and the Global Metabolic Rift: Unequal Exchange and the Guano/Nitrates Trade," *International Journal of Comparative Sociology* 50, no. 2–3 (2009): 311–34.
68. Hughes, *Big Sea*, 112.
69. Hughes, *Big Sea*, 112.
70. Omri Moses, *Out of Character: Modernism, Vitalism, Psychic Life* (Stanford, CA: Stanford University Press, 2014). Moses analyzes how modernist writers "focused on creating individuals [characters and personas] who set store by their openness to circumstance.

These characters think and act on the basis of attitudes that are not shaped in advance" (2).

71. Rampersad, *Life of Langston Hughes*, 377; see also Lindon Barrett, "The Gaze of Langston Hughes: Subjectivity, Homoeroticism, and the Feminine in *The Big Sea*," *Yale Journal of Criticism* 12, no. 2 (Fall 1999): 383; and Brian Loftus, "In/Verse Autobiography: Sexual (In)Difference and the Textual Backside of Langston Hughes's *The Big Sea*," *Auto/Biography Studies* 15, no. 1 (2000): 141–61.
72. Ziarek, *Feminist Aesthetics*, p. 176.
73. Hughes, *Big Sea*, 4.
74. Hughes, *Big Sea*, 4.
75. Hughes, *Big Sea*, 4.
76. Loftus, "In/Verse Autobiography," 152.
77. Omise'eke Natasha Tinsley, "Black Atlantic, Queer Atlantic: Queer Imaginings of the Middle Passage," in *GLQ* 14, no. 2–4 (2008): 199.
78. Tinsley, "Black Atlantic, Queer Atlantic," 199.
79. Glissant, *Caribbean Discourse*, 66–67; see also Snorton, *Black on Both Sides*, 7, 10.
80. Snorton, *Black on Both Sides*, 6.
81. Hughes, *Big Sea*, 7.
82. Hughes, *Big Sea*, 7.
83. Hortense J. Spillers, "Mama's Baby, Papa's Maybe: An American Grammar Book," *Diacritics* 17, no. 2 (Summer, 1987): 67.
84. Snorton, *Black on Both Sides*, 8, quoting Stryker, Currah, and Moore.
85. Hughes, *Big Sea*, 107–8.
86. Hughes, *Big Sea*, 108.
87. Reid-Pharr, *Archives of Flesh*, 122–23.
88. Zora Neale Hurston, *Their Eyes Were Watching God* (1937; reprint New York: HarperCollins, 1990), 129.
89. Isabel Hofmeyr, "Provisional Notes on Hydrocolonialism," *ELN*, ed. Laura Winkiel, 57, no. 1 (April 2019): 15.
90. Hofmeyr, "Provisional Notes," 15.
91. Brian Russell Roberts, "Archipelagic Diaspora, Geographical Form, and Hurston's *Their Eyes Were Watching God*," *American Literature* 85, no. 1 (March 2013): 138.
92. The hurricane in Hurston's novel is based on the September 12, 1928 historical event in which a massive hurricane approached the lake from the northwest. In Susan Scott Parrish, "Zora Neale Hurston and the Environmental Ethic of Risk," in *American Studies, Ecocriticism, and Citizenship: Thinking and Acting in the Local and Global Commons*," ed. Joni Adamson and Kimberley N. Ruffin (New York: Routledge, 2012): 21–36, Parrish relates that this hurricane, "sloshed a 10-foot wall of water over its bottom rim and breaking down the paltry dike across a 21-mile expanse" (31). Between 2,500 and 3,000 people died in the event, more than three-quarters of whom were African American and Afro-Caribbean (31). This flood risk was well-known to the industrial agribusinessmen who carried out the land reclamation project. The massive Okeechobee drainage project begun in the 1880s, Parrish explains, redirected the flow

of the Kissimmee River that had previously emptied into the lake. Entrepreneurs dug canals on three sides of the lake to drain "vast and arable acres to the south. What was laid bare south of the Lake was nine-foot-deep fertile earth-'the muck'-which in turn yielded large crops of beans, citrus trees, tomatoes, and most of all, sugar cane" (29). In an attempt to mitigate the flood risk, "the state built a 5-foot high dike along forty-seven miles of the Lake's southern border" (29). But this effort fell far short of what was needed to protect the mostly Black migrant laborers who lived in squatter camps along the southern rim of the lake during harvest season.

93. Hurston, *Their Eyes Were Watching God*, 131.
94. Spillers, "Mama's Baby, Papa's Maybe," 67–68; see also Joshua Bennett, *Being Property Myself: Blackness and the Ends of Man* (Cambridge, MA: Harvard University Press, 2020), especially chapter 3, for an extended discussion of Spillers's notion of vestibular.
95. Spillers, "Mama's Baby, Papa's Maybe," 67.
96. Hurston, *Their Eyes Were Watching God*, 132.
97. Hurston, *Their Eyes Were Watching God*, 16.
98. Hurston, *Their Eyes Were Watching God*, 16; For an excellent discussion of animality in *Their Eyes*, see Cherene Sherrard-Johnson, "High Water and the Limits of Humanity in Zora Neale Hurston's *Their Eyes Were Watching God*," in *Animals in the American Classics: How Natural History Inspired Great Fiction*, ed. John Cullen Gruesser (College Station: Texas A&M University Press, 2022): 178–98.
99. Hurston, *Their Eyes Were Watching God*, 14.
100. See Cherene Sherrard-Johnson, "High Water and the Limits of Humanity," for a generative exploration of human and animal relations in the novel.
101. Glissant, *Poetics of Relation*, 54–55.
102. Sonya Posmentier, *Cultivation and Catastrophe: The Lyric Ecology of Modern Black Literature* (Baltimore, MD: Johns Hopkins University Press, 2017), 164.
103. Zora Neale Hurston, *Dust Tracks on the Road: An Autobiography* (1942; reprint New York: HarperCollins, 1996), 159.
104. Hurston, *Their Eyes Were Watching God*, 154.
105. Hurston, *Their Eyes Were Watching God*, 155.
106. Bennett, *Being Property Myself*, 135.
107. Bennett, *Being Property Myself*, 137.
108. Hurston, *Their Eyes Were Watching God*, 138.
109. Hurston, *Their Eyes Were Watching God*, 160.
110. Hurston, *Their Eyes Were Watching God*, 161; For a discussion of the Barracoon, see Zora Neale Hurston, *Barracoon: The Story of the Last "Black Cargo,"* ed. Deborah G. Plant (New York: HarperCollins, 2018).
111. Hurston, *Their Eyes Were Watching God*, 161–62.
112. Hurston, *Their Eyes Were Watching God*, 162.
113. Hurston, *Their Eye Were Watching God*, 164.
114. Hurston, *Their Eyes Were Watching God*, 170.
115. Posmentier, *Cultivation and Catastrophe*, 164.
116. Hurston, *Their Eyes Were Watching God*, 183.

117. Claude McKay, *Romance in Marseille*, ed. Gary Edward Holcomb and William J. Maxwell (New York: Penguin, 2020), 76.
118. "The slave ship was a strange and potent combination of war machine, mobile prison, and factory.... Sailors ...'produced' slaves within the ship as factory, doubling their economic value as they moved them from a market on the eastern Atlantic to one on the west and helping to create the labor power that animated a growing world economy in the eighteenth century and after. In producing workers for the plantation, the ship-factory also produced 'race'" (Rediker, *Slave Ship*, 9–10). To be sure, this process began even before embarkation, on the shores of West Africa, where captives were first purchased and made fungible. See Stephanie Smallwood, *Saltwater Slavery: A Middle Passage from Africa to American Diaspora* (Cambridge, MA: Harvard University Press, 2007), chapter 2.
119. These questions allude to the infamous Zong case as well as to the large numbers of suicides during the Middle Passage; see, for instance, Ian Baucom, *Specters of the Atlantic: Finance Capital, Slavery, and the Philosophy of History* (Durham, NC: Duke University Press, 2005); and Terri L. Snyder, *The Power to Die: Slavery and Suicide in British North America* (Chicago: University of Chicago Press, 2015). Christina Sharpe argues that contemporary refugees frequently meet similar fates on board overcrowded, unsafe, and unwanted vessels in *In the Wake: On Blackness and Being* (Durham, NC: Duke University Press, 2016); See also Marcus Rediker, Cassandra Pybus, and Emma Christopher, eds., *Many Middle Passages: Forced Migration and the Making of the Modern World* (Berkeley: University of California Press, 2007).
120. Darieck Scott, *Extravagant Abjection: Blackness, Power, and Sexuality in the African American Literary Imagination* (New York: New York University Press, 2010). On finding power through trauma, Scott asks, "What is the potential for useful political, personal, psychological resource in racialization-through-abjection as historical legacy, as ancestral experience?" (6). Specifically, his book explores Black sexuality "as a vehicle for, and the realization of, Black freedom and power" (7); On lateral relations with the nonhuman, Dana Luciano and Mel Y. Chen, "Introduction: Has the Queer Ever Been Human?," *GLQ* 21, no. 2–3 (June 2015), explores how photographer Laura Aguilar questions what constitutes the human through positing an erotic, queer relation to the nonhuman land. Queer theory, Luciano and Chen state, tends to interrogate the nature of the "human" in its relation to the queer, both in their attention to "how sexual norms ... constitute and regulate hierarchies of humanness, and as they work to unsettle those norms and the default forms of humanness they uphold" (186). This unsettling of norms, they argue, extends to relations with nonhuman surrounds.
121. A useful definition of things as opposed to objects is as follows from Bill Brown, "The Secret Life of Things (*Virginia Woolf and the Matter of Modernism*)," *Modernism/modernity* 6, no. 2 (1999): 1–28. Brown writes "The passage into materialism ... requires acknowledging 'things' outside the subject/object trajectory, which means thinking sensation in its distinction from cognition to the degree that the 'thing' registers the undignified mutability of objects, and thus the excess of the object (a capacity to be other than it is), the 'thing' names a mutual mediation (and a slide between

objective and subjective predication) that appears as the object's difference from itself" (1–2).

122. We can also understand fungibility-as-resistance as having always accompanied the slave ship masters' attempts to render African captives into pure, exchangeable quantities of human labor. The slave ship used the depersonalizing nowhere of the waters, the violent threat of drowning and animal violence, and the horrendous confinement in the holds to commodify humans into racialized refuse. But something else occurred on board those ships: namely what Tinsley, in "Black Atlantic, Queer Atlantic," refers to as "the brown-skinned, fluid-bodied experiences now called *Blackness* and *queerness* [that] surfaced in intercontinental, maritime contact hundreds of years ago: in the seventeenth century, in the Atlantic Ocean. The Black Atlantic has always been the queer Atlantic" (191). That queerness arose from the need to survive captivity and to resist commodification, Tinsley says, "by feeling and feeling for their co-occupants [in the sex-segregated holds] on these ships" (192). This eroticism took place against the backdrop of violent dehumanization on board ship and against the threat of death by drowning.

123. Saidiya V. Hartman, *Wayward Lives, Beautiful Experiments: Intimate Histories of Social Upheaval* (New York: Norton, 2019), 61–62.

124. Glissant defines "transversality" as submerged forms of relationality that need not be visible to have effects" (*Caribbean Discourse*, 66–67). Transversality also encompasses the quality of open-ended activity and affectivity: passing, cruising, flopping, feeding, loving. The "trans" here, as Snorton poses it, is a transitive grammar, "the expression of an action that requires a direct object to complete its sense of meaning" (*Black on Both Sides*, 6). See Snorton's discussion of transversality, *Black on Both Sides*, 9–11.

125. Meg Samuelson, "Coastal Form: Amphibian Positions, Wider Worlds, and Planetary Horizons on the African Indian Ocean Littoral," *Comparative Literature* 69, no. 1 (2017): 17; and Hofmeyr, "Provisional Notes."

126. McKay, *Romance in Marseille*, 102.

127. Hester Blum, "Introduction: Oceanic Studies," *Atlantic Studies* 10, no. 2 (2013): 151.

128. Jeremy Chow and Brandi Bushman. "Hydro-eroticism," *ELN*, ed. Laura Winkiel, 57, no. 1 (April 2019): 98.

129. McKay, *Romance in Marseille*, 77.

130. I use the term "entanglement" following Karen Barad, in *Meeting the Universe Halfway: Quantum Physics and the Entanglement of Matter and Meaning* (Durham, NC: Duke University Press, 2007), "Matter and meaning are not separate elements. They are inextricably fused together and no event, no matter how energetic, can tear them asunder.... Mattering is simultaneously a matter of substance and significance, most evidently when it is the nature of matter that is in question, when the smallest parts of matter are found to be capable of exploding deeply entrenched ideas and large cites. Perhaps this is why contemporary physics makes the inescapable entanglement of matters of being, knowing and doing, of ontology, epistemology, and ethics, of fact and value, so tangible, so poignant" (3). While Barad's archive consists of subatomic particles and wave theory, feminist new materialism has taken up her work on the

undecidability of matter and meaning and the question of subjective perspective vis à vis the object being studied to foreground the liveliness of matter. This liveliness transforms received notions of causality and agency and highlights the ways in which subjectivity is situated within a complex, interlocking multitude of systems that are both internal and external to the subject.

131. McKay, *Romance in Marseille*, 19.
132. McKay, *Romance in Marseille*, 11–12.
133. McKay, *Romance in Marseille*, 22.
134. McKay, *Romance in Marseille*, 44.
135. I thank Professor Sophia Azeb for clarifying these terms in an email exchange on April 15, 2021.
136. McKay, *Romance in Marseille*, 44.
137. McKay, *Romance in Marseille*, 45.
138. McKay, *Romance in Marseille*, 42.
139. On Afro-Orientalism in McKay's work, see Allan G. Borst, "Signifyin(g) Afro-Orientalism: The Jazz Addict Subculture of *Nigger Heaven and Home to Harlem*," *Modernism/Modernity* 16, no. 4 (2009): 685–707; and more broadly, see Bill V. Mullen, *Afro-Orientalism* (Minneapolis: University of Minnesota Press, 2004).
140. McKay, *Romance in Marseille*, 122.
141. McKay, *Romance in Marseille*, 122.
142. McKay, *Romance in Marseille*, 127.
143. McKay, *Romance in Marseille*, 125.
144. Hartman, *Wayward Lives*, 17, 34.
145. McKay, *Romance in Marseille*, 107.
146. McKay, *Romance in Marseille*, 107.
147. On "racial memory," see note 170.
148. McKay, *Romance in Marseille*, 108.
149. McKay, *Romance in Marseille*, 108.
150. McKay, *Romance in Marseille*, 108.
151. McKay, *Romance in Marseille*, 41.
152. Hartman, *Wayward Lives*, 61.
153. Jennifer F. Wang, "Anachronistic Life: Racial Vitalism and 'Unhistorical' Temporality in Claude McKay's *Home to Harlem*," *Modernism/Modernity* 26, no. 4 (November 2019): 791.
154. McKay, *Romance in Marseille*, 41.
155. Hartman, *Wayward Lives*, 274–75.
156. Hartman, *Wayward Lives*, 17.
157. McKay, *Romance in Marseille*, 76.
158. Hartman, *Scenes of Subjection*, 80.
159. McKay, *Romance in Marseille*, 91, 123. It is notable that Lafala is also labeled a stranger by Aslima when she recounts his first arrival in Marseille and why she thought it was appropriate to steal his money (33). Hartman uses the term "stranger" to define a slave in *Lose Your Mother: A Journey Along the Atlantic Slave Route* (New York: Macmillan

Press, 2008), 5; See also Orlando Patterson, *Slavery and Social Death: A Comparative Study*, rev. ed. (1982; repr., Cambridge, MA: Harvard University Press, 2018), 39.
160. McKay, *Romance in Marseille*, 90.
161. McKay, *Romance in Marseille*, 91.
162. King, *Black Shoals*, 25.
163. King, *Black Shoals*, 24.
164. King, *Black Shoals*, 22–23.
165. McKay, *Romance in Marseille*, 113.
166. Audre Lorde, *Sister Outsider: Essays and Speeches* (Berkeley, CA: Crossing Press, 2007), 53.
167. Lorde, *Sister Outsider*, 55.
168. Lorde, *Sister Outsider*, 55.
169. McKay, *Romance in Marseille*, 60–61.
170. While the phrase "racial memory" suggests a problematic racial essentialism, it is important to historicize the term. It partakes of a project of racial vitalism most closely associated with Négritude writers, Aimé Césaire, Léopold Sédar Senghor, and Léon Gontran Damas. Claude McKay's novel *Banjo* (1929) was highly regarded by this group. Racial vitalism attempts to know and describe the category of life as something beyond the mechanical, the rational, and the dualist subject-object split. In so doing, it seeks to define the human in terms other than those developed in post-Enlightenment Europe. Its modern sources include Romantic organicism and, slightly later, the development of evolutionary biology. The latter had especial relevance for McKay's reclamation of Black life. In *Racial Discourses of Life Philosophy: Négritude, Vitalism, and Modernity* (New York: Columbia University Press, 2010), Donna V. Jones writes, "Biology opened up the possibility of defining life in terms of memory, and the discovery of a deep ethnological past in the context of social Darwinian anthropology made it possible to speculate on the memories of racial groups" (6). In short, vitalism, as it was formulated in the early twentieth century and used by writers including McKay, involved an intuition of racial memory. Access to this memory could only be known "through aesthetic experience or deeper and immediate self-knowledge," a recovery of authentic existence through an active wresting of truth out of memory (114).
171. Glissant, *Poetics of Relation*, 6
172. McKay, *Romance in Marseille*, 62.
173. Hartman, *Wayward Lives*, 259.
174. King, *Black Shoals*, 22; McKay, *Romance in Marseille*, 130.
175. McKay, *Romance in Marseille*, 125.

(INTERLUDE)

1. W. E. B. Du Bois, *The Souls of Black Folk* (New York: Dover, 1994), 155.
2. Du Bois, *The Souls of Black Folk*, 157.

3. Du Bois, *The Souls of Black Folk*, 157.
4. Julie Beth Napolin, *The Fact of Resonance: Modernist Acoustics and Narrative Form* (New York: Fordham University Press, 2020), 143. I'm indebted to her discussion of "The Sorrow Songs" for my analysis.
5. Anna Kornbluh, "Freeing Impersonality: The Objective Subject of Psychoanalysis in *Sense & Sensibility*," in *Knots: Post-Lacanian Psychoanalysis, Literature and Film*, ed. Jean Michel Rabaté (New York: Routledge, 2019), 35.
6. Kelly Sultzbach, *Ecocriticism in the Modernist Imagination: Forster, Woolf, and Auden* (New York: Cambridge University Press, 2016), 2.
7. Virginia Woolf, *To the Lighthouse* (New York: Harcourt Brace, 1927), 125–26.
8. Woolf, *To the Lighthouse*, 126.
9. Woolf, *To the Lighthouse*, 132.
10. Woolf, *To the Lighthouse*, 135.
11. Hortense J. Spillers, "Mama's Baby, Papa's Maybe: An American Grammar Book," *diacritics* 17, no. 2 (Summer, 1987): 72.
12. J. M. Coetzee, *Foe* (New York: Viking, 1986), 156.
13. Coetzee, *Foe*, 156.
14. Coetzee, *Foe*, 157.
15. J. S. Bolin, "Thresholds of the Novel: Realism, the Inhuman, the Ethical in J. M. Coetzee's *Foe*," *Novel: A Forum on Fiction* 51, no. 3 (2018): 452.
16. Coetzee, *Foe*, 157.
17. Stefano Harney and Fred Moten, *The Undercommons: Fugitive Planning and Black Study* (New York: Autonomedia, 2013), 93.
18. I borrow from Brent Hayes Edwards, *The Practice of Diaspora: Literature, Translation, and the Rise of Black Internationalism* (Cambridge, MA: Harvard University Press, 2003), his use of the term diaspora that "implies neither that it offers the comfort of abstraction, an easy recourse to origins, nor that it provides a foolproof antiessentialism: instead it forces us to articulate discourses of cultural and political linkage only through and across difference in full view of all the risks of that endeavor" (13). This formulation bears a striking resemblance to Glissant's *relation*.
19. Marlon James, "Worthless Women: Marlon James on Jean Rhys and Her Female Characters," *CRB: The Caribbean Review of Books* (blog), August 13, 2007, www.caribbeanreviewofbooks.com/crb-archive/13-august- 2007/worthless-women.
20. James, "Worthless Women," n.p.
21. James, "Worthless Women," n.p.
22. Elizabeth M. DeLoughrey, *Roots and Routes: Navigating Caribbean and Pacific Island Literature* (Honolulu: University of Hawai'i Press, 2007), 61.
23. My discussion of Patterson's parasitism is indebted to Ewa Płonowska Ziarek, *Feminist Aesthetics and the Politics of Modernism* (New York: Columbia University Press, 2012), chapter 5.
24. Orlando Patterson, *Slavery and Social Death: A Comparative Study* (Cambridge, MA: Harvard University Press, 1982), 335.
25. Patterson, *Slavery and Social Death*, 335.

26. Ziarek, *Feminist Aesthetics*, 166. I take the term "bare life" from Giorgio Agamben, *Homo Sacer: Sovereign Power and Bare Life* (Stanford, CA: Stanford University Press, 1998). Bare life for Agamben is traceable to Aristotle's distinction between *zoe* "the simple fact of living common to all living beings (animals, men, or gods) and *bios*, which indicated the form or way of living proper to an individual or group" (1). Bios is also glossed as political life. Humans who are reduced to bare life serve as a founding exclusion demarcating political life of "the city of men" (7).
27. Ziarek, *Feminist Aesthetics*. Parasitism, she argues, fundamentally revises "Agamben's theory of sovereignty [by foregrounding] the unstable dependence of power on bare life" (166).
28. Ziarek, *Feminist Aesthetics*, 160.
29. Ziarek, *Feminist Aesthetics*, 159.
30. Ziarek, *Feminist Aesthetics*, 157.
31. Ziarek, *Feminist Aesthetics*, 163.
32. Ziarek, *Feminist Aesthetics*, 162
33. Djuna Chappell Barnes, "How It Feels to be Forcibly Fed," *New York World Magazine*, September 6, 1914, Djuna Barnes Papers, https://hdl.handle.net/1903.1/14687.
34. Barnes, "How it Feels to be Forcibly Fed," 5.
35. Barnes, "How it Feels to be Forcibly Fed," 5.

3. WAVES

1. Hester Blum, "The Prospect of Oceanic Studies," *PMLA* 125, no. 3 (2010): 670–77.
2. Karen Barad, "Transmaterialities: Trans*/Matter/Realities and Queer Political Imaginings," *GLQ* 21, no. 2–3 (June 2015): 151.
3. Karen Barad, *Meeting the Universe Halfway: Quantum Physics and the Entanglement of Matter and Meaning* (Durham, NC: Duke University Press, 2007), 137; See also Serenella Iovino and Serpil Oppermann, "Material Ecocriticism: Materiality, Agency, and Models of Narrativity," *Ecozon@* 3, no. 1 (Spring 2012): 77.
4. Stefan Helmreich, "The Genders of Waves," *WSQ: Women's Studies Quarterly* 45, no. 1–2 (Spring/Summer 2017): 30.
5. Barad, *Meeting the Universe*; Rosi Braidotti, *The Posthuman* (Malden, MA: Polity Press, 2013); Jane Bennett, *Vibrant Matter: A Political Ecology of Things* (Durham, NC: Duke University Press, 2010); Stacy Alaimo, *Bodily Natures: Science, Environment, and the Material Self* (Bloomington: Indiana University Press, 2010); Stacy Alaimo and Susan Hekman, eds. *Material Feminisms* (Bloomington: Indiana University Press, 2008).
6. Diana Leong, "The Mattering of Black Lives: Octavia Butler's Hyperempathy and the Promise of the New Materialisms," *Catalyst: Feminism, Theory, Technoscience* 2, no. 2 (2016): 8.
7. Leong, "The Mattering of Black Lives," 6.
8. Braidotti, *The Posthuman*, 100–101. Thanks to Axelle Karera, "Blackness and the Pitfalls of Anthropocene Ethics," *Critical Philosophy of Race* 7, no. 1 (2019): 41, for bringing this example to my attention.

9. Leong, "The Mattering of Black Lives," 19–20.
10. Hortense J. Spillers, "Mama's Baby, Papa's Maybe: An American Grammar Book," *Diacritics* 17, no. 2 (Summer 1987): 67.
11. Leong, "The Mattering of Black Lives," 21.
12. Leong, "The Mattering of Black Lives," 22, quoting Spillers, "Mama's Baby," 67.
13. Spillers, "Mama's Baby," 80.
14. Spillers, "Mama's Baby," 80, 67; See also Karera, "Blackness and the Pitfalls of Anthropocene Ethics," 43–44, where she associates new materialism with Saidiya Hartman's statement in "The Position of the Unthought: An Interview with Saidiya V. Hartman Conducted by Frank B. Wilderson, III," *Qui Parle* 13, no. 2 (Spring/Summer 2003) that "the white bourgeois family can actually live with murder in order to reconstitute its domesticity" (191).
15. Tiffany Lethabo King, *The Black Shoals: Offshore Formations of Black and Native Studies* (Durham, NC: Duke University Press, 2019), xii.
16. I was unable to acquire a high resolution of the image for inclusion in this book. I ask that readers consult the image online at: https://commons.wikimedia.org/wiki/File:Vignetta_satirica_del_Tacoma_Times,_Washington,_1914.jpg.
17. Helmreich, "Genders of Waves," 34.
18. Helmreich, "Genders of Waves," 34, quoting Spillers, "Mama's Baby," 72, 68.
19. Édouard Glissant, *Poetics of Relation* (Ann Arbor: University of Michigan Press, 1997), 6; On the "residence time" of salt from human blood in the ocean, see Christina Sharpe, *In the Wake: On Blackness and Being* (Durham, NC: Duke University Press, 2016), 41.
20. Gillian Beer, "Excerpts from *The Waves* with discussion by Gillian Beer," *Daedalus* 143, no. 1 (Winter 2014): 56.
21. Virginia Woolf, *A Room of One's Own* (New York: Harcourt, Brace, 1929), 113–14.
22. Woolf, *Room of One's Own*, 48.
23. Woolf, *Room of One's Own*, 114.
24. Woolf, *Room of One's Own*, 114.
25. Woolf, *Room of One's Own*, 114.
26. Nicole Rizzuto, "Maritime Modernism: The Aqueous Form of Virginia Woolf's *The Waves*," *Modernist Cultures* 11, no. 2 (July 2016): 289.
27. Vron Ware, in *Beyond the Pale: White Women, Racism, and History* (New York: Verso, 2015), writes: "The existence of a popular movement against the slavery of blacks in the Caribbean and later in America provided a cornerstone for the building of a women's rights movement in Britain. Concepts of equality, legal, and economic bondage, liberation and all the metaphors of servitude where were freely used by abolitionists were consistently borrowed by pioneers for women's rights to link their struggle to the wider one of human rights. As the movement for women's rights progressed, women were able to exploit the power of the slavery analogy in interpreting their own servitude but without needing any longer to refer to the slaves whose bondage had once outraged and inspired them" (109); See also Laura Nym E. Mayhall, "The Rhetorics of Slavery and Citizenship: Suffragist Discourse and Canonical Texts in Britain, 1880–1914," *Gender & History* 13, no. 3 (November 2001): 481–97.

28. Howard Winant coined this term, and it is quoted by Sylvia Wynter, "Unsettling the Coloniality of Being/Power/Truth/Freedom: Towards the Human, After Man, Its Over-representation—An Argument," *The Centennial Review* 3, no. 3 (Fall 2003): 263.
29. Jane Marcus, "Britannia Rules The Waves," in *Decolonizing Tradition*, ed. Karen Lawrence (Champaign-Urbana: University of Illinois Press, 1991), 136–37, argues that *The Waves* presents "the submerged mind of empire" that "keep[s] alive the myth of individualism and selfhood that fuels English patriotism and nationalism"; Jessica Berman, *Modernist Fiction, Cosmopolitanism, and the Politics of Community* (New York: Cambridge University Press, 2001), 117, explores how Woolf constructs alternative models of community in *The Waves* that are cosmopolitan rather than nationalist and that can intervene in political life in Britain.
30. Bonnie Kime Scott, *In the Hollow of the Wave: Virginia Woolf and Modernist Uses of Nature* (Charlottesville: University of Virginia Press, 2012), 9.
31. Judith Butler, "Critically Queer," in *Performance Studies*, ed. Erin Striff (New York: Palgrave Macmillan, 2003), 228.
32. Heather Love, *Feeling Backward: Loss and the Politics of Queer History* (Cambridge, MA: Harvard University Press, 2009), 20.
33. Queer also resists the recent surge of interest in "modernist inhumanisms," which, too often, quickly leaves gendered, sexed, and raced bodies behind, along with ethical and political zones of engagement.
34. A version of this paragraph has been previously published in Laura Winkiel, "Afterword: Modernism Beside Itself," *Modernism/Modernity* Vol. 3, Cycle 4 (December 2018), https://doi.org/10.26597/mod.0082, n.p.
35. Dana Luciano and Mel Y. Chen, "Introduction: Has the Queer Ever Been Human?," *GLQ* 21, no. 2–3 (June 2015): 185.
36. Virginia Woolf, *A Writer's Diary* (New York: Harcourt, Brace, 1953), 108.
37. Meg Samuelson, "Coastal Form: Amphibian Positions, Wider Worlds, and Planetary Horizons on the African Indian Ocean Littoral," *Comparative Literature* 69, no. 1 (March 2017): 17.
38. Virginia Woolf, *The Waves* (New York: Harcourt, Brace, 1931), 8.
39. Luciano and Chen, "Introduction," 184.
40. Catriona Mortimer-Sandilands and Bruce Erickson, "Introduction: A Genealogy of Queer Ecologies," in *Queer Ecologies: Sex, Nature, Politics, Desire*, eds. Catriona Mortimer-Sandilands and Bruce Erickson (Bloomington: Indiana University Press, 2010), 5.
41. Greta Gaard, "Toward a Queer Ecofeminism," *Hypatia* 12, no. 1 (Winter 1997): 115, 122.
42. Luciano and Chen, "Introduction," 185.
43. Luciano and Chen, "Introduction," 185; See also Gaard, "Toward a Queer Ecofeminism"; and Timothy Morton, "Guest Column: Queer Ecology," *PMLA* 125, no. 2 (March 2010): 273–82.
44. Luicano and Chen, "Introduction," 185.
45. Barad, "Transmaterialities," 387. The full quotation reads: "Matter is promiscuous and inventive in its agential wanderings: one might even dare say, imaginative."

46. Kandice Chuh, "It's Not about Anything," *Social Text* 32, no. 4 (Winter 2014): 125–26.
47. Rizzuto, "Maritime Modernism," 272.
48. Philip E. Steinberg and Kimberley Peters, "Wet Ontologies, Fluid Spaces: Giving Depth to Volume through Oceanic Thinking," *Environment and Planning D: Society and Space* 33, no. 2 (April 2015): 248.
49. Woolf, *Writer's Diary*, 139.
50. See also the discussion of "moments of being" as Woolf's concern with world-making in Derek Ryan, *Virginia Woolf and the Materiality of Theory: Sex, Animal, Life* (Edinburgh: Edinburgh University Press, 2013), 1.
51. Benjamin D. Hagen, "Feeling Shadows: Virginia Woolf's Sensuous Pedagogy," *PMLA* 132, no. 2 (2017): 269.
52. Hagen, "Feeling Shadows," 269.
53. Woolf, *Moments of Being* (New York: Harcourt, Brace, 1985), 72.
54. Woolf, *Waves*, 7.
55. Melba Cuddy-Keane, "Afterword: Inside and Outside the Covers: Beginnings, Endings, and Woolf's Non-Coercive Ethical Texts," in *Woolfian Boundaries: Selected Papers from the Sixteenth Annual International Conference on Virginia Woolf*, ed. Anna Burrells and Steve Ellis (Clemson, SC: Clemson University Press, 2007), 175.
56. Woolf, *Writer's Diary*, 149–50.
57. Steve Mentz, *Shipwreck Modernity: Ecologies of Globalization, 1550–1719* (Minneapolis: University of Minnesota Press, 2015), x.
58. Woolf, *Moments of Being*, 71.
59. Braidotti, *The Posthuman*, 71.
60. By queer ecological ethics, I mean, following Braidotti in *Posthuman*, "an ethics based on the primacy of the relation, of interdependence, which values non-human or a-personal life" (95).
61. Ewa Płonowska Ziarek, *Feminist Aesthetics and the Politics of Modernism* (New York: Columbia University Press, 2012), 28.
62. Ziarek, *Feminist Aesthetics*, 102.
63. Ziarek, *Feminist Aesthetics*, 103.
64. Qtd. in Gillian Beer, *Virginia Woolf: The Common Ground* (Ann Arbor: University of Michigan Press, 1996), 83.
65. Frederick Burkhardt, Sydney Smith, et al., eds. *The Correspondence of Charles Darwin*, Vol. 8 (New York: Cambridge University Press, 1993), 29; see also Stacy Alaimo, *Exposed: Environmental Politics and Pleasures in Posthuman Times* (Minneapolis: University of Minnesota Press, 2016), 114–27.
66. Elizabeth Grosz, *The Nick of Time: Politics, Evolution, and the Untimely* (Durham, NC: Duke University Press, 2004). Grosz comments on this queer latency in Darwin's evolutionary theory: "The individuals who never developed into maturing adults—the evolutionary residue, those that leave no trace, no progeny—cannot simply be regarded as the losers, the inferior, in the evolutionary battle for adaptation. They remain the undeveloped, the latent, the recessive, a virtual forever unactualized, or perhaps actualized outside the traditional lines of genealogy" (50).

67. Woolf, *Waves*, 16.
68. Woolf, *Mrs. Dalloway* (New York: Harcourt, Brace, 1924), 117.
69. Woolf, *Waves*, 16.
70. Woolf, *Waves*, 17. In Elvedon, the gardeners' futile, but endlessly repeated, labor of keeping the garden tidy and distinct from the chaotic fecundity of nature signals the class-based nature of literature. The lady writer depends upon her servants for leisure to write. But it also "re-marks" the dividing line between nature and culture. Timothy Morton, *Ecology without Nature: Rethinking Environmental Aesthetics* (Cambridge, MA: Harvard University Press, 2009), defines the re-mark as "a kind of echo. It is a special mark (or a series of them) that makes us aware that we are in the presence of (significant) marks" (48). The sweeping announces a border or demarcation between the wild and the cultivated (the scene of writing significant "marks"). These zones are artificially produced through the dualistic structures of Western thought. The exuberance and exorbitance of what Morton calls "ecomimesis," or the ways in which writing evokes an environment, is explicitly thematized through the way in which the re-mark "establishes [the difference between subjectivity and objectivity] out of an undifferentiated ground" (49). More than providing domestic labor, the gardeners enact the very possibility of art.
71. Jack Halberstam, *The Queer Art of Failure* (Durham, NC: Duke University Press, 2011), 120.
72. Woolf, *Waves*, 17.
73. José Esteban Muñoz, *Disidentifications: Queers of Color and the Performance of Politics* (Minneapolis: University of Minnesota Press, 1999), 78.
74. Kimberly Engdahl Coates, "Virginia Woolf's Queer Time and Place: Wartime London and a World Aslant," in *Queer Bloomsbury*, ed. Brenda Helt and Madelyn Detloff, (Edinburgh: Edinburgh University Press, 2016), 277.
75. Sarah Ahmed, *Queer Phenomenology: Orientations, Objects, Others* (Durham, NC: Duke University Press, 2006), 65. I am indebted to Coates's discussion of Ahmed's phenomenology. See Coates, "Virginia Woolf's Queer Time and Place," 277.
76. Woolf, *Waves*, 200.
77. See Elizabeth DeLoughrey, *Routes and Roots: Navigating Caribbean and Pacific Island Literatures* (Honolulu: University of Hawai'i Press, 2007), 68.
78. Woolf, *Waves*, 75.
79. Rizzuto, "Maritime Modernism," 288–89.
80. Woolf, *Waves*, 9.
81. Woolf, *Waves*, 75.
82. This formulation follows Fredric Jameson's influential account of modernism and imperialism. See his "Modernism and Imperialism," in *Modernism, Colonialism, and Literature*, eds. Terry Eagleton, Fredric Jameson, and Edward Said (Minneapolis: University of Minnesota Press, 1990). As discussed in this book's chapter 1, he argues: "Colonialism means that a significant structural segment of the economic system as a whole is now located elsewhere, beyond the metropolis" (50). As a result, modernists, including Woolf, attempt to compensate for this absence, as Richard Begam and Michael

Valdez Moses argue, in their "Introduction" to the edited collection *Modernism, Postcolonialism, and Globalism: Anglophone Literature, 1950 to the Present* (New York: Oxford University Press, 2019), "by way of style, a false or artificially constructed version of wholeness, harmony, and beauty" (7).

83. Woolf, *Waves*, 232.
84. DeLoughrey, *Routes and Roots*, 54–55.
85. Margaret Cohen's *The Novel and the Sea* (Princeton, NJ: Princeton University Press, 2010) compellingly accounts for the rise of the novel through the seafaring narratives and craft of the British, French, and American maritime navies.
86. Rizzuto, "Maritime Modernism," 284.
87. DeLoughrey, *Routes and Roots*, 61.
88. Beer, *Virginia Woolf*, 14.
89. In Virginia Woolf, *The Voyage Out* (New York: Harcourt, Brace, 1920), the heroine, Rachel Vinrace, travels across the Atlantic aboard the *Euphrosyne*, named after the muse of joy. As the trip begins, the sea embodies the wild freedom of the romantic quest: "All the smoke and the houses had disappeared, and the ship was out in a wide space of sea very fresh and clear though pale in the early light. They had left London sitting on its mud. They were free of roads, free of mankind, and the same exhilaration at their freedom ran through them all" (27). But as the voyage continues and both a conventional marriage and sexual assault await Rachel, the allure of the sea becomes a nightmarish trap. Rachel dreams of a "long tunnel [where a] little deformed man squatted on the floor gibbering, with long nails" (77). Marianne DeKoven, in *Rich and Strange: Gender, History, Modernism* (Princeton, NJ: Princeton University Press, 1991) argues that the deformed man, "is a figure of the distortion of the female in patriarchal culture: as Freud reveals, woman in patriarchy can only be visible or explicable as a 'deformed man'" (106). Woolf's novel, according to DeKoven, demonstrates how "the maternal ocean has become the site of patriarchal suppression, distortion, and occupation of the feminine" (106). As the heroine discovers that she is imprisoned by gender expectations even at sea, it becomes clear that the British empire subordinates women at every turn.
90. Beer, *Virginia Woolf*, 18.
91. Elizabeth Grosz, *Chaos, Territory, Art: Deleuze and the Framing of the Earth* (New York: Columbia University Press, 2008). Grosz notes that "the first gesture of art, its metaphysical condition and universal expression, is the construction or fabrication of a frame" (10). That Woolf undoes this frame points to its contingency and her understanding of art's relation to the elements of earth and sea.
92. DeLoughrey, *Routes and Roots*, 54.
93. Ahmed, *Queer Phenomenology*, 65.
94. Virginia Woolf, *The Cambridge Edition of the Works of Virginia Woolf: The Waves*, ed. Michael Herbert and Susan Sellers (New York: Cambridge University Press, 2011), xlvii.
95. Woolf, *Waves*, 33.
96. Woolf, *Waves*, 27.
97. Quoted in Ahmed, *Queer Phenomenology*, 4.

98. Coates, "Queer Time and Place," 277.
99. Woolf, *Waves*, 21–22.
100. Woolf, *Waves*, 26.
101. Woolf, *Waves*, 28.
102. Woolf, *Waves*, 57.
103. Rhoda's alienation takes on aspects of abjection. Louis, who is most closely associated with the commercial forces of globalization, describes Rhoda as having "eyes the colour of snail's flesh" (Woolf, *Waves*, 220). In the fourth interlude, the violence of empire is projected onto the natural world: "[The birds] spied a snail and tapped the shell against a stone. They tapped furiously, methodically, until the shell broke and something slimy oozed from the crack" (Woolf, *Waves*, 109).
104. Woolf, *Waves*, 120.
105. Woolf, *Waves*, 105.
106. Woolf, *Waves*, 64.
107. As argued in Kathy J. Philips, *Virginia Woolf Against Empire* (Knoxville: University of Tennessee Press, 1994), Virginia Woolf was well aware of the atrocities and unsustainability of British imperialism in Africa, given that she read closely and commented on Leonard Woolf's *Empire and Commerce in Africa* (1920).
108. Woolf, *Waves*, 203–4.
109. Patrick McGee, "The Politics of Modernist Form: Or, Who Rules *The Waves*?," *Modern Fiction Studies* 38, no. 3 (Autumn 1992): 648. McGee notes the limits of Woolf's imperial critique as follows: "That modernist works have exposed the limits of European culture does not necessarily mean they have articulated the space in which the voice of the other can be heard—the other whose exclusion from the discourse of modernism is one of the grounds of its authority" (648). Although the new modernist studies challenges what counts as the "discourse of modernism," McGee's caution vis à vis Woolf and racial difference stands.
110. Woolf, *Waves*, 9.
111. Woolf, *Waves*, 150, 75.
112. Woolf, *Waves*, 206.
113. Woolf, *Room of One's Own*, 114.
114. Woolf, *Waves*, 291.
115. Woolf, *Waves*, 288.
116. Woolf, *Waves*, 294.
117. Laura Doyle, *Freedom's Empire: Race and the Rise of the Novel in Atlantic Modernity, 1640–1940* (Durham, NC: Duke University Press, 2008), 442.
118. Doyle, *Freedom's Empire*, 443.
119. Woolf, *Waves*, 297.
120. Woolf, *Room of One's Own*, 42.
121. Malachi McIntosh, Video interview with Kabe Wilson, April 25, 2014, accessed June 1, 2020, video no longer available on YouTube.
122. Susan Stanford Friedman initially brought Wilson's work to the attention of modernist scholars, and she has also facilitated this author's contact with the artist. I am

grateful for her assistance. See Susan Stanford Friedman, "Alternatives to Periodization," *Modern Language Quarterly* 80, no. 4 (2019): 379–402; Friedman, "Recycling Revolutions: Remixing *A Room of One's Own* and Black Power in Kabe Wilson's Performance, Installation, and Narrative Art," in *Contemporary Revolutions: Turning Back to the Future in 21st Century Art*, ed. Susan Stanford Friedman (New York: Bloomsbury Academic, 2020), 21–47; and Friedman with Kabe Wilson, "Of Words, Worlds, and Woolf: Recycling *A Room of One's Own* into *Of One Woman or So*," an unpublished interview, n.d.

123. For more on the Dreadlocks Hoax, see Kabe Wilson, "The Dreadlocks Hoax," *Studies in the Maternal* 6, no. 1 (2014): 1. https://doi.org/10.16995/sim.15.
124. Friedman and Wilson, "Of Words, Worlds, and Woolf," 10.
125. Kabe Wilson, *Of One Woman or So, by Olivia N'Gowfri*, an art installation on scroll and unpublished typescript, 2014, 88. Used by permission of the author.
126. Wilson, *Of One Woman or So*, 131.
127. Wilson, *Of One Woman or So*, 131.
128. Wilson, *Of One Woman or So*, 131–32.
129. Katherine McKittrick, "Mathematics Black Life," *The Black Scholar* 44, no. 2 (Summer 2014): 18–28.
130. Friedman and Wilson, "Of Words, Worlds, and Woolf," 5.
131. Friedman and Wilson, "Of Words, Worlds, and Woolf," 9.
132. Friedman and Wilson, "Of Words, Worlds, and Woolf," 10.
133. Friedman and Wilson, "Of Words, Worlds, and Woolf," 10; see also Simon Gikandi, *Slavery and the Culture of Taste* (Princeton, NJ: Princeton University Press, 2011).
134. Rebecca L. Walkowitz, *Born Translated: The Contemporary Novel in the Age of World Literature* (New York: Columbia University Press, 2015).
135. Wilson, *Of One Woman or So*, 131.
136. Wilson, *Of One Woman or So*, 131.

4. ARCHIPELAGO

1. Elizabeth M. DeLoughrey, *Routes and Roots: Navigating Caribbean and Pacific Island Literature* (Honolulu: University of Hawai'i Press, 2007). DeLoughrey writes that "The notion of the isolated island has material and metaphorical meanings derived from a complex history of European expansion into contained space.... Islands were especially sought for colonization by all the major maritime powers because their long coastlines provided multiple access points for trade and defense, they provided necessary stopover points for the refitting and the restocking of ships, and their contained spaces facilitated greater control of colonized and enslaved populations who, without access to maritime vessels, were less likely to escape" (8).
2. Omise'eke Natasha Tinsley, *Thiefing Sugar: Eroticism between Women in Caribbean Literature* (Durham, NC: Duke University Press, 2010), 76.

3. See Edward Kamau Brathwaite, *Contradictory Omens: Cultural Diversity and Integration in the Caribbean* (Kingston: Savacou Press, 1974), 64, for his dictum, "Unity is submarine"; See also Édouard Glissant, *Caribbean Discourse: Selected Essays* (Charlottesville: University of Virginia Press, 1989), 67.
4. Epeli Hau'ofa, "Our Sea of Islands," in *Inside Out: Literature, Cultural Politics, and Identity in the New Pacific*, ed. Vilsoni Hereniko and Rob Wilson (New York: Rowman & Littlefield, 1999), 31.
5. Édouard Glissant, *Poetic Intention* (Callicoon, NY: Nightboat, 2010), 18.
6. Joshua Bennett, *Being Property Once Myself: Blackness and the End of Man* (Cambridge, MA: Harvard University Press, 2020), 133.
7. Brian Russell Roberts and Michelle Ann Stephens, "Introduction: Archipelagic American Studies: Decontinentalizing the Study of American Literature," *Journal of Transnational American Studies* 5, no. 1 (May 2017): 7.
8. Roberts and Stephens, "Archipelagic American Studies," 7.
9. Roberts and Stephens, "Archipelagic American Studies," 7.
10. Roberts and Stephens, "Archipelagic American Studies," 8; See also Amy Clukey and Jeremy Wells, "Introduction: Plantation Modernity," *The Global South* 10, no. 2 (Fall 2016): 1–10, doi:10.2979/globalsouth.10.2.01. Clukey and Wells list "Cherokee-owned plantations in Oklahoma, British tea plantations in the Himalayas, Arab cotton plantations in Egypt, Fordian rubber plantations in Latin America, corporate coffee plantations in Tanzania" as instances of the global plantation system (8).
11. Antonio Benítez-Rojo, *The Repeating Island: The Caribbean and the Postmodern Perspective* (Durham, NC: Duke University Press, 1996), 2.
12. Benítez-Rojo, *Repeating Island*, 3.
13. Benítez-Rojo, *Repeating Island*, 2.
14. Benítez-Rojo, *Repeating Island*, 6.
15. Roberts and Stephens, "Archipelagic American Studies," 24.
16. Benítez-Rojo, *Repeating Island*, 27.
17. Warwick Research Collective, *Combined and Uneven Development: Towards a New Theory of World-Literature* (Liverpool: Liverpool University Press, 2015). The Warwick Research Collective (WReC) has theorized uneven development within the global circulation of literature from a world-systems perspective.
18. In addition to the WReC, see James Graham, Michael Niblett, and Sharae Deckard, "Postcolonial Studies and World Literature," *Journal of Postcolonial Writing* 48, no. 5 (December 2012): 465–71; and Benita Parry, "Aspects of Peripheral Modernisms," *ariel* 40, no. 1 (2009): 27–55.
19. Urmila Seshagiri. "Modernist Ashes, Postcolonial Phoenix: Jean Rhys and the Evolution of the English Novel in the Twentieth Century," *Modernism/modernity* 13, no. 3 (September 2006): 487–505. Seshagiri argues that Rhys occupies the interregnum between modernism and postcolonialism in a manner that keeps the categories intact but is generative for assessing the transnational asymmetries in her work. Most critics focus either on Rhys's modernist qualities (González, for instance) or her postcolonial

ones (DeGuzman, Emery, Gregg, Lai, Rosenberg, Thomas). While partial to the latter, my attempt is to rethink the categories of modernism through the racial longue durée.

20. Rhys's novels frequently present Black people as either indifferent or hostile and surly laborers, without any contextualization of their history or consideration of the possibility for their self-determination. At other times, her protagonists idealize them. In Jean Rhys, *Voyage in the Dark* (New York: Norton, 1994), for instance, Anna describes Black people as "warm and gay," stating, "I always wanted to be black" (31). Omise'eke Natasha Tinsley, in *Thiefing Sugar*, comments on another white modernist Creole author, Eliot Bliss, in a manner that is useful for assessing Rhys: "For the white woman 'blackening' is always a choice for herself—a choice that draws on rather than forfeits race privilege—while for the black woman it never is" (79). Further, Rhys neglects to interrogate her protagonists' white privilege and to write history from an Afro-diasporic perspective.

21. Recent work on the United Kingdom (and beyond) North Atlantic archipelago includes the Nicolas Allen, Nick Groom, and Jos Smith, introduction to *Coastal Works: Cultures of the Atlantic Edge*, Oxford Scholarship Online (July 2017): 1–20, https://www.doi.org/10.1093/oso/9780198795155.001.0001; J. G. A. Pocock, *The Discovery of Islands: Essays in British History* (New York: Cambridge University Press, 2005); John Brannigan, *Archipelagic Modernism: Literature in the Irish and British Isles, 1890-1970* (Edinburgh: Edinburgh University Press, 2014).

22. Benítez-Rojo, *Repeating Island*, 4.

23. Benítez-Rojo, *Repeating Island*, 3.

24. Benítez-Rojo, *Repeating Island*, 25.

25. On the developmental aspect of the modernist and postcolonial bildungsroman, see Jed Esty, *Unseasonable Youth: Modernism, Colonialism, and the Fiction of Development* (New York: Oxford University Press, 2012).

26. Jean Rhys, "Black Exercise Book," (unpublished manuscript), Jean Rhys archive 1976-011, University of Tulsa McFarlin Library, Department of Special Collections & University Archives. The copyright holder declined to grant permission to reproduce from this work.

27. Jean Rhys, "Black Exercise Book," in *Wide Sargasso Sea*, ed. Judith L. Raiskin, (New York: Norton, 1999), 155. I also paraphrase from this material in respect of the wishes of the Rhys literary estate. The reader may consult the Norton Critical Edition to see the actual language.

28. Katherine McKittrick, *Demonic Grounds: Black Women and the Cartographies of Struggle* (Minneapolis: University of Minnesota Press, 2006), ix.

29. In linking the melancholy of Caribbean history to literary innovation, I draw from Ewa Płonowska Ziarek, *Feminist Aesthetics and the Politics of Modernism* (New York: Columbia University Press, 2012). She traces "how the destructive muteness and the erasure of the feminine, this 'pressure of dumbness' of unrecorded women's lives and their destroyed bodies, can be transformed into a process of writing, into a possibility of inventing new ways of speaking, community, and acting" (2).

30. Wally Look Lai, "The Road to Thornfield Hall: An Analysis of Jean Rhys' *Wide Sargasso Sea*," *New Beacon Review*, Collection One, ed. John La Rose (London: New Beacon Books, 1968): 40.
31. Caryl Phillips concurs that Rhys was entirely invested in Caribbean place. See Caryl Phillips, *A View of the Empire at Sunset* (New York: Farrar, Straus and Giroux, 2018), especially its ending.
32. Ann Cvetkovich, *Depression: A Public Feeling* (Durham, NC: Duke University Press, 2012), 138; Ziarek, *Feminist Aesthetics*, 79.
33. Saidiya V. Hartman, *Lose Your Mother: A Journey Along the Atlantic Slave Route* (New York: Farrar, Straus and Giroux, 2008), 16; also cited in Cvetkovich, *Depression*, 126; See also Jenny Sharpe, *Immaterial Archives: An African Diaspora Poetics of Loss* (Evanston, IL: Northwestern University Press, 2020).
34. Yogita Goyal, *Runaway Genres: The Global Afterlives of Slavery* (New York: New York University Press, 2019), 144.
35. Cvetkovich, *Depression*, 120.
36. Ann Anlin Cheng, *The Melancholy of Race: Psychoanalysis, Assimilation, and Hidden Grief* (New York: Oxford University Press, 2001), 19–20.
37. Glissant, *Caribbean Discourse*, 14.
38. Françoise Lionnet, *Le su et l'incertain: Cosmopolitiques creoles de l'océan Indien* (Trou d'eau Douce, Ile Maurice: Aé, 2012), 66.
39. Lionnet, *Le su et l'incertain*, 68.
40. Veronica Marie Gregg, *Jean Rhys's Historical Imagination: Reading and Writing the Creole* (Chapel Hill: University of North Carolina Press, 1995), 102. For instance, in Rhys's *Wide Sargasso Sea*, Antoinette's husband assesses his new bride: "Long, sad, dark alien eyes. Creole of pure English descent she may be, but they are not English or European either" (39). "May" expresses possibility, but not certainty, already inviting fears about Antoinette's racial contamination and mental stability.
41. Glissant, *Caribbean Discourse*, 144.
42. Rhys, *Voyage in the Dark*, 123; Rhys, *Wide Sargasso Sea*, 111, 109; Rhys, *Voyage in the Dark*, 162; and Jean Rhys, *Quartet* (New York: Norton, 1997); see Mary Lou Emery, *Jean Rhys at "World's End": Novels of Colonial and Sexual Exile* (Austin: University of Texas Press, 1990). Emery writes that in Rhys's *Wide Sargasso Sea*, Antoinette's references to flying, including "[a]s I ran or perhaps floated or flew" (112), allude to "the traditional slave wish for wings with which to fly 'home' or becoming like the Anancy flying trickster" (57).
43. John E. Drabinski, *Glissant and the Middle Passage: Philosophy, Beginning, Abyss* (Minneapolis: University of Minnesota Press, 2019), 41.
44. Philip E. Steinberg, "Of Other Seas: Metaphors and Materialities in Maritime Regions," *Atlantic Studies* 10, no. 2 (2013): 156–69. Steinberg writes, "Movement, instead of being subsequent to geography, *is* geography. . . . In other words, objects come into being as they move (or unfold) through space and time" (160).
45. Drabinski, *Glissant and the Middle Passage*, 45.
46. Rhys, *Voyage in the Dark*, 98.

47. Ziarek, *Feminist Aesthetics*, 53.
48. Rhys, *Voyage in the Dark*, 98.
49. Jean Rhys, *The Letters of Jean Rhys*, ed. Francis Wyndham and Diana Melly (New York: Viking Penguin, 1984), 25.
50. Bonnie Kime Scott, *The Gender of Modernism: A Critical Anthology* (Bloomington: Indiana University Press, 1990), 385. This material was originally edited and introduced by Nancy Hemond Brown in *London Magazine*, Vol. 25, no. 1 (1985): 40–59.
51. Scott, *Gender of Modernism*, 385, 387.
52. Scott, *Gender of Modernism*, 387.
53. Scott, *Gender of Modernism*, 387.
54. Scott, *Gender of Modernism*, 388.
55. Scott, *Gender of Modernism*, 387.
56. See J. S. Bolin, "Thresholds of the Novel: Realism, the Inhuman, the Ethical in J. M. Coetzee's *Foe*," *Novel: A Forum on Fiction* 51, no. 3 (2018): 438–60, where he argues, "*Foe* stages a confrontation with such a form's [the novel] precise obverse [of individual perfection]. That this obverse is figured as the 'dark' subject of an enslaving violence suggests that, contra Toni Morrison, the English novel, too, relied on what Herman Melville called 'the power of blackness' in a manner that was nothing short of fundamental to its structure and meaning" (439). In *Runaway Genres*, Goyal suggests along the same lines, "Today the political value of slavery, as a world historical event that forces disciplinary knowledge to reorganize itself—for history to confront the limits of knowledge, for novels to break their own frame—is everywhere visible" (212–13).
57. In the excised, published version, the youthful Anna states, "I know why the masks are laughing," but the rest of her anticolonial statement, "at the idea that anybody black would want to be white," is omitted. Scott, *Gender of Modernism,* 387. She also thinks, "I'm going to fall," but eliminates the place on which she'll land. Scott, *Gender of Modernism*, 388. The sexual seduction by her uncle is also deleted; Rhys, *Voyage in the Dark*, 184–87.
58. Rhys, *Voyage in the Dark*, 187. I allude here to Esty, *Unseasonable Youth* and his argument regarding the colonial bildungsroman.
59. Benítez-Rojo, *Repeating Island*, 2.
60. Rhys, *Voyage in the Dark*, 52.
61. Rhys, *Voyage in the Dark*, 53.
62. Roberts and Stephens, "Archipelagic American Studies," 26.
63. There is biographical evidence of Rhys's sexual proclivities toward masochism that she figuratively (and inaccurately) linked to slavery. Rhys was seduced by a seventy-four-year-old man, called Mr. Howard in the black exercise book, when she was fourteen. Touched inappropriately at the start of the affair and possibly raped at its conclusion, Mr. Howard entertained Rhys by telling her a series of pornographic fantasies in which she is abducted to another Caribbean island and becomes his sex slave. She serves him and his guests dinner while naked; her hands are tied with a flower-covered rope; she is punished and forced into sexual submission. Rhys is debased, called his "little saleté" (filth, dirt). She is to be humiliated, placed in bondage, and

made to perform sexualized menial labor while stripped of clothing. The servile roles of these fantasies enact cross-racial as well as sexual transgressions. Rhys recounts that this experience fitted with all that she had ever known on the island. David Dabydeen reminds us that "the British Empire was as much a pornographic as an economic project [energized by the] perverse eroticism of black labor and the fantasy of domination, bondage, and sado-masochism," quoted in Sue Thomas, *The Worlding of Jean Rhys* (Westport, CT: Greenwood Press, 1999), 31; See Elizabeth Freeman, *Time Binds: Queer Temporalities, Queer Histories* (Durham, NC: Duke University Press, 2010), especially chapter 4, for a reading of S/M that "in its very insistence on reanimating historically specific social roles, in the historically specific elements of its theatrical language, and in using the body as an instrument to rearrange time, becomes a kind of *écriture historique*. S/M becomes a form of writing history with the body in which the linearity of history itself may be called into question" (139). While I cannot do justice to this suggestive reading here, I am arguing that Rhys's melancholy and her protagonists' zombie-like states insist on the afterlife of the slave past.

64. On Black surrogacy, see Toni Morrison, *Playing in the Dark: Whiteness in the Literary Imagination* (New York: Vintage, 1992), where she defines Black surrogacy as a white form "of power without risk" and a white desire for "a *safe* participation in loss, in love, in chaos, in justice" (28); See also Goyal's discussion of how Toni Morrison's play *Desdemona* "amplifies these fraught dynamics of substitution, ventriloquism, and exchange" in *Runaway Genres*, 160.

65. Margaret Cohen, "Literary Studies on the Terraqueous Globe," *PMLA* 125, no. 3 (2010): 661.

66. DeLoughrey, *Routes and Roots*, 68.

67. John Hearne, *The Sure Salvation* (Boston: Faber & Faber, 1981), 7.

68. Jean Rhys, *Good Morning, Midnight* (New York: Norton, 1999), 168.

69. Rhys, *Good Morning*, 168.

70. Cheryl I. Harris, "Whiteness as Property," *Harvard Law Review* 106, no. 8 (June 1993): 1710–91. Harris argues that "Possession—the act necessary to lay the basis for rights in property—was defined to include only the cultural practices of whites. This definition laid the foundation for the idea that whiteness—that which whites alone possess—is valuable and is property" (1721). This foundation is not merely exclusionary but encodes whiteness itself as exclusionary property: "The law has established and protected an actual property interest in whiteness itself, which shares the critical characteristics of property and accords with the many and varied theoretical descriptions of property" (1724).

71. Rhys, *Good Morning*, 169.

72. In *Quartet*, Miss Nicolson who "despised women from the Southern states," avoids confronting the patriarchy of her own Southern family's history by instead claiming that she "adored Beauty, that she lived for Beauty" (159).

73. *Quartet* anatomizes the whiteness of the Heidlers, the well-meaning, solidly bourgeois expatriate couple (modeled after Ford Madox Ford and his wife, Violet Hunt), who

invite Marya to stay with them while her husband is in jail: "They were fresh, sturdy people" (10). Mr. Heidler, in fact, "looked as if nothing could break him down.... His shoulders were tremendous, his nose arrogant.... The wooden expression of his face was carefully striven for. His eyes were light blue and intelligent, but with a curious underlying expression of obtuseness—even of brutality" (10–11). Heidler is narcissistically self-regarding, shut in upon his privilege. Hence, he is described as "obtuse," "wooden," with hints of "brutality," even when expressing his love for Marya; See Octavio R. González, "The Narrative Mood of Jean Rhys' *Quartet*," *ariel* 49, no. 1 (2018): 107–41, for a remarkable essay on *Quartet's* narrative technique that draws attention to the Heidlers' characteristics.

74. Simon Gikandi, *Slavery and the Culture of Taste* (Princeton, NJ: Princeton University Press, 2011). Gikandi, remarking on the genesis of his book, states, "It occurred to me that the strange and incomprehensible signs of a black presence in the making of high culture often tended to slip away, not because of the invisibility of the enslaved but because the construction of the ideals of modern civilization demanded the repression of what it had introjected—the experience or phenomenon that it had unconsciously assimilated" (xii).
75. I take the term "slave-ship factories" from Marcus Rediker, *The Slave Ship: A Human History* (New York: Viking Penguin, 2007), 9.
76. Gikandi, *Slavery and the Culture of Taste*, 122.
77. Benítez-Rojo, *Repeating Island*, 4.
78. Rhys, *Good Morning*, 44.
79. Rhys, *Good Morning*, 9; Rhys, *Wide Sargasso Sea*, 9.
80. Jean Rhys, *After Leaving Mr. McKenzie* (New York: Norton, 1997), 27.
81. Rhys, *After Leaving Mr. Mckenzie*, 27.
82. Rhys, *Quartet*, 117.
83. Within the context of revolutionary longing following the Haitian Revolution, see Monique Allewaert, *Ariel's Ecology: Plantations, Personhood, and Colonialism in the American Tropics* (Minneapolis: University of Minnesota Press, 2013) and her reading of Leonora Sansay's travelogue *Secret History* (1808) and novel *Zelica* (1820). "The portents of destructivity, ruination, fragmentation, and death that she so persistently accumulates in her works make clear a desire for a destructive difference that breaks the conventions of life and personhood so dominant in postrevolutionary Philadelphia. This is not evidence of a death drive or masochism, but rather is the only way possible to stage her desire for a dramatic shift from existing models of agency and social life" (170).
84. Benítez-Rojo, *Repeating Island*, 4.
85. C. L. R. James, "Lecture on Federation (West Indies and British Guiana)," (Demarara, Guyana: Argosy, & Co., n.d.), Marxists.org/archive/james-clr/works/1958/06/federation.htm.
86. Rhys, *Wide Sargasso Sea*, 145.
87. Glissant, *Caribbean Discourse*, 105–6.
88. Benítez-Rojo, *Repeating Island*, 27.

89. Michael T. Taussig, *Shamanism, Colonialism, and the Wild Man: A Study in Terror and Healing* (Chicago: University of Chicago Press, 1991), refers to a "colonial unconscious," as a Latin American surreality, "with its phantoms of various shapes and guises stalking each other in the thicket of their differences" (91).
90. Rhys, *Wide Sargasso Sea*, 47; see also Kathleen DeGuzman, "*Wide Sargasso Sea*'s Archipelagic Provincialism," *small axe* 23, no. 2 (July 2019): 1–16.
91. Rhys, *Wide Sargasso Sea*, 9.
92. Rhys, *Wide Sargasso Sea*, 10.
93. Rhys, *Wide Sargasso Sea*, 9.
94. Rhys, *Wide Sargasso Sea*, 9.
95. The name of the house, Coulibri, derives from a Carib word meaning "humming bird." In this and other references to the Caribs, Rhys insists on a multilayering of history that reaches back to the pre-Conquest Indigenous settlement and also recognizes the ongoing presence of Caribs in Dominica. Carib, or Kalinago, Territory is a 3,700 acre settlement on the Atlantic coast of Dominica and home to approximately 3,000 Carib Indians. Rhys's interest in the Caribs' history and culture included a planned novel called *Wedding in the Carib Quarter* and featured a cross-racial marriage. Carole Angier, *Jean Rhys: Life and Work* (New York: Viking, 1985), quotes Rhys regarding this nonexistent novel, "This feeling I have about the Caribs & the Carib Quarter is very old & very complicated. . . . When I try to explain the feeling I find I cannot or do not wish to" (33).
96. Rhys, *Wide Sargasso Sea*, 10–11.
97. Taussig, *Shamanism, Colonialism, and the Wild Man*, 91.
98. Jack Halberstam, "Wildness, Loss, Death," *Social Text* 32, no. 4 (Winter 2014): 147.
99. Jean Rhys, *Smile, Please: An Unfinished Autobiography* (New York: Harper & Row, 1979), 23.
100. Taussig, *Shamanism, Colonialism, and the Wild Man*, "The importance of this colonial work of fabulation extends beyond the nightmarish quality of its contents. Its truly crucial feature lies in the way it creates an uncertain reality out of fiction, giving shape and voice to the formless form of the reality in which an unstable interplay of truth and illusion becomes a phantasmatic social force" (121).
101. Rhys's figuration of the post-slavery plantation as an overgrown Garden of Eden echoes the early model of imperial conservation in which, as Elizabeth M. DeLoughrey and George Handley, eds., *Postcolonial Ecologies: Literatures of the Environment* (New York: Oxford University Press, 2011), put it, "colonial violence was mystified by invoking a model of conserving an untouched (and often feminized) Edenic landscape" (12). Here, though, there is no need to conserve nature, as it has reverted on its own to wildness—untamed, failed, chaotic—and expresses the shadowy underside of the modern/colonial system.
102. Halberstam, "Wildness, Loss, Death," 147.
103. Matter, in this instance, is a site of narrativity. It grows, floats, reproduces, and absorbs oxygen when decomposing, as with sargassum algae. Some might point to how anthropomorphic language appropriates nonhuman materialism for human knowledge. Plants lack a linguistic self-awareness of their own activity; they do not narrate their

own stories. By necessity, because humans use language to highlight the agency of inert substances and plant life, anthropomorphism must occur. Serenella Iovino and Serpil Oppermann, in "Material Ecocriticism: Materiality, Agency, and Models of Narrativity," *Ecozon@* 3, no. 1 (2012), argue that an element of human likeness is a "narrative expedient intended to stress the agentic power of matter and the horizontality of its elements" (82). Going further, Eduardo Kohn argues that matter thinks and signifies. Anthropomorphism, in this instance, is not a ploy to make nonhuman materiality more like humans. Rather, it fires the human imagination to understand humanity's entwined, transcorporeal relationship to its environmental surrounds, in *How Forests Think: Toward an Anthropology Beyond the Human* (Berkeley: University of California Press, 2013). Through this language, the reader comes to perceive that, as Susan Hekman, in *The Material of Knowledge: Feminist Disclosures* (Bloomington: Indiana University Press, 2010), puts it, "the linguistic, social, political and biological are inseparable" (25). Likewise, the activities and geographies of the sea demand a rethinking of conceptual paradigms.

104. Rhys, *Wide Sargasso Sea*, 141.
105. See Aaron Pinnix, "Sargassum in the Black Atlantic: Entanglement and the Abyss in Bearden, Walcott, and Philip," *Atlantic Studies* 16, no. 4 (2018), https://www.doi.org/10.1080/14788810.2018.1510700, for a consideration of the Sargasso Sea in Black Atlantic literature and art.
106. DeGuzman, "*Wide Sargasso Sea's* Archipelagic Provincialism," 15.
107. Rhys, *Wide Sargasso Sea*, letter to Francis Wyndham, 139. Republished from *The Letters of Jean Rhys*, selected and edited by Francis Wyndham and Diana Melly (New York: Viking, 1984).
108. Rhys's letter to Francis Wyndham. In it, Rhys ventriloquizes the Afro-Caribbean phrase, "she *magic* with him," (*Wide Sargasso Sea*, 139).
109. In Jamaica, it wasn't until Tacky's Rebellion (1760) that obeah was criminalized by colonists. Prior to and even after obeah's criminalization, African and Afro-diasporic botanical medicine was an important source of healing for Blacks and whites alike. Emily Senior, in *The Caribbean and the Medical Imagination, 1764–1834: Slavery, Disease, and Colonial Modernity* (New York: Cambridge University Press, 2018), argues that obeah was often more effective than European medicine in treating tropical diseases and other ailments (163–66). She writes, for enslaved Africans and African-descended persons, proficiency in "medical and natural knowledge [was] a way to gain power and privilege on the plantation" as well as to continue African religious practices (164). These practices articulate an alternative worldview from that of the colonizer. Senior continues, "In the north-west region of Africa from which obeah originates, disease and death were often attributed to supernatural causes, and the physical, spiritual and moral aspects of the disease were unified in obeah practice. While slaves in the British Caribbean often explained minor illnesses in naturalistic terms, major illnesses and death were more frequently thought to be caused by specific agents such as malevolent spirits, acts of God(s), the breaking of religious rules or taboos, the displeasure of ancestral spirits and magic or sorcery. This unified approach to healing and

spiritual practices, which worked in opposition to Enlightenment movement towards the separation of medicine and religion ... suggests one way in which obeah emerged as a form of conceptual resistance to the colonial slave system" (166). Rhys was aware of this history, evident through the reference she makes to Père Labat in *Wide Sargasso Sea*; See Diana Paton, *Cultural Politics of Obeah: Religion, Colonialism and Modernity in the Caribbean World* (New York: Cambridge University Press, 2015). Paton argues that white Caribbean beliefs in the occult outlasted their European counterparts as exemplified by the French Dominican priest Jean-Baptist Labat. "Born in the 1660s, Labat lived through the period in which witchcraft was decriminalized, but maintained belief in the power of the supernatural. As Doris Garraway notes, his application of 'the discourse of colonial demonology to African practices of magic' indicates 'the persistence of colonial beliefs in the occult supernatural at the beginning of the eighteenth century, when the European witch craze was undeniably in decline'" (27, quoting Doris Garraway, *The Libertine Colony: Creolization in the Early French Caribbean*, Durham: Duke University Press, 2005, 165). Labat is also infamous for modernizing and expanding the sugar plantation system in Martinique and was a particularly brutal slave master. In her reference to Labat, Rhys probably drew upon Lafcadio Hearn's travelogue, *Two Years in the French West Indies* (1890), that recounts how, upon banishment from Martinique, Labat cursed the island and promised to return. The free Blacks on the island believe he is a "revenant" who haunts the island. *The Revenant* was a working title for what became *Wide Sargasso Sea*.

110. Danielle N. Boaz, "'Instruments of Obeah:' The Significance of Ritual Objects in the Jamaican Legal System, 1760 to the Present," in *Materialities of the Black Atlantic*, ed. Akinwumi Ogundiran, Amanda Tang, Paula Saunders, et al. (Bloomington: Indiana University Press, 2014), 144.

111. Paton, in *Cultural Politics of Obeah*, explains, "Protection against spiritual attack was a necessary aspect of daily life. Physical substances could have powerful effects, and these often depended on the ritual context in which they were consumed, touched, or simply placed in proximity to a person" (23).

112. Monique Allewaert, "Super Fly: François Makandal's Colonial Semiotics," *American Literature* 91, no. 3 (September 2019): 470.

113. Robert Farris Thompson, *Flash of the Spirit: African and Afro-American Art and Philosophy* (New York: Vintage, 1983). Thompson cites a Cuban Santeria practice in which, "one places to the side a piece of sugarcane filled with sea water, sand and mercury, stoppered with wax, so that the *nkisi* will always have life, like the flow of quicksilver, so that it will be swift and moving, like the waters of the ocean, so that the spirit in the charm can merge with the sea and travel far away" (122). Quoting Lydia Cabrera, *El Monte: Igbo Fina Ewe Orisha, Vititinfinda* (Havana: Edicones C. R., 1954), 136; see also Allewaert, *Ariel's Ecology*, 131.

114. Thompson, *Flash of the Spirit*, 117. Thompson describes the religious practices of the West African Bakongo but states that they "reappeared in the Americas in the form of the *nkisi*-charm. An *nkisi* (plural: *minkisi*) is a strategic object in black Atlantic art" (117); Zora Neale Hurston, *Tell My Horse: Voodoo and Life in Haiti and Jamaica* (New

York: Harper & Row, 1990). Hurston disputes the meaning of grave dirt by citing doctors who have found germs of yellow fever, scarlatina, typhoid, and other infectious diseases within the dirt (238). Besides its indexical relation to spirits, then, grave dirt can directly cause harm through contamination.

115. Stephen Nathan Haymes, "An Africana Studies Critique of Environmental Ethics," in *Racial Ecologies*, ed. LeiLani Nishime and Kim D. Hester Williams (Seattle: University of Washington Press, 2018), 36.
116. Haymes, "Africana Studies Critique," 36–37.
117. Haymes, "Africana Studies Critique," 37.
118. Rhys, *Wide Sargasso Sea*, 65.
119. Rhys, *Wide Sargasso Sea*, 66.
120. Rhys, *Wide Sargasso Sea*, 71.
121. Allewaert, *Ariel's Ecology*, 134; See also William Pietz, "The problem of the fetish, I," *Res* 9 (Spring 1985): 5–17. He writes that the fetish institutes "the subjection of the human body (as the material locus of action and desire) to the influence of certain significant material objects that, although cut off from the body, function as its controlling organs at certain moments" (10).
122. Allewaert, *Ariel's Ecology*, 132.
123. Rhys, *Wide Sargasso Sea*, 64.
124. Rhys, *Wide Sargasso Sea*, 140.
125. Rhys, *Wide Sargasso Sea*, 107.
126. Rhys, *Wide Sargasso Sea*, 109; See also Emery, *Jean Rhys at "World's End,"* for her compelling reading of this scene to which I'm indebted.
127. Rhys, *Wide Sargasso Sea*, 112.
128. Rhys, *Wide Sargasso Sea*, 107.
129. Olaudah Equiano, *Equiano's Travels*, ed. Paul Edwards (Portsmouth, NH: Heinemann, 1967). See Equiano's encounter with the talking book, which he approaches with curiosity "to learn how all things had a beginning" (40). Surely, Equiano is thinking of the biblical book of Genesis here, but perhaps there is also an ironic echo of postcolonial critique: how colonial narratives begin with the native's fierce resistance rather than from the colonizer's initial aggressive incursion into the territory, may also be heard. If ironic, then Equiano, as well as Rhys, work to demystify the book as fetish, how, in Rhys's words in *Wide Sargasso Sea*, "there is always the other side, always" (77).
130. Rochester, whose experience in the West Indies is largely mediated by the ethnographic texts and slanderous letters he reads, describes the contents on the bookshelves in his dressing room: "Byron's poems, novels by Sir Walter Scott, *Confessions of an Opium Eater*, some shabby brown volumes, and on the last shelf, *Life and Letters of*. . . . The rest was eaten away" (*Wide Sargasso Sea*, 44). Romantic exoticization is crumbling in the Caribbean. The narratives that sustained the plantocracy can no longer uphold the stable subject position of the European master. Rochester soon after begins to hallucinate as he is untethered from European systems of meaning. Only his access to the power of colonial law allows him to regain his authoritative footing.
131. Rhys, *Voyage in the Dark*, 9, my emphasis.

132. See Isabel Hofmeyr, *Dockside Reading: Hydrocolonialism and the Custom House* (Durham, NC: Duke University Press, 2022), for a related methodology of reading the book as object.
133. Taussig, *Shamanism, Colonialism, and the Wild Man*, 132.
134. Srinivas Aravamudan, *Tropicopolitans: Colonialism and Agency, 1688–1804* (Durham, NC: Duke University Press, 1999), 281.
135. In Rhys, *Voyage in the Dark,* Anna freely associates about her unintended pregnancy: "And all the time thinking round and round in a circle that it is there inside me, and about all the things I had taken so that if I had it, it would be a monster. The Abbé Sebastian's Pills, primrose label, one guinea a box, daffodil label, two guineas, orange label, three guineas. No eyes, perhaps. . . . No arms, perhaps. . . . Pull yourself together" (168). The seriality of money, itself an echo of the slave trade's conflation of Black bodies with West African gold and geographical region (Guinea), stands in direct contradiction with the circularity of gestation and the formlessness of the monstrous fetus.
136. Marlon James, *The Book of Night Women* (New York: Riverhead, 2009), 6.
137. Brathwaite, in *Contradictory Omens*, commenting on both the final pages of *Wide Sargasso Sea* and Wally Look Lai's assessment of *Wide Sargasso Sea* writes: "The 'jump' here is a jump to death; so that Antoinette wakes to death, not to life; for life would have meant dreaming in the reality of madness in a cold castle in England. But death was also her allegiance to the carefully detailed exotic fantasy of the West Indies. In fact, neither world is 'real.' They exist inside her head. Tia was not and never could be her friend. . . . White creoles in the English and French West Indies have separated themselves by too wide a gulf and have contributed too little culturally, as a group, to give credence to the notion that they can, given the present structure, meaningfully identify or be identified, with the spiritual world on this side of the Sargasso Sea" (36–38). In "A Post-Cautionary Tale of the Helen of Our Wars," *Wasafiri* 11, no. 22 (1995), Brathwaite clarifies that his work "has never even **hinted** at any form of cultural or other apartheid" (75). Instead, he says, "We have to begin the great work of plantation psychocultural reconstruction by first of all knowing as clearly & as carefully as we can, where we each of us COMING from & the nature & complexity—often complicity—of the BROKEN dispossessed sometimes alienated GROUND on which we at 'first' find ourselves" (75).
138. James, *The Book of Night Women*, 63.
139. James, *The Book of Night Women*, 3.
140. James, *The Book of Night Women*, 3.
141. James, *The Book of Night Women*, 112.
142. James, *The Book of Night Women*, 112.
143. James, *The Book of Night Women*, 113.
144. James, *The Book of Night Women*, 114.
145. James, *The Book of Night Women*, 115.
146. Jamaica Kincaid, *The Autobiography of My Mother* (New York: Penguin, 1996), 3–4.
147. Kincaid, *The Autobiography of My Mother*, 228.
148. Rhys, *Wide Sargasso Sea*, 38.
149. Kincaid, *The Autobiography of My Mother*, 87.

150. Kincaid, *The Autobiography of My Mother*, 16.
151. While Kincaid's novel begins to recover Carib history in the Caribbean, Tiffany Lethabo King's, *The Black Shoals: Offshore Formations of Black and Native Studies* (Durham, NC: Duke University Press, 2019), problematizes the binary between land-based natives and Black watery geographies. Her metaphor of the shoal "as simultaneously land and sea . . . fracture[s] this notion that Black diaspora studies is overdetermined by rootlessness and only metaphorized by water and . . . disrupt[s] the idea that Indigenous studies is solely rooted and fixed in imaginaries of land as territory" (4). Building upon Brathwaite's tidalectics, King's shoals, at once material and metaphorical, emphasizes embodied rhythms and practices of Black remembrance as a watery rerooting on shore.
152. Kincaid, *The Autobiography of My Mother*, 35–36.
153. Kincaid, *The Autobiography of My Mother*, 36.
154. Valérie Loichot, in *Water Graves: The Art of the Unritual in the Greater Caribbean* (Charlottesville: University of Virginia Press, 2020), argues that given the casual, unritualized disposal of Black bodies in slavery and its aftermath, "the border between the dead and the living is not properly sealed, and the angry and suffering dead, in the form of zonbis [sic] or ghosts, become unpredictable and threaten living humanity" (12). The drowning (un)death of the boy in Kincaid's novel also signifies the silence of the archive on the issue of Black disposability in slavery and its aftermath and, at the same time, configures a space of Black possibility; See also Sharpe, *Immaterial Archives*.
155. Kincaid, *The Autobiography of My Mother*, 37.
156. Kincaid, *The Autobiography of My Mother*, 37.
157. Kincaid, *The Autobiography of My Mother*, 37–38.
158. Kincaid, *The Autobiography of My Mother*, 51.
159. Kincaid, *The Autobiography of My Mother*, 83.
160. Kincaid, *The Autobiography of My Mother*, 97–98.
161. Zakiyyah Iman Jackson, *On Becoming Human: Matter and Meaning in an Antiblack World* (New York: New York University Press, 2020), 45.
162. Jackson, *On Becoming Human*, 39.
163. Hortense J. Spillers, in "Mama's Baby, Papa's Maybe: An American Grammar Book," *diacritics* 17, no. 2 (Summer 1987), uses the term "pornotroping" to conflate both the violence and sexualization of the female captives (porno) and the metaphoric proliferation of meanings, symbols, fantasies, and desires (troping) that attached to the female captive body (67).

5. DELTA

1. My description of the origins of petroleum is drawn from https://www.eia.gov/energyexplained/oil-and-petroleum-products/ (last accessed on 8/14/24).
2. Sharad Chari, "Detritus," in *Fueling Culture: 101 Words for Energy and Environment*, ed. Imre Szeman, Jennifer Wenzel, and Patricia Yeager (New York: Fordham University Press, 2017), 101.

3. Stephanie LeMenager, *Living Oil: Petroleum Culture in the American Century* (New York: Oxford University Press, 2016), 5. Quoted in Kathryn Yusoff, *A Billion Black Anthropocenes or None* (Minneapolis: Minnesota University Press, 2018), 6; See also Timothy Mitchell, "Economentality: How the Future Entered Government," *Critical Inquiry* 40, no. 4 (Summer 2014): 479–507.
4. Yusoff, *A Billion Black Anthropocenes*, 14.
5. Yusoff, *A Billion Black Anthropocenes*, 2.
6. Kathryn Yusoff, *Geologic Life: Inhuman Intimacies and the Geophysics of Race* (Durham, NC: Duke University Press, 2024), 8.
7. Yusoff, *A Billion Black Anthropocenes*, xii.
8. Yusoff, *A Billion Black Anthropocenes*, xii.
9. Sylvia Wynter, in *Black Metamorphoses: New Natives in a New World* (Institute of the Black World Papers, Schomburg Center for Research in Black Culture, n.d.), comments on the Haitian ethnologist Jean Prince-Mars's folklore, "The creation of . . . Haitian culture was the result of a 'transplantation' on a 'stranger soil' of essential African cultural patterns. It is this process of transplantation that we label 'indigenization'. . . . The physical and geographic disruption of the Middle Passage, by the change of continent and by a total conditioning power of the plantation, made him [the Caribbean "native" and American Black] the first to experience a near total alienation. It was the totality of this change which occasioned a cultural response of such magnitude. This response was great enough to transform him into the indigenous inhabitant of his new land" (17).
10. On the Niger Delta, see, for instance, Ike Okonta and Oronto Douglas, *Where Vultures Feast: Shell, Human Rights and Oil in the Niger Delta* (San Francisco: Sierra Club Books, 2001); Jennifer Wenzel, *The Disposition of Nature: Environmental Crisis and World Literature* (New York: Fordham University Press, 2019), especially chapter 2; Cajetan Iheka, *Naturalizing Africa: Ecological Violence, Agency, and Postcolonial Resistance in African Literature* (New York: Cambridge University Press, 2018), especially chapter 3; Tekena N. Tamuno. *Oil Wars in the Niger Delta 1849-2009* (Ibadan, Nigeria: Stirling-Horden Publishers, 2011). On the Mississippi Delta, see Clyde Woods, *Development Arrested: The Blues and Plantation Power in the Mississippi Delta* (New York: Verso, 1998); and Susan Scott Parrish, *The Flood Year 1927: A Cultural History* (Princeton, NJ: Princeton University Press, 2017).
11. Achille Mbembe, "Necropolitics," *Public Culture* 15, no. 1 (2003): 24.
12. Hannah Arendt, *The Origins of Totalitarianism* (New York: Harvest, 1966), 192. Quoted in Mbembe, "Necropolitics," 24.
13. Mbembe, "Necropolitics," 25–26.
14. Mbembe, "Necropolitics," 34.
15. See Peter Kalliney, *Commonwealth of Letters: British Literary Culture and the Emergence of Postcolonial Aesthetics* (New York: Oxford University Press, 2013).
16. The etymology of Yoknapatawpha is taken from https://en.wikipedia.org/wiki/Yoknapatawpha_County (last accessed 8/27/24).

17. Philip Gordon, "The Delta and Yoknapatawpha: The Layering of Geography and Myth in the Works of William Faulkner," *Study the South* (2016), 16.
18. Jay Watson's "Fictions of Capture: William Faulkner in an Era of Fugitive Energy," *American Literary History* 34, no. 2 (Summer 2022): 477–509, and *Fossil Fuel Faulkner: Energy, Modernity and the U.S. South* (New York: Oxford University Press, 2022) are notable exceptions. Watson's newest work interrogates the South's energy cultures and histories, including their link to race.
19. On the lure of oil wealth to replace white dependency on resistant Black labor in Faulkner's fiction as well as on the boom and bust cycles of resource "capture," see Watson, "Fictions of Capture."
20. George S. King, *The Last Slaver* (New York: G. P. Putnam's Sons, 1933), 54.
21. Sarah Gleeson-White, *William Faulkner at Twentieth Century Fox: The Annotated Screenplays* (New York: Oxford University Press, 2017), 283; In comparing the novel to multiple versions of the screenplay, I am indebted to Jeff Karem, "Fear of a Black Atlantic? African Passages in *Absalom, Absalom!* and *The Last Slaver*," in *Global Faulkner: Faulkner and Yoknapatawpha*, ed. Melanie R. Benson (Oxford: University of Mississippi Press, 2006), 166.
22. Gleeson-White, *William Faulkner at Twentieth Century Fox*, 337; See also Karem's discussion of the passage in "Fear of a Black Atlantic," 170.
23. Karem, "Fear of a Black Atlantic," 170.
24. Karem, "Fear of a Black Atlantic," 171.
25. Édouard Glissant, *Faulkner, Mississippi* (New York: Farrar, Straus and Giroux, 1999), 10.
26. Glissant, *Faulkner, Mississippi*, 30.
27. Woods in *Development Arrested*, describes this process of settler colonialism as follows: "Between the Native American expulsion known as the Trail of Tears [in the 1830s] and the Great Depression of the 1930s, the Yazoo-Mississippi Delta was carved out of an impenetrable complex of swamps and hardwood forests. Prior to colonization, the Lower Mississippi Valley was imagined by Easterners as a future empire that would eventually rival the Nile Valley Civilizations. Consequently, allusions to those ancient empires are still scattered throughout the valley: Cairo, Illinois; Luxora, Arkansas; Memphis, Tennessee; Alexandria, Louisiana. . . . For African Americans, the Delta came to represent a slavery within slavery and oppression of biblical proportions. . . . Because of the high cost of clearing undergrowth, building levees, and digging draining canals, only large-scale operators even attempted to make a go of planting in Tunica [Mississippi]. They brought in thousands of slaves to clear and cultivate the land. Those Blacks not killed by cholera or weakened by swamp-bred disease, dug ditches, felled huge cypress trees, and made dazzling crops of cotton, a bale or more to the acre" (40, 47); See also Sonya Posmentier, *Cultivation and Catastrophe: The Lyric Ecology of Modern Black Literature* (Baltimore, MD: Johns Hopkins University Press, 2017); Parrish, *The Flood Year 1927*; and Zora Neale Hurston, *Mules and Men* (Bloomington: Indiana University Press, 1978).
28. William Faulkner, *Absalom, Absalom!* (New York: Vintage, 1986), 210.

29. For an analysis of Faulkner's views on integrating the South, see Kristen Lee Over, "Nation, Narration, and Race: William Faulkner and the Discursive Limits of the Southern Condition," *Arizona Quarterly* 77, no. 1 (Spring 2021): 57–82.
30. Faulkner, *Absalom*, 14.
31. Faulkner, *Absalom*, 7.
32. William Faulkner, *The Big Woods* (New York: Random House, 1955), 1–2.
33. Faulkner, *Absalom*, 126.
34. Faulkner, *Absalom*, 126.
35. Faulkner, *Absalom*, 126.
36. Ryan Heryford, "Thomas Sutpen's Geography Lesson: Environmental Obscurities and Racial Remapping in Faulkner's *Absalom, Absalom!*," in *Faulkner's Geographies*, ed. Jay Watson and Ann J. Abadie (Oxford: University Press of Mississippi, 2015), 102.
37. Faulkner, *Absalom*, 295, 280.
38. Julie Beth Napolin, in *The Fact of Resonance: Modernist Acoustics and Narrative Form* (New York: Fordham University Press, 2020), writes that "in reading *The Nigger of the 'Narcissus*,' Faulkner contacts a grounding acoustical unconscious of the formation of the Americas. Faulkner remarked that *The Nigger of the 'Narcissus'* was the book he wished he had written more than any other, and he kept a copy on his nightstand" (104). Napolin tracks the enduring echo of the violent catastrophe of racializing slavery in the Americas, from James Wait's piercing cries at the advent of his death, across to Benjy's moaning in *The Sound and the Fury* (1929) and Jim Bond's final cry in *Absalom*. As the plantation house burns down, "there was only the sound of the idiot negro left." Faulkner, *Absalom*, 301.
39. Faulkner, *Absalom*, 201–2.
40. See Elizabeth DeLoughrey, *Roots and Routes: Navigating Caribbean and Pacific Island Literatures* (Honolulu: University of Hawai'i Press, 2007).
41. See Heryford, "Thomas Sutpen's Geography Lesson," 98.
42. Karem, "Fear of a Black Atlantic," 164.
43. Compare Faulkner's delta imaginary *Absalom* with the geography the novel uses to describe Quentin Compson and his friend at Harvard, Shrevlin McCannon: "Born half a continent apart yet joined, connected after a fashion in a sort of geographical transubstantiation by that Continental Trough, that River which runs not only the physical land of which it is the geologic umbilical, not only runs through the spiritual lives of the beings within its scope, but is very Environment itself which laughs at degrees of latitude and temperature" (208). Unlike climatological theories of racial groups and their fitness for tropical climates, Shreve and Quentin transcend environments and are connected by means of a "spiritual" river. For more on Faulkner's racializing geography, see Heryford, "Thomas Sutpen's Geography Lesson."
44. Jay Watson, *William Faulkner and the Faces of Modernity* (New York: Oxford University Press, 2019), 243.
45. Watson, *William Faulkner*, 214, quoting Paul Gilroy, *The Black Atlantic: Modernity and Double Consciousness* (Cambridge, MA: Harvard University Press, 1993), 63.

46. Susan Buck-Morss, *Hegel, Haiti, and Universal History* (Pittsburgh, PA: University of Pittsburgh Press, 2009), 56.
47. Terry L. Synder, *The Power to Die: Slavery and Suicide in British North America* (Chicago: University of Chicago Press, 2015), 13.
48. George Hutchinson, "Tracking Faulkner in the Paths of Black Modernism," in *Faulkner and the Black Literatures of the Americas: Faulkner and Yoknapatawpha*, ed. Jay Watson and James G. Thomas Jr. (Jackson: University of Mississippi Press, 2016), 59–73. See Watson's discussion of this essay as well as the historical influences on Faulkner's representations of Black resistance in *William Faulkner*, 283–85.
49. Watson, *William Faulkner*, 219.
50. Faulkner, *Absalom*, 57.
51. Faulkner, *Absalom*, 28.
52. Faulkner, *Absalom*, 30.
53. Faulkner, *Absalom*, 163.
54. Faulkner, *Absalom*, 67.
55. James C. Cobb, in *The Most Southern Place on Earth: The Mississippi Delta and the Roots of Regional Identity* (New York: Oxford University Press, 1992), draws on Mississippi Delta inhabitants' recollections of living through the frequent floods on the delta: "On the one hand, Deltans eagerly anticipated the recession of the flood waters. On the other, they knew the frustrating, discouraging, and distasteful process of cleaning up and returning to normalcy awaited them once the flood was over. [Florence Ogden] Sillers described the scene in the wake of the 1897 flood as the town of Rosedale lay 'plastered in slimy mud. The streets and lawns were littered with the corpses of dead animals washed in by the current. Broken remains of fences and plank walks lay helter-skelter over the town. The stink of dead things, drying mud, rotting plant life, and human refuse lay thick on the air. The streets were bogs of greenish mud. Crawfish squirmed about in the mud and as it dried, they died and added their bit to the stench'" (127).
56. Faulkner's letter is quoted in Richard Godden, *Fictions of Labor: William Faulkner and the South's Long Revolution* (New York: Cambridge University Press, 1997), 61.
57. Faulkner, *Absalom*, 293.
58. Faulkner, *Absalom*, 295.
59. Faulkner, *Absalom*, 298.
60. Faulkner, *Absalom*, 298.
61. Faulkner, *Absalom*, 300.
62. Faulkner, *Absalom*, 300, 144.
63. Faulkner, *Absalom*, 300.
64. William Faulkner, *Collected Stories of William Faulkner* (New York: Random House, 1950), 327–28.
65. Faulkner, *Collected Stories*, 318.
66. Faulkner, *Collected Stories*, 315.
67. Watson, *William Faulkner*, 223.
68. Yusoff, *Geologic Life*, 55.

69. Faulkner, *Collected Stories*, 315.
70. Faulkner, *Collected Stories*, 329–30.
71. Watson, *William Faulkner*, 222.
72. Faulkner, *Collected Stories*, 330.
73. Faulkner, *Collected Stories*, 328–29.
74. Faulkner, *Collected Stories*, 334.
75. Cited in Watson, *William Faulkner*, 227. Watson speculates as to whether his ceremonial word has its origins in West Africa, as Thompson suggests, or "Perhaps we are to understand that the black manservant learned the rite from his enslavers—or perhaps he teaches it to them" (227). The muddy origins of Indigenous and diasporic practices present fascinating historical and cultural questions rather than primitivist essentialisms.
76. Faulkner, *Collected Stories*, 335.
77. Watson, *William Faulkner*, 224.
78. Watson, *William Faulkner*, 225.
79. Faulkner, *Collected Stories*, 338.
80. William Faulkner, *Go Down, Moses* (New York: Random House 1942), 37–38.
81. Watson, "Fictions of Capture," 488.
82. Faulkner, *Go Down, Moses*, 38.
83. Faulkner, *Go Down, Moses*, 99.
84. Faulkner, *Go Down, Moses*, 120.
85. Faulkner, *Go Down, Moses*, 241.
86. Faulkner, *Go Down, Moses*, 253.
87. Faulkner, *Go Down, Moses*, 254.
88. Faulkner, *Go Down, Moses*, 254.
89. Faulkner, *Go Down, Moses*, 255.
90. Faulkner, *Go Down, Moses*, 257.
91. Faulkner, *Go Down, Moses*, 184–85.
92. Iheka, *Naturalizing Africa*, 1.
93. Okonta and Douglas, *Where Vultures Feast*, 23; See also Omolade Adunbi, *Oil Wealth and Insurgency in Nigeria* (Bloomington: Indiana University Press, 2015).
94. Iheka, *Naturalizing Africa*, 99–100.
95. Jennifer Wenzel, "Petro-magic-realism: Toward a Political Ecology of Nigerian Literature," *Postcolonial Studies* 9, no. 4 (2006): 450, 455. I base these points on Vaclav Paris's summary of Wenzel's argument in "Tutuola in the Bush of Primitivism," *Comparative Literature* 76, no. 2 (2024): 210.
96. Wenzel, "Petro-magic-realism," 457. Wenzel is speaking about Ben Okri's "What the Tapster Saw" but it is applicable as well to Tutuola's work.
97. Paris, "Tutuola in the Bush," 216.
98. Ato Quayson, *Strategic Transformations in Nigerian Writing: Orality and History in the Work of Reverend Samuel Johnson, Amos Tutuola, Wole Soyinka and Ben Okri* (Bloomington: Indiana University Press, 1997), 58.
99. Matthew Omelsky, "The Creaturely Modernism of Amos Tutuola," *Cultural Critique* 99 (Spring 2018): 66–67.

100. Omelsky, "Creaturely Modernism," 89.
101. Achille Mbembe, "Life, Sovereignty, and Terror in the Fiction of Amos Tutuola," *Research in African Literatures* 34, no. 4 (Winter 2003): 1.
102. Omelsky, "Creaturely Modernism," 67.
103. Laura Murphy, *Metaphor and the Slave Trade in West African Literature* (Athens: Ohio University Press, 2012), 55–56; See also Quayson, *Strategic Transformations*, for his exploration of the interrelationships between West African orality and literature that result in hybrid literary genres.
104. Amos Tutuola, *The Palm-Wine Drinkard and My Life in the Bush of Ghosts* (New York: Grove Press, 1994), 167; see also 18.
105. Murphy, *Metaphor and the Slave Trade*, 51.
106. Murphy, *Metaphor and the Slave Trade*, 51; See also Michael Thelwell's introduction to Tutuola's *The Palm-Wine Drinkard*, where he writes, "According to local legend a small band of refugees, fleeing the destruction of their town during a wave of slave-taking, were guided by a spirit to a cave in the side of a hill that was capped by a spectacular granite formation. There in the cave, 'under the rock,' or in Yoruba 'Abeokuta,' they found refuge" (179).
107. Murphy, *Metaphor and the Slave Trade*, 49.
108. Tutuola, *The Palm-Wine Drinkard*, 174.
109. Murphy, *Metaphor and the Slave Trade*, 74.
110. Tutuola, *The Palm-Wine Drinkard*, "These slave-wars were causing dead luck to both old and young of those days, because if one is captured, he or she would be sold into slavery for foreigners who would carry him or her to unknown destinations to be killed for the buyer's god or to be working for him" (18).
111. Tutuola, *The Palm-Wine Drinkard*, 30.
112. Tutuola, *The Palm-Wine Drinkard*, 281.
113. For example, in Tutuola, *The Palm-Wine Drinkard*, the protagonist in *My Life in the Bush of Ghosts* describes his encounter with a barber after fourteen years of wandering the bush. After having been barbered, the protagonist watches him cut the hair of the "Flash-eyed Mother" and her millions of heads (just like a baby's head): "I noticed carefully that uncountable beetles, bees, wasps and many other kinds of biting insects were living inside the hair of these heads as their homes and also their mother's head was full up with numerous small birds which built their nests inside the hair of her head as on trees" (106). The narrator is a "careful" observer of the strange creatures.
114. Tutuola, *Palm-Wine Drinkard*, 109.
115. Iheka, *Naturalizing Africa*, 26.
116. Iheka, *Naturalizing Africa*, 27.
117. Tutuola, *Palm-Wine Drinkard*, 205.
118. Wenzel, in *The Disposition of Nature*, says of Harry Garuba's argument in favor of contemporary African animism, "Central to Garuba's conceptually ambitious argument is the notion that animist thought, contrary to Weberian narratives of modernization as disenchantment, opens itself to 'the continual re-enchantment' of the world" (125).
119. Tutuola, *The Palm-Wine Drinkard*, 246.

120. Tutuola, *The Palm-Wine Drinkard*, 248–49.
121. Tutuola, *The Palm-Wine Drinkard*, 249.
122. Omelsky, "Creaturely Modernism," 86.
123. Tutuola, *The Palm-Wine Drinkard*, 249–50.
124. On modernity's "bad infinity," see Jed Esty, *Unseasonable Youth: Modernism, Colonialism, and the Fiction of Development* (New York: Oxford University Press, 2012), where he says, "spurious [bad] infinity is one defined in direct and full contradistinction to the finite, so that it could be exemplified by a numerical series that goes on forever or, indeed, by a temporally blank conception of history as moments unfolding into the future without end" (27).

CODA

1. Ben Raines, "Wreck Found by Reporter Might be Last American Slave Ship, Archaeologists Say," *Alabama Local News,* January 23, 2018, https://www.al.com/news/mobile/2018/01/alcom_reporter_may_have_found.html (accessed January 27, 2023).
2. Richard Fausset, "Alabama Historians: The Last Known Slave Ship Has Been Found," *New York Times,* May 23, 2019, https://www.nytimes.com/2019/05/23/us/clotilda-slave-ship-alabama.html (last accessed January 27, 2023).
3. At the 2022 Sundance Film Festival, the documentary film *Descendant* premiered. This film traces the history and triumphs of the African-descended people whose ancestors were brought to the United States on the *Clotilda* and who settled in Africatown, Alabama. It also details the finding of the *Clotilda* and the debates among the community on the proper way to memorialize the remains of the last transatlantic forced passage from Africa (Benin) to the United States; See also Hannah Durkin, *The Survivors of the* Clotilda: *The Lost Stories of the Last Captives of the American Slave Trade* (New York: Amistad Press, 2024), epilogue.
4. On the "slave sublime," see Paul Gilroy, *The Black Atlantic: Modernity and Double Consciousness* (Cambridge, MA: Harvard University Press, 1993), chapter 6. It names how the Middle Passage turn toward death "emerges continually in the literature and expressive cultures of the black Atlantic . . . as a non-traditional tradition, an irreducibly modern, ex-centric, unstable, and asymmetric cultural ensemble" (198). These practices comprise a counterculture of modernity that holds open a space for utopian longings; Michelle M. Wright, in *Physics of Blackness: Beyond the Middle Passage Epistemology* (Minneapolis: University of Minnesota Press, 2015), warns against constructing Blackness as "Middle Passage Blackness," defined "through an unbroken chain of ancestors whose experiences inform our contemporary outlook" (10); Yogita Goyal, in "Afrofuturist Speculations and Diaspora," affirms Wright's caution, stating that "invoking slavery does as much to divide the Black diaspora as it once did to unify it" (113). In *Diaspora and Literary Studies*, ed. Angela Naimou (New York: Cambridge University Press, 2023), 112–25.

5. Kerry Bystrom and Isabel Hofmyer, "Oceanic Routes: (Post-it) Notes on Hydro-Colonialism," *Comparative Literature* 69, no. 1 (2017): 1–6; Joseph R. Slaughter and Kerry Bystrom, "The Sea of International Politics: Fluidity, Solvency, and Drift in the Global South Atlantic," in *The Global South Atlantic* (New York: Fordham University Press, 2017), 1–30; Françoise Lionnet,"World Literature, Postcolonial Studies, and Coolie Odysseys: J.-M.G. Le Clézio's and Amitav Ghosh's Indian Ocean Novels," *Comparative Literature* 67, no. 3 (2015): 287–311; Elizabeth DeLoughrey, "Toward a Critical Ocean Studies for the Anthropocene," *English Language Notes* 57, no. 1 (April 2019): 21–36, and *Routes and Roots: Navigating Caribbean and Pacific Island Literatures* (Honolulu: University of Hawai'i Press, 2009); Epeli Hau'ofa, *We are the Ocean: Selected Works* (Honolulu: University of Hawai'i Press, 2008); Maebh Long and Matthew Hayward, *The Rise of Pacific Literature: Decolonization, Radical Campuses, and Modernism* (New York: Columbia University Press, 2024); Sarah Nuttall, "Pluvia Time/Wet Form," *New Literary History* 51, no. 2 (Spring 2020): 455–72; Meg Samuelson and Charne Lavery, "The Oceanic South," *English Language Notes* 57, no. 1 (April 2019): 37–50; Meg Samuelson, "Coastal Form: Amphibian Positions, Wider Worlds, and Planetary Horizons on the African Indian Ocean Littoral," *Comparative Literature* 69, no. 1 (2017): 16–24; Alice Te Punga Somerville, *Once Were Pacific: Maori Connections to Oceania* (Minneapolis: Minnesota University Press, 2012).

6. W. E. B. Du Bois, *Darkwater: Voices from Within the Veil* (New York: Dover Publications, 1999), 22.

7. Hannah Arendt, *The Origins of Totalitarianism* (New York: Harcourt, Brace, 1951), see especially the later preface to part 2 (written in 1967) where she writes, "This book deals only with the strictly European colonial imperialism whose end came with the liquidation of British rule in India. It tells the story of the disintegration of the nation-state that proved to contain nearly all the elements necessary for the subsequent rise of totalitarian movements and governments. Before the imperialist era, there was no such thing as world politics, and without it, the totalitarian claim to global rule would not have made sense" (xxi); see also Aimé Césaire, *Discourse on Colonialism*, trans. Joan Pinkham (New York: Monthly Review Press, 2000), 36.

8. Arendt, *The Origins*, 267.

9. Du Bois, *Darkwater*, 18.

10. Neferti X. M. Tadiar, *Remaindered Life* (Durham, NC: Duke University Press, 2022), 66.

11. Tadiar, *Remaindered Life*, 67.

12. Ellen Gallagher, "Interview: Characters, Myths, and Stories," *Art21*, July 10, 2005, https://art21.org/read/ellen-gallagher-characters-myths-and-stories/ (accessed April 8, 2025).

13. https://www.discogs.com/release/1545133-Drexciya-The-Quest (accessed October 5, 2024).

14. M. NourbeSe Philip, *Zong!* (Middletown, CT: Wesleyan University Press, 2008), 203.

15. Gallagher, "Interview," n.p.

16. Suzanna Chan, "'Alive . . . again.' Unmoored in the Aquafuture of Ellen Gallagher's Watery Ecstatic," *WSQ: Women's Studies Quarterly* 45, no. 1–2 (Spring/Summer 2017): 246.
17. Chan, "Alive . . . again," 248.
18. Chan, "Alive . . . again," 254.
19. Chan, "Alive . . . again," 249.

INDEX

Page numbers in *italics* refer to figures.

abolitionism: lexicon of, 8, 110–11; modernist appropriations of, 36; modernity/coloniality and, 108, 207; testimony for, 46; Woolf and, 138
Absalom, Absalom! (Faulkner), 197–98, 200–210
Achebe, Chinua, 12
Adichie, Chimamanda Ngozi, 230
Adorno, Theodor, 30–31, 62, 63
Aeschylus, 207
Afrofuturism, 233–35
Afro-Orientalism, 91–92, 99, 100
Afro-Pessimism, 239n21
Agamben, Giorgio, 262n26
agency: in *Absalom, Absalom!* (Faulkner), 204, 208–9; in *The Autobiography of My Mother* (Kincaid), 190–91; in *Barracoon* (Hurston), 50–54; being human as praxis and, 36; in *The Big Sea* (Hughes), 67–69; in *Feeding the Ghosts* (D'Aguilar), 48; in *Go Down, Moses* (Faulkner), 217; in *To the Lighthouse* (Woolf), 104–7; nonliving objects and, 103–7. *See also* animism; in

"Of One Woman or So" (Wilson), 147–48; in *Romance in Marseille* (McKay), 88, 91–94; slavery and, 27, 194; water and, 23–24, 89; in *The Waves* (Woolf), 116, 120, 130, 134, 138
Ahmed, Sara, 135–36
Alaimo, Stacy, 17, 34, 116–17
Alexander, M. Jacqui, 157
Alexander VI, Pope, 37
Allewaert, Monique, 275n83, 279n121
alluvium: concept of, 19, 31, 60–66; deltas and, 196; Glissant on, 60–64, 66, 70–71, 84, 99, 118; Hughes and, 7, 63–66. *See also Big Sea, The* (Hughes); Hurston and, 63–64, 65, 79–87; McKay and, 7, 18, 63–64, 65, 87–101; ports and, 80–81
Americanah (Adichie), 230
animism: in *Feeding the Ghosts* (D'Aguilar), 48; in modernist literature, 24, 31, 32–34, 229; in *Romance in Marseille* (McKay), 91, 98–99; Tutuola and, 220, 224–26. *See also* books and literary texts
Anthill, Diana, 169

Apter, Emily, 13
archipelago: concept of, 19, 31, 150–54; chaos and, 152–54, 162–63, 167–71; deltas and, 196; Glissant on Caribbean as, 150–51, 156; racialized abjection and, 164–68. *See also* Rhys, Jean
Arendt, Hannah, 197, 231–32, 245n50
Aristotle, 262n26
assemblage, 237–38n4
Autobiography of My Mother, The (Kincaid), 185–91
autopoiesis, 40

Bachelard, Gaston, 39
Baker, Houston A., 11, 68
Bandung Conference (1955), 99
Banjo (McKay), 260n170
Barad, Karen, 34, 116–17, 126, 242n58, 258–59n130
Barnes, Djuna, 112–14, 235
Barr, Caroline, 214
barracoon (barrier wall), 43
Barracoon (Hurston), 5–6, 18, 50–54, 58, 85–86, 233
Barthes, Roland, 39
Beer, Gillian, 121, 139
Begam, Richard, 266–67n82
being human as praxis: concept of, 9–10, 31, 34–36; alluvium and, 65; Middle Passage and, 42–49; in *The Nigger of the 'Narcissus'* (Conrad), 56
Benítez-Rojo, Antonio, 152–53, 154, 162, 168, 170
Benito Cereno (Melville), 164–65
Benjamin, Walter, 18–19
Bennett, Jane, 17, 34, 116–17
Bennett, Joshua, 42, 84–85
Bergson, Henri, 117
Berman, Jessica, 122
Big Sea, The (Hughes), 67–69, 70–71, 73–79, 101, 235
Big Woods, The (Faulkner), 103, 202–3
biopolitics, 111–12, 194

Birth of Venus, The (Botticelli), 119
Black fungibility: concept of, 12, 27–29; alluvium and, 63–66; in *The Autobiography of My Mother* (Kincaid), 190–91; being human as praxis and, 35; female bodies and, 49, 82–83; forcible feeding and, 112; Hughes and, 68–69, 78–79; Hurston and, 82–84; McKay and, 88, 94, 97–100; sexual violence and, 27, 49, 63–64; in *Wide Sargasso Sea* (Rhys), 184
Black maternity: in *The Autobiography of My Mother* (Kincaid), 185–86, 189–90; in *The Book of Night Women* (James), 184; as monstrous, 41, 49, 182–83; in "The Negro Mother" (Hughes), 69–70; in *The Souls of Black Folk* (Du Bois), 103; in "Watery Ecstatic" (Gallagher), 234–35
Black Reconstruction (Du Bois), 6
Black Thunder (Bontemps), 7
Bliss, Eliot, 271n20
Blum, Hester, 24, 89, 116
Bolin, J. S., 273n56
Bontemps, Arna, 7
Book of Night Women, The (James), 183–85
books and literary texts: in *The Big Sea* (Hughes), 34, 67–69, 70, 76; in "Red Leaves" (Faulkner), 212; Rhys and, 154, 171, 181–82; Talking Book trope and, 34, 67–69, 212
Botticelli, Sandro, 119
Braidotti, Rosi, 116–18, 130
Brand, Dionne, 16
Brathwaite, Edward Kamau, 183, 230, 280n137
British Petroleum, 218–19
Brodber, Erna, 229
Brontë, Charlotte, 154, 171, 181
Brown, Bill, 257–58n121
Brown, H. Rap, 146
Brown, Vincent, 44–45
Buck-Morss, Susan, 206–7
Burnham, Michelle, 39, 246n59
Butler, Judith, 35, 124

Butler, Octavia E., 235
Bystrom, Kerry, 230

Caribbean Discourse (Glissant), 61–62
Caribbean Federation (1958–1962), 168–69
"Caribbean Sunset" (Hughes), 69
Carmichael, Stokely, 146
Castro-Gómez, Santiago, 38
Césaire, Aimé, 231–32, 260n170
Chan, Suzanna, 234–35
chaos: archipelago and, 152–54, 162–63, 167–71; in *The Autobiography of My Mother* (Kincaid), 190–91; in *The Big Sea* (Hughes), 73; eros and, 97–101; in *Romance in Marseille* (McKay), 89; in sea-travel narratives, 39, 49; in Woolf's novels, 105, 141, 143
Chari, Sharad, 193
Cheah, Pheng, 13
Chen, Mel Y., 34, 52, 124, 126, 257n120
Cheng, Anne Anlin, 157, 158
"Children of the Sea" (Danticat), 230
Claxton, Ecroyde, 47, 253–54n47
climate change, 4, 15–16, 196, 228
Clotilda (slave ship), 228. See also *Barracoon* (Hurston)
Clukey, Amy, 270n10
Cobb, James C., 285n55
Coetzee, J. M., 106–7, 230–31, 235
Cohen, Margaret, 164, 267n85
Collingwood, W. G., 119
coloniality. *See* modernity/coloniality
colonization, concept of, 238n5
commodity fetishism: in *The Big Sea* (Hughes), 75, 78; in *The Last Slaver* (Faulkner), 200; Rhys and, 171, 181–82; slavery and, 29–31, 75, 165
Conrad, Joseph: animism and, 33–34; Faulkner and, 7, 203–4, 206, 218; free indirect discourse and, 103–4; racial supremacy and, 14. See also *Nigger of the 'Narcissus,' The* (Conrad)
Constable & Co., 161
Co-operative Women's Guild, 121

Couto, Mia, 230–31
"Craftsmanship" (Woolf), 145
Creole culture and creolization: in *The Book of Night Women* (James), 183–85; Faulkner and, 200–202; Glissant on, 61–62; obeah practices and, 33, 154–55, 171, 174–82, 184–85; Rhys and, 153–55, 158–60, 169–70, 174–82
Cuddy-Keane, Melba, 129
Cvetkovich, Ann, 157

Dabydeen, David, 273–74n63
D'Aguilar, Fred, 48
Damas, Léon Gontran, 260n170
Danticat, Edwidge, 230
Darkwater (Du Bois), 231–32
Darwin, Charles, 133, 173–74
Dawson, Kevin, 45–46, 249n91
de Gennaro, Mara, 14, 42
death: in *Absalom, Absalom!* (Faulkner), 209–10; in *The Autobiography of My Mother* (Kincaid), 185–86, 188, 190–91; in *The Big Sea* (Hughes), 74–76; in *The Book of Night Women* (James), 184; in *To the Lighthouse* (Woolf), 104–7; in "Red Leaves" (Faulkner), 213–14; in Tutuola's novels, 226–27; in *Voyage in the Dark* (Rhys), 162–63; in *The Waves* (Woolf), 122, 138, 141–44; in *Wide Sargasso Sea* (Rhys), 171–73, 180–82. See also suicide
Deepwater Horizon oil spill (2010), 218–19
Defoe, William, 106–7
DeGuzman, Kathleen, 175
DeKoven, Marianne, 267n89
Deleuze, Gilles, 117, 237–38n4
DeLoughrey, Elizabeth M., 15, 110–11, 164, 230, 269n1, 276n101, 284n40
deltas: concept of, 19, 31, 191, 192–96; in *Absalom, Absalom!* (Faulkner), 197–98, 200–210; Faulkner and, 197–99; in *Go Down, Moses* (Faulkner), 198, 214–18; in "Red Leaves" (Faulkner), 198, 199, 210–14, 215; slave trade and extractive industries in, 196–97; Tutuola and, 194–96, 197–98, 219–27

Descendant (2022 documentary film), 288n3
Diedrich, Maria, 8
"Discourse Concerning Western Planting, A" (Hakluyt), 252n27
Discourse on Colonialism (Césaire), 231–32
Douglass, Frederick, 29–30, 67–69
Doyle, Briohny, 230–31
Doyle, Laura, 11, 12, 144, 242n59
Drabinski, John E., 32, 159
"Dreadlocks Hoax, The" (Wilson), 145
Dreadnought Hoax (1910), 145
Drexciya, 233–34, 237n3
DS (2) (Dreamstories), 230
Du Bois, W. E. B., 6, 102–3, 231–32
Durkin, Hannah, 249n106
Dussel, Enrique, 241n48

ecocriticism and ecological thought, 16–17, 35, 203, 225. *See also* new materialism
ecofeminism, 123
ecology, 124. *See also* queer ecology
Edwards, Brent Hayes, 261n18
Emery, Mary Lou, 272n42
entour, 61–62
Equiano, Olaudah, 34, 53, 67–69, 212, 223, 279n129
Erikson, Bruce, 125
eros, 97–101
Erzulie's Skirt (Lara), 230
Esty, Jed, 17–18, 154, 162, 288n124
extraction: oil industry and, 191, 193, 195, 197, 218–19; slavery as, 192–96. *See also* deltas

Faber and Faber, 198
Fagunwa, D. O., 198
Fanon, Frantz, 9, 35
Faulkner, William: animism and, 33–34; Conrad and, 7, 203–4, 206, 218; delta in *Absalom, Absalom!* (Faulkner), 197–98, 200–210; delta in *Go Down, Moses* (Faulkner), 198, 214–18; delta in "Red Leaves" (Faulkner), 198, 199, 210–14, 215; delta in *The Last Slaver* (Faulkner), 6–7,

197–98, 199–200; free indirect discourse and, 103–4; interludes and, 202–3; Mississippi Delta and, 194–96, 197–99; racial supremacy and, 14, 203–9; *Salvage the Bones* (Ward) and, 229–30
Feeding the Ghosts (D'Aguilar), 48
Feinsod, Harris, 74–75
Felski, Rita, 243n6
First World War, 8, 71–72, 103–7, 231–32
Foe (Coetzee), 106–7
Fons Americanus (Walker), 1–5, 2, 6, 19, 228–29
forcible feeding, 112–14
Ford, Ford Madox, 274–75n73
Forest of Thousand Daemons (Fagunwa), 198
Forster, E. M., 229
free indirect discourse, 57, 96, 103–6, 229. *See also* stream of consciousness
Friedman, Susan Stanford, 148, 243n6, 268–69n122

Gaard, Greta, 126
Gallagher, Ellen, 19, 233–35, 235
Garraway, Doris, 277–78n109
Garuba, Harry, 33, 288n118
Garvey, Marcus, 91
Gates, Henry Louis, Jr., 8, 68, 252–53n28
geography, 24, 31–32, 62–63, 65. *See also* alluvium; archipelago; deltas; waves
Ghosh, Amitav, 230–31
Gikandi, Simon, 11, 15, 167, 247n74, 275n74
Gilroy, Paul, 15, 69, 138, 195, 212, 230, 247nn73–4
Glissant, Édouard: on alluvium, 60–64, 66, 70–71, 84, 99, 118; on Caribbean as archipelago, 150–51, 156; on Faulkner, 201; McKay and, 91–92; on Other of Thought, 83; on poetics of landscape, 32; on poetics of relation, 9–10, 61–64, 169–70, 196; on slave ship as womb abyss, 60, 64, 73, 99, 158, 196; on transversality, 77, 258n124
Go Down, Moses (Faulkner), 198, 214–18
Good Morning, Midnight (Rhys), 165–68

Gordon, Avery, 66
Gordon, Philip, 198–99
Goyal, Yogita, 7, 273n56, 274n64, 288–89n4
Graham, Shane, 69, 70
Grain of Wheat, A (Ngũgĩ), 12
Great War, 8, 71–72, 103–7, 231–32
Grosz, Elizabeth, 265n66, 267n91
Grove Press, 224
Guattari, Félix, 237–38n4
Gulf Stream, The (Homer), 5
Gurnah, Abdulrazak, 230–31

Hagen, Benjamin, 127
Haiti, 200, 203–7
Hakluyt, Richard, 252n27
Halberstam, Jack, 135, 173–74
Hall, Radclyffe, 123
Handley, George, 276n101
Harney, Stefano, 108
Harris, Cheryl I., 274n70
Hartman, Saidiya: Afro-Pessimism and, 239n21; on Black fungibility, 27, 88, 94; on trope of beached whale, 99–100; on critical fabulation, 5; on experiments in freedom, 88, 92, 94, 95; Glissant and, 66; on Hughes, 68; on melancholy, 157; new materialism and, 263n14; on sexual violence, 96; on slave trade, 8; on slavery archive, 42–43; on slavery's afterlife, 4; Spillers and, 26–27; use of "stranger" and, 259–60n159. See also *Lose Your Mother* (Hartman)
Harvey, Graham, 245n47
Hau'ofa, Epeli, 151, 230
Haymes, Stephen, 177
Hayward, Matthew, 230
Hearn, Lafcadio, 277–78n109
Hearne, John, 164–65
Heart of Darkness (Conrad), 7, 56–57
Hegel, Georg Wilhelm Friedrich, 111–12, 206–7
Heimdal and His Nine Mothers (Collingwood), 119

Hekman, Susan, 116–17, 276–77n103
Heryford, Ryan, 203
Historic Sketches of the South (Roche), 228
Hofmeyr, Isabel, 80–81, 230
Home to Harlem (McKay), 95
Homer, Winslow, 5
hooks, bell, 146
Howard's End (Forster), 229
Hudibras (slave ship), 44–45
Hughes, Langston: alluvium and, 7, 63–66. See also *Big Sea, The* (Hughes); animism and, 34; free indirect discourse and, 103–4
Hulme, Keri, 230–31
humanism, 9–10, 17, 34–35
hunger striking, 111–14
Hunt, Violet, 274–75n73
Hurricane Katrina, 229–30
Hurston, Zora Neale: alluvium and, 63–64, 65, 79–87; ethnography of slave trade and. See *Barracoon* (Hurston); free indirect discourse and, 103–4; *Louisiana* (Brodber) and, 229; on obeah practices, 278–79n114; *Salvage the Bones* (Ward) and, 229–30
Hutchinson, George, 11, 207

Iheka, Cajetan, 218–19, 220, 225–26
Ihimaera, Witi, 230–31
Indigenous peoples: alluvium and, 80; deltas and, 195, 197; genocide of, 37, 185, 193, 197; in "Red Leaves" (Faulkner), 210–12; wildness and, 170–71
interludes: Faulkner and, 202–3; in *The Souls of Black Folk* (Du Bois), 102–3; Woolf and, 103–10, 125, 128–29, 136–37, 268n103
Iovino, Serenella, 276–77n103
Islam, 98–99

Jackson, Zakiyyah Iman, 16, 41, 190
Jacob, Harriet, 212
James, C. L. R., 146, 169
James, Marlon, 109, 110, 151, 183–85
Jameson, Fredric, 11–12, 266–67n82

Jane Eyre (Brontë), 154, 171, 181
Jones, Donna V., 260n170
Julius II, Pope, 37

Karem, Jeff, 200, 206
Katrina (hurricane), 229–30
Kincaid, Jamaica, 110, 151, 185–91
King, George S., 199
King, Tiffany Lethabo: Afro-Pessimism and, 239n21; on autopoiesis, 40; being human as praxis and, 36; on Black fungibility, 12, 27–28, 49, 97; Glissant and, 66; on shoal as metaphor, 281n151; on Whiteness, 118–19
Kohn, Eduardo, 276–77n103
Kornbluh, Anna, 103
Kossula, Oluale (Cudjo Lewis). See *Barracoon* (Hurston)
Krik? Krak! (Danticat), 230

Labat, Jean-Baptiste, 277–78n109
Lai, Wally Look, 156–57
Lara, Ana-Maurine, 230
Larsen, Nella, 12
Last Slaver, The (Faulkner), 6–7, 197–98, 199–200
Last Slaver, The (King), 199
Latour, Bruno, 17
Lavery, Charne, 230
LeMenager, Stephanie, 193
Leong, Diana, 117–18
Lewis, Cudjo (Oluale Kossula). See *Barracoon* (Hurston)
liberal subjectivity: alluvium and, 66, 68; archipelagos and, 155, 174–78, 182–83; being human as praxis and, 35–36; deltas and, 88; ending of slavery and, 40–42; geography and, 31–32; poetics of relation and, 9–10, 106–7, 109; weak modernisms and, 14
Life as We Have Known It (Woolf), 121
Ligon, Richard, 27–28
Lilith's Brood (Butler), 235

Lionnet, Françoise, 158, 230
Loftus, Brian, 77
Loichot, Valérie, 61–62, 281n154
Long, Maebh, 230
Lorde, Audre, 97–98
Lose Your Mother (Hartman), 8, 230
Louisiana (Brodber), 229
Lowe, Lisa, 40
Luciano, Dana, 124, 126, 257n120
Lyell, Charles, 133

"Mama's Baby, Papa's Maybe: An American Grammar Book" (Spillers), 118, 281n163
Mao, Douglas, 247–48n75
Marcus, Jane, 122
Mariátegui, José Carlos, 241n48
Marshall, Paule, 230
Marx, Karl, 29
maternity. See Black maternity
Mbembe, Achille, 197, 221, 240n32
McGee, Patrick, 268n109
McKay, Claude: alluvium and, 7, 18, 63–64, 65, 87–101; animism and, 91, 98–99
McKittrick, Katherine, 31, 35, 64–65, 66, 155–56, 239n21
Mda, Zakes, 230–31
melancholy, 46, 151, 153, 156–60, 168
Melville, Herman, 164–65
Mentz, Steve, 24, 130
Middle Passage: being human as praxis and, 42–49; commodification of Black bodies and, 24, 25–31, 40–42; geography and, 24, 31–32, 62–63, 65. See also alluvium; archipelago; deltas; waves; origins and use of term, 110–11; World War One and, 105–7. See also Black fungibility; slave ship(s)
Mignolo, Walter D., 38–39, 240n27, 241n48
Mills, Ernestine, 19, 132–33, *132*
Mississippi Delta: in *Absalom, Absalom!* (Faulkner), 197–98, 200–210; Faulkner and, 194–96, 197–99; in *Go Down, Moses* (Faulkner), 198, 214–18; in "Red Leaves"

(Faulkner), 198, 199, 210–14, 215; slave trade and extractive industries in, 196–97
modernity/coloniality: concept of, 36–42; Africa and, 195; alluvium and, 86; Black and postcolonial modernisms and, 12, 19, 66; Conrad and, 50; Glissant and, 169–70; Haitian Revolution and, 207; Rhys and, 108–10; Tutuola and, 220; Woolf and, 108–10, 123
Morgan, Jennifer L., 27–28, 31
Morrison, Toni, 45, 146, 274n64
Mortimer-Sandilands, Catriona, 125
Morton, Timothy, 266n70
Moses, Michael Valdez, 266–67n82
Moses, Omri, 76
Moten, Fred, 29–30, 108, 239n21
motherhood. *See* Black maternity
Mrs. Dalloway (Woolf), 134
Mufti, Aamir, 13–14
Murphy, Laura T., 8, 220, 221–23, 238n12
Mustakeem, Sowande' M., 43, 47–48
My Life in the Bush of Ghosts (Tutuola), 198, 221–23, 224–25

Naipaul, V. S., 169
Nana (Zola), 182
Napolin, Julie Beth, 103, 249n117, 284n38
Narrative of the Life of Frederick Douglass, an American Slave (Douglass), 29–30
Native Son (Wright), 207
natural resources. *See* extraction
necropolitics, 197
Négritude, 260n170
"Negro Mother, The" (Hughes), 69–70
"Negro Speaks of Rivers, The" (Hughes), 69
New Masses (journal), 70
new materialism: race blindness of, 16, 64–65, 116–19; Woolf and, 119–21, 122–23. *See also* specific authors
"New Mrs Partington (of the Anti Suffrage Society), The" (Mills), 132–33, 132
Ngũgĩ wa Thiong'o, 12
Nietzsche, Friedrich, 117

Niger Delta: extractive industries in, 218–19; slave trade and extractive industries in, 196–97; Tutuola and, 194–96, 197–98, 219–27
Nigger of the 'Narcissus,' The (Conrad), 6, 50, 54–59, 203–4, 206, 218
Nile River, 192
North, Michael, 11, 57–58
Nurhussein, Nadia, 42, 71, 73, 254n57
Nuttall, Sarah, 230

obeah practices, 33, 154–55, 171, 174–82, 184–85
"Of One Woman or So" (Wilson), 110, 120, 145–49
oil industry, 191, 193, 195, 197, 218–19
Omelsky, Matthew, 220–21, 227
Omeros (Walcott), 230
On Beauty (Smith), 229
Oppermann, Serpil, 276–77n103
Oresteia (Aeschyus), 207
Origin of Species (Darwin), 173–74
Orlando (Woolf), 121, 123

Palm-Wine Drinkard, The (Tutuola), 198, 223–27
parasitism, 111–12
Paris, Vaclav, 219
Parrish, Susan Scott, 255–56n92
Paton, Diana, 277–78n109, 278n111
patriarchal violence: Rhys and, 156; slavery and, 111–12, 116–19, 139–44; water and, 119–20; women's suffrage movement and, 111–14, 119, 130–33, 132
Patterson, Orlando, 25, 30, 111–12, 237n2, 239n21
Pedersen, Carl, 8
Perez, Craig Santos, 230–31
Peters, Kimberley, 127
petrofiction, 219
petroleum. *See* oil industry
Philip, M. NourbeSe, 234
Philips, Kathy J., 268n107

Phillips, Caryl, 272n31
Philosophie de la Relation (Glissant), 61–62
Plant, Deborah G., 52
Plato, 237–38n4
pornotroping, 190
Posmentier, Sonya, 42, 84, 86
Posthuman, The (Braidotti), 117–18
posthumanism, 16–17, 117–18
poststructuralism, 117
Postures (Quartet) (Rhys), 154, 168, 274–75nn72–73
Praisesong for the Widow (Marshall), 230
primitivism, 33, 69, 99, 174, 232
Prince-Mars, Jean, 282n9

Quayson, Ato, 220
queer ecology: concept of, 123; Darwin and, 133; women's suffrage movement and, 130–32, 132; Woolf and, 109–10, 121–35, 143
queerness: in *The Big Sea* (Hughes), 76–79, 235; origins and use of term, 124; "Watery Ecstatic" (Gallagher) and, 234–35
Quest, The (Drexciya), 233–34
Quicksand (Larsen), 12
Quijano, Anibal, 241n48

racial memory, 93, 98–99
racial vitalism, 260n170
Rajiva, Jay, 33, 34
Ramazani, Jahan, 11
Rampersad, Arnold, 73
rape. *See* sexual violence
"Red Leaves" (Faulkner), 198, 199, 210–14, 215
Rediker, Marcus, 43, 251n2, 257n118, 275n75
Reid-Pharr, Robert, 65–66, 71, 79
relation, poetics of, 9–10, 61–64, 169–70, 196
Rhys, Jean: Creole culture and, 153–55, 158–60, 169–70, 174–82; James and, 151, 183–85; Kincaid and, 151, 185–91; modernity/coloniality and, 108–10; obeah practices and, 154–55, 171, 174–82; racial supremacy and, 6, 14, 153–54; racialized

abjection and, 165–68; slave abyss and, 155–63
Rizzuto, Nicole, 122, 127, 137
Roberts, Brian Russell, 81, 151–52, 153
Robinson Crusoe (Defoe), 106–7
Roche, Emma Langdon, 19, 228
Romance in Marseille (McKay): agency in, 88, 91–94; alluvium in, 18, 87–101; animism in, 91, 98–99; sexuality in, 88–89, 92–97
Room of One's Own, A (Woolf): fictional Judith Shakespeare in, 121, 139, 143; queer ecology and, 125, 127; *The Waves* (Woolf) and, 143; Wilson and, 110, 120, 145–49; Ziarek on, 131
Royal Dutch Shell, 219

Sackville-West, Vita, 121
Saint-Amour, Paul, 13–14
Salvage the Bones (Ward), 229–30
Samuelson, Meg, 125, 230
Saturday Evening Post (newspaper), 199
Schmitt, Carl, 37–38
scientific method, 38–40
Scott, Bonnie Kime, 123
Scott, Darieck, 257n120
"Sea Charm" (Hughes), 69
Selvon, Sam, 169
Senghor, Léopold Sédar, 260n170
Senior, Emily, 277–78n109
Seshagiri, Urmila, 270–71n19
Sexton, Jared, 16–17
sexual violence: in *Absalom, Absalom!* (Faulkner), 203, 217; as afterlife of slavery, 96; in *The Big Sea* (Hughes), 78–79; Black fungibility and, 27, 49, 63–64; in *The Book of Night Women* (James), 184; forcible feeding as, 112–13; Middle Passage and, 49; Rhys and, 273–74n63; in *Their Eyes Were Watching God* (Hurston), 79–80; in *Wide Sargasso Sea* (Rhys), 173
Sharpe, Christina, 4, 15, 66, 257n119
Slaughter, Joseph R., 230

slave ship(s): dehumanization and, 77, 106, 167, 184; as demonic grounds, 64–65; *Fons Americanus* (Walker) and, 1–5, 2, 6, 19, 228–29; Gilroy's chronotope of, 15, 138–39; hunger striking and, 111; living conditions on, 42–49, 51–53, 60–61; racialized abjection and, 164–68; ruins of, 228; Spillers on, 25–27, 82–83, 118, 119–20; suicide on, 60, 180; wake and, 4; as womb abyss, 60, 73, 99, 158, 196. See also *Clotilda* (slave ship)
Slave Ship (1937 film), 199. See also *Last Slaver, The* (Faulkner)
Smallwood, Stephanie, 25–26, 43–44
Smith, Harrison, 208
Smith, Zadie, 146, 229
Snorton, C. Riley, 64, 66, 78, 258n124
social constructivism, 117
sociogeny, 35
Somerville, Alice Te Punga, 230
Souls of Black Folk, The (Du Bois), 102–3
"Souls of White Folk, The" (Du Bois), 232
Spillers, Hortense J.: Afro-Pessimism and, 239n21; Glissant and, 66; on Middle Passage, 25–27, 82–83, 105–6, 118, 119–20; on pornotroping, 281n163
Spinoza, Baruch, 117
Spivak, Gayatri, 237–38n4
Steinberg, Philip E., 23–24, 39, 127, 246n55, 272n44
Stephens, Michelle Ann, 151–52, 153
stream of consciousness, 201–2, 204–5. See also free indirect discourse
suicide: as antislavery act, 207; in *Go Down, Moses* (Faulkner), 198, 217; in *A Room of One's Own* (Woolf), 121, 143; on slave ships, 60, 180; in *The Waves* (Woolf), 122, 138, 141–44; in *Wide Sargasso Sea* (Rhys), 180–82
Sultzbach, Kelly, 103–4
Sure Salvation, The (Hearne), 164–65
Synder, Terri L., 207

Tadiar, Neferti X. M., 232–33
Talking Book trope, 34, 67–69, 212

Tang, Yan, 242n59
Taussig, Michael, 170–71, 173–74
Their Eyes Were Watching God (Hurston), 79–87
Things Fall Apart (Achebe), 12
Thompson, Robert Farris, 213, 278–79nn113-4
Till, Emmet, 5
Tinsley, Omise'eke Natasha, 77, 258n122, 271n20
Titian, 119
To the Lighthouse (Woolf), 103, 104–7, 120
"To the Little Fort of San Lazaro on the Ocean Front, Havana" (Hughes), 70
Tordesillas, Treaty of (1494), 37
totalitarianism, 231–32
transgendering, 64
transgenerational trauma, 7–8, 196, 202
transmateriality, 126
transversality, 64, 66, 69–70, 77–78, 88
trauma: in *Absalom, Absalom!* (Faulkner), 202; animism and, 33–34; deltas and, 194, 196; in *Feeding the Ghosts* (D'Aguilar), 48; geography and, 32, 62; in modernist literature, 29, 31, 106. See also queer ecology; transgenerational trauma
Tropic Death (Walrond), 74–75
True and Exact History of the Island of Barbados, A (Ligon), 27–28
Tuck, Eve, 241n48
Tutuola, Amos, 7, 194–96, 197–98, 219–27
Twentieth-Century Fox, 199
Two Years in the French West Indies (Hearn), 277–78n109

Uphaus, Maxwell, 55

Venus Anadyomene (Titian), 119
Victoria Memorial, 1, 3, 5
violence: in *The Big Sea* (Hughes), 72, 74–76, 78–79; in *To the Lighthouse* (Woolf), 104–6; in *Their Eyes Were Watching God* (Hurston), 79–80, 83. See also patriarchal violence; sexual violence

Voyage in the Dark (Rhys): *The Autobiography of My Mother* (Kincaid) and, 185–91; book as fetish in, 181–82; *The Book of Night Women* (James) and, 183–85; race and racialized abjection in, 6, 168, 271n20; slave abyss and, 159–63; unintended pregnancy in, 280n135
Voyage Out, The (Woolf), 267n89

Walcott, Derek, 230
Walker, Alice, 249n121
Walker, Kara, 1–5, 2, 6, 19, 228–29
Walkowitz, Rebecca L., 247–48n75
Walrond, Eric, 74–75
Wang, Jennifer F., 95
Ward, Jesmyn, 229–30
Ware, Vron, 263n27
Warwick Research Collective (WReC), 270n17
water: in *Absalom, Absalom!* (Faulkner), 201–2; in African spiritual traditions, 45–46; agency of, 23–24, 89; in *The Autobiography of My Mother* (Kincaid), 189; in *Barracoon* (Hurston), 52; in *The Big Sea* (Hughes), 67–69; *Fons Americanus* (Walker) and, 1–5, 2, 6; in *The Nigger of the 'Narcissus'* (Conrad), 57–59; white femininity and, 119–20. *See also* waves
"Watery Ecstatic" (Gallagher), 233–35, 235
Watson, Jay, 198, 206, 212, 286n75
waves: concept of, 19, 31, 115–16; deltas and, 196; women's suffrage movement and, 119, 132–33, 132. *See also Waves, The* (Woolf)
Waves, The (Woolf): empire and, 6, 134–44; interludes in, 103, 125, 128–29, 136–37; queer ecology and, 109–10, 120, 122–30, 133–36, 143; women's suffrage movement and, 131–32; writing of, 121, 129–30
weak modernisms, 13–14
"Weary Blues, The" (Hughes), 71–73
Weary Blues, The (Hughes), 69, 71–73

Weheliye, Alexander G., 10, 36, 66, 237–38n4, 242n57
Well of Loneliness, The (Hall), 123
Wells, Jeremy, 270n10
Wenzel, Jennifer, 13, 219, 241n44
"Wharf Rats" (Walrond), 74–75
white femininity: policing of. *See* patriarchal violence;
Wide Sargasso Sea (Rhys): *The Autobiography of My Mother* (Kincaid) and, 185–91; *The Book of Night Women* (James) and, 183–85; creolization in, 272n40; flying in, 272n42; *Jane Eyre* (Brontë) and, 154, 171, 181; obeah practices in, 174–82; polyvocality and wildness in, 168–74; slave abyss and, 156
Wilderson, Frank B., III, 26, 239n21
wildness, 170–74
Wilson, Kabe, 110, 120, 145–49
Wilson, Thomas, 46–47
Winant, Howard, 264n28
women. *See* Black maternity; patriarchal violence; sexual violence
Women's Social and Political Union (WSPU), 132
women's suffrage movement, 111–14, 119, 130–33, 132
Woods, Clyde, 283n27
Woolf, Virginia: on composting technique, 63, 129–30; interludes and, 103–10, 125, 128–29, 136–37, 268n103; modernity/ coloniality and, 108–10. *See also* queer ecology; queer ecology and, 121–35, 143; race blindness of new materialism and, 119–21, 122–23; racial supremacy and, 14; Wilson and, 110, 120, 145–49; women's suffrage movement and, 119, 130–32. *See also To the Lighthouse* (Woolf); *Waves, The* (Woolf)
World Magazine, The, 112–14
World War One, 8, 71–72, 103–7, 231–32
Wright, Michelle M., 288–89n4
Wright, Richard, 207

Wyndham, Francis, 174–75, 179
Wynter, Sylvia: Afro-Pessimism and, 239n21; on being human as praxis, 9–10, 35; on Black relationality to land, 194; on Blackness, 16; on demonic grounds, 11, 64–65; Glissant and, 66; on new natives in a new world, 60; Yountae An, 241n48

Yang, K. Wayne, 241n48
Yoruba oral traditions, 198, 221–23
Yountae, An, 61, 62, 241n48

Yusoff, Kathryn, 193–94

Ziarek, Ewa Płonowska: on materialist aesthetics, 76; on melancholy, 157, 271n29; on parasitism, 111–13; on relation, 62; on trauma, 29–30; on women's suffrage movement, 131
Zola, Émile, 182
zombies, 179–80
Zong! (Philip), 234
Zong (slave ship), 175